MW01089931

Ann Dvorak

Ann Dvorak

Hollywood's Forgotten Rebel

CHRISTINA RICE

UNIVERSITY PRESS OF KENTUCKY

Copyright © 2013 by The University Press of Kentucky

Scholarly publisher for the Commonwealth,
· serving Bellarmine University, Berea College, Centre College of Kentucky,
Eastern Kentucky University, The Filson Historical Society, Georgetown
College, Kentucky Historical Society, Kentucky State University, Morehead
State University, Murray State University, Northern Kentucky University,
Transylvania University, University of Kentucky, University of Louisville,
and Western Kentucky University.
All rights reserved.

Editorial and Sales Offices: The University Press of Kentucky
663 South Limestone Street, Lexington, Kentucky 40508-4008
www.kentuckypress.com

17 16 15 14 13   5 4 3 2 1

Library of Congress Cataloging-in-Publication Data

Rice, Christina, 1974-
    Ann Dvorak : Hollywood's forgotten rebel / Christina Rice.
        pages cm. — (Screen classics)
    Includes bibliographical references and index.
    Includes filmography.
    ISBN 978-0-8131-4426-9 (hardcover : alk. paper) —
    ISBN 978-0-8131-4439-9 (epub) -- ISBN 978-0-8131-4440-5 (pdf)
    1. Dvorak, Ann, 1912-1979. 2. Motion picture actors and actresses—
United States—Biography. I. Title.
    PN2287.D885R53 2013
    791.4302'8092—dc23
    [B]   2013026546

Unless otherwise noted, photographs are from the author's collection.

This book is printed on acid-free paper meeting the requirements of the American
National Standard for Permanence in Paper for Printed Library Materials.

Manufactured in the United States of America.

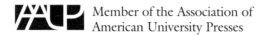 Member of the Association of
American University Presses

For Josh and Gable.

I hope I inspire you as much as you inspire me.

Contents

Preface

When I first encountered Ann Dvorak in the mid-1990s, I'd never have guessed she would become so ingrained in my life. I had checked out a VHS copy of *Three on a Match* from my local library, expecting only to enjoy a short, snappy, minor pre-Code film with Humphrey Bogart and Bette Davis. Instead, I was blindsided by Ann Dvorak's performance as a society wife who throws away wealth, motherhood, and security for hot sex with Lyle Talbot and a lot of drugs. Her long slide to hell was mesmerizing and her ultimate demise shocking. I was so floored by this actress I had never heard of that when the film ended, I hit the rewind button and watched it again. Ann Dvorak was officially on my radar.

Viewings of *Scarface* and *"G" Men* soon followed and there she was again, with those large eyes, distinct voice, and mannerisms that seemed contemporary rather than dated. I found myself desperately wanting to know why this beautiful and talented actress had not become a bigger star. This was in the early days of the Internet and I was a clueless twenty-something, so my efforts to find information on Ann or more of her films were fruitless. I gave up quickly, and Ann Dvorak went on the back burner.

In the fall of 1997, I was interning at a Beverly Hills talent agency alongside a fellow named Darin, the first classic-film buff I had ever encountered. I felt like an old-movie hack compared to him, and in a desperate attempt to sound like I knew something about obscure 1930s actors, I pulled Ann Dvorak out of my hat. It worked. He was impressed and intrigued by my interest in this actress he was only vaguely familiar with, so Ann ended up forging a lasting bond between us. Darin quickly introduced me to the various movie memorabilia shops that were still around in those days before eBay took off, and I quickly discovered that even though I was a starving college student, I could afford to collect gorgeous vintage posters from Ann's films. Why? Well, because no one else wanted them. Ann Dvorak was mine to claim if I wanted to—so I did.

Preface

Somewhere along the line, I decided to become Ann's biographer, though it soon became apparent that this was not going to be easy. She retired from the entertainment industry so long ago that most people she worked with are long gone. Those whom I did track down had only hazy memories of working briefly with Ann on forgettable productions. There were no children, no siblings, no close friends to be found, and she outlived her three husbands. There were no personal papers donated to a research institution, and since she spent the last twenty years of her life living in obscurity in Hawaii, she was never interviewed by film scholars in the 1960s and 1970s.

I'm not one to believe in spirits or ghosts, but at times I felt as if Ann was continuing to play a role in her story. When two different people gave me large collections of letters written by Ann and her mother, Anna Lehr, it was sheer serendipity. I poured over the 1960s correspondence of these two women, who both wrote in an excited, desperate, breathless fashion, using multiple ellipses to string together sentences describing an action as mundane as feeding the cat. And while these letters sometimes reflected a very troubled side of both, I still felt like I had Ann's seal of approval on my project. When I was permitted to have my wedding ceremony and reception at Ann's 1930s San Fernando Valley ranch home, how could I not imagine her smiling down on me?

On other occasions, Ann seemed to actively oppose my prying into her life. There are no photos of her third, and last, husband to be found in these pages, because the snapshots that a member of the Wade family mailed to me never showed up. Three weeks after I turned in the final draft of this book to the publisher, I received a cryptic message from a person claiming to have Ann's personal possessions, including letters, photos, and a journal—items I had dreamed of finding for over a decade. After two frustrating months of haggling, the box arrived on the day my final edit approvals were due. In the eleventh hour, I found myself frantically scanning photos, writing captions, and revising the final chapters to reflect new information and insight gained about her final years. Maybe Ann was willing to throw me a few bones, but only on her terms and she was not going to make it easy for me.

My quest to uncover the life of Ann Dvorak has not always been a smooth ride, but for all the frustrations I endured, there were also moments of sheer joy, like uncovering another piece of the Dvorak puzzle or discovering something new about Ann that made her even more fascinating. Along the way, I was introduced to many wonderful people because of Ann, and I cannot deny the part she played in turning this insecure college student into a confident professional. It may have taken a long time to get to this point, but I like to think I finally captured Ann Dvorak as she was.

I hope she would agree.

Introduction

April 4, 1936, was a typical sunny day in Southern California as Ann Dvorak made her way toward the all-too-familiar entrance of the Los Angeles Superior Courthouse. Here, over the past two months, she had endured pointed questions from Warner Bros.' lawyers and watched as X-rays of her inner organs were put on display. The proceedings had not gone her way so far, and this last-ditch effort to get the judge to void her contract would probably fail. Still, maybe this time she would at least find out how long her servitude to Warner Bros. would continue. If nothing else, she was no longer the lone rebel lashing out against the serfdom known as the Hollywood studio system. Her fellow Warner costar, James Cagney, had followed her lead by filing his own lawsuit in late February, and rumor had it Bette Davis was also becoming increasingly unhappy. The three actors may have had their own reasons for being discontented, but the underlying motive was the same: to gain control over their own careers. The contracts they had signed early on gave Warner Bros. a stranglehold on their professional livelihood, dictating what roles they would play, loaning them out to other studios without their consent—and in Ann's case, suspending them indefinitely (without cause, as far as she was concerned) and tacking the unpaid suspension time onto the end of contract, which could extend the termination date by months. These contracts were no different than the ones most actors in Hollywood signed, but Warner Bros. seemed to be the worst offender when it came to overworking its talent, and frequently in mediocre films.

Ever since Ann had walked out on the studio in 1932 to go to Europe with her husband, Leslie Fenton, she had been punished with a string of unmemorable supporting roles. Not that Warner Bros. would ever admit to this, but to Ann it seemed clear. The drab leading-lady roles they subjected her to were bad enough, but many times the studio went so far as to relegate her to small supporting parts. When Ann had costarred in *Scarface* in 1932, she never dreamed it would be the best film she would make, that her subsequent roles would be less and less significant. Then

Ann meets with Mary Jane Viall before entering court in April 1936. (Courtesy of the University of Southern California, on behalf of the USC Special Collections)

again, she also could have never predicted that Howard Hughes would sell her contract with his Caddo production company to Warner Bros. The Burbank-based studio had shelled out $10,000 more to Hughes for possession of her than MGM had spent for Jean Harlow, but look at how Harlow's career had prospered. The platinum blonde was costarring with Clark Gable and Franchot Tone, while she was billed fifth, playing opposite Dick Foran. Yes, Ann was convinced that the only way to salvage her career was to get away from Warner Bros. Unfortunately, after six months without a paycheck, Ann also had to admit that she needed to go back to work, even if it was for the studio she was currently suing. As a freelance actor, Leslie Fenton's income could be unpredictable, and the profits from their walnut ranch were not enough to sustain them. If they hadn't had that investment property in Van Nuys to sell, they'd be in real trouble by now. At this point, as much as Ann wanted some sort of resolution, she mainly needed to get back in front of the cameras.

Before making her way to the courtroom where Judge Archibald was presiding, Ann stopped to meet five-year-old Mary Jane Viall, whose mother was a jury clerk at the courthouse. When the youngster had learned her favorite actress was making another appearance at her mom's workplace, she asked to meet Dvorak. The bailiff approached Ann about a meeting, and she was more than happy to oblige. Though fairly reclusive in her personal life, Ann didn't mind interacting with the occasional fan and the introduction to little Mary Jane would also be a good photo op. The press had painted her as "difficult" after the Europe incident, and this lawsuit wasn't helping her reputation. Maybe a smiling photo with Mary Jane would soften her image a bit. Ann took a few moments to sit down and chat with the youngster while posing for the newspaper photographers. But the pleasantries soon had to come to an end. Ann stood up, and with her head held high, she entered the courtroom to find out the verdict on her war with Warner Bros.

Ann Dvorak was only twenty years old when she seduced George Raft, and audiences, in the 1932 classic *Scarface*, but it seemed as if she had spent her entire life on the silver screen. She had, in fact, appeared in a handful of movies as a child and spent two years hoofing her way through many an MGM musical as a member of the chorus. *Scarface*, however, was the first chance she had to really act in a movie and she made the most of it. This was an era when many actors struggled to tone down the exaggerated styles that had been appropriate for the stage and silent screen, while others enunciated dialogue with bizarre accents taught by diction coaches. Dvorak, however, played the role of Cesca Camonte with a natural ease that was ahead of its time and remains potent even today. By the time the notorious gangster film was released in March 1932, entertainment gossip columnists had been touting Ann as "Hollywood's New Cinderella," Warner Bros. had developed an intense infatuation with her, and she seemed destined to land at the top of the A-list.

Compared to thousands of Hollywood hopefuls, success in Tinseltown came easily, it seemed, to Ann Dvorak. Perhaps these early triumphs were the reason she was not afraid to thumb her nose at a potentially phenomenal film career, believing she could play the Hollywood game by her own rules. Contemporaries like Bette Davis endured countless leads in B films before being given the chance to carry an A picture. Ann, on the other hand, was given decent-sized parts right out of the gate and seemed certain to have a long and fruitful career. Both Ann and Bette had signed with Warner Bros. around the same time, possessed arresting large-eyed beauty, were well suited for similar dramatic roles, and had very public battles with their studios. However, it was Bette Davis who became a legend, while Ann Dvorak faded into the footnotes of cinema history. As much as Ann wanted to be a film actress, she also sought to be an ideal wife and often put her career on the back burner to concentrate on her marriages, something Bette would never have allowed during her ascent. Ann's actions against Warner Bros. tended to be reactionary, started early in her career, and were usually influenced by those in her inner circle. Bette's battles were much more calculated and came after she had established herself as a box-office draw and Academy Award winner. Ann conjured a sort of a regretful contempt from studio head Jack Warner, while Bette earned his begrudging respect. Ann lived day to day with a wavering focus, while Bette always had her eye on her career.

Ann Dvorak never had the chance to tackle the heavy roles Bette Davis did, but she still appeared in over fifty films, was ahead of her time in many respects, and her contributions to cinema, both onscreen and off, should be acknowledged. Ann walked out on her contract when most would never have considered such an action, battled a major studio in court before her more successful contemporaries did, and spent the better part of her career freelancing at a time when others anxiously sought the stability of a long-term deal with one studio. Her lawsuit against Warner

Bros. paved the way for Cagney, Davis, and even Olivia de Havilland, who in 1944 succeeded in getting the courts to declare the studio practice of extending contracts due to suspension time illegal. When war broke out in Europe, Ann followed her British-born husband to England a full year before the United States became officially involved in the conflict.

Ann Dvorak's filmography may not be overwhelmingly significant as a whole, but there are enough isolated moments of brilliance that her contributions to film deserve to be recognized. Onscreen, she injected life into the many uninteresting roles she was stuck playing and could hold her own opposite vibrant personalities like James Cagney, Paul Muni, Joe E. Brown, and John Wayne. When the part was strong and the director was good, Ann Dvorak could be electrifying. She arrived on the big screen during the heyday of the pre-Code era, that brief but glorious period in the early 1930s when American cinema got away with storytelling not dictated by tight social mores. The female roles were strong, daring, admirable, and a lot of fun to watch. Ann's live-wire energy exploded in characters like the free-willed Cesca in *Scarface*, the soft yet jaded Molly Louvain in *The Strange Love of Molly Louvain*, the repressed Myra in *Heat Lightning*, and the self-destructing Vivian Revere in *Three on a Match*. Ann made movies into the early 1950s, but she is mainly known for her scant few gems from the early 1930s. These films are all now pre-Code primers, and they stand up today, in part, because of Ann's presence.

Even during the latter part of her career, she proved she was more than capable of taking a small part and walking off with an entire film. Her turn as a washed-up fashion model opposite Lana Turner in *A Life of Her Own* resonates long after the character throws herself out a high-rise window. Her portrayal in *Our Very Own* of Gert, a working-class gal blindsided when the child she gave up for adoption shows up years later, is heartbreaking. Ann steals *Out of the Blue* away from George Brent, Carole Landis, and Virginia Mayo with one of her few comedic performances as the lovable drunk Olive, and nearly does the same as the loathsome drunk Belle in *The Walls of Jericho* opposite Cornel Wilde, Linda Darnell, and Anne Baxter. Ann Dvorak almost always made the most of what she was given to work with, and on the rare opportunity when she was given something good, her performance was unforgettable.

Unfortunately, the good parts did not come often enough, and perhaps Ann needs to shoulder some of the blame for this. As bold and rebellious as her actions may have been in the heyday of the Hollywood studio system, her timing was always premature and her efforts seldom beneficial. It is difficult to ascertain how much of her independent streak originated from within, and how much of it resulted from the bad advice of those she put her trust in. For someone who projected such self-reliance, she tended to attach herself to people who had tremendous influence over her—namely, her three husbands. Despite many self-inflicted setbacks, she always worked steadily, but finally turned her back on it all, opting for obscurity and, ultimately, near poverty in Hawaii.

But for a brief moment in the spring of 1932, Ann Dvorak had the world at her feet, and one cannot help but speculate what would have happened if only she had embraced her opportunity.

I

Vaudeville Days

The actress known to movie audiences as Ann Dvorak was born as the less exotic-sounding Anna McKim. Unlike many aspiring starlets who journeyed to Hollywood from small towns and humble beginnings, Ann Dvorak was born amid the hustle and bustle of Manhattan. At the time of her birth in 1911, New York City was the country's epicenter of live entertainment and a burgeoning film industry. This was the exciting and unpredictable world into which her vaudevillian parents brought her.

Dvorak's father did not play a prominent role in her life—he was completely absent from it from her early childhood into her twenties. Depending on what newspaper you read in 1934 when father and daughter were reunited, his name was either Edward, Samuel, or Edwin McKim. His given name was in fact Samuel, but he later opted to go by Edwin S. McKim. He was born in Pittsburgh, Pennsylvania, in October 1869 to John McKim, a Scot by birth who had emigrated from Ireland, and Margaret Keasey, a Keystone State native who was born around 1843 and was a year younger than her husband. Ann Dvorak would later claim she was a direct descendent of Vice President John Caldwell Calhoun, but this seems untrue. Three of Dvorak's grandparents were immigrants, so the only connection to Calhoun would be through her paternal grandmother. Margaret Keasey's parents were also natives of Pennsylvania, whereas Calhoun's children and grandchildren were all born in the South. If there is some sort of distant connection to the southern politician, that link is not "direct," as Dvorak liked to claim.

When John met Margaret in the mid-1860s, she was a widow who, unable to support financially more than herself, had been forced to place two daughters in an orphanage. The couple was able to get one child, Annie, out of the orphanage, but the other girl had already been adopted. Alexander and Edwin were the first two children born to the McKims,

Ann's father, Edwin S. McKim, who could have risen up the ranks of Pittsburgh government but opted for acting instead.

followed by John Jr., Ellen, Wilson, Blanche, Walter, Alice, and Cora. John McKim supported his ever-growing family mostly by working as a millwright, though for a time he was employed by the Baltimore & Ohio Railroad. Nineteenth-century Pittsburgh was a thriving city due to the coal and steel industries, and all the McKim boys eventually contributed to the family purse by finding work as laborers—except Edwin. Exhibiting a more genteel nature than the rest of the McKim men, he instead sought out office jobs, including a clerk position with the B&O Railroad and another at the local courthouse. He moved his way up to become the superintendent of sewers, working at Pittsburgh's city hall, and appeared to have a promising future in local government. This potential career was cut short when Edwin discovered the theater.

He made an early stage appearance in November 1889 as a member of the Curry School of Elocution and Dramatic Culture, which presented a "very creditable rendering" of *Damon and Pythias*.[1] While still working in Pittsburgh government, Edwin pursued his interest in the theater, putting on local productions to benefit charities.[2] McKim would frequently recruit family members to appear in his productions, including sister Cora, who was a trained dancer. In 1904 Edwin left city hall forever and became a full-time actor, joining a traveling company in a production of Shakespeare's *Twelfth Night* starring celebrated actress Marie Wainwright. The tour lasted for over a year, as the troupe performed in cities across the country. Most reviewers reserved their praise for the popular Miss Wainwright, though some applauded the supporting male cast: "Orsino the duke of Illyria, master of Viola, was well interpreted by Edwin McKim."[3] Following the yearlong tour, McKim moved to New York, and by the end of 1905 he was starring in a production of the melodrama *When the World Sleeps* at the Star Theater in East Harlem. The *New York Dramatic Mirror* found McKim to be a "manly chap" with a smile that "is winning and worth cultivating."[4]

On Saturday afternoons, a small group of students from a nearby private school attended matinees at the Star Theater. McKim, then in his mid-thirties, became smitten with one of the visiting pupils, a teenager named Anna Lehr who also had a taste for the theater. For the starry-eyed schoolgirl, the older thespian was "the most attractive man I had ever met in my life; that he was also an actor made him practically superlative."[5] Lehr failed to understand how McKim could fall in love with someone so young, but he indeed did, and the actor and aspiring teenaged actress soon were an item.

If Ann Dvorak's father was missing for most of her life, then the opposite can be said of her mother. Anna Lehr was a constant, if sometimes overbearing, presence in her daughter's life. Dvorak's view of her mother would range from idol to nuisance to savior. In turn, Lehr would look upon her daughter with varying degrees of amusement, pride, and pity. In contrast to Dvorak's low-key and serious personality, Anna Lehr always projected a grandiose persona along the lines of *Sunset Blvd.*'s Norma Desmond, even though she later became a cash-poor and obscure figure of the silent-film era. As much as Ann may have respected and even at times revered her mother, she broke loose from her the first opportunity she got. However, in the end when all others failed her, Ann would find herself running back to her mother for moral courage.

Anna Lehr was the youngest daughter of Frank Lehr and Emile (Emma) Freisinger, who hailed from Austria-Bohemia, an area now part

Ann's mother, Anna Lehr, was a driving force in her daughter's life.

of the Czech Republic. Over the years, the family name would be spelled Lehr, Lajer, or Layer. Like many immigrants of the late nineteenth century, thirty-six-year-old Frank Lehr made the journey to America alone, arriving in New York City in 1888. After setting up shop as a tailor for a year, he was able to send for Emile and their six children, Frank Jr., Louis, Emma, Mary, Flo, and Helen. The brood settled in Manhattan's Upper East Side and added two more members to the clan. Anna was born in November 1890, followed by Willie in 1892. Despite being "uninterruptedly poor," the family was not unhappy.[6] According to family lore, the Lehrs sometimes exhibited eccentric behavior, which was exemplified by Flo, who embarked on an unsuccessful vaudeville career at Coney Island. She would at times require assistance after getting stuck in yoga positions, and she once tried to alter the shape of her nose by attaching a clothespin to it. A trip to the hospital was required to remove it.[7] The

Lehr family eccentricities would be evident in Anna later on in life, and to a degree in Ann Dvorak.

Anna Lehr later recalled a childhood of near poverty, but her father's meager earnings as a tailor were apparently enough to pay for his youngest daughter to attend the private school through whose activities she was introduced to Edwin McKim. Even before she was swept off her feet by the actor from Pittsburgh, she had ambitions to make a name for herself on the stage. In March 1905 she was singing between acts at the Third Avenue Theater, proving to be a crowd pleaser when belting out Ted S. Barron and Felix F. Feist's "Honey I'm Waiting."[8] By May 1907 Lehr had left school and was performing at Chase's Theater in Washington, DC, with legendary vaudevillian/songwriter/publisher Gus Edwards. Known as the cowriter of songs such as "By the Light of the Silvery Moon" and "In My Merry Oldsmobile," Edwards has also been credited over the years with discovering entertainment luminaries such as Groucho Marx, Eddie Cantor, and George Jessel. In 1907 Edwards was capitalizing on the success of his song "School Days (When We Were a Couple of Kids)" by putting on stage shows set in a classroom. It was in one of these one-act shows, entitled *Primary No. 23*, that Anna Lehr was cast in the role of Daisy Fair. A local newspaper noted that she "scored a hit," and that "with her winning way and pleasing smile Miss Lehr does much to bring the act to a successful conclusion."[9]

McKim and Lehr spent 1908 pursuing their careers, and each other, in a traveling production of the musical drama *The Little Organ Grinder.* The show, which featured McKim as the villain and Lehr in a supporting role, arrived in Pittsburgh in January. McKim's hometown welcomed their wayward son back with open arms, declaring that Edwin was the "most suave villain" ever to tread the boards of the Bijou Theater.[10] By the end of 1908, the eighteen-year-old Lehr and the thirty-nine-year-old McKim had made their relationship official. When the *Little Organ Grinder* made a return engagement to the Iron City in November, the *Pittsburgh Post* reported that McKim's "wife, Anna Lehar, is also with the company, assuming an important role."[11] The newlyweds forged ahead with their careers, appearing in various vaudeville shows in New York and Washington, DC, and the following year developed a magic and comedy act.[12] In the summer of 1910, Lehr almost performed on Broadway in a comedy produced by William C. deMille, older brother of Cecil B. DeMille. Lehr had a small role in deMille's *High Life in Jail,* which previewed in Atlantic City under the altered title *The Simple Life*. The production was supposed to start its official run at the Hackett Theater in New York City, but was indefinitely postponed when it was bumped in favor of a play starring Clara Lipman. As a consolation, Lehr again had the opportunity to work with her husband in a show called *The Man of the Hour* at the Academy Theater in the nation's capital. She would look back on this period of traveling and performing alongside her husband with great fondness.

Married life did not slow down the pair in the least. By 1911 Lehr had developed her own act and was getting solo billing as a singing comedienne and receiving positive reviews. Even the impending birth of a child did not cause Lehr to withdraw from center stage. At seven months pregnant she was still making the rounds of New York vaudeville houses with a nine-minute act. Apparently the later stages of pregnancy agreed with her, as one reviewer claimed she was "good to look at and has a cute little voice."[13] Lehr and McKim's dedication to the performing arts would continue after their child was born, and this environment would set the stage for Ann Dvorak to follow in their footsteps.

2

Child Actress

Most sources give Ann Dvorak's birth date as August 2, 1912. However, the New York City Birth Index confirms that Anna McKim was born on August 2, 1911. Throughout her career, Ann would claim 1912 as the year of her birth, though in later years she would begin listing 1911. Shaving off a few years has always been a common practice in Hollywood, though the origin of this discrepancy is probably Anna Lehr. Dvorak's mother frequently subtracted anywhere from four to fourteen years off her own age, even fudging the numbers on her application for a Social Security card. More than likely, Lehr either purposely gave her daughter an incorrect date for reasons of personal vanity or absentmindedly stated the misinformation early on in Dvorak's life. Whatever the reason may have been, 1912 stuck until Ann found out otherwise.

Dvorak was born at the Murray Hill Sanitarium on Thirty-fifth Street, and mother and baby were released from the hospital four weeks later. Lehr admitted that she "hadn't been particularly thrilled over the idea of motherhood," but she quickly warmed up to the infant, whom she described as "an amazingly good baby. No more trouble than a pet pup."[1] Lehr later also claimed her baby daughter learned to speak early and never engaged in "baby talk," an indicator of the serious and studious personality Dvorak would come to exhibit. From her mother Ann inherited dark hair, a prominent nose, and startlingly large blue-green eyes. Her strong chin and smile came courtesy of the McKim side of the family.

Now that they were grounded in New York with an infant, Lehr and her husband put their vaudeville road engagements on hold; however, a mere six months after giving birth, Lehr was back onstage. Given the addition to the family, the next logical step was to turn their attentions to the flourishing film industry. The movies, a mere novelty a few years before, were rapidly gaining steam as the prominent form of entertainment for the masses. The year 1912 proved to be a landmark one for motion pictures: Carl Laemmle founded Universal Pictures; William Fox started the Fox Film Foundation (which eventually became 20th Century-Fox); and Adolph Zukor formed the Famous Players Film Corporation, a forerunner to Paramount Pictures. Dvorak's parents were in an ideal position to take advantage of the numerous film production companies operating in New York, and Edwin McKim played a minor role in that milestone year when he was cast as "Monks" in H. A. Spanuth's production of *Oliver Twist*, generally believed to be the first full-length American feature film screened for audiences. *Oliver Twist* presented audiences with a full five reels of storytelling and featured famed stage actor Nat C. Goodwin reprising his role as Fagin. Despite Edwin McKim's fairly auspicious beginning as a film actor, *Oliver Twist* is his only credited role in movies, though he later claimed to have been regularly employed for two years as a leading man alongside Pearl White with the Powers Motion Picture Company. When the Powers outfit merged into Universal Pictures, McKim went behind the camera to direct a series of films for the obscure Crystal Motion Picture Company.[2]

Anna Lehr's film career showed plenty of early promise: she signed with the Majestic Motion Picture Company and appeared in a series of comedy shorts. Lehr's early film efforts seem to have gone over well; the newly established fan magazine *Photoplay* reported, "Her grace, beauty and cleverness always cause a sigh of satisfaction to steal over an audience when she appears on the screen."[3] Lehr had the opportunity to appear in a feature-length film when the short-lived Victory Film Company cast her in *Victory*, a large-scale war picture featuring battleships and hydroplanes provided by the U.S. Navy. The movie was filmed on location in Cuba, and Lehr was accompanied by her husband and baby daughter. It is unclear if McKim was employed on the film, but he definitely was on hand with a camera to document his daughter's first big trip. The movie, which featured combat scenes in a Cuban harbor, also cast real naval officers and received the navy's official endorsement, via a statement by Acting Secretary Franklin Delano Roosevelt.

Lehr made one more feature for the Victory Film Company, then returned to the stage with the Orpheum Vaudeville Circuit. She headed a small cast in the melodramatic playlet *Little California*, which dealt with racial strife in the region's early history. The tour started just after Christmas in 1913 and continued for three months, with performances in

Anna Lehr (left) and Arline Pretty in *Valley of Doubt.*

Canada, California, and Nebraska. Ann, two years old at the time, joined her mother on the road. Sharing the bill with Lehr was comedian Charles "Chic" Sale, who would eventually appear onscreen with Dvorak in the Warner Bros. comedy *Stranger in Town.* Sale later recalled that Lehr would set up a crib in her dressing room so the tot could nap during performances. On the long train rides between engagements, Sale would sit the young girl on his knee and feed her candy. He also noted that Dvorak made her theatrical debut during the Orpheum tour when she snuck out of her crib and onto the stage during one of her mother's performances. The toddler chose the dramatic climax of the show as the ideal time to tug at her mother's skirts and yell, "Mama!" which caused the cast and audience to convulse with laughter—and Lehr to end the night's performance early, hastily carrying her daughter offstage.[4]

The Orpheum tour marked the end of Anna Lehr's stage performing, as she now settled into a film career that lasted around a decade. Upon her return from the road, she immediately had the opportunity to work with her husband, who had given up acting for directing and scenario writing. McKim directed his wife in the Ivan Film Productions feature *Should a Woman Divorce*, which tackled the "greatest social problem of the day" and proved to be rather prophetic for Dvorak's parents.[5] By the end of 1915 their marriage was showing signs of strain as they both accepted steady film work on opposite ends of the country. Lehr relocated to Los Angeles with her daughter and made a string of features at the newly constructed Universal Studios. McKim returned to his home state to write and direct comedy shorts for the Lubin Manufacturing Company in Philadelphia.

The move west was lucrative for Anna Lehr, who gradually received more prominent roles at Universal, including a handful of costarring stints with film pioneer Hobart Bosworth. Lehr's presence in Los Angeles also proved to be the springboard for her daughter's short-lived career as a child actor. In late 1915 a four-year-old Dvorak was recruited to appear in a film adaptation of Helen Hunt Jackson's novel, *Ramona*. Set in California in the aftermath of the Mexican-American War, *Ramona* is the purely fictional tale of a half-Scottish, half–Native-American orphan who endures immense hardships because of her Indian lineage. The heavily romanticized story, an enormous success when first published in 1884, had been embraced by Southern California residents as a sort of regional mythology. D. W. Griffith had made a short film of the story in 1910 with Mary Pickford in the title role, but producer William H. Clune, who had helped finance Griffith's *The Birth of a Nation*, decided that the time was right for a *Ramona* of epic proportions. Donald Crisp was enlisted to direct the feature, which was partially filmed on "authentic" Ramona locations around the Southland. Dvorak appeared briefly in the film's prologue as the title character at age four. She was billed as "Baby Anna

Four-year-old Ann makes her film debut in *Ramona*, credited as "Baby Anna Lehr." (Courtesy of Marc Wanamaker)

Lehr," a decision that still causes her childhood film credits to be confused with her mother's. The finished product ran between ten and fourteen reels and had its world premiere in February 1916 at Clune's Auditorium (later known at the Philharmonic Auditorium) in downtown Los Angeles.

Reviews for the film were generally positive, although the reception on the West Coast was much more enthusiastic than in other parts of the country. Los Angeles newspapers were particularly taken with Ann's acting debut; the *Evening Herald* reported, "The most disappointing feature of the entire production is the fact that this sweet youth remains on the canvas only a few brief moments."[6] The *Los Angeles Express* was especially impressed by Dvorak and proved it by running a large portrait of her under the headline "Anna Lehr Great Hit in *Ramona,* 4-Year-Old Prodigy Proves Film Wonder" and gushing, "The talent of Anna is wonderful, and when linked with her uncommon beauty makes her, in the opinion of many, the greatest child actress yet seen on the screen."[7] Unfortunately, no copies of Ann Dvorak's film debut are known to exist. Both parents escorted their young daughter to the New York premiere of *Ramona,* where audiences and newspaper reporters alike were dazzled by the poise and charm of the precocious four-year-old. This exciting event marked one of the last times Dvorak would see her father until the mid-1930s, as McKim resumed his work with Lubin in Philadelphia while mother and daughter remained in New York.

Anna Lehr's film career continued at full speed. Thomas H. Ince signed her to a contract with the Triangle Motion Picture Company and she began dividing her time between both coasts for different productions. This employment also led to her daughter's second screen appearance, courtesy of Triangle, which cast the youngster in a 1917 comedy/drama called *The Man Hater.* In her second outing as an actress, Dvorak had a modest role as the younger sister of the film's star, Winifred Allen, with whom she formed an offscreen bond. In between scenes, Ann helped Allen knit items to send to the soldiers fighting overseas in the First World War.[8] The film, about a young woman who becomes a "man hater" at the hands of an abusive father, was, oddly, a lighthearted and family-friendly feature that received favorable reviews, though Dvorak was not singled out as she had been for her appearance in *Ramona.* Like her first film, *The Man Hater* is also lost.

Shortly after Dvorak completed *The Man Hater,* Lehr decided that a bicoastal career and motherhood were too much to juggle. Furthermore, Ann had arrived at an age to begin her formal education, so arrangements were made for her to enter St. Catherine's Convent on Madison Avenue in New York City. When the day came for Lehr to drop Ann off at her new home, she was so unsure how her daughter would react to the separation that she arranged for one of the nuns to distract the young girl with a story while she slipped away unnoticed. Lehr was surprised and a bit ashamed when, upon arriving at the convent, Dvorak, whom her mother described as "solemn, yet humorous and wholly independent," looked her in the eye and simply said, "Goodbye, Mother," and gave her a quick hug before turning away to enter the building.[9] Lehr was even more surprised at how quickly and intensely her daughter took to convent school life. Though she had not been raised Catholic, Ann grew to love her surroundings, and despite her young age she spent hours in deep, reverent prayer. This would mark the beginning of a pattern in Ann Dvorak's life: she would throw herself into whatever her immediate circumstances were—marriage, acting, walnut farming, war reporting, or bacteriology— and absorb every bit of information available. A friend later commented, "Whatever [Ann] does, she does intensely," adding, "She is the victim of a consuming ambition that will not let her rest."[10] When Ann began expressing an interest in becoming a nun, Lehr became concerned that her daughter was becoming too religious at too young an age and removed her from St. Catherine's.

After leaving the convent, Ann was enrolled at the Clark School for Girls on West End Avenue and went to live with family members, most likely her aunt Helen, who lived four miles away from the school. Most of the Lehr family was still living in New York and Ann enjoyed getting to know her relatives. She especially reveled in her grandmother's tales of life in eastern Europe, which seemed so exotic to the young girl. It was also during this time that she supposedly discovered "Dvorak" was a surname somewhere on the family tree and began referring to herself as "Anna Dvorak," which sounded much more exciting than "Anna McKim." Ann would later claim to be a cousin of the famed Czech composer Antonin Dvorak, but this remains unsubstantiated. Edwin McKim later told an acquaintance of Ann's that she admired Antonin Dvorak's music so much that she took the name as a tribute to him.[11] So as not to confuse the two Annas, the Lehr family referred to mother and daughter as "Big Anna" and "Little Anna," though to Ann, her mother would always be "Mama."[12] During this period of separation from her mother, Ann frequently went to the movies with a young cousin to see films starring Mama Lehr, where the giggling children would be hushed by the other theatergoers. The experience of seeing larger-than-life images of her mother projected on the big screen most certainly made a tremendous impression on Ann and

Advertisement for the 1917 Triangle feature *The Man Hater,* starring Winifred Allen and a six-year-old Ann.

cast Lehr in an almost mythical light. There is little doubt these viewings, at least in part, led her to pursue film acting later on.

When Lehr was in town, she did make the effort to see Ann on her free Saturdays, taking her out to lunch at one of the big uptown hotels or fashionable cafes. She remembered Ann at these outings as being "intensely interested in her surroundings, noticing the clothes worn by the women lunchers and gossiping over them with me." Lehr also explained that as much as Ann enjoyed the realities of her immediate environment, she also loved to hear fairy tales: "It has always been possible to reach Ann through her imagination."[13]

While living in the East, Ann received another opportunity to appear in a motion picture. She was selected to costar with Herbert Rawlinson in a 1920 short called *The Five Dollar Plate,* which was filmed in New York City and produced by the short-lived Oliver Films. Ann adored Rawlinson, who was a fairly big star in the silent era and became a reliable character actor, appearing in almost four hundred films during his career. He appeared with Anna Lehr a year later in a Universal production called

Cheated Hearts, and Ann worked with him again on film in the 1930s and on radio in the 1940s. A personally inscribed photo of the actor was one of Dvorak's prized childhood possessions. *The Five Dollar Plate* was one of a handful of shorts based on the real-life experiences of William J. Flynn, who had served as chief of the Secret Service and director of the Bureau of Investigation, later known as the Federal Bureau of Investigation. Ann was more than happy to be chaperoned from her school to the film set, where she was costumed in ragged clothing for her role. As Lehr remembered, "When she wasn't needed on the set, Ann could always be found in front of the studio (which was located in a tenement section of the city) playing with children whose clothes were as ragged and unkempt as her costume."[14] This third go at onscreen acting marked the end of Ann's early film career. It also is considered a missing title.

Back in Philadelphia, Edwin McKim had been busy at the Lubin studio writing and directing a series of comedy shorts starring Davy Don. The demand for Davy Don comedies was so great that McKim welcomed the general public to send him scenario submissions.[15] After Dvorak made a name for herself in the 1930s, her father would usually be credited as a director for the better-known Biograph Company. However, all available filmographies disprove any association between McKim and Biograph; the bulk of his film work consists of the more than thirty shorts he wrote and directed for Lubin during 1915 and 1916. At one point McKim also claimed to have at least one hundred pictures in the Vitagraph vaults although, as is the case with so many credits of the industry's pioneering days, these claims are nearly impossible to verify.

After the Lubin Manufacturing Company folded, McKim returned to his hometown of Pittsburgh and attempted to use his reputation to launch an interesting business venture called the Advanced Photo Play Corporation. Advanced Photo Play aimed to bring filmmaking to Pittsburgh by offering stock to residents of the city and neighboring areas for $10 a share. The company promised to give the people of Pittsburgh the chance to view film productions in progress and to "develop whatever talent [is] latent in young Pittsburghers," which was too often "killed through a lack of opportunity."[16] McKim intended to kick off his company's inaugural feature with a bang by staging the first day of filming at the Motor Square Garden, a massive open-space building with plenty of natural sunlight. Billed as a "$100,000 Super Feature Production," the event would be open to the general public for a price of admission ranging from 50¢ to $1. Whoever came up with the best title for the film would receive a $300 prize. Established film stars like Carlyle Blackwell and Anna Lehr would be on hand for the attendees to gawk at. Despite any difficulties the McKims had been experiencing in their marriage, Lehr was still willing to use her name to help make her husband's slightly harebrained business idea a success. After a nearly six-month buildup, production finally commenced on July 2, 1920, in which "two scenes were laid, one in a hotel lobby, the other a cabaret scene."[17] Three days later, however, production came to a standstill; the cast and crew were dismissed. Less than two weeks later, Carlyle Blackwell filed suit against the company, claiming a $10,000 breach of contract. That was the end of the Advanced Photo Play Corporation Company, and it seems to have been the end of Edwin McKim's show-business career.

After fulfilling her obligation to Advanced Photo Play, Lehr went back to Los Angeles sometime in the latter half of 1920, leaving her daughter behind in New York. However, once she had established that she would be staying in California for an indefinite period, Lehr decided to resume her motherly duties. At the time of the reunion Dvorak was nine years old and had endured extended separations from her mother as well as various living arrangements in New York. Despite these challenges, Lehr maintained that her daughter was a well-adjusted and confident child with a strong sense of adventure. Dvorak had the opportunity to put this to the test when, at Lehr's request, Ann's grandmother put her on a train for a solo cross-country trip. When Ann arrived in Los Angeles five days later, Lehr found her daughter dirty, bedraggled, and hungry, but in high spirits. The money Lehr had wired for the journey had been stolen by a porter, so Ann had lived off cookies and dill pickles the entire trip and, unsupervised, she had avoided the washbasin completely. But such circumstances only added to the excitement of the journey in the young girl's eyes. Lehr could not stop herself from laughing as Ann "hopped about the station platform like a little witch, her black, curly, *dirty* hair flying, her blue eyes dancing with excitement."[18]

From 1918 to 1920, Anna Lehr had appeared in close to twenty films. Nearly a year and a half after settling in Los Angeles with her daughter, she had made only three movies. It is not entirely clear if Lehr's career was winding down due to choice or to circumstance, but by the spring of 1921, financial difficulties were starting to become apparent. This was evident when Lehr was taken to court by the high-end dressmaker

Chapell, Inc., which accused her of not paying a $916 bill in a reasonable amount of time. Lehr claimed she had every intention of paying the bill but, indignant when Chapell involved the sheriff and bill collectors, decided to wait until she was good and ready. When she appeared in court in July 1921, she was blindsided by the plaintiff's lawyer, who named her estranged husband as an additional defendant in the suit. Lehr reportedly stood and dramatically confronted the lawyer: "Why are you trying to drag my husband into this simple case at law? You are trying to make a personal matter of it and the more personal it becomes the more I will fight you."[19]

The 1921 lawsuit seems to have finally convinced the pair that a formal divorce was in their best interest. The union was officially dissolved shortly after. Lehr and Ann returned to New York in 1922 and although McKim was now living in the city, it does not appear that he had much contact with his daughter at this time. In the meantime, Anna Lehr embarked on a new romantic relationship with a local advertising executive. Mother and daughter were about to enter a new phase in their lives.

3

Schoolgirl

Upon returning to New York in early 1922, Lehr did not obtain film work, though it is not clear if she was looking for such opportunities. She had always made her career her top priority since she was a teenager, and toward the end of her life she frequently expressed an interest in making a big comeback, so her sudden retirement remains a mystery. Perhaps she had finally become burned out after working nonstop for fifteen years. Or maybe, now that she was over thirty, roles were becoming harder to land. Lehr must have felt at least a little guilty over having missed so much of Ann's childhood, so it is possible she believed it was time to settle down and concentrate on raising her daughter. Whatever her reasons, one thing was apparent; she no longer needed to work to earn income, as she had entered into a new relationship with a man not affiliated with the entertainment industry. Interestingly, Anna Lehr's film career was not unlike her daughter's. Both appeared in a steady stream of movies, gave consistently solid performances that received positive reviews, but never became big stars. Since most of Lehr's films no longer exist, she has, at best, become a minor footnote in the annals of silent cinema.

The man who facilitated Anna Lehr's early retirement was Arthur Rutledge Pearson, though he usually went by the more fashionable "A. R." Seven years Lehr's senior, Pearson was an Arkansas native, raised in Baltimore, who entered New York society in 1909 by marrying Jeanette Chomley, the niece and ward of early feminist Jeanette Gilder, who had founded the *Critic,* a literary magazine. The union with Chomley dissolved after a handful of years, and sometime around 1922 he became involved with Anna Lehr, although since the pair ran in completely different social circles, it's not evident how they first crossed paths. While Lehr frequently referred to Pearson as her husband, no official marriage records have surfaced. Decades later, Lehr would make the bizarre claim that she never married Pearson because he was already legally wed to an invalid. This is not only untrue, as Chomley remarried in 1917 and there are no indications that he was ever wed to anyone else, but it also mirrors one of the plot points of Ann's later film *A Life of Her Own*. Why Lehr would fabricate such a tale is anyone's guess, though maybe she harbored some Victorian shame at having lived with a man for a number of years without marrying him.

The couple decided to relocate to Los Angeles, with Ann in tow, and this time the move would be permanent. Anna Lehr acquired work in the Famous Players–Lasky production of *Ruggles of Red Gap*, which would prove to be her last film of any significance. Ann's new stepfather secured employment with the Smith & Ferris Advertising Agency in downtown Los Angeles. As Pearson worked his way up the ranks of the ad agency, the family settled into modest quarters above a garage at 733 N. Harvard in Hollywood. Ann immediately took to her new life in sunny Southern California, thrilled to be living so close to the numerous movie studios sprouting up around the city. This included the Robert Brunton Studio, located less than a mile away, which eventually became the home of Paramount Pictures. The influence of living in the midst of what had rapidly become the film capital of the world prompted Ann to start talking about her desire to become a motion-picture actress. Ann grilled her mother about all aspects of the film industry down to the operation of a camera. Lehr was dubious about her daughter's looks, observing later, "She had an arresting face but I didn't think she was pretty."[1] Secretly, Lehr did not believe that Ann, who was becoming tall, thin, and gawky, could ever be beautiful or stylish enough to have a successful film career.

In addition to her interest in the movies, Ann also started to show a passion and talent for writing. Poetry was her special love; she would fill reams of paper with her verse, which she usually hid away until she was in the mood to perform select readings for her mother. During these performances Lehr would briefly see her daughter in a different light: "Sometimes she read with such fervor and voice-beauty that I began to wonder if Ann were not really beautiful after all. When she was in one of her inspired moods she was like some heady red wine. But another day would bring another mood—and Ann was just Ann." Ann never lost her desire to write; it would be a common theme throughout her life and one she pursued long after her film career was over. Ann's parents wholeheartedly encouraged authoring over acting, especially Pearson, whose job at the ad

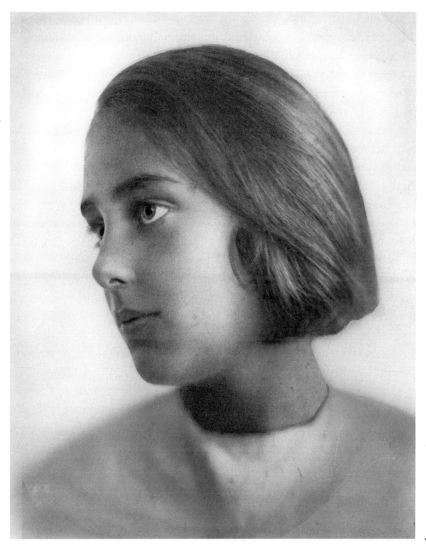

Ann, age nine. Her mother did not think she was pretty enough to be an actress.

agency was commercial writing. "You stick to writing, Ann," he advised. "That's your line. Forget about being an actress."[2]

Seeking to continue the private-school education Ann had been receiving in New York, Lehr enrolled her in the Elliott School for Girls, located at Pico Boulevard and Gramercy Place, five miles southwest of downtown Los Angeles. Under the tutelage of Principal Martha Weaver, the school emphasized "character building with educational advantages, for it is only through this perfect combination that the girls can attain a full and harmonious development." Weaver's curriculum also stressed music, art, and dance because "the proper blending of cultural studies polishes the rougher elementary subjects of the school."[3]

Ann would spend the weekdays on campus at boarding school, then take the streetcar back to her parents' house on weekends. Because she was so young, the principal would have Leona Cary, one of the older students, accompany her home. Three years Ann's senior, Leona came to look upon the younger girl as a kid sister. Years later, writing to Ann, Leona recalled the mischief they got into: "I . . . remember our mid-nite suppers and being caught. You putting both hands in a yellow crock bowl for ripe olives they had ready for the next day—lunch or dinner. You ran through the front hall and reception room up the lovely stairs to our room dripping juice every place. I of course took a chocolate pie, had it behind me (my robe) when my ballet slippers slipped on those back stairs—the house mother Mrs. Genrick was at the top of the stairs. I'm sure they gave her that bedroom to guard the stairs and back sleeping porch."[4]

Cary noted that Ann always did well in her French classes, but at times had her fingers rapped with a ruler when she hit a wrong key during piano lessons. She remembered Ann as a nervous kid, reminding her years later how she would "take your round comb out of your hair every few minutes then replace it. Even when we would skate in front of that lovely old house."[5] The two girls became close friends and their relationship would endure for nearly sixty years.

For reasons unknown, Ann's tenure at the Elliott School did not last long, and she was then enrolled in the Page School for Girls, a boarding school located in a Los Angeles suburb. The school had been founded in 1908 by sisters Emma and Della Page with the goal to "prepare its pupils for honorable and useful womanhood."[6] It had originally been located near downtown Los Angeles, but the Page sisters moved the campus to Highland Park, an upper-class residential neighborhood dotted with Victorian homes that complemented the natural beauty of the Arroyo Seco watershed running through the area. The dormitory and kitchen were set up inside a three-story mansion that housed, in addition to faculty and staff, between forty and sixty students aged six through nineteen, with an additional forty or so pupils living off campus. Classes were held in a separate building located at the rear of the large property, which sat at the corner of North Pasadena (now Figueroa) and Avenue 45. In addition to preparing its pupils for useful womanhood, the Page School for Girls also emphasized dancing, drama, and music, frequently putting on large-scale pageants in which most students participated. While at the school, Ann learned to dance, act, and play the piano, which would be the only formal training she received before entering the movies. During the time Ann was attending the Page School, her classmates included the nieces of Vivian and Rosetta Duncan, a popular vaudeville duo known as the Duncan Sisters. In June 1927, the two were promoting their first film, *Topsy and Eva*, by performing a prologue at Grauman's Egyptian Theatre in Hollywood. After one of these performances, the sisters decided to pay their nieces, and the rest of the Page student body, a visit. The pair showed up unannounced at one of the school's many evening pageants and treated the audience to a preshow routine. The Duncans promised the girls they would return to the school with the entire cast of the *Topsy and Eva* prologue and give a special performance.[7]

Ann immediately took to life at the school, relishing the semirural surroundings and excelling in her studies, which incorporated both her passion for writing, via the school newspaper, the *Pagette*, and her desire to follow in her mother's theatrical footsteps. However, Ann could not always restrain herself when she disagreed with what was being presented in class and sometimes got into hot water with the school's administrators. A friend later recalled, "At least once a month she would come over to my house to tell me she had been expelled for arguing with her teachers. She never would accept anything without discussion, not even her own personal opinions. She is keenly analytical by nature, and demands proof of everything she is told. She was decidedly radical."[8] After she had been attending the school for a little over a year, Ann's adventurous side got the best of her when she and a fellow student ran away just to see what it felt like. They got as far as the adjacent neighborhood of Eagle Rock before Ann decided that "running away is no good," and turned around.[9] At least, this was the lighthearted story Anna Lehr presented. Jeanne de Kolty, who knew Ann at the time, remembered it differently. "One of her friends, it seems, had been seen away from school with a boy, a crime strictly forbidden, except when a pupil had obtained a leave of absence. The girl was about to graduate and any sort of trouble would be disastrous. Feeling very noble, Ann had told the teachers that she, not her friend, was the culprit. Since nobody was sure just who the girl had been, they took Ann's word for it. She was threatened with expulsion, but she didn't wait to be sentenced. She ran away." De Kolty continued, "She spent the night with me, after my mother had telephoned her parents and explained the situation, and the next morning I convinced her that she'd better go home and have it out with her mother. She did and was roundly scolded."[10] Ann escaped expulsion from school, though this would not be the last time she would find herself running away from a situation she did not want to face head-on.

As Ann entered adolescence, she was excelling intellectually but had yet to blossom physically, usually dressing in baggy, mismatched clothes and wearing her long hair in thick braids. She later described herself as "the school's most consistent wallflower."[11] Shortly after the Page School for Girls opened, Della Page left the institution in the hands of her sister and established the all-male Page Military Academy with her husband, Robert Gibbs. The two schools would coordinate and hold dances where the boys and girls could intermingle. An alumnus of the boys' school later recalled seeing Ann at these dances, remembering her as "a curious-looking youngster with great excited eyes, always bent a little forward from her wall-seat as though hopeful for an attention that never came."[12] A friend of Ann's at the time also later confirmed this description: "That Ann was a skinny child and not very pretty, except her glorious eyes, is true."[13] As much as Ann was enjoying her time spent writing and editing the school paper, she was harboring a desire to appear in motion pictures. Her mother, who still felt that Ann lacked the necessary polish to appear before the cameras, did not have the heart to discourage her teenaged daughter's aspirations.

Toward the end of Ann's tenure at the Page School for Girls, Arthur Pearson abruptly stopped working for the Smith & Ferris Advertising Agency, and the family fell on hard times. Pearson's inability to quickly land another job prompted Anna Lehr to come out of retirement. Unfortunately, after her four-year absence from the movies, Hollywood was not exactly welcoming her back. In the fall of 1927, Lehr made a desperate plea to producer/director Hal Roach, begging to be used as part of his "stock company" and stressing she'd be "glad to take any salary at all," adding, "If you will just give me half a chance and gamble with me, I know I can stage a nice big 'come back.'"[14] Lehr never did become a part of Roach's stock company, and it is unknown if he even responded to her. Considering that Roach and Lehr had never worked together when her career was flourishing, he was probably not the only producer Lehr contacted for work. Ideal Pictures finally cast her as the Virgin Mary to Philip Van Loan's Messiah in the feature *Jesus of Nazareth*, which quietly came and went in 1928 and would be Lehr's last acting job.

Dvorak adapted to the family's change in fortunes by going to work. Since her family could no longer afford the tuition, the Page School agreed to employ Ann on campus in lieu of payment. She arose every school day at 4:30 a.m. and worked until 7:30 a.m. answering phones in the front office and assisting the staff. She also earned a few extra dollars tutoring fellow students in French, a language in which she had become fluent. While Ann took care of her own livelihood at the boarding school, her mother and stepfather were on less stable ground, just getting by and changing residences every year or two.

Ann was only fifteen when she graduated in 1927, and although following in her mother's footsteps professionally was never too far from her thoughts, she began focusing her ambitions in other directions, which included a higher education and a career as a writer. Occidental College had previously occupied a campus up the street from the Page School for Girls, and even though it had been moved to the neighboring Eagle Rock, it remained a logical destination for Page School graduates. As much as Ann may have wanted to enroll in classes at the school, her parents' precarious finances made this impossible, a blow she seems never to have fully recovered from. In the mid-1940s Ann began claiming she had attended Occidental College and had been editor of the school's newspaper. However, Occidental has no record of Ann attending, even temporarily, and she is nowhere to be found on the roster of newspaper editors and writers for those years.[15] Long after she retired from films, Ann would continue to claim this false association with Occidental. Her lack of a college education would always haunt Ann, who occasionally took night classes after she became a film actress and tried to ingrain herself in the world of academia much later on in life by undertaking what she deemed to be a significant scholarly project.

With her dreams of college dashed, Ann decided that the next best thing was to pursue her interest in writing. Another claim she later frequently made about her pre-Hollywood years is that she worked for the *Los Angeles Times* as a cub reporter but was fired by a particularly critical editor when she added an extra "e" to the word "resiliency" in a piece.[16] Since cub reporters did not get bylines, we'll have to take Ann's word that she very briefly was a newspaperwoman. After her abbreviated tenure at the *Times*, Ann pounded the pavement, trying to find employment at one of the many newspapers that existed in Los Angeles in the late 1920s, but none were willing to hire a teenaged girl with virtually no experience. She later recalled, "I wore myself out looking for the kind of work I wanted. Then I tried reading the want ads in the paper, and following them up every morning. Nothing came of that either."[17] During this time, she supposedly sold a poem to *Cosmopolitan* magazine, then a literary publication. Unless she submitted the poem under a pseudonym, it appears that it was never actually published—this may be another of Ann's false claims about this period in her life. It's not clear why Ann would fabricate so many details of this time, though the extreme financial instability her family was enduring may have been too painful to relive later on.

For nearly two years after graduating, Ann attempted to jump-start a writing career without success. By 1928 Arthur Pearson had finally gained employment as a manager at the Honig & Cooper Company, another advertising agency. This helped slow the flow of red ink running through the household, but the family still found itself hurting financially and Ann felt pressure to find some sort of work. The three soon moved into an apartment at 6366 Orange Street in the Fairfax District of Los Angeles, and with Ann's writing career having ended before it began, she turned her attention to what for her was the next logical place . . . the movies.

4

Chorus Cutie

With her writing ambitions unrealized, at least for the moment, Ann turned to the business she had been surrounded by her entire life. She was banking on her mother to help her break through the studio doors. Always one to put Lehr on a pedestal, Ann reflected, "I'm lucky that's all, in having a mother who knows these people personally." Lehr was unofficially retired, but still had enough connections to arrange for her daughter to meet with Douglas Fairbanks, who would soon be entering production on his last silent film, *The Iron Mask*. Ann was excited to meet the swashbuckling superstar, whom she described as "a very courteous and interesting man. He is very handsome too." She added, "He has a very pleasant laugh which I found out through his amusement over my extreme youth and inexperience." She was especially impressed that the busy actor would take the time to meet with her, observing, "I have found out that the really big people—that is those who amount to something and who have a great deal of responsibility—are the ones most likely to be tolerant and understanding. Some little fortieth assistant director would probably have just taken my name and address, shooed me out of the studio, and thrown away the paper he had written it on." Once she became a prominent film star, Ann was always conscious of extending similar courtesies to aspiring actors. Fairbanks was impressed, or amused, enough with Ann to offer her a screen test; he turned her over to his secretary, who attended to the "details of my costume, and wigs etc. for a test. You see, they are making a picture of the Louis XIII and XIV period. Oh God, I hope I photograph well enough."[1]

Ann did not get called back for *The Iron Mask*, so she persuaded her mother to help arrange screen tests at other studios. She tried her luck at MGM, but according to Ann, the casting man "said the test was no good. That's lovely and encouraging!" She fared better when she "took the test at Lasky's. Saw it. It was wonderful. From the depths to the heights!"² Nothing came from any of these screen tests either, and as Ann later recalled, "I received no encouragement. Casting directors said I was too young. They also said I was self-conscious, and not particularly good looking." Still, she did her best to remain optimistic: "No use being downcast and all that rot. I'll make these studios or bust!" Breaking into the movies started to become an obsession for Ann; she admitted that during this period "I lived in a dream, thinking about nothing but motion pictures. I kept John Barrymore's picture on my dresser. At last I got a chance to meet him. I found myself so tongue-tied that I could hardly talk. Afterward, I cried about it."³ As time went on with no word from any of the studios, Ann started to feel desperate, especially because she needed to contribute financially at home. As she recorded in a journal, "Good Lord, I simply *must* get work. I hate money but one must have it."⁴ As it turned out, Ann did not need to despair. The movie industry was changing before her eyes, and her luck was about to change with it.

Hollywood had been turned on its ear in 1927 when Warner Bros. released *The Jazz Singer,* featuring Al Jolson actually singing and (occasionally) speaking onscreen. These "talking pictures" were at first considered a novelty by many industry insiders, but an overwhelmingly positive audience reaction quickly dictated the death of the silent-film era and forced the studios to make a mad scramble to get sound features into theaters. With the switch to sound came the need for a new wave of film talent. Many stars of the silent screen were not able to make the transition to the new format because of unintelligible foreign accents or voices that did not register well on the newly developed recording equipment. The purging of screen talent opened a door of opportunity for acting hopefuls with strong voices as Hollywood tried to meet the moviegoing public's insatiable desire for sound films.

Under the leadership of mogul Louis B. Mayer and production chief Irving Thalberg, Metro-Goldwyn-Mayer (MGM) had been establishing itself as one of the premier studios since its formation in 1924. The studio had been slow to follow Warner Bros.' lead into the realm of talking pictures but quickly recovered ground by releasing the first movie musical, *The Broadway Melody.* Advertised as "All Talking, All Singing, All Dancing," the film, featuring Bessie Love and Anita Page as sisters living and loving under the hot lights of Broadway, dazzled audiences when it was released in early 1929 and won an Academy Award for Best Picture.

Seeking to follow up the success of *The Broadway Melody,* MGM immediately launched *Revue of Revues* into production. Ultimately released as *The Hollywood Revue of 1929,* the film would again be all talking, all singing, and all dancing, and it provided the studio with a platform to show off the impressive stable of stars it had under contract, including Norma Shearer, Marion Davies, Joan Crawford, John Gilbert, William Haines, Buster Keaton, and Marie Dressler. The movie was to be structured like a vaudeville/variety show, with Jack Benny and Conrad Nagel serving as emcees and a large chorus of dancers performing multiple routines. MGM began holding auditions to fill spaces in the lineup and Ann, despite the rejections of the previous few months, including one from MGM, saw the chorus auditions as good a way as any to get film work. When a friend pointed out that Ann really did not know how to dance, she shot back, "What's the difference? I'm limber, I can do a split and a cartwheel. Maybe I can get someone to teach me a time-step. I'm going to try, anyway."[5] Lehr, still unimpressed with her daughter's physical appearance, was probably not surprised that her attempts to acquire work in the movies up to this point had fallen flat. Still, she had to admit that the teenager was fairly confident and self-possessed, and she couldn't help but admire Ann's gumption.

Before heading to the Culver City studio for the big audition, Ann asked her mother to write a letter of introduction to Harry Rapf, an acquaintance from Lehr's acting days who was the producer of *The Hollywood Revue* and would be sitting in on the chorus auditions. Ann's continued faith in her mother's influence is touchingly naive. With the exception of *Jesus of Nazareth,* Lehr had not made a film in over six years and was by this time a relic in an industry with a short attention span and even shorter memory. Anna often harbored delusions of grandeur in looking back at her former career, but even she was well aware that a letter of introduction to Rapf would do little to assist her seventeen-year-old daughter in landing a job at MGM. Not wanting to be too discouraging, she fulfilled Ann's request and drafted the letter, which was as ineffective as Lehr predicted. When she showed up at the audition, Dvorak further established her belief in her mother's influence by discarding her own name in favor of "Anna Lehr." Ann also demonstrated a lack of clothing sense by showing up in an unfashionably long pleated skirt and thick-soled shoes. She may have had enough confidence to show up at the audition, but she was too modest to show off her legs. At this point she also saw no need to wear any makeup or to style her hair, which she was still wearing in two thick braids. Not surprisingly, Ann was one of the first girls told to go home. Instead of leaving as instructed, however, she simply walked to the end of the line of hopefuls and auditioned again. Once again she was told to go home, and again she moved to the back of the line and auditioned once more. After this had gone on for awhile, Ann finally marched up to either Rapf or director Christy Cabanne (who was ultimately replaced by Charles F. Reisner) and proclaimed she was "as good as the ones you chose. Why didn't you pick me? I'm going to get somewhere. I'm sincere. I work. I have ambition." Ann's chutzpah impressed Rapf enough that he hired her as a substitute in case one of the other girls was injured. As luck would have it, an injury occurred almost immediately, and Ann soon found herself standing before movie cameras for the first time in almost ten years.[6]

Ann was thrilled to have a job, and while Anna was still skeptical of her daughter's chances of making a career in the movies, she was happy to get the $37.50 a week Ann brought home. Despite the family's continued financial struggles, Arthur Pearson was vehemently opposed to his step-daughter's chosen vocation, and their Orange Street apartment was constantly disrupted by bickering over Ann's employment at MGM. Ann ignored these objections and continued to make the short trip from her home to Culver City. She was determined to prove her worth among the other ladies of the chorus.

Rehearsals for *The Hollywood Revue of 1929* started on February 4 and proved a grueling routine for the dancers, who appeared in many of the film's scenes. Overseeing the bevy of chorus girls and boys was Sammy Lee, a successful dance director who had choreographed Broadway hits such as *Lady, Be Good, No, No, Nanette,* and *Show Boat.* MGM had lured Lee away from New York in November 1928 to stage some uncredited dance numbers for *The Broadway Melody.* He proved to be so adept at his job that choreography of *The Hollywood Revue* was handed over to him even though George Cunningham had originally been announced as dance director.[7] Lee expected a lot from his dancers, noting that "it's mighty tough work. They have to be troupers, in perfect physical condition, willing to work hard and to learn."[8] He meant what he said. By the end of her first week on the job, Ann was so stiff she could hardly walk, joking to a friend that she had "a Charley horse in every muscle."[9] She admitted that the work was "frantically hard" and exhausting, but was

Ann (far right) exchanges glances with MGM choreographer Sammy Lee on the set of the short *The Doll Shop*.

also "a lot of fun," and she was pleased to be contributing at last to her family financially. On her first payday, she recorded in her journal, "I had the pleasure of giving mother $37.50 tonight. Hurrah! I'm actually earning some money. It's about time I did that."[10] In the weeks leading up to production, Sammy Lee had been dealing with remaining commitments in New York, so he was not present at Ann's spunky audition. But she made a big impression on him after he'd been working with her for a short period of time. Ann may not have been the best dancer in the chorus, but Lee noticed her stamina and strong work ethic. He also picked up on her ability to effectively teach routines to her fellow hoofers, a holdover from her pageant days at the private school. When Ann fell sick with the flu a couple of weeks into rehearsal and was sidelined for ten days, she feared the worst, but Lee held her place in the chorus and she got back to work as soon as she was able.[11]

Once the cameras started rolling, Ann found the work far less fun as she settled into an exhausting routine: she arrived at the studio by 9:00 in the morning and left so tired she would go straight to bed as soon as she got home. She also discovered the monotony of movie making: "Waiting around on the set is demoralizing in every way. People just sit around and look at each other. There is positively no mental work at all. But I am trying to keep my head above water. I know that what I am now doing is molding my future career, but oh gosh, it's hard!" Still, she found the work gratifying, and when the chorus wrapped up its scenes on *Hollywood Revue*, Ann recorded in a journal, "All the boys and girls felt rather sad about leaving after being together all of every day for eleven weeks. I certainly do. It has meant the beginning of everything for me." For the girl who had shown up for the audition in a long, modest skirt, the experience had been life altering; as she wrote, "A good part of my self-consciousness has left me, and I now feel at ease among people."[12]

Production on *The Hollywood Revue of 1929* continued after the chorus was dismissed, wrapping up on June 11. Amazingly, it was edited and ready to go for its big Los Angeles premiere a mere nine days later. MGM pulled out all the stops for promoting the film and on June 18, two days before the premiere, set up a "human billboard" at the corner of Wilshire Boulevard and Shatto Place. The advertisement, which was hidden behind a massive curtain, was unveiled at 8:30 p.m. and spelled out METRO-GOLD-WYN-MAYER'S HOLLYWOOD REVUE, GRAUMAN'S CHINESE THEATRE. The letters of the film's title were large enough to support the sixteen scantily clad chorus girls put on display for passing onlookers to gawk at. Existing photos reveal that Ann was one of the chosen girls; she can be seen perched atop the first "O" in "Hollywood," looking extremely bored. None of the dancers seemed too thrilled to be stuck thirty-plus feet above ground without any visible safeguards, and newspapers documenting the evening do not state how long they had to endure the display. This bizarre stunt would

A "living billboard" at the corner of Wilshire Boulevard and Shatto Place, advertising the *Hollywood Revue of 1929*. Ann is on top of the first O in Hollywood.

be repeated on a much larger scale at the film's New York premiere at the Astor Theatre two months later. Fortunately for Ann and the other girls, there were more than enough dancers in the Big Apple to handle the job, and the MGM hoofers were spared a repeat performance. On June 20, Ann attended the big gala at Grauman's Chinese Theatre with her mother by her side, but the event seemed to have been bittersweet. She later recorded, "I felt terribly small and inconsequential among all those stars. Mother looked lovely, but I felt sorry that more people did not take notice of her. She certainly looked much prettier than anyone else I saw."[13] Ann was finally coming to the realization that others did not view her mother in the same bright spotlight she did.

    The Hollywood Revue of 1929 proved to be as successful as MGM had anticipated and earned a Best Picture nomination alongside *The Broadway Melody*. Watching the movie today prompts a mixed assessment; largely filmed from one angle, it is static, sometimes boring, and many of the jokes are dated and fall flat. On the other hand, the film is a fascinating document of the industry's awkward transition to sound as well as a permanent record of the dying art form that was early twentieth-century vaudeville. Plus, this marked the first time the song "Singin' in the Rain" appeared in a film, presented as a splashy two-color Technicolor number featuring the cast and chorus singing away in yellow rain slickers. Considering that Ann earned her place in the lineup by the skin of her teeth, she is amazingly prominent throughout the film, which demonstrates how big an impression she made on Sammy Lee. She really is the standout among the group as the girl smiling the widest, flailing her arms the highest, and tapping the hardest. This would be true of all her nearly thirty appearances in MGM films over the next two years. In *The Hollywood Revue* she even speaks two words, "Pardon me," and slaps Jack Benny in the face.

Following the success of *Broadway Melody* and The *Hollywood Revue of 1929*, MGM launched a number of musical features and shorts into production. Despite her minor triumph in *The Hollywood Revue*, Ann was not offered a contract with the studio. She experienced a "heavy failure feeling" once she found herself without a job again: "I woke and started to dress for work—and then I realized that it is over!" Fortunately, she was called back to appear as a dancing student in *So This Is College*, featuring Robert Montgomery and Cliff Edwards. Ann was ecstatic to be employed in front of the camera again but seemed conflicted about the type of work she was doing, saying,

I really love the studios and everyone there. I know they don't realize how much I appreciate the chances they have been giving me. I love it and I hope I can get a little part of some kind. O, God, please give me the courage to keep up the right spirit towards my work. I don't mean that I'm not still ambitious about it, but I mean that I don't want to fall into that mental rut that so many do, who find themselves still on the "small end" of the profession. I *want* to start at the bottom. In fact, I'd rather. Anyway, I *have* to. But I want to keep myself *good*—and intelligent and alert, most of all.

Ann's ambitions may have been to be cast in a speaking part, but she had to settle for another chorus job when she was called to appear in the short feature *The Doll Shop* as a dancing toy soldier. As dismayed as she may have been with yet another dancing role, she became even more discouraged when over a month went by without her being offered any more work, other than the gig on the living billboard. When MGM finally contacted her in late July, it was for another chorus job in the feature *Chasing Rainbows*, a comedy/drama about the highs and lows of a traveling road show. *Chasing Rainbows* was followed by *Devil-May-Care*, a big-budget musical set in Napoleonic France and starring Ramon Novarro. Ann was not happy with continued chorus work and began to harbor concerns that she was getting stuck in a rut, commenting, "I supposed if they ever do sign me, it will be merely along with the rest of the chorus, just as a dancing girl. I'm not so good as I thought I was. But that, too, is part of the game. I'll stick to it like an octopus until, finally, in my old age they'll take pity and sign me for a character woman." Still, Ann was not one to be held down for too long and added, "But there I go, mooning with self-pity! I'll just keep working and remember that one can never hold a job too small—that is, if we aren't big enough to do little things, we certainly aren't big enough to do big things. And then, too, a ladder must be climbed, not flown."[14]

Just as Ann predicted, when she was finally offered a six-month contract, MGM was interested only in her services as a hoofer. On the bright side, after working with Ann multiple times, Sammy Lee had become convinced of her worth as a hardworking dancer and an even harder working dance instructor. He wanted to sign her on as his assistant. Ann may have not been thrilled at the prospect of being tied to the chorus for an indefinite period, but the opportunity to have a stable job at the studio in any capacity was too good to pass up. She signed the contract on August 10, 1929, and received a bump in pay to $50 a week.[15] Curiously, the contract lists her date of birth as 1910, but even this slight boost in age did not prevent Ann from having to appear before a judge to have the contract approved, as she was still a minor. Ann, still going by the stage name Anna Lehr, showed up at the courthouse on December 20 with her mother and received official approval along with twelve other minors, including ingénue Mary Carlisle, who remembered Ann from that day as "the tall brunette with the big feet."[16]

Immediately following her promotion to assistant choreographer, Ann was working alongside Vivian and Rosetta Duncan, who had been signed by MGM to appear in their first (and only) sound feature, ultimately released as *It's a Great Life*. The Duncan Sisters had originally been pegged to play the leads in *The Broadway Melody*, but a scheduling conflict had prevented this from happening. Instead, they starred in this virtual remake of the successful film, and Ann ended up sharing center stage with the pair who had performed at her school only two short years before. Ann worked privately with the sisters on a step called the "Hoosier Hop," which she had supposedly choreographed herself.[17] During this number, the Duncans exit the screen and a particularly proud-looking Ann and another dancer become the focal point. Despite any misgivings Ann may have had about the chorus work, she seemed determined to make the most of it.

As 1930 began, there was no letup on the number of large-scale musicals going into production. Even though she had become Lee's assistant, Ann was still showing up among the chorus dancers in a number of features, such as *Children of Pleasure*, *Lord Byron of Broadway*, and *The Woman Racket*, along with musical shorts such as *Manhattan Serenade*, *The Flower Garden*, *Pirates*, and *The Snappy Caballero*. She is highly visible during the "Varsity Drag" number in *Good News*, and she is the chorine Buster Keaton singles out in *Free and Easy*. A photo of Ann along with a few other half-clothed dance hall girls from the William Haines picture *Way Out West* made it on the cover of sheet music for the film. She still had the appearance of an awkward teenager and was a far cry from the beauty she would later become, but Ann is easy to pick out in these films with her large eyes, slightly lopsided smile, and an enthusiasm unmatched by anyone else in the chorus. Even in the still photographs for these films, she pops out among the others as the girl very aware of the camera, looking straight into it. No matter how discouraged Ann may have been by the string of chorus work MGM was casting her in, she never let it show when she was on camera.

When she wasn't working long hours at the studio, Ann could usually be found at the beach. This was partially to avoid the unpleasant atmosphere that had developed at home since she became an MGM employee, but mainly because she genuinely loved being outdoors. She spent so much time at the ocean that Clarence Sinclair Bull, head of the MGM Stills Department, spent an afternoon photographing Ann and fellow contract player Marjorie King (alleged namesake of the margarita cocktail) frolicking on the beach. The one drawback to Ann's extracurricular activities was the deep tan she developed from hours under the sun. As she later

Chorus Cutie

Always the sun worshipper, a very tanned Ann (fourth from left) is instructed by Busby Berkeley, circa 1930.

recalled, "About the only marked notice I got—and that was scarcely complimentary—was from the cameramen telling me that my skin, nearly all of which was exposed by our so-called costumes, was too dark." She continued, "I was so tanned that it took three coats of body make-up before I would photograph as white as the other girls."[18]

Her spare days may have been spent at the ocean, but the evenings tended to find her on Orange Street, as Anna Lehr maintained a tight leash on her only child. Ann complained, "I can't stand sitting around. That's all I can do you know, because mother won't let me go anywhere. She's worried I'll be around too sophisticated a crowd. I get so tired of seeing this house and I'd give *any*thing for a nice dance floor and a good dancing partner. Pretty soon I'll forget what it's like to go out and I won't care. If it weren't for my work, I'd go insane—that comes from my heart too." Lehr couldn't watch her daughter round the clock, and Ann proved that, like most teenagers, she wasn't above giving into the habits of some of her peers when she expressed, "Every time I smoke a cigarette I get sick, and yet every once in a while I do it. I must have an idea that I look cute or something when I smoke. I'm so dumb."[19] Eventually, the arguments in the household over Ann's employment at MGM became so heated that Lehr found "I had to make the unhappy choice between my husband . . . and my daughter. Her stepfather was dead set against Ann becoming an actress. Ann was equally determined to continue with her 'career.'"[20] Pearson moved out and Ann and Anna were soon relying solely on each other.

Ann's position as assistant choreographer continued and she ended up becoming a sort of mother hen to the other dancers. In 1930 a young girl from the Midwest named Anna Swensen came to Los Angeles to take care of a sick aunt and through a friend found employment as a dancer on *Free and Easy*. Ann quickly took the girl under her wing. As her son, Dick Peterson, recalls, "My mom was a wide-eyed seventeen-year-old from a small city in the Midwest and their relationship was big sister to little sister." He continues, "At the studio, everyone that worked with Ann thought very highly of her. She was very protective of the other dancers and wasn't afraid to challenge any director or studio flunky if they criticized anyone in her group." Swensen had relayed one particular incident to her son that occurred on the set of *Free and Easy*, when the on-set orchestra kept ruining takes by flubbing the music. "One day, after an exasperating number of retakes because of musical goofs, Ann walked over to the orchestra leader and gave him a verbal lashing, saying that her girls were tired and their feet were sore and they didn't need the orchestra's lack of professionalism." He adds, "Then she walked over to the director and told him how disgusted she was because her girls had rehearsed over and over again and came on the set well prepared and that a few drunken clowns in the orchestra were upsetting everything. The director then called for lunch and had the orchestra rehearse over and over on set until they had it right. My mom said that was typical Ann Dvorak."[21]

On another occasion Ann proved her willingness to aid other Hollywood hopefuls. Over eighty years later, actress Mary Carlisle remembered, "My uncle's name was Grant Whytock, who was an editor and worked with producer Edward Small. Edward knew everyone at MGM and heard they were signing chorus girls, so he told my uncle to get me over to the studio for an audition. I wasn't a dancer, so someone—I think it was Mr. Small—arranged for me to learn how to dance. I was up all night with that nice girl who taught me a time step." She continued, "It was Ann Dvorak; she was a good dancer. I did the audition and got the contract."[22]

As much as Ann enjoyed working with her girls, she was becoming bored with the work and hated the chorine label, complaining, "And it hurts too, being a chorus girl and branded as such. Not that I don't like dancing. It's just the undignified something about it. It sort of keeps you from doing anything else." In what had become her typical fashion of not allowing herself to be down for too long, Ann followed up this sentiment with "But I *will*, anyway—and just let someone try and stop me!"[23] After appearing in over a dozen features and shorts as a dancer, she longed for more substantial film roles, sick of doing the same thing over and over. Coincidentally, the moviegoing public was also tiring of what one movie magazine writer referred to as "those all-singing-all-dancing-all-pretty-terrible affairs that were one of the first microphone plagues."[24] Audiences had so quickly and violently turned on these early musical revues that MGM scrapped the release of the grandiose *The March of Time*, which was nearly completed. Bits from this film would later be recycled and inserted into shorts features and the 1933 release *Broadway to Hollywood*. The last number shot before the project was killed was "The Lock Step," featuring what was then the highest set ever built inside a soundstage, accommodating over fifty chorus girls, including Ann, dressed as jailbirds. As soon as the project was shelved, Sammy Lee was released from his contract, and he returned to New York.

With Sammy Lee gone and musical revues making an exit, Ann was eager to expand her MGM repertoire and was willing to try almost anything for a change of pace. True to her personality, she was most interested in actually acting onscreen, but she was also open to scriptwriting. She had become friendly with many people around the lot and was well liked and admired for her strong work ethic. However, after more than a year of appearing in musicals, she carried the stigma of being a mere chorus girl and was not thought of as someone who would rise above the ranks. Even after she became a film actress of note, she still seemed to carry some resentment from this period, complaining, "Our Hollywood chorines are nice kids, all of them, and to my personal knowledge, many of them have ability beyond the average. But it's hard to believe that the talent in these youngsters would remain unnoticed by those who are constantly on the lookout for it. Our producers and directors must have their own reasons for not choosing these girls from the ranks. But what are they?"[25]

During her time at MGM, she also came to notice that not all employees on the lot were as affable as she was. "People at the studio are very strange. One day they are smiling and friendly. The next day they are cold and distant. . . . People are very, very cruel when they have success, and God forbid that I ever get that way when I succeed!" Ann never named individuals who acted this way, but this treatment made a huge impression on the teenager. "And when I reach the top, I won't be high-hat like all the rest. I'd rather die. Even if there are people I am not interested in, I won't hurt them by letting them know it." As Ann grew more frustrated with her lack of options at MGM, she also started to abandon whatever spiritual faith she had carried over from her convent days, commenting, "I don't think about God much. I try to put all my faith in myself. My God, if I have one, is beauty and love and music combined. Everything is beautiful, even what we call ugliness. If a mountain is beautiful, one can't say it is partly ugly because it is made of dirt or because there are bugs and worms living on it."[26]

With the large-scale musical on the wane, Ann started being cast as a background extra, though she continued to instruct actors on smaller-scale numbers and occasionally still danced onscreen herself, most notably as the Indian girl Ramon Navarro stumbles upon in *Son of India*. Ann was so determined to shake the chorus girl label that she even changed her name in an attempt to reinvent herself. It was sometime during these latter months at MGM that she ditched the stage name Anna Lehr in favor of Ann Dvorak, the moniker she had sometimes adopted as a child in New York. The name Dvorak had always intrigued her and she probably felt it now gave her an air of sophistication that would help alter her standing as a lowly hoofer. If nothing else, the name proved to be difficult for the MGM publicity department, which identified her in the C. S. Bull beach photos as "Ann Devorak."

Instead of an acting part, Ann was next assigned to instruct Joan Crawford in two dance numbers the actress was to perform in *Dance, Fools, Dance*. Like Ann, Joan had been a chorus dancer, hoofing her way through various revues on New York stages. She was signed by MGM in 1924, first appearing as Norma Shearer's double in *Lady of the Night*. By the time Ann was coaching Crawford on dance steps, she had become one of the biggest stars on the lot. Ann would eventually find herself unsuited for long-term contracts with one studio, but Joan Crawford was the ultimate studio-system star who embraced everything that came with it, both

Famed MGM photographer Clarence Sinclair Bull captures contract player Ann "Devorak" in 1931. Months later, the slightly awkward teenager would be transformed into a movie star.

good and bad. The pair took an instant liking to each other, as Joan identified with Ann's determination to succeed, and Ann admired the actress whose star burned so brightly. During the early stages of Ann's friendship with Crawford, Anna Lehr began to notice a transformation in her daughter's appearance and manner that was clearly due to her association with the actress. She noted, "For several weeks I suspected her of attempting to look as much like Joan Crawford as possible. It seemed to me that she was even beginning to talk like Joan. Her clothes were selected with an eye toward a 'Crawford flair' and I must say that Ann's style sense seemed to improve. During this marked Crawford influence she began to think more and more of her figure and carriage. In the next two months the change in my tall, ungainly Ann was quite remarkable."[27] Lehr wasn't the only one who saw the resemblance between the two young women. On the lot Ann was sometimes referred to as the dancer who looked like Joan Crawford, though Ann remarked after they became friends, "People thought we looked alike when they saw us separately. They never think we look alike when they see us together."[28] Crawford tried to use whatever influence she had to secure more substantial roles for her protégée, but to no avail. Ann appreciated the efforts, noting "She did everything she could to get me my chance. But nobody would get interested. Perhaps we were too good friends—perhaps people thought Joan was too greatly influenced by that friendship." Crawford's husband at the time, Douglas Fairbanks Jr., had also taken a shine to Ann, but admitted, "We introduced her to any number of directors, producers and executives. No one would give her a chance it seemed. I guess we were poor salesmen, because we both thought Ann had the goods."[29] Crawford did manage to get Ann into a couple of her own starring vehicles, as a party crasher in *This Modern Age* and as one of four girls fawning over Robert Montgomery in *Our Blushing Brides*.

By mid-1931 Ann's career at MGM had stalled. Occasional photos would be released by the studio touting her as "Ann Devorak, MGM featured player," but there were no plans to do anything with her beyond the extra work she was still being assigned. It was during these waning months in Culver City that she became close friends with another actress on the lot. Ann could have never guessed that this friendship would be the catalyst for her acting career and lead her to the role of a lifetime.

5

Scarface

By 1931 the Hollywood film industry was getting over the growing pains brought on by sound films and had entered one of its most notorious periods, now known as the pre-Code era. As the country shifted from strict Victorian moral codes to the looser attitudes of the Jazz Age, the movies reflected these social changes and became increasingly more daring with the subject matter presented on the screen. The majority of film fans who flocked to the theaters reveled in these tales of crime, sex, drugs, and the like, but more vocal religious groups took exception to the lurid themes and emerging real-life Hollywood scandals, and began putting pressure on the studios to clean up their act. The industry had initially responded to these moral rumblings in 1922 by forming the Motion Picture Producers and Distributors of America (MPPDA) and appointing former postmaster general William (Will) H. Hays as head of the organization, whose goal was to instill a system of self-regulation, allowing the studios to proceed without government intervention. Hays was able to stave off federal meddling, but the state censorship boards that sprang up frequently reedited films to suit their own moral standards.

As outside pressures for cleaner films mounted, the MPPDA adopted a set of guidelines in 1927 for the studios to follow to help them steer clear of objectionable material. By 1930 this list of "Don't's" and "Be careful's" morphed into the more comprehensive "Hays Code" or "Production Code." The Code clearly spelled out what the movies could and could not portray, but these restrictions on taboo topics were generally ignored by the studios until 1934, when the industry was essentially strong-armed into adopting the Code by religious groups. The brief but glorious period between the drafting and adoption of the Production Code would see the studios producing films that were shocking, even by today's standards, but also gave audiences some of the most interesting female characters in film history. Actresses like Jean Harlow, Barbara Stanwyck, Ruth Chatterton, and Miriam Hopkins blazed across the screen in *Red-headed Woman, Baby Face, Female,* and *The Story of Temple Drake,* with characterizations that still stand up decades later as fresh and daring. This period of strong, self-possessed, sexually liberated screen dames is when Ann Dvorak finally broke out of the chorus ranks and made her small but indelible mark on the movies.

Ann had been at MGM for almost two and a half years by mid-1931. She had proved reliable and was willing to undertake whatever the studio threw at her, but she now felt as if she was spinning her wheels. Splashy chorus-filled musicals were officially out of vogue, and Sammy Lee was no longer employed at the Culver City lot. There seemed to be little for Ann to do besides show up as a background extra in films like *Just a Gigolo* and *A Tailor Made Man.* During this period, Ann was becoming so discouraged that she began to rethink her career plans and was on the verge of leaving the film industry.

One of her extra jobs at the time was as a member of a political rally in the Marie Dressler/Polly Moran proto-feminist feature *Politics.* The film costarred an up-and-coming actress named Karen Morley. Morley had moved to Los Angeles from Iowa at a young age and started her acting career at the Pasadena Playhouse. While on the MGM lot for a screen test in 1930, she caught the eye of director Clarence Brown, who gave her the ingénue role in the Greta Garbo vehicle *Inspiration.* She was soon signed to a contract with the studio and named a "baby star" by the Western Association of Motion Picture Advertisers (WAMPAS). Much like Dvorak, Morley was considered unconventional in both her looks and acting style, and she also had a hard time accepting the restraints of the studio system. Both women ended up fighting their studios to gain early release from their contracts, and both would spend the bulk of their careers freelancing. The two women also came to be extremely influenced by their husbands. For Ann, this sway extended primarily to hobbies and career decisions, while Karen's two unions would shape her in becoming a vocal political activist. Dvorak and Morley both saw their film careers end in 1951, with Ann opting for retirement and Karen winding up on the blacklist after being named a Communist during the McCarthy-era witch hunts.

Shortly after arriving at MGM, Karen was introduced to Ann Dvorak, and even though she was a full-fledged actress and Ann was a mere chorus dancer, they must have recognized their similar temperaments. The two became fast friends. They frequently had lunch together, and Ann often visited Karen in her dressing room where they discussed Ann's chances of leaving the chorus behind. As had Joan Crawford, Morley identified a great deal of potential in her friend; she soon became Ann's most ardent cheerleader. As was the case with Crawford, people on the lot also began commenting on how Ann and Karen resembled each other physically.[1] Morley, who was a couple of years older than Dvorak, was always quick with words of support, and Anna Lehr later recalled that if it hadn't been for Karen's "constant, almost dogged, encouragement," Ann would have turned her back on the movies.[2] As Morley continued her acting career at MGM, Ann was equally supportive, and when Karen landed a plum role in an upcoming gangster film at another studio, Ann was sincerely happy for her friend, although she thought it would mean Karen would be far too busy to socialize.

Karen's new film was being produced by Howard Hughes, who had rapidly emerged as a force to be reckoned with in Hollywood. The versatile Texan had come to Los Angeles in the mid-1920s with an inherited family fortune and a desire to make movies. He formed the Caddo Company and made a name for himself by producing and directing the epic *Hell's Angels*, featuring spectacular feats of aviation and a barely covered Jean Harlow in a breakout role. Despite this early triumph, Hughes was not embraced by the movie moguls, who viewed the twenty-something producer as an arrogant outsider. This attitude only encouraged him to push the envelope on the types of films he was making. In 1930 Hughes optioned the rights to the Armitage Trail novel *Scarface*, published the previous year. The Chicago-based story focused on two brothers: one inspired by the real-life exploits of gangster Al Capone, the other residing on the right side of the law as a police officer. Hughes envisioned the story as an epic gangster film. He approached Howard Hawks to direct it. Like Hughes, Hawks was an arrogant and independent man, on the precipice of a phenomenal career, who welcomed the opportunity to make a film outside the studio system. In January 1931 Warner Bros. released *Little Caesar*, starring Edward G. Robinson, which brought the gangster flick into vogue. That same month Howard Hawks was officially contracted to direct *Scarface*, and Ben Hecht was brought in to write the screenplay.

Neither Hawks nor Hecht was thrilled by the idea of making a gangster film and basically abandoned the plot of the Armitage Trail novel early on. Instead, they decided to use the scandalous Renaissance-era Borgias as a model for their modern-day Camonte family. Hawks imagined their updated version of one of the Borgia brothers as "Al Capone, and his sister does the same incest thing as Lucretia Borgia."[3] The Hays Office immediately began expressing concerns over the content of Howard Hughes's latest production, and while the office may have been facing resistance to the recently adopted Production Code, it still had enough teeth to schedule a conference with Hughes and Hawks in March 1931 to discuss their plans for the film. This was to be the first in a long line of legendary censorship battles for a movie that Hays's assistant Colonel Jason S. Joy viewed as "the most harsh and frank gangster picture" the office had seen. Additionally, Joy expected that *Scarface* would not pass any of the state censorship boards.[4]

Censorship wasn't the only obstacle in Hughes and Hawks's way to getting *Scarface* made. Given the negative attitude the studio heads harbored toward the Texas millionaire and his independent productions, the pair had little chance of borrowing any notable talent from the major studios. Instead, Hawks set out for New York to see if he could spot any suitable actors on the Great White Way, and here he discovered Paul Muni. At first Muni was more interested in the stage than motion pictures, but Hawks was able to persuade him to do a screen test. Muni was pleased enough with the results to sign on to play the lead character, Tony Camonte, and come to the West Coast. For the role of Camonte's loyal sidekick, Guino Rinaldo, Hawks selected George Raft, a struggling actor whom the director had encountered at a prizefight. Stage actor Osgood Perkins (father of Anthony) was selected to play Camonte's betrayed mentor, and Boris Karloff, whose role as Frankenstein's monster would delight film fans later that year, was bought on for a small but memorable part as a rival gang member. The script contained two strong female characters; Cesca, Tony's younger independent-minded sister, for whom he harbors uncomfortably close feelings, and Poppy, moll to Tony's boss whom he ultimately woos into his corner. Karen Morley was under contract to MGM, but Hawks was good friends with Eddie Mannix, a high-ranking executive at the studio who allowed the actress to be loaned out for the production. Years later, Morley would recall that she had her pick of either role. Even though Cesca was the stronger part and the blonde actress would have worn "the prettiest wig, full of black curls," she chose the role of Poppy. She still hadn't given up on a film career for Ann; realizing that her friend was all wrong for Poppy, she thought Dvorak might have a serious shot at landing Cesca. Almost seventy years later, Morley would look back at her actions as "probably the nicest thing I did in my life."[5]

Now that Karen was signed on for *Scarface*, she had to figure out a way to introduce Ann to Howard Hawks. Fortunately, the director was having a hard time finding an actress he liked for Cesca and opportunity presented itself one night when Hawks threw a party at his home for the cast of his upcoming production. Morley wasted no time in calling Ann, instructing her to dress to the nines and come over to Hawks's house immediately. Karen had opened the door for her friend, but it would be up to Ann to make an impression. When she arrived at the party, Ann zeroed in on George Raft, who would be playing Cesca's love interest in the film. Howard Hawks later recalled, "Ann asked [Raft] to dance with her, but he said he would rather not. She was a little high and right in front of him starts to do this sexy undulating dance, sort of trying to lure him on to dance with her. She was a knockout. She wore a black silk gown, almost cut down to her hips. I'm sure that's all she had on. After a while George couldn't resist her suggestive dance and in no time they were doing a sensational number which stopped the party."[6]

Hawks was more than impressed with Ann, and even though he had reservations about casting a chorus girl in such an important role, invited her to come see him the next day to do a screen test. Morley and Dvorak returned to Ann's home after the party and stayed up the rest of the night, prematurely planning the look and behavior of Cesca. Karen's hunch about her friend proved to be spot-on, and as Ann later recalled, "I was anxious to do it and knew I could play it, but how to get it. I knew Karen Morley and I got her to introduce me to Howard Hawks, and . . . then I just talked myself into it. He was very kind but not really convinced. He thought of me as a dancing girl. He didn't think I would act, but I guess I just wore him down, and he sort of thought if I was so keen about it, perhaps I could do it. Anyway, he gave me a test and I got the part."[7] On July 8 Ann recorded in her journal, "Although I haven't bothered to write in such a childish thing as a diary for a long time, I feel as though this is one of the big thrill days of my life! After several days of agonizing suspense, I have a lovely, grand part in Howard Hughes' 'Scarface.' Little Karen Morley was responsible to a great degree for the whole thing. I'm

Ann undergoes an incredible transformation for the role of Cesca Camonte in *Scarface*.

too happy to think clearly."[8] Ann was at the right place at the right time, with the right connections, but she also credited her own single-minded drive in landing the role. As she later reflected, "I believe you can do anything in the world, if you really want to hard enough. It isn't even intelligence perhaps it's a sense of values. A peasant woman in Jugo-Slavia decides to send her boy to school. It's the most important thing in her life. Somehow she manages it. That's the way it was with me about the Cesca part with Paul Muni in 'Scarface.'"[9] Once again, Hawks turned to his pal Mannix at MGM and asked to borrow her, adding, "I don't mean just borrow her and then you get her back. I want her after this is over."[10] Considering that MGM had no immediate plans for Ann, the studio had no problem releasing her from her contract and turning her over to Hawks, who would indeed use her subsequently in *The Crowd Roars.* Just when she had been ready to give up, it seemed that two and a half years as a dancer, fashion tips from Joan Crawford, and relentless encouragement from Karen Morley had finally paid off for Ann Dvorak.

Film columns in the numerous Los Angeles newspapers began breaking the news of Ann winning the role of Cesca in mid-July 1931. Within a couple of months, papers around the country would be commonly referring to her as "Hollywood's New Cinderella." Dvorak was thrilled to see her name in print, and as her mother recalled, "Ann would read to me with delight the columnist hints of a new actress, said to be the most colorful personality since Joan Crawford."[11] Howard Hughes immediately saw Ann's potential as a bankable actress; a few weeks after her twentieth birthday, he signed her to a long-term contract with the Caddo Company. Under the provisions of the contract, Ann would receive $300 a week for her work in *Scarface*, which was expected to last three weeks. If Hughes decided to keep her on, her rate would drop to $200 a week with options every six months that would eventually see her pay go up to a weekly sum of $1,200. Because Ann was still a minor, Anna Lehr had to cosign the Caddo contract.[12] Two weeks after signing with Hughes's company, Ann once again found herself in Superior Court to receive official permission to work under the newly inked deal as a minor. Among the small group of juveniles appearing before the judge that day was future pinup queen Betty Grable.[13] Of her newfound professional fortune, Ann was quoted as saying, "It's what I want; It's what I've worked for. I'm going to keep on working for it. And always, I'll remember the biggest lesson I've learned in Hollywood—that is: 'Keep Your Head.' That means keep it when you're down, and keep it even more when you're going up."[14]

Now that Ann was making a name for herself, questions started springing up about her surname, which seemed to be confounding a lot of people. One newspaper reported that the young actress had been "nicely stripped of her foreign accent by careful tutelage," while another referred to her as the girl "whose name sounds like a typographical error." Ann herself was amused by the misinformation, noting, "Just the other day, I read in a paper that 'Ann Dvorak, the European actress is rapidly losing her accent.' Imagine—and I've never been any farther outside the United States than Agua Caliente!"[15] Columnist Jimmy Starr insisted that Howard Hughes was going to make her change her name, and even threw in "Ann Castle" as his preference. Hughes may have toyed with a name change, but in the end he let Ann keep it, noting that it was unusual enough to be interesting, and "when she's famous she can drop the Ann and just be Dvorak."[16] Ann herself was a bit undecided about her stage name; she signed her Caddo contract "D'Vorak," though this spelling was not implemented elsewhere. She may have still been wavering on the spelling, but had decided that "Vor-shak" was the correct way to say it. Unfortunately, no one else seemed to be aware of this, and the common pronunciation quickly became "Da-vor-ak." After "having been called practically everything from Balzac to Bickelsrock," Ann conceded defeat, stopped correcting people, and lived with being called "Da-vor-ak." To many friends and family, including her mother, she was often referred to as "Ann-D."

The filming of *Scarface* was an incredibly positive experience for Ann, and this first performance is one of her best. Karen Morley also had fond memories of the movie, later recalling it was "the most fun I had making a picture. Everybody was in awe of Paul Muni, he was so great. I was just barely of age, and that set was an exciting place to be. It was all men, and there I was prancing around in gowns that barely got past the censors."[17] The film was shot quickly, and Morley later remembered that the director had very little input into her characterization of Poppy. Perhaps Howard Hawks felt that with a few movies under her belt, Morley didn't require too much direction. However, he seems to have taken the time with his novice film actors to guide them through their interpretations of the characters. As George Raft later recalled, "We would often sit around, Howard Hawks, Ann Dvorak, Paul Muni, and myself, and discuss a scene for hours."[18] Ann responded positively to the director, and a few months after filming ended reflected, "I often wonder what the status of my career at this moment might have been had Howard Hawks not given me the encouragement and help so important to me at that time. He was so patient—so thoughtful and understanding. He told me I was an actress who had much to give the screen. I shall be forever grateful to him all my life for his fine trust and encouragement."[19]

Hawks drew upon his actors' individual talents to enhance their characters, and in one scene Ann was allowed to show off her musical talents by playing piano and gleefully singing the lyrics to the rather gruesome "The Wreck of the Old '97." In one of the film's many notable scenes, Hawks had Dvorak and Raft re-create the real scene from the party, with Ann attempting to lure him onto the dance floor. Hawks later remarked, "The scene played like a million dollars because it was something that really happened between George and Ann."[20] Under Hawks's direction, Ann was able to convincingly get through intense scenes, like the killing of Raft's character at the hands of Muni, or her own death scene, which could easily have been overplayed. From the moment she first appears on the screen, Ann exudes the independence, confidence, and sexuality that would become trademarks of the "Hawksian Woman," and the extra time the director spent with his actors clearly paid off for Ann. She bursts off the screen and demands attention with what one modern writer describes as her "intelligent eyes and clear voice incapable of conveying cheap emotion."[21] Ann's debut performance was so strong that despite having less screen time than many of the other actors, she was given second billing, right after Paul Muni. In retrospect, Ann proved to be her own harshest critic: "I got the part in *Scarface* by what amounted to an out-and-out fluke—a test and the part was mine—and I actually had no business to have it. I managed to give, I was told, a creditable performance."[22]

Ann's physical transformation for the role was amazing. Gone was the slightly awkward teenager from the MGM chorus. Her hair was teased into a massive mound of wild curls, and the amount of makeup she wore made her blue-green eyes appear enormous onscreen. The slinky black evening gown she wears in the nightclub scene is a far cry from the bulky skirt she had worn to hide her legs for the *Hollywood Revue* audition only a couple of years before. Once reports of Ann's performance started being printed, Anna Lehr reflected, "It did not seem possible that this vivid creature the critics described as Ann Dvorak could be the girl who was my daughter and friend."[23] Warner Bros.' makeup guru Perc Westmore, who had encountered Ann during her chorus days, possibly while visiting Marion Davies on the MGM lot, commented, "When I first saw [Ann] about six months ago, she looked just like a little peasant girl. She wasn't particularly well groomed, she used no cosmetics. But she was striking. In six months' time, she has learned how to carry her head to best advantage, the best expressions of her eyes." Westmore, whose brother Monte worked on *Scarface,* added, "Ann Dvorak has a peculiar type of beauty. She appears to have vitality in great quantities, strength, the wholesome qualities of the sturdy women of Europe."[24] Going forward, she would always carry the appearance of polished beauty, but never again did she look quite as striking as in *Scarface.*

Ann, anxious for her film debut to arrive in theaters, would show up at the Caddo Company offices to view rushes or to see how publicity stills had turned out. Despite the confidence she exuded as Cesca on the screen, she could still be reserved in person, and early interviewers noticed her nervous energy. Anna Lehr claimed that Ann's emotional portrayal of Cesca could not have been drawn from actual personal experience, but Ann felt differently, noting, "It was easy for me to understand my role in Scarface because of my own childhood experiences. I knew at first hand the clannishness [that] holds a foreign family together in the atmosphere of a new country. I knew how suspicious and fearful they are of outside people and influences, how they regard everything strange as dangerous." She continued, "And I understand how, no matter what a member of such a group has done, the others will stand by him to the bitter end." She concluded these sentiments about her family with, "When I was a child, I saw much of my grandparents. They were Austrian immigrants, very poor. They spoke the language of their native land. I could understand it, but not speak it. I, myself have that feeling of clannishness. Family ties mean much to me. My mother and I have always been close together."[25] On another occasion, Ann contradicted herself somewhat by stating, "I knew I had registered on the screen. My own personal self was not a part of it. I could separate *me* entirely from my work, and I believe that is the greatest thing an actress can accomplish." When it was pointed out that intense foreign roles like that of Cesca would frequently be measured against performances by the Swedish Greta Garbo or German Marlene Dietrich, Ann responded, "Oh, I wouldn't know how to imitate anybody. I can only be myself, whatever that may be."[26] Ann's portrayal of the Italian Cesca was that of an Americanized girl of a younger generation, which provided a stark contrast to Muni's accented Camonte and prevented any comparisons to Garbo or Dietrich, whose performances did not contain the high-wire energy Ann brought to the screen.

During production Hawks and Hughes found themselves constantly meeting with the Hays Office to discuss revisions to the script, but *Scarface* still managed to be shot and assembled at an amazingly fast pace. A rough cut was screened for the Production Code Administration (PCA) in early September 1931. Over the next month and a half, the film was also shown to members of the California Crime Commission and police officials, who endorsed the movie wholeheartedly, failing to see how the exploits of Tony Camonte would encourage moviegoers to embark on a life of crime. Industry insiders were also privy to advanced screenings, including MGM production wiz Irving Thalberg, who proclaimed it to be one of the strongest pictures he had ever seen.[27] Despite the positive feedback from these initial viewings, the Hays Office continued to insist on numerous changes before it issued final approval. Hughes relented on some points, like toning down the violence and tentatively agreeing to change the title to *Yellow* or *The Shame of the Nation* to prevent glamorizing Al Capone. He would ultimately backtrack and go with the original title, but all references to the name "Scarface" were removed from the final print. This is why in one scene, Ann mouths the word "Scarface" but "murderer" is what is heard on the soundtrack. Interestingly, the PCA made very little mention of the bond between Tony and Cesca, whose feelings for each other clearly went beyond the realm of brotherly/sisterly love. In fact, Hays's staff even made the suggestion that further scenes should be shot "to change the idea of a protective brother-sister relationship to that of jealousy," essentially reinforcing the incestuous nature of their relationship.[28] These censorship battles between Hughes, the Hays Office, and various state boards dragged on for months, and it started to look like *Scarface* might never make its way onto movie screens.

Howard Hughes had earned the reputation as a man about town, but there is little evidence to suggest there was much to the relationship between him and Ann beyond employer and contract player. According to Anna Lehr, Hughes did try to initiate something with the young actress by inviting Ann to accompany him to the famed Cocoanut Grove at the Ambassador Hotel. Though excited by the prospect of spending a night on the town with the Texas playboy, Ann believed Hughes was really interested in the exotic, uninhibited Cesca he had been viewing during the daily *Scarface* rushes and not the real her. Ann still saw herself as mousy and dull and feared that if Hughes found her ordinary and inexperienced, he would lose interest in putting her over on the screen. Whenever Hughes telephoned her home, Ann would have her mother make excuses

Ann and Paul Muni as Tony and Cesca Camonte get uncomfortably close in
Scarface.

for her, concocting false stories of her daughter's lavish social life, when in
fact Ann would be sitting there, "shivering and shaking with excitement
. . . her face cold-creamed, eating a ham sandwich."[29] Hughes eventually
lost interest and stopped calling. Lehr also claimed that during this period

men in general had little interest in her daughter, and she did not have a single beau. However, it is possible that Ann and Howard Hawks carried on an affair during the making of *Scarface*. Writer John Lee Mahin, who worked on the *Scarface* set, providing dialogue and continuity, confirmed the relationship to Hawks biographer Todd McCarthy, claiming everyone who worked on the film was well aware of the relationship.[30] For Hawks to have a fling with one of his actresses was very much in character for the director, who was immersed in a frequently troubled marriage to Athole Shearer, sister of screen queen Norma. If Ann was as inexperienced as her mother liked to suggest, it isn't hard to believe that she could be drawn into a relationship with a man fifteen years her senior who had been guiding and nurturing her through her first major role as an actress.

No matter what was going on in her private life, it was her professional existence that had Ann on pins and needles. The constant delays on *Scarface* had Ann convinced the picture would never be released and that her big break had been too good to be true. Anna Lehr described her daughter's state as that of "a person going through the wild hysteria of a nightmare," and Ann toyed with asking for clips of her performance to shop around to other producers, which would have been futile as she was under contract to Hughes. As the battle for *Scarface* raged on, Hughes finally occupied a restless Ann by casting her in *Sky Devils*.

Sky Devils is a slight World War I comedy starring Spencer Tracy and William Boyd (not to be confused with the William Boyd of Hopalong Cassidy fame) as members of the army's aviation branch who get into a series of misadventures while AWOL in France. Ann shows up halfway through the film as an American dancer, and both men vie for her attentions. Compared to *Scarface*, Ann's role in *Sky Devils* is a bit of a letdown. Besides a Busby Berkeley dance routine, she has little to do but parade around in a slip and exchange drab dialogue with Tracy and Boyd. Dvorak was pleased enough with the part, which was a radical departure from the young and defiant Cesca Camonte, remarking, "I am glad it is a different type of role. I do not want to be a type."[31] Despite script input from humorist Robert Benchley, the film is remarkably unfunny and recycles aviation footage from *Hell's Angels*. Because of the ongoing delays with *Scarface*, the public would unfortunately get its first taste of Ann Dvorak in *Sky Devils*, which started appearing in theaters in January 1932. Reviews were not terribly enthusiastic, and Ann's notices ranged from "definitely interesting" to "Dvorak is the inevitable girl" to no mention at all.

Censorship had denied Ann the opportunity to make a truly striking film debut.

Scarface finally hit screens in March 1932. Hughes did end up making some compromises, including an opening disclaimer, a preachy and out-of-place scene involving city officials (not directed by Hawks), and an alternate ending with Tony going to the gallows (again, not directed by Hawks). Enough of the film remained intact that it did have trouble playing in some places, most notably in New York State. Nevertheless, *Scarface* proved to be a hit with audiences and reviewers alike, and many took notice of Hughes's newest discovery, Ann Dvorak.

The film would enjoy a couple of reissues into the 1940s, but Howard Hughes eventually pulled it from circulation. Ann's true acting debut would be virtually unseen for nearly forty years until it was made available again in 1979. For modern audiences, *Scarface* is still one of the most riveting gangster films of the early 1930s and the performances hold up, particularly those of Dvorak and Raft, who play well off of each other. In 1983 *Scarface* received an update when Brian De Palma directed a screenplay adapted by Oliver Stone, starring Al Pacino in the Paul Muni role and Michelle Pfeiffer and Mary Elizabeth Mastrantonio taking over for Karen Morley and Ann Dvorak respectively. This remake has come to have a massive cult following, but its graphic violence packs less of a punch than Hawks's original presentation and Pacino's over-the-top performance makes Paul Muni come off as positively understated.

Despite Ann's position as a contract player with the Caddo Company, *Scarface* and *Sky Devils* were the only films she would make for Howard Hughes. The company renewed her contract in December 1931, but rumors started popping that the actress would be making her way to the Fox studios on loan for *Devil's Lottery*. Instead, Ann would soon find herself working once again with Howard Hawks at a studio in Burbank run by three brothers named Warner.

6

Hollywood's New Cinderella

Warner Bros. had ushered in the era of talking pictures in 1927, and by 1932 had established itself as a studio to be reckoned with. The four Warner brothers had originally started out as film exhibitors and had moved into the distribution side of the business before deciding that creating their own movies was the way to go. They made a name for themselves in 1918 by producing the controversial *My Four Years in Germany*, which depicted atrocities committed by the Germans during World War I. The production established the fledgling production company as an entity willing to take risks and pursue unconventional subject matter for the screen. Following the success of *The Jazz Singer* and the unexpected death of brother Sam, they merged with First National in 1928 and in the process acquired a massive studio in Burbank. Films like *Little Caesar* and *The Public Enemy* exemplified Warner Bros.' willingness to tackle socially conscious issues, which frequently mirrored a country suffering through the Great Depression. With her unconventional good looks and unaffected acting style, Ann Dvorak seemed to be a perfect fit for the Warner films of the early 1930s.

While Ann anxiously awaited the release of *Scarface* in the waning days of 1931, Howard Hawks moved on to his next project, *The Roar of the Crowd*, and was determined to work with Dvorak again. The drama, set in the world of professional race-car driving, was to be made by Warner Bros. and star James Cagney, who had broken out earlier in the year with a dynamic performance in *The Public Enemy*. Production was set to begin in December 1931 with a script that called for two female leads. One would play the long-suffering girlfriend of the callous Cagney character, and the other would ruffle Cagney's feathers by having the hots for his kid brother. Likable Warner contract player Joan Blondell was cast to play the main love interest, and Hawks brought Ann over to the Burbank studio to play the second female lead. Howard Hughes was not one to shy away from turning a profit, and as he had nothing in the pipeline for Dvorak, he gladly loaned her out to Warner Bros., earning $600 a week for the use of her services while Ann received the $200 stipulated in her contract.[1] When Dvorak and Blondell got a look at the script, they both agreed they had been miscast and went to Hawks, with Blondell stating, "I can't play a neurotic," and Dvorak seconding the motion with "I can't play an ingénue."[2] The director had no problem allowing the women to switch roles, and Ann was soon working opposite one of the hottest stars on the Warner lot. Ann would be one of the few actresses Howard Hawks worked with more than once during his fifty-year career. However, this would be their last pairing, even though he later expressed an interest in using her in another Cagney vehicle, *Ceiling Zero*. If Dvorak and Hawks were indeed involved romantically, this relationship cooled down after they stopped working together and Hawks took an extended vacation with his wife shortly after the production wrapped.[3] During filming, writer Niven Busch frequently came by the set to drop off newly scripted pages to the cast, later admitting, "I developed a big crush on [Ann Dvorak] which got me nowhere."[4]

Ultimately released as *The Crowd Roars*, the film is notable mainly for its racing sequences and for casting professional drivers, whose lack of acting experience comes across as oddly charming. As Lee Merrick, this was the first time Ann played the levelheaded and devoted girlfriend, a role she would find herself in time and again during her tenure with Warner Bros. Cagney's character is so dismissive of Lee that at times it's hard to believe she would tolerate that much emotional abuse. However, in one scene where Cagney has a guilt-ridden breakdown following an unfortunate chain of events, both he and Dvorak truly shine. Hawks later recalled that Cagney's crying in this scene was unscripted, and admitted that the scene played great because of it.[5] As was true of their work in *Scarface*, Hawks and Dvorak bring a level of intense emotion to her character without going overboard. However, the relatively reserved and weak-willed Lee is far less interesting than the uninhibited Cesca Camonte and is the type of female character Hawks would eliminate from subsequent films. Ann and Joan Blondell worked well together, but unfortunately were not paired up more often. Lee Merrick in *The Crowd Roars* is not Dvorak's strongest role, but for only her third appearance as a full-fledged film actress it is more than respectable. The performance sparked reviews calling her anything from "an extremely accomplished little actress" to a "slightly unexperienced portrayer of a somewhat unlettered bachelor girl."[6] Ann clearly had raw talent, but even she was able to identify her shortcomings. "Untrained as I am, I must work three and four times as hard as the people with whom I play, the theatrically trained ones. I'm doing my best and giving the job everything I have."[7] Significantly, with *The Crowd Roars*, Ann was introduced to the studio that would dominate her career for the next five years.

Howard Hughes didn't have any immediate plans for Ann, but her contract with the Caddo Company was still extended by three months at the end of 1931.[8] Following production of *The Crowd Roars*, Warner Bros. quickly developed a serious infatuation with the young actress, and the studio decided it wanted a monopoly on her services. The company signed a deal with Howard Hughes to borrow her exclusively from February 1 to June 1, 1932, and immediately wanted her for *The Rich Are Always with Us*, with Ruth Chatterton, followed by *Tinsel Girl*, opposite Lee Tracy. Caddo would receive $400 for the first seven weeks of this loan-out and $450 for the remaining time.[9] Hughes was more than happy to oblige and make a modest profit off his young discovery as long as his company had script approval for anything Ann was to appear in, and only if his actress had first-class transportation and accommodations for any location shoots. Warner Bros.' lawyers cautioned the studio against launching into such a deal with Hughes, but it was interested enough in Ann to agree to the terms. Therefore, every time Warner Bros. considered using her in a film, a copy of the script was couriered to the Caddo Company offices across town a minimum of two weeks before a movie was expected to go into production. To skirt around the other provision, the notoriously cheap studio steered clear of casting her in anything not shot on one of its lots. Additionally, the exclusive agreement called for Ann not to be cast in anything less than the leading lady role, and to receive billing second only to the male star of any films she appeared in.

As Warner Bros. was finalizing its plans for Dvorak, Hughes finally found a vehicle he deemed worthy of her talents. The character of Sadie Thompson in the United Artists' production of *Rain* would be a showcase role for the actress who landed it, and entertainment columnists had a field day predicting who would play the infamous prostitute. Gossip grande dame Louella Parsons even stated on a couple of occasions that Dvorak definitely had the part, and Hughes was so sure of the project that the exclusive agreement with Warner Bros. included another clause stating that the deal would be temporarily suspended as soon as *Rain* went into production.[10] Despite Hughes's best efforts to get Dvorak the choice role in the Lewis Milestone–directed film, the part ended up going to Ann's friend and former mentor, Joan Crawford. The intense part was a departure for Crawford, and fans of the MGM star did not take kindly to the film. Crawford would come to distance herself from *Rain* because of its poor box-office take, later proclaiming, "I hope they burn every print of this turkey that's in existence." In retrospect, the movie and Crawford's performance are at times riveting, so Joan's claim that it was an "unpardonably bad performance" does not ring true.[11] Still, it's hard not to imagine what Ann Dvorak would have done with Sadie Thompson. Ann had already proven with *Scarface* that she could handle an intensely emotional role, and she never possessed the extreme self-consciousness that Joan Crawford did. Ann would never again have the chance to play a role of this caliber, and in hindsight, the loss of *Rain* was a major missed opportunity, though it's unclear if Ann realized what had slipped through her fingers. In the meantime, Warner Bros. decided to use Adrienne Dore for the role of Allison in *The Rich Are Always with Us*, and while it was preparing *Tinsel Girl* for production, Ann was sent down to the Agua Caliente resort in Mexico with a studio photographer for some rest and publicity shots with parrots.

Ann's second film with Warner Bros. finally went into production the first week of February, and the title was changed from the catchy-sounding *Tinsel Girl* to the head-scratching *The Strange Love of Molly Louvain*. Directed by Michael Curtiz, *The Strange Love of Molly Louvain* is classic pre-Code, with Dvorak playing a girl from the wrong side of the tracks trying to make good. Her rich boyfriend gives her the big brush-off, leaving her broken hearted and pregnant with an illegitimate child (who, as a toddler, inexplicably speaks with a British accent). In defeat, she hooks up with a small-time hood who mixes her up in a life of petty crime and pushes her into the arms of a wisecracking newspaper reporter played by Lee Tracy. Though not the strongest of pre-Code films, *Molly Louvain* has the obligatory lingerie shots, premarital sex, drunkenness, crime, and, most important, a strong and interesting female lead character, albeit in a bad blonde wig. Ann more than holds her own with Lee Tracy and she dominates her scenes with Richard Cromwell, who plays a sniveling bell-hop who has a crush on her.

This film would be one of the few times Ann had the opportunity to play the central character, and it contains one of the most memorable scenes of her career. After being jilted, Molly drowns her sorrows in the hotel room of the small-time crook, played by Leslie Fenton, who has been making advances toward her. She sits at a piano with Fenton, morose, drunk, and performing a scat version of the song "Penthouse Serenade." As in *Scarface*, Dvorak is actually playing the piano and singing, and the audience gets a tiny taste of what an all-around talent she really was. As she guzzles down champagne and alternates between breaking down and reveling in her drunkenness, the audience can empathize with her disappointment as well as dread the road she is about to go down. The scene ends with Ann launching into one of her own compositions, a ditty called "Gold Digger Lady," which Warner Bros. had to get official permission from Dvorak to use in the final cut.[12]

The Production Code Administration had some objections to the amount of skin visible in Ann's disrobing scenes early in the film, and cautioned against some of the double entendres in the exchanges between Dvorak and Tracy, but overall *The Strange Love of Molly Louvain* seems to have reached the theaters with only minimal cuts.[13] For a photo shoot to promote the film, studio photographer Elmer Fryer posed Ann in a skimpy dress with a champagne glass that may have been full of the real stuff. The resulting images are striking, with Ann appearing more seductive and uninhibited than she would in any other photos taken during the course of her career. The photos from this session, in which Ann looks more than a bit tipsy, are the embodiment of the pre-Code female.

Jacquie Lyn, who portrayed Ann's daughter in the film, had little memory of making *Molly Louvain* at the age of four, but Ann did make an impression on her. "It was the first picture I did, I think, so my memory isn't too clear. I do remember being introduced to Ann Dvorak before my part was filmed. My impression of her is pleasant, but not very friendly. I didn't particularly like her. She was just someone on the set, and I gather she felt the same. I do remember, though, that she must have been filming when we met, because she was wearing that teddy and gown from the first couple of scenes, and I remember thinking how rude she was to meet strangers in her underwear!"[14]

The Strange Love of Molly Louvain is an important film for Ann

Warner Bros. photographer Elmer Fryer catches Ann at her sultriest.

Dvorak, not only because it is one of her most substantial roles in terms of screen time, but it's also where she fell for Leslie Fenton, the man who was arguably the love of her life.

Nearly ten years Ann's senior, Leslie Carter Fenton was born in Liverpool, England, and immigrated to the United States when he was six. The family, which included six sons, settled in Mifflin, Ohio, where

Fenton found work as an office clerk when he was a teenager. In the mid-1920s he switched professions and relocated to Los Angeles, where he began appearing in local theater productions. He soon began making motion pictures, mainly for the Fox Film Corporation, working with such notable directors and actors as Raoul Walsh, Howard Hawks, Clara Bow, and Dolores Del Rio. He was a serious and studious person, and while appearing in a Los Angeles stage production of *An American Tragedy*, likened himself to the play's protagonist, whom he was portraying: "I feel like I can play Clyde Griffiths because I am him." He added, "Mentally I can appreciate everything Clyde felt. I am much like him." This was an odd comparison, considering that Clyde is a crass opportunist who plots to murder his pregnant girlfriend in order to upgrade to a high-society debutante. His further claim that "I think as he did in regard to women. Not a commendable thing to admit—but unfortunately true," makes the statement even more bizarre.[15] Of his chosen vocation, Fenton stated, "Unless he's doing it for a while just to make money, as I believe most of them are, I can't imagine a man making a profession of putting this muck on his face and making a fool of himself looking romantic."[16]

Fenton was frequently described as having "the wanderlust," and he baffled the film community in 1929 by turning down long-term studio contracts and halting the momentum of his screen career in order to travel abroad until he was flat broke and had to borrow money to get back from Europe. He had some regard for the stage, but as for the film industry, "Hollywood, you see, is like a bank to me. It is a place to go and get money. I'll stay here not a minute more than two years—perhaps less. Then I'm gone again. For you see, I don't want any of the things that actors have. I want none of their elaborate households, none of their social system that has sprung up in Hollywood, none of their ambitions."[17] Despite the nearly two-year absence from movie theaters, Fenton was able to pick up his film career when he returned, and in 1931 appeared in his most famous role as the doomed Nails Nathan, opposite James Cagney, in *The Public Enemy*. The film community more than expected Fenton to disappear once again to the ends of the earth, but the last thing anyone anticipated was that he'd be roped by a mere mortal woman. Ann Dvorak would soon prove them wrong.

Ann had actually met Fenton a few weeks prior to the filming of *Molly Louvain*. As she later recounted:

It was New Year's Eve and a lot of gaiety everywhere. We had just finished *The Crowd Roars* and I hurried over to Perc Westmore's make-up shop to wish him 'Happy New Year' before rushing home to dress for a party Mother was giving. Leslie was there. Perc introduced me. We said 'How do you do?' and suddenly I, who had been in such a hurry, sat down. I wasn't in a hurry any-more. Leslie was complaining to Perc that he'd lost his automo-bile keys, so I offered to drive him home. He refused. Later he confessed to me that he had felt the same way about me then— you know, that sort of overcome feeling. And that was why he refused my offer. He'd been boasting about being too smart to get trapped, and when he met me he sensed danger! It was quite a while before I saw him again, but I didn't forget him. Proof of that was that I tried to forget him. Then they cast me as the lead in *The Strange Love of Molly Louvain* and he was cast as the bad boy in the same picture. Just about the second day we were together in scenes of the picture we knew we were hooked.[18]

Sparks had flown during that first meeting, but once they started act-ing opposite each other their relationship turned into a full-blown whirl-wind romance. At first Fenton tried to find excuses to visit with Ann, namely, by sharing riddles with her, which had become a minor craze around Hollywood. Soon he did not need to find reasons to talk to Ann and could be found daily on the set of *Molly Louvain*, even if he was not scheduled to work.[19] The real-life courtship was an intense one, and it shows onscreen. Scene stills of the pair from *The Strange Love of Molly Louvain* show Ann gazing upon Leslie Fenton with absolute devotion, and the offscreen relationship may be one reason why the aforementioned scene at the piano is so effective. For the twenty-year-old Dvorak, Fenton must have seemed both accomplished and worldly, appealing to her own desires to be better educated and well traveled. If she was indeed coming out of an affair with the married Howard Hawks, the notion of being in a relationship with an older and actually available man would have appealed greatly to her emotions. Ann Dvorak fell hard for Leslie Fenton—and much to everyone's surprise, he reciprocated her feelings.

Even before Ann revealed this new relationship to her mother, Anna Lehr noticed all the "restless, ecstatic symptoms," observing, "Love hit Ann like a ton of bricks . . . from out of nowhere . . . without warning!"[20]

She was not particularly happy over the pairing, though it's hard to imagine she would have approved of anyone dating her daughter. As Ann's star was ascending, Lehr was enjoying a brief return to the spotlight as journalists began noting that Hollywood's New Cinderella was the child of a former film actress. Anna had always been skeptical about her daughter's ability to appeal to film audiences, but she no doubt enjoyed reaping the benefits of Ann's growing fame and did not welcome any outside intrusions. Plus, she was alarmed by the intensity of Ann's feelings for Fenton, later noting, "I was afraid, terribly. She was so young. She had had so little experience. Life was just beginning for her. And Leslie, I felt, was a man of the world. What could a young, unsophisticated girl have in common with a man who had experienced every sensation life had to offer?"[21] Still, Lehr could probably understand, at least in part, why her daughter had fallen so helplessly in love with this older man, as she herself had experienced similar emotions when she met and married Edwin McKim over twenty-five years earlier. She quickly saw how the tales of life abroad Fenton told to entertain Ann must have made him seem "like a character out of a book," to her daughter. Lehr herself admitted, "There is something almost fictional about Leslie. He is like one of the heroes in the novels of your favorite authoress. Nothing conventional, about his views of life, love, marriage, or civilization." Lehr may have been worried about Ann's emotional well-being, plunging into such an intense relationship, but she was also terrified by how Fenton's views on Hollywood would affect her daughter's career. She had no problem expressing these fears when she lamented, "It seemed sheer tragedy that such an overwhelming love should have sprung up between these two. Ann had worked so hard for all these things that Leslie despised. Ann was soaring up into the Hollywood heavens, and Leslie's only desire was to be rid of it all."[22]

One more reason Anna Lehr was uneasy with the relationship was revealed decades later when Leslie Fenton's brother Howard stated, "Leslie dated the actress Mother before Ann—then married Ann—so Anna Lehr (Ma) always hated Leslie."[23] If this were true, it must have been during a period of separation between Anna and Arthur Pearson. It's not clear if Ann was ever aware of any romantic ties between Fenton and her mother, and Lehr wasn't about to go public with that piece of information. When it became clear that Ann had every intention of remaining with Leslie Fenton, Lehr started refuting reports that she was opposed to her daughter's love interest and very publicly stated that she considered Leslie "one of the most charming men I have ever met."[24]

Another person who was vehemently opposed to the union was Arthur Pearson, who by this time had come back into Lehr's life. He apparently had made peace with the fact that Ann was committed to a screen career and had moved back into the apartment on Orange Street. Now, Ann's new romance reignited Pearson's battles with his stepdaughter. Lehr, who would serve as referee between the two, remarked, "He had no particular reason except that his great fondness for Ann had convinced him that there are very few things, and practically no men, good enough for her." Pearson was well aware of Leslie Fenton's nomadic reputation, and Lehr remembered one particularly heated argument that concluded with Pearson shouting at Ann, "What do you know about him? From what I learn he is sort of a vagabond . . . working just long enough to get money ahead to support him while he lives the life of a beachcomber in the South Seas . . . or China . . . or wherever he cares to go. Is that the kind of life you plan for yourself?" Ann dramatically shot back, "I want to be with him wherever he is" and, as these confrontations usually ended, she stormed out of the house to the waiting arms of Leslie Fenton.[25]

At first Ann talked to her mother about Leslie, but then Lehr noticed that "Ann seemed to lock even his name in her heart."[26] The pair began spending every waking moment together, though Ann seldom invited him into the apartment, where her disapproving parents were waiting. On many nights during their courtship Dvorak and Fenton would sit in his car in front of her home, engaged in long conversations over cigarettes. There is something oddly touching in the thought of Ann Dvorak, who was rapidly becoming the toast of Hollywood and had been appearing onscreen as a sexy spitfire, parked out in front of her parents' place, delaying the end of an evening with Leslie Fenton.

While Ann's love life was in full bloom, Warner Bros. cast her as the second female lead in *Love Is a Racket*, starring Douglas Fairbanks Jr., Frances Dee, Lee Tracy, and Lyle Talbot, and directed by William Wellman. The film tells the tale of a fast-talking reporter (Fairbanks), who inadvertently gets mixed up with unsavory characters while trying to clear up some bad checks written by the high-society dame he's nutty about. Douglas Fairbanks Jr. was not impressed with his involvement in the picture, noting, "I was not very good in a part that was meant for the more

The real-life attraction between Ann and Leslie Fenton is apparent in this image from *The Strange Love of Molly Louvain*.

important Warner star Jimmy Cagney, but a logjam of schedules pushed it my way—really too bad for all concerned." He continued, "Still, it was joyous to make because of two wonderfully attractive and intelligent leading ladies, Frances Dee and Ann Dvorak."[27] Ann plays Fairbanks's pal who has eyes for him and inexplicably hangs out at his apartment all day wearing his bathrobe. Ann is not the main female lead, but hers is the more interesting role of the two. That said, her character in the Rian James novel the film was based on was a coked-up call girl, so the part could have been much more interesting. This seemed to have crossed the line even for pre-Code Hollywood, as her profession and any unsavory habits are not even remotely alluded to. Since her role in *Love Is a Racket* is a secondary one, it's interesting that Howard Hughes agreed to let her appear in it, though the deal between Warner Bros. and the Caddo Company explains why she received second billing after Douglas Fairbanks Jr. even though Frances Dee has more screen time. After she had played the title character in *The Strange Love of Molly Louvain*, this secondary role is a bit of a letdown, but as Warner Bros. contract player Glenda Farrell so aptly put it, "They might star you in one movie and give you a bit part in the next. . . . You were still well paid and didn't get a star complex."[28] Unlike Ann's former studio, MGM, which carefully nurtured its actors with the hope of finding a formula that would strike a chord with film audiences, Warner Bros. was in the business of making movies, not movie stars. As the studio would soon find out, this attitude would cause it to experience the greatest number of revolts from its contract players.

When filming of *Love Is a Racket* wrapped up on March 16, 1932, onscreen billing was probably of little consequence to Ann Dvorak as she was preparing to become Mrs. Leslie Fenton.

7

Mrs. Leslie Fenton

In the early hours of St. Patrick's Day in 1932, Ann Dvorak and Leslie Fenton made their way to the United Airport in Burbank where they were scheduled to a catch a chartered flight to Yuma, Arizona, at 9:30 a.m. Arizona had become a popular place for Hollywood notables to elope, not only because it was far from the prying eyes of Tinseltown's gossip columnists, but because amorous couples could thereby bypass California's three-day waiting period. The day before, Ann had finished her scenes on *Love Is a Racket* early but had to sit for a scheduled interview before leaving the studio. She tried to skirt the journalist's questions about marriage before finally admitting that she was in love, "dreadfully, and for the first time. I've been too busy before."[1] She spent the afternoon shopping for new clothes and in the evening confided to a few friends what the next day would bring.

By noon on March 17, the pair had been joined as husband and wife by the Reverend Herbert Brooke, with his wife, Vera, and a Miss Jewell L. Cypert standing in as witnesses.[2] Leslie later relayed the events of the simple ceremony: "We went into the little parsonage to be married. A baby sat crying on the floor; an older child was nursing a bruised knee. And the minister called his wife, and the housemaid to witness the ceremony. The maid came in from the kitchen, wiping her hands on her apron. And there they stood, and even before her hands were quite dry, we were married."[3] The bride wore a simple blue skirt with a tailored tweed jacket, and the groom donned a light-colored suit. Ann, who had promised her mother she would wait at least three months before getting married, was hesitant to alert her to the planned elopement, but finally revealed her plans the night before. Lehr claimed, "They wanted me to go along—but I felt that I wouldn't have the courage to go through it like a trouper. So I gave them my blessing—and let them go," adding,

"After all, we live in a modern age. *I saw that it was either an affair or marriage*—and I was glad that her life would start with marriage."[4] Apparently Lehr had, at least publicly, resigned herself to thinking that if her daughter had to be with a former flame, at least it would be a respectable union.

Instead of rushing back to Los Angeles to meet reporters and a none-too-happy mother of the bride, the newlyweds took a detour to Mexico for some postmarital fun in Agua Caliente. Unfortunately, they had failed to notify anyone of this side trip. When they didn't show up at the appointed time and reports started appearing that a plane had crashed into a mountain near the border town of El Centro, the worst was feared. The safety of the happy couple was quickly confirmed, and when the two returned to Burbank at 6:30 p.m., the press was there to greet them, along with a photographer from Warner Bros. Images from that evening show Ann, wearing very little makeup, looking tired but happy as she clings to her new husband, making sure her ring finger with its new wedding band is visible for the cameras. Fenton, who had always loudly proclaimed how much his freedom meant to him, justified his actions by saying, "There's something missing when you see things and do things alone," adding, "There's no one to share your ecstasy over a lovely sunrise. No one with whom you can laugh over passport trouble, and your sad mistakes in ordering from a foreign bill of fare, or even your entanglements with the police. Everything is an experience and worthwhile—and often amusing—if there is someone with you, sensing, feeling, undergoing similar emotions and reactions." He concluded, "We'll do things together—Ann and I—that lacked flavor when I did them alone!"[5] For Ann, marriage was the definition of freedom, even in a post–Jazz Age world. As she explained, "Now I've really found my independence. The dropping of a lot of petty restrictions has given me a new sense of freedom. As a young lady living with her mother I had to be wary of companionships, hours I kept, places I visited. Now I have the only companion I wish."[6] As for the inevitable questions about starting a family, Ann was quick to respond, "Children? No, that wouldn't do at all—because then I could no longer be a companion to Leslie. No anchors—nothing to tie us down! Not for years, anyway."[7] The only time Ann seems to have expressed an interest in having children was three years into the marriage, though her attitude was more clinical than maternal: "I should like to have a baby someday—because I prefer not to miss any of the vital experiences."[8]

Ann and Leslie Fenton land at United Airport in Burbank after eloping in Yuma, Arizona.

Despite the occasional rumor that the Fentons were expecting a "blessed event," Ann would never become a mother.

Anna Lehr wasn't the only one dismayed by Ann's sudden elopement, as the actress revealed. "The men who had been instrumental in my success, from Howard Hughes down to Monte Westmore, who instructed me in make-up, were wild when they heard I had married. All of Hollywood thought I was crazy. They thought me a product of pictures, and therefore belonging to them. But they did not stop to think that although many men may be important in a woman's career, there is just *one* to make her completely happy and successful." As for juggling marriage and a career, Ann was confident in stating, "I married recently because I was so sure an actress and a woman could be two distinct and different people." She added, "If I ever attain the heights I hope to some day, it will be because of Leslie Fenton, my husband. He is a fine actor, a traveler, a writer, a learned man. From his own experience he will inspire me." Married for mere weeks, Ann felt comfortable doling out wisdom:

"Any advice I might give to the woman seeking that fine state in marriage is this: Marry the man you love and don't expect too much. Be like *him* within your soul. Adopt his masculine strength of will, and thereby understand his mind. Outwardly, be the woman, the very effeminate woman he married. Be his confidante and pal. Work at being happy."[9]

The couple moved into a charming Spanish Colonial Revival home at 3339 Troy Drive in the Hollywood Hills. However, their newlywed bliss was short-lived. Five days after the elopement, nineteen-year-old Gladys Freeman came out of the woodwork to file a breach of promise suit against the groom. Freeman was an aspiring actress who resembled Ann, though she was far less striking. She had appeared in a handful of films, most notably portraying a Native American maiden in the 1929 feature *Redskin* under the stage name Julie Carter, a surname that happened also to be Fenton's middle name. To a local gossip columnist, Freeman described herself as having "no sense of humor, loathes exercise, bleached blondes, earthquakes, and radios. Likes candy, dogs and cats, Warner Baxter, Helen Hayes, swimming and tangos. And tolerates the goldfish someone gave me some months ago."[10] Judging from her looks and career standing, it seems Leslie Fenton had an eye for brunette actresses he could mentor. In her suit Freeman claimed she had been romantically involved with Fenton since she was seventeen, and had been induced to live with him out of wedlock with promises of marriage. She was suing for a total of $250,000, with half the amount covering damages and the other half recompense for asserted betrayal.[11] Many were surprised by the accusations, also questioning Freeman's breach of promise suit, which Louella Parsons thought had "sort of gone out of style . . . it is not often that the modern girl resorts to that method to show her broken heart."[12] Ann quickly came out publicly in support of her husband stating, "Leslie's yesterdays—any man's past, for that matter—are his concerns. Only his tomorrows belong to me."[13] She added, "How could she help loving him . . . and wanting him? It's too bad there aren't enough Leslies to go around for every woman!"[14] Privately, she commented to her mother that Julie Carter bore a resemblance to her and left it at that. Fenton chose to keep his mouth shut on the matter. His lawyers soon issued a demurrer stating that the suit was ambiguous and unintelligible, though the judge allowed the complaint to proceed. By the end of May, Freeman decided to drop the suit and disappeared from Fenton's life. She went on to have a rocky marriage with gossip columnist Jimmy Starr, appeared in a number of uncredited parts into the 1940s, attempted suicide in 1948, was briefly married Robert Livingston in the early 1960s, and then faded into obscurity.

As the dust cleared on the Freeman affair, Ann settled into married life. For someone who had been so devoted to her burgeoning career and was on the cusp of success as a film actress, marriage quickly became a top priority for Ann. After the wedding, Lehr saw less and less of her daughter, bemoaning, "I began to pick up as much information about my child from the gossip of the movie columnists as I actually learned when I visited her." The sudden loss of her daughter must have been painful for Lehr, who tried to put up a good front by claiming she did not care to see Ann because "I hope I am too wise in the ways of the world to form a 'three' in that paradise of 'two,' a honeymoon."[15] At first Ann seemed to be able to juggle her personal and professional life. As much as Leslie Fenton loathed the Hollywood scene, in the weeks after their marriage he seemed to have no problem being seen around town with his bride and accompanying her for studio publicity purposes. The happy couple was seen attending screenings of *The Crowd Roars* and *Scarface* and was also spotted at boxing matches in both Hollywood and Tijuana. For one personal appearance, Ann mistakenly showed up at the Warner Bros. Theater in Huntington Park, when she really should have been at an identical sister theater in San Pedro.[16] By all accounts the newlyweds seemed happy, which is especially apparent in a photo that ran in one of the fan magazines showing them walking arm in arm down Hollywood Boulevard, Ann wearing Fenton's overcoat, whose sleeves were way too long for her.

They seemed perfectly happy residing in the film colony, but Hollywood insiders began to wonder if Fenton's "wanderlust" was starting to bubble—and if it were contagious. Dvorak quickly confirmed those rumors. "Lots of people were surprised, I guess, when Les and I married. They said, 'that boy has the wanderlust. What will Ann do?' My answer is, 'Dvorak has the wanderlust too. Always has had it.' So we'll wander all over the earth together. Isn't that a fine thing to anticipate?" She even indicated that her immediate film work could possibly be short-lived, echoing her husband's sentiments: "Two or three busy years of film work, a cheerful bank balance and then a long trip with my husband to Europe and the South Seas."[17] Hollywood's new Cinderella had found her prince and seemed ready to permanently ride off into the sunset. Anna Lehr continued to be concerned about Ann's career, admitting, "I had only to look into Ann's eyes to realize that for the first time not even I could reach through to her. Her whole world revolved around Leslie and his icono-clastic talk. He never talked to Ann of Hollywood . . . or her career. The names and places he painted for her imagination were the white beaches of Papeete, the dewey slopes of Ireland, and the sun in the South of France." Lehr ruefully said, "The world of the studios seemed as far apart from her now as though she had never been a part of it."[18]

No matter what her short- and long-term marriage plans were, the fact was that Ann had a contract with the Caddo Company, which in turn had an exclusive deal with Warner Bros. Plus, the young couple needed money, so Ann got back to work. Warner Bros. had gotten approval for two more features, the first being *Central Park*, costarring Wallace Ford. Studio executives frequently pegged actors for certain roles and then changed their minds and shuffled them around with little or no explana-tion. This was the case with *Central Park*, which saw Joan Blondell plugged into the part originally assigned to Ann. Instead, Dvorak was cast in *Stranger in Town* opposite David Manners, who had recently appeared in Universal's *Dracula* and was soon to be cast in *The Mummy*. *Stranger in Town* was a reunion of sorts for Ann and the star of the film, Chic Sale, who had traveled on the same vaudeville circuit as Anna Lehr in 1914, when Ann was just a tot. Although Sale was only in his forties at the time, he assumed the role of an octogenarian in the film. Sale plays the founder/postmaster/merchant of a small town whose world is thrown upside down when David Manners rolls in and opens a competing grocery store across the street. Ann plays Sale's granddaughter, who is torn between her loyalty to her grandfather and her interest in the new kid in town, with whom she has fallen head over heels in love. Ann's role is a slight variation on the devoted girlfriend she played in *The Crowd Roars*, only this time she didn't have James Cagney and Howard Hawks to help make the char-acter interesting. The part in *Stranger in Town* is one essentially any young and pretty contract player could have stepped into, though Ann probably inserts a bit more intelligence than the character deserves. There are flashes of charm in some of her flirtatious scenes with Manners, but for the most part, it's a waste of Ann's talents.

After *Stranger in Town* Warner Bros. next planned on casting Ann as Nordie Lord, the saucy daughter of a southern plantation owner in an adaptation of Harry Harrison Kroll's novel, *The Cabin in the Cotton*.[19] In what would prove to be another missed opportunity in the career of Ann Dvorak, the studio once again changed its plan. Instead of having Ann play the character, who had been rechristened Madge Norwood, the studio gave the role to an up-and-coming contract player named Bette Davis, who had herself been suffering through a slew of drab roles at Warner Bros.[20] Davis considered the part of this "downright, forthright bitch" her "best role to date," and it did indeed turn out to be a showcase role for the young actress, giving her the memorable line, "I'd love to kiss ya but I just washed mah hair."[21]

What made the loss of Madge Norwood even more frustrating was that the part Ann was cast in instead was another blandly devoted girlfriend, this time in the farcical *Crooner*. She was teamed again with David Manners (with a singing voice doubled by Brick Holton), playing a struggling bandleader who inadvertently discovers that when he sings through a megaphone his normally weak voice becomes silky smooth and irresistible to the ladies. His newfound success quickly goes to his head and for some reason causes him to become exceedingly effeminate. Once again, Ann has very little to do, and in the end she reunites with a humbled and repentant David Manners when she should have ridden off with the more affable music promoter, played by Ken Murray. The film itself is a mildly amusing take on the popularity of crooners of the day such as Rudy Vallee, but Ann's talents are once again underutilized. However, in one scene where she tells off her ego-fueled crooner we are briefly reminded of the live wire who had dazzled audiences a few months earlier in *Scarface*. In preparation for the role, Ann reportedly spent many evenings at KFWB, the Warner radio station in Hollywood, an experience said to have aided her greatly when the cameras started rolling, though it's questionable if anything could have helped her with the thin part.[22] She also allegedly wrote words and music for a tune called "A Pair of Arms" that was to be performed in the film, though the only songs that seem to have been used are "Sweethearts Forever" and "Three's a Crowd," which are played over, and over, and over.[23] Even though her screen time is minimal in *Crooner*, it is Ann's portrait that graces the sheet music for the ubiquitous songs as well as the one-sheet poster for the film, indicating that Warner Bros. had high hopes for the young actress, in whom the studio was beginning to invest a fair amount of money and time, even if the quality of the roles was starting to become questionable.

For her next film, Warner Bros. finally gave Ann a role she could sink her teeth into: the doomed Vivian Revere in *Three on a Match*. The film featured a stable of familiar Warner faces: Joan Blondell, Lyle Talbot,

Ann gives onscreen husband Warren William the brush-off in the pre-Code classic *Three on a Match*.

Edward Arnold, Warren William, Allen Jenkins, and Jack La Rue, and even a young Bette Davis and Humphrey Bogart. *Three on a Match* is a mere sixty-three minutes long, but it packs more in that hour than most modern films do at twice the running time. This pre-Code gem finds Ann going from bored society wife and mother to good-time party girl to pathetic junkie who must make the ultimate sacrifice to save her young son (played by the overly precocious Buster Phelps) from the thugs she has gotten mixed up with. Joan Blondell is the spunky showgirl who accidentally introduces Ann to the smooth-talking crook who will launch her undoing, and Bette Davis serves little purpose other than appearing in lingerie and allowing the film to be called *Three on a Match*. Years later, Bette looked back on the film as "a dull 'B' picture," though she may have felt differently if she had instead played the heavier lead role.[24]

At the time it was released, *Three on a Match* came and went with little fanfare. The *Daily Variety* was not inspired by the film and negatively singled out Ann's performance, noting, "Miss Dvorak has the heaviest part, but plays it unimpressively and is subservient to Miss Blondell."[25] It seems that even Ann herself was quick to dismiss the film. Of all the features she made in 1932, *Three on a Match* is one she barely discussed with her mother, who referred to it in passing as "another feature whose title slips my mind," adding, "Certainly Ann must have not been enthused about this part for I heard so little about it."[26] Unexpectedly, the only person who seemed to be excited about *Three on a Match* was Jason Joy at the Production Code Administration. With the abduction of the Lindbergh baby still making headlines, Joy viewed the film as a strong indictment against kidnapping, gushing, "In this case, the kidnappers come to grief. They can't get away with it! And it seems to me there is clearly presented a moral to the effect that kidnapping is one business the American people will rise, as one man, to overthrow."[27] Joy felt so strongly about the film that he took extra steps to get it past New York's strong censorship boards, though this endorsement from the PCA did little to boost its meager box-office receipts.

The passage of time has been very kind to *Three on a Match* and Ann Dvorak, as the film now is considered a quintessential pre-Code classic, complete with sex, drugs, booze, skin, kidnapping, suicide, and magnified nose-hair plucking. For modern audiences aware of the ultra-sanitized scenarios that would plague American films for decades once the Production Code was aggressively enforced, *Three on a Match* stands out as a delightfully shocking and racy example of early 1930s Hollywood. Ann is only mildly effective as the society wife but comes to dominate the film once her downfall begins, and the train wreck that is Vivian Revere is mesmerizing. Any pent-up nervous energy Ann may have had in real life is unleashed through Vivian and she isn't afraid to look like hell to bring this character to life. In one scene, as she waits for Blondell to exit a beauty parlor in order to hit her up for cash, Ann appears emaciated with dark circles under her eyes, wearing little or no makeup, and biting her nails (a habit she possessed in real life). Later in the film, as her life completely unravels, she is a pathetic mess, disheveled, going through withdrawal, battered, bruised, and clad in a dirty nightgown she has been wearing for days. As the film climaxes, she realizes the gangsters who have been holding her and her son hostage are getting ready to kill the boy, and her frantic attempts to find a way out of the high-rise apartment cause viewers to sit perched on the edge of their seats. Her final interaction with her child is heart wrenching, and her last scene is both haunting and devastating. *Three on a Match* is a prime example of what Ann Dvorak was capable of as an actress when given a decent role and a solid director, in this case Mervyn LeRoy. Interestingly, despite the riveting performance he got out of Ann, LeRoy was most impressed with one of her costars, noting, "They gave me three unknown girls in that one—Joan Blondell, Bette Davis and Ann Dvorak. I made a mistake when the picture was finished. I told an interviewer that Joan Blondell was going to be a big star, that Ann Dvorak had definite possibilities, but that I didn't think Bette Davis would make it. She's been cool to me ever since."[28] Though underappreciated at the time, Vivian Revere has proven to be one of Ann's most unforgettable roles and has served as a fitting introduction to the actress for many modern-day fans of classic cinema.

Before the first half of 1932 had passed, Ann had appeared in six films for Warner Bros., and the studio decided it had enough faith in the young actress's potential to purchase her contract outright from Howard Hughes rather than dealing with the Caddo Company as a middleman for use of her services. Hughes had recently sold the contract of another discovery, Jean Harlow, to MGM for $30,000 and didn't have a problem releasing Ann, if the price was right. Hughes ultimately agreed to turn Ann's contract over to Warner Bros. for $40,000, an impressive sum given the Warner reputation for penny-pinching and the fact that the effects of the Great Depression were finally starting to show up in the box-office receipts.

Hughes agreed to release Ann in early May 1932, but the deal would not be finalized for another month and a half. Even so, Warner Bros. quickly began making plans for its latest acquisition. Every spring, Warner Bros. made preparations to shut down for a few weeks during the summer months, and while this may have meant a vacation for studio brass, the talent would frequently be loaned out to other studios in order to maximize profits for the time the lot was dark. Warner Bros. agreed to let the independent Jefferson Pictures borrow Ann for $4,000 to star in *Halls of Justice* to be filmed on the Pathé lot, and there were rumors that she would also be going over to the Goldwyn studio to costar with Ronald Colman in *Cynara*.[29] The summer of 1932 was shaping up to be a busy one for Ann Dvorak, and so it transpired—but not in the way Warner Bros. had planned.

8

Sold Down the River

If there was ever a crossroads in the career of Ann Dvorak, it was in early July 1932. She had been making films nonstop for more than six months, was a darling of the Hollywood press, and seemed positioned to have a long and fruitful career with Warner Bros., the studio that had just forked over $40,000 to Howard Hughes for her contract. The Production Code was still largely ignored by filmmakers, and opportunities for Ann to appear in daring roles like Cesca Camonte and Vivian Revere were still possible. By July her films were regularly showing in theaters to mostly positive reviews, and stories about Ann were turning up in the movie magazines. Having one's name mentioned in the Hollywood columns of the daily papers was always welcome, but appearing in the fan magazines signified a whole new level of success, given the lengthy articles, beautifully reproduced photos, and nationwide distribution of these publications with names like *Photoplay, Modern Screen,* and *Movie Mirror.* Unlike the studio-invented backstories of many film personalities, Ann's show-business upbringing was ready-made for the fan magazines, needing little alteration other than minor fibs like claiming she had attended Hollywood High School. The writers at these magazines could not get enough of Ann's rags-to-riches story and sudden elopement, and after three years of hard work and dogged determination, she seemed to be on the precipice of a phenomenal career as a dramatic film actress. This was the exact moment Ann Dvorak chose to walk out on her contract and leave the country, essentially killing her chances of becoming a major star at Warner Bros.

Over the years, Ann's sudden walkout has usually been attributed to salary issues with Warner Bros., specifically because she discovered that Buster Phelps, the child actor who portrayed her son in *Three on a Match,* was making the same amount per week, $250, as she was. This perception permeated the industry at the time. As Bette Davis stated decades later, "I even understood Ann Dvorak for disappearing from town because an infant in one of her films was earning more money than she."[1] This injustice no doubt played some part in Ann's hasty departure, but there were many other factors at play. To perceive the walkout as some grand gesture against the servitude of the Hollywood studio system is simplistic and probably gives Ann too much credit. *Three on a Match* was the first film Ann made for Warner Bros. after it had agreed to the Caddo deal, but the studio was still in the process of drawing up a new contract for her. When filming began in June, she was still working under the terms and salary she had agreed to in August 1931, and what she had agreed to was $250 a week. When she left the country in early July, Warner Bros. had still not drafted a new contract.

A more pressing reason for the walkout stemmed from Leslie Fenton being offered a part in the English-language version of *F.P.1*. The movie was to be filmed in Germany later in the year and Fenton viewed this as the perfect opportunity to show his new bride the world. Shortly after their elopement, Fenton briefly went out of town for the Universal Pictures production *Air Mail*, directed by John Ford. As Ann admitted, "The time Leslie went to Bishop in California on location was enough. We were both so unhappy that we decided [being separated] isn't worth it."[2] Contract or no contract, the notion of Fenton traveling abroad without Ann was simply not an option for the couple. Furthermore, Leslie seemed unfazed by his wife's studio obligations.

Ann may have been more concerned with contractual obligations than her husband, but she was not happy with the way her career was going. Later on, Ann would sum up this early part of her career: "I stayed there [MGM] three years and never played a part. Then Karen Morley took me to Howard Hawks, who put me in 'Scarface' with Paul Muni— the first and best part I have ever had. Howard Hughes put me under a seven-year contract. Then he loaned me out to Warner Brothers for six months at the end of which he sold them my contract, although he had promised he would not. I made nine pictures in eight months—quantity, not quality."[3] As much as Ann may have wanted a career as an actress, she was clearly not pleased with Howard Hughes's decision to make her the property of Warner Bros. Given the roles her new bosses were starting to cast her in, maybe she figured she wasn't going to be missing out on much by skipping town for a few months.

Another factor in Ann's decision to breach the contract was exhaustion. As much as she had wanted a successful film career, the past year had been a whirlwind for the young actress and she had barely had time to catch her breath. In ten months' time, she had gone from lowly MGM chorus girl to second billing in a high-profile feature film to Warner Bros. workhorse. On top of the breakneck filming schedule, she had possibly had an affair with a married man, and had met and wed Leslie Fenton after an incredibly short courtship. This all happened before she was twenty-one. Initially, Ann was thrilled by her sudden change in fortune, stating, "There I was, a dancing girl—the same girl I'd been for three years—and then all of a sudden, *zoom!* Is it, or is it not, all sort of breathtaking?"[4] However, a few days before taking off with Fenton, she had confided at a lunchtime interview, "I can't go on. They're pushing me too hard. I tell you I'm tired of seeing so much Ann Dvorak around—on the billboards, in the magazines. If they keep on, there will be nothing left of me. I'll be dead so far as movies are concerned. And something in me will die too."[5] Had this been the story presented to the public, that of an overwhelmed young actress appreciative of the opportunities of the past year but desperate for rest and time alone with her new husband, she may have survived the walkout unscathed, with a slap on the hand from Warner Bros. and the sympathy of the press. Instead, outside influences would steer her in the wrong direction, causing her promising career to plateau at a studio none too amused by her actions.

Warner Bros. may have been blindsided by the actress's sudden departure, but columnists reported that Ann and Leslie had been studying French and German in preparation for an impending honeymoon. The two themselves were anything but quiet about their desire to travel abroad as soon as the opportunity arose. There had also been grumblings for a few weeks about Ann possibly "pulling a Cagney," in reference to Ann's former costar who had recently gone on a personal strike against the studio in an attempt to increase the pay terms of his contract. This would be the first of many disputes Cagney would have with the studio, and many other Warner contract players would follow suit over the years. Ann was now beholden to Warner Bros.; "pulling a Cagney" at this point in the game does seem ill advised. James Cagney had already proven himself an audience favorite and his films were clearly profit makers. Ann, on the other hand, while definitely a major up-and-comer, had yet to prove her box-office clout and was really not in a position to make these types of demands on the studio. Unfortunately, the people looking out for her career interests didn't realize this.

When Ann eloped to Yuma with Leslie Fenton, she not only gained a husband, she also acquired an agent. Charles Feldman had left his legal practice in the late 1920s to become an agent and created the Famous Artists agency. He specialized in the representation of freelance talent, and Leslie Fenton was on his roster at the time of the marriage. With Ann's star on the rise and Warner Bros. on the verge of drafting a new contract for the actress, Feldman saw big dollar signs and got to work on a plan to net a higher salary for Ann. Her situation was unique because most actresses with her lack of previous experience would probably not have received roles like Cesca Camonte and Vivian Revere. With the steep price tag Warner Bros. had paid for her contract, there was no way of knowing if Charles Feldman would be able to maneuver the studio payroll in Ann's favor. When the opportunity arose for the couple to travel to Germany, Feldman did nothing to discourage Ann from skipping town; it seems he viewed her departure as a way to gain leverage over the studio. He presumably thought that having paid such a large amount for her contract, Warner Bros. would certainly want to keep the actress happy in order to start earning a return on its investment. It's unknown if Warner Bros. actually intended to increase Ann's salary on the new contract or merely roll over the options on the Caddo deal, but Feldman clearly felt a raise was due and he was more than willing to play hardball with the studio by sending her out of town.

On July 3 Ann sent a handwritten note to the studio's accounting department asking that all forthcoming checks be sent directly to the First National Bank of Los Angeles in Hollywood, as "I will be out of town for a few weeks."[6] The following morning Ann and Leslie headed to the Port of Los Angeles to catch the SS *Virginia*, which would take them to New York City via the Panama Canal. The adventure Ann Dvorak had dreamed about from the time she was a child was finally beginning.

Shortly after boarding the ship, Fenton sent a Western Union telegram to Feldman's Hollywood office at 11:30 a.m.: "Going to Europe via New York Ann unhappy over studio conditions she must have rest take care of things for us see you later May = Leslie and Ann."[7] After receiving the message, Feldman headed to the Burbank studio to personally deliver the telegram to Jack Warner himself. He told the boss he could get Dvorak to come back if he was willing to double her salary. He further suggested

Ann with her mother, Anna Lehr, in 1932. Any control mother may have had over daughter completely disappeared when Ann departed for New York with Leslie Fenton.

that Warner personally cable Ann on the boat requesting that once she arrived in New York, they turn around and come back to the West Coast. It is unknown how Warner responded to the salary request, but he did send the message to Ann asking her to return as soon as she docked. Feldman sent his own cable, instructing her to pay no attention to the message from Warner and to enjoy Europe while he dealt with her salary.

Warner and Feldman were not the only ones sending messages to the SS *Virginia*. Anna Lehr was also caught off guard by her daughter's actions and began sending tearful messages begging Ann to leave the boat at Balboa and fly back to Hollywood to resume her career before it was too late. This was one time Ann gave no indication to her mother about what her plans were, and Lehr would later comment, "I felt as though a good friend had failed me—had failed *us!*" She added, "A good trouper never walks out on his 'curtain.' Ann knows that."[8]

During Ann's two-week journey to the East Coast, the press had a field day speculating what would happen next in the unfolding saga. Ann followed Feldman's advice, ignoring Jack Warner's telegram along with everyone else's, and settled into her delayed honeymoon. When Ann and Leslie docked in New York on July 18, the press was anxiously awaiting their arrival. They emerged from the boat well tanned and all smiles, but Ann seems to have been well prepped by her agent and husband—she came out swinging. When questioned about her decision to walk out on the studio that had invested so much money in her, Ann responded uncharacteristically, attacking Warner Bros., Howard Hughes, and Hollywood in general. She claimed she was "sold down the river" by Hughes when he unloaded her contract on Warner Bros., and that he had been making a profit of $1,000 a week from her during the previous six months. She further bemoaned the injustice that the baby in her last picture earned $500 a week to her scant $250. The comments were harsh and out of character for Ann, who had spent over two years at MGM patiently waiting for her big break and who, mere months earlier, had been fretting for her career because of the delayed release of *Scarface*. Leslie Fenton was quick to back up his wife's statements. "Producers look at you for how much money they can squeeze out of you. A contract's a sentence to hard labor. There's no regard for personality. Stars are being sent to sanatoriums because they can't stand the pace. That's not going to happen to Ann."[9] Also joining in the fight was fellow shipmate Victor Varconi, a Hungarian actor who added his two cents that Hollywood producers were "slave drivers": "There is little culture in Hollywood. I hope I shall be able to arrange my affairs so that I will not have to return there."[10]

Ann's comments were ill advised for a number of reasons, not least of which was that most of her information was incorrect. Howard Hughes was only making a $200 a week in profit from the deal with Warner Bros., not $1,000. As for Master Phelps, he was making the same amount per week as Ann, and while that certainly must have been an insult, it wasn't the $250 extra she claimed he was earning. Warner Bros. was surprised by the actress's comments as the studio seemed genuinely unaware she was that unhappy. Studio executives were also confused by her rant against Howard Hughes and suspected that he may have been paying her additional cash under the table while she was under contract to him and being loaned out to them. Considering that the Caddo deal was netting the

Ann and Leslie arrive in New York, where they denounce the "slave drivers" of the film industry.

company such a small profit, it seems unlikely Hughes would have been handing anything extra over to Ann. Hughes himself was irritated enough by Ann's comments to issue a lengthy press statement about the matter. He was quick to correct the inaccuracies of Ann's numbers and even defended little Buster by pointing out that "Miss Dvorak should not forget that during the year there would be many weeks when that baby would not be working and would not receive anything, whereas she receives her salary every week whether she was working or not." Overall, Hughes decided to shame Ann by taking the high road and complimenting her many talents:

> Of course, some producers might be highly indignant at Miss Dvorak's statement if they were in my position and denounce Miss Dvorak's ingratitude, proclaiming loudly, "Miss Dvorak would still be unknown, receiving $75.00 a week if we had not given her the part in *Scarface*." However, I do not feel that way about it. I don't think that producers are ever entirely responsible for the success of stars. They may give the artist opportunities, but if the actress hasn't what it takes to get over with the public she will not succeed no matter how many opportunities she is given. I think the credit for Miss Dvorak's success lies entirely in her own ability. In *Scarface* she gave a superb performance which was almost universally lauded by the critics. I do not feel that we were kind to Miss Dvorak in giving her this part, because I know of no one else in the world whom we might have put in her place who could have possibly improved on the performance she gave.
>
> So if, by any chance, Miss Dvorak feels any appreciation for the opportunity I hope she will remove any such thoughts from her mind as I am sure that if she had not played this part she would unquestionably have risen to the same prominence through some other part in some other picture. A really fine artist with true dramatic talent, like Miss Dvorak, could not long stay undiscovered even in Hollywood, the "place of no culture and slave driving producers" according to Mr. Varconi.

As for Victor Varconi, who did indeed return to Hollywood to enjoy a film and television career that lasted well into the 1950s, Hughes concluded:

> Incidentally, in regard to this remark of Mr. Varconi's. I will have to confess I do not know exactly what Mr. Varconi refers to in this instance by the word "culture." If he means learning, certainly he

will have to admit that the California Institute of Technology and the Mt. Wilson Observatory have made appropriate contributions. If he refers to table manners, I remember a very enjoyable evening which I spent at his house wherein what is commonly known as culture seemed to be flowing at its height. Certainly he will have to admit that the climate here leaves little to be desired, which, in a measure, may compensate for any other faults he might find. Personally, I do not know of a better place to live, and I have yet to see a producer with a whip.

With that, Howard Hughes was officially done with Ann Dvorak, and no doubt with Victor Varconi as well.

If Charles Feldman and the Fentons honestly thought taking Ann's troubles to the press was going to garner public support, they were sorely mistaken. The backlash was immediate and at times harsh. Feldman had grossly misjudged how much clout Ann had as a box-office draw, and the press portrayed her as an ungrateful brat who had been given the opportunity of a lifetime and was whining about it. For a large percentage of the American population, $250 a week was akin to a king's ransom. Elizabeth Yeaman with the *Hollywood Citizen News* lambasted Ann for the misinformation she was spouting, noting, "Ann should get her facts straight the next time she starts airing her grievances. It's altogether too easy to check up on figures."[11] Relman Morin over at the *Los Angeles Record* figured that with her rant, which had been picked up by the syndicates, Ann had "harmed herself immeasurably." He continued, "To the man on the street, any girl of Ann Dvorak's age—she's not 21 yet—who would complain over a salary of 250 dollars a week is a strange, grasping thoroughly disagreeable sort of person." He concluded, "There are dozens of actors and actresses in Hollywood who feel that they're getting a raw deal from the boss. But the smart ones don't air their injuries in public. They realize that the salary which seems small to them seems terrific to the fans. So they keep quiet, and complain to the people who can, if they will, change the situation."[12] Perhaps the most scathing commentary came from Delight Evans of *Screenland* magazine who penned an editorial titled "Watch Your Step, Ann Dvorak!" In this two-page tirade he lectured, "Ann Dvorak, you have not yet 'arrived.' And I think you should get wise to yourself—while there's still time." Evans recapped her hard work leading up to *Scarface*, but pointed out that she had toiled for far less time than Joan Crawford, and detected that following a bit of success, "something happened to you. In a Barrymore it's temperament; in a little, new actress it's—something else." He continued, "You, Ann Dvorak, are not yet important enough to get away with it. And when you are important enough, you won't want to. The motion picture industry is bigger than you are. It can get along without you, but you can't, excuse me, get along without it." He concluded, "You may wonder why, since I feel this way about you, I take the trouble and the space to spank you. It's because I think you have the real stuff. That's why I say to you, Ann Dvorak. 'Be a trouper!'"[13]

But how much of this was really coming from Ann? She had exhibited nothing but the strongest work ethic since she was at the Page School for Girls and had proven on numerous occasions that she did not expect things to come too easily. As much as Ann's heart desired to go on this trip with her bridegroom, for her to feel guilty over breaching her contract was much more in character for her and if anything, the salary issues possibly helped her feel justified in her actions. There is little doubt that two weeks on a ship through Panama was more than enough time for Fenton and Feldman to thoroughly convince Ann that attacking Hughes and Warner Bros. was the sound thing to do. Fenton did sincerely have his wife's best interests in mind, but there is some question as to exactly what those interests may have been. It seems that Ann did come to regret the public outburst. After returning from her travels, she backpedaled, taking a much more philosophical approach to the events.

> It wasn't a question of money. I could have had a salary raise then if I wanted it. You see, I had found out a startling thing. There is no place in Hollywood now for just an ingénue. . . . I was one. I hadn't lived enough to be anything else. And by living I don't mean the hey hey, goodtime sort of thing. I mean building up a background for yourself. Getting out of ruts so you won't be fashioned to any standard pattern. It is girls like Katharine Hepburn—the ones who take what they want from life and dare to be personalities—that forge ahead the fastest. I knew when I left. I knew I had to bring color and glamour into my own life in order to give a semblance of them on the screen.

She reinforced this point about life experience salvaging her acting by remarking,

I had done a number of pictures, of course—too many. . . . As I look back, I believe I had played parts too important for my abilities and age. After all, what range, what depth can a girl of eighteen have—a girl who hadn't been out of Hollywood since she was nine years old? I had always, you see, played *myself*. I was very young. I was very introspective. I've always been interested in abnormal psychology and mordant subjects and I put myself into every role I played. I took the parts too seriously. I took the parts I played and made them into—*me*.

She concluded this thought with, "When Leslie and I were married and went away I was very tired. I had been working steadily. I knew just enough to know that I had been giving poor performances. I was enough of a critic of myself to realize that despite the kindness of reviewers and of fans." Just to drive home the point about the walkout not being about the money, she added, "People thought, among other things, that I wanted more money. Well, I didn't want it so badly ever to ask for it. I was afraid I might get it!"[14] As she further explained, "I did thirteen pictures in a year [it was actually eight]. I didn't have anything more to give a part. All my enthusiasm was gone. All the thrill. It has been said that I risked everything on a whim of the moment. Let me tell you something: I would have risked everything if I'd stayed."[15]

As for Warner Bros., it was in the middle of its annual studio shutdown and had remained silent, preferring to let Ann and Howard Hughes duke it out in the public arena. According to Anna Lehr, one of the executives at Warner Bros. contacted her the day Ann walked out to find out what was going on. He claimed the studio had every intention of giving her a raise, and in his view had given her "the very finest roles any newcomer had ever drawn on this lot." To Lehr, the studio seemed genuinely surprised by Ann's stated unhappiness.[16] Given the strong words Ann had directed at Hughes, Warner Bros. executives continued to wonder if the pair did have some sort of verbal agreement and if they in turn should withhold the remainder of the balance they owed the producer until they received some sort of clarification. Ultimately, the money was paid, the deal was officially closed, and Ann Dvorak was completely Warner Bros.' problem. The studio quietly put her on suspension in order to halt her paychecks. All it could do after that was closely monitor Ann's actions and hope she would come home soon.

For Ann, the damage had been done and there was no turning back. The couple spent a few days in New York so she could renew ties with members of the Lehr clan and introduce them to her new husband. She had spent the past few years dreaming of and working toward being a successful film actress, but she had spent a lifetime dreaming of seeing the world. Now she had a companion who wanted that for her as much as she wanted it for herself. The dust would settle on her film career and she would deal with that when the time came. As far as Ann Dvorak was concerned, her immediate future lay at the other side of the Atlantic Ocean.

9

Happy Vagabonds

When Ann Dvorak walked out on her contract in July 1932, she may have done irrevocable damage to her relationship with Warner Bros., but she also embarked on an incredible journey that exceeded even her wildest dreams. The couple was absent from Hollywood for over eight months and spent the majority of the time roaming around Europe, journeying as far as Africa. Ann would travel abroad many times during the course of her life, but none of the subsequent trips would hold the wonder and romance this first one did. The memory of her honeymoon with Leslie Fenton proved to be a strong one and remained with her long after her career and marriage were over.

While Ann was gone, the Great Depression would finally affect the film industry, causing the studios to make dramatic cuts in their payrolls, a further indicator that her foul cries of salary were ill timed. Additionally, the Hays Office began to grow sharper teeth, and Hollywood would soon see the content of its films severely sanitized. Ann was not around to see her paycheck slashed during this period, but she also lost the opportunity to appear in additional pre-Code films, which were winding down in production by the time she returned. This was probably all of little importance to Ann Dvorak, who was now half a world away from Hollywood.

The couple arrived on White Star Line's SS *Olympic* passenger ship in Southampton on July 28 and immediately traveled to London, where they checked into the historic Savoy Hotel. Leslie Fenton was not expected in Germany for the filming of *F.P.1* until late fall, so they had plenty of time to explore the continent. Within days of arriving in England, rumors started circulating that Ann had been approached by the Gaumont-British Picture Corporation, which was coproducing *F.P.1* with the German production company UFA, and offered a two-picture deal. She reportedly would be receiving £300 a week, roughly $1,500 and a substantial increase

99

Ann and Leslie relax at a European cafe.

over what she was making at Warner Bros.[1] There was some validity to the speculation, which Ann confirmed when she wrote to her mother, "They wanted me to play the lead in Les' picture. I'd have loved it—but even if my contract is jeopardized already, I wouldn't take it."[2] Ann may have been on the other side of the world and thrilled to finally be fulfilling her childhood dream of traveling to Europe, but the future of her career still loomed over her.

Happy Vagabonds

The couple stayed in England for a few weeks and then moved on to France. When rumors of Ann's impending employment persisted, Warner Bros. finally felt compelled to take action and a cable was sent to Robert Schless, the studio's foreign department head in Paris, reading, "Understand Ann Dvorak on continent seeking engagement. Please advise local producers she is under contract to us." Schless made sure word got out that Ann Dvorak was spoken for and alerted his bosses, "No producer in Paris is making other than French talker, and unless Miss Dvorak speaks good French, there will be no market here for her services."[3] Ann did in fact speak good French, and as intriguing as an appearance in a foreign-language film may have been, Ann remained a mere tourist in Europe, which was fine with her. She was absorbing every bit of her surroundings and was especially taken with France's most famous locale, commenting, "I think the whole attraction of Europe lies in its color and variety—the oldness of things and traditions that a newcomer is always conscious of. I am, anyway. *Paris* is *the city*. It is unbelievably beautiful."[4]

During the trip, Ann also experienced times of quiet introspection. As she reflected once she returned to the States, "I thought I had experienced every human emotion here in Hollywood. I'd had the heart taken out of me so many times. I knew tragedy. Poverty. Hate—yes, there were occasions when I hated terribly! Revenge. The joy of first success. And *love*." She continued, "But there have been moments during these last twelve months that gave me sensations I didn't know I was capable of. When we went over the war-torn section of France, I came upon two gold-star mothers from America in a little cemetery one afternoon. They were standing beside their white crosses; I saw the expression on their faces. And I had believed that *I* knew suffering."[5]

From France, the couple traveled to Vienna, Stockholm, Copenhagen, Munich, and Hamburg. Ann wrote often to her mother, excitedly describing each step of the adventure and sending snapshots. Never one to shy away from the spotlight, and not wanting her daughter to be forgotten by film fans, Lehr designated herself Ann's unofficial PR representative and shared many of her daughter's letters and photos with the press, which was more than happy to publish them. Lehr was still disappointed by Ann's decision to breach her contract, but tried her best to put on a positive public face with comments like, "Whether Ann made a business error or not, she is completely happy. Judging from her letters, one would think

Ann and the cast of *F.P.1* between scenes. From left to right: Ann, Leslie Fenton, Jill Esmond, Jean Murat (from the French-language version), and Donald Calthrop.

that she and Leslie discovered love and have an absolute monopoly on it. I have no worries about their future."[6]

Finally, the time came for Leslie to report for work on *F.P.1*. The science fiction/spy drama set on a floating air station was a massive undertaking, with Gaumont, UFA, and Les Productions Fox Europa coproducing English-, German-, and French-language versions simultaneously. The English production starred Conrad Veidt and Jill Esmond in the role Ann claimed she had been offered. Leslie Fenton played a supporting role as the architect of Floating Platform 1 (F.P.1). Filming commenced in Berlin, and after a couple of weeks, the production moved to the island of Greifswalder Oie in the Baltic Sea. Ann came to the set often with her husband and she soon joked that the members of the crew "call us 'the inseparables,' and I guess we deserve the name."[7]

Although away from the bright lights of Paris and Berlin, Ann reveled in her environment, even when the elements were detrimental to the production. In one letter to her mother, she wrote, "We're on a barren little island which boasts only this one little hotel. It's only used for a lighthouse base, really. They have built quite a large set at one end of the island. They have terrible storms here—and even without rain, there is too much wind for proper recording." The weather soon took a turn for the worse, though it did not seem to put too much of a damper on the cast and crew, as Ann reported, "We're having lots of fun. There was a hurricane on the sea and it damaged the floating set where the company has been working. Everyone is so good-natured. Even having production delayed so long by bad weather doesn't seem to bother them."[8] She further described their time on the little Baltic island as "the most primitive life you can imagine. No hot water, no heat, no bathroom—absolutely nothing—except cold water."[9]

As much as Ann may have been enjoying the overall experience, the fate of her career hung over her like a black cloud at times, especially when she was observing the other actors in action. As she later explained, "And I suffered as I watched them work. I resented the fact that I wasn't playing the feminine lead. I was restless. I kept thinking I should be back in Hollywood where I belong. What am I doing here? What have I thrown away? I should not be sitting on the side-lines, a part of the audience . . . I don't belong in the audience."[10] Although Ann did not play the lead role of the wealthy sophisticate, which would have been an interesting part for her, it's possible she still made an appearance in *F.P.1*. In the film's opening party scene, a svelte brunette in a black evening gown can be seen in the background—and she bears a striking resemblance to Ann as she looked as Cesca Camonte.

When Fenton wasn't busy filming, the couple explored the small island at great length, which took Ann's mind off the film industry. As she described, "We are getting lots of exercise—we walked sixteen miles the other day and twelve the day before. We hiked according to the only decent map we could get, to the top of a mountain in the middle of a forest, and found there a lonely old castle." She continued, "All this walking and sea air is making new people of us. We are beginning to look like a couple of confirmed German hikers. We have bought a couple of heavy wool roughneck sweaters that are ideal for this Baltic climate. I never imagined there would be so many interesting things to do and see in a little seacoast village." When the production moved to Cuxhaven, Ann was still impressed with what she saw, commenting, "There's a place here about three hours out of Cuxhaven called 'Helgoland.' It's rather like a fairytale to me. It's on an island that rises sheer from the sea on every side. The boat only goes out every other day, so we had to stay overnight. There's another little island called Menewerk, and at night, when the tide goes out—it runs for miles—we take a horse and buggy and drive right through a foot or so of water in order to reach it. It's nearly twenty miles off shore."[11] As much as Ann may have been enjoying herself, the remote filming locations seemed to have finally worn on her when she wrote, "Fun is fun, but I think we will be glad to get back to Berlin where we can sit down to a nice cup of tea and say, ''Twas a grand experience.'"[12]

Back in Berlin, Ann continued her explorations. "I do a lot of walking—seeing as much of the town as possible. I've been through dozens of shops and department stores, as well as most of the art galleries and museums. I feel that I'm acquiring knowledge and experience of real value." Of the many hours spent in the galleries, Ann stated, "I had never heard of any of the artists and didn't know one picture from another, but I studied until the things I saw really began to mean something to me."[13] While in Berlin, she also observed, "There's a street here that reminds me of Hollywood Boulevard—Kurfürstendamm—but much nicer, with better stores and wider sidewalks. But it is brilliantly lighted, like Hollywood Boulevard, and everyone parades up and down it in just the same way." After spending so many weeks in Germany, Ann was rapidly becoming trilingual, commenting, "I am speaking German fairly well now. I spent most of the time studying it as we travelled around. Leslie, of course, speaks German fluently, so we talk to each other, half the time in German and half the time in English. Everyone kids us about our obvious happiness, and certainly we never make any effort to hide it." Ann had the opportunity to test her recently learned language skills when "we went to the Metropole Opera House the other night to see Fritz Massary, the German idol, in an operetta. This Massary is sixty-five years old—and *what* a personality! It was all in German, of course, but we both understood every word. It was a great thrill to me to realize that our study has produced results."[14]

The experience of being in foreign countries was exhilarating for Ann, but this was largely due to her traveling companion. In one of the many letters she wrote to her mother, she gushed,

Everything's quite rolling in a buttercup, as Leslie says. We are having a grand time and are unbelievably happy. I never dreamed that anyone could be as thoughtful as Leslie has been during this entire trip. He is continually planning something for my pleasure and seems to take even more joy in my enthusiasms than I do, myself. All in all, I wouldn't have missed this wonderful experience for any amount of personal success. Leslie and I want our marriage to be completely happy—and what better start could we possibly have made than to share so many pleasures? We fall more deeply in love every day.[15]

Ann may have been enjoying her honeymoon, but she had not forgotten about the career she had thrown into limbo. She later admitted, "Nearly everyone thought I was foolish to run away. Once in a while I got panicky too, wondering if I had completely lost my chance at a career in Hollywood."[16] She was feeling some apprehension over what her actions might mean for her and Warner Bros., but seemed to be having an inner battle over how she felt about her career. As much as she may have "suffered" watching actors engaged in their craft during the filming of *F.P.1*, when writing to Anna Lehr, she claimed, "Not for one moment have I regretted 'running away' from Hollywood. I suppose I have been guilty of poor business judgment. Perhaps I've endangered, or even ruined my career—but what of that? I'll always have these gay exciting, carefree months to look back on. Leslie and I are the happiest people in the world—and what does a career matter in view of that all-important fact?" Ann was having the time of her life, and believed the experience could only help her performances onscreen, noting, "After this we will be willing to settle down and work for a while, anyway! I feel as though I would be a better actress for having seen a little of the world. You know what a narrow life I have always led. I felt when I was working in pictures that I hadn't had enough experience and background." Even as the weeks of the trip stretched into months, and *F.P.1* was wrapping up production, Ann remained resolved that she had done what was best for her, commenting, "Leslie is almost through with his work, so I suppose that before many more weeks have passed, we'll be on our way home. I know I'll bring back with me a great many more memories that I'll treasure as long as I live. I wonder how I'll be greeted when I report to the studio? No matter what happens, it's been worth it—and I know that I'll be able to do much better work, for I'm completely rested and fit as a fiddle."[17]

Once Leslie Fenton was done working, the two decided they were not quite ready to go home, so they made their way to St. Moritz, Switzerland, where they spent New Year's Eve, which also marked the one-year anniversary of their first meeting.[18] They went skiing in the Alps.

Ann enjoying the landscape, possibly in St. Moritz, Switzerland.

Here they experienced one of the more harrowing adventures of the trip. As Ann later recalled, "[We] were in an Alpine mountain cabin when an avalanche came crashing through the far end of the cabin. For a moment both of us sat there transfixed waiting for the director to shout 'cut' and stop the terrifying roar and crash. But neither director or his assistant came running with blankets and hot cups of coffee. Only more snow and rocks came crashing down from above." She continued, "'What does the script say?' shouted Leslie. Then he seized me, laughed and kissed me and we ran out through the door to the road. It was a perfect 'take,' but no cameras were there to film it, and somehow we thought very little more about it—it was so much like a movie situation."[19]

The pair made their way down to Monaco. According to Ann, "It was in Monte Carlo, I think, that we decided suddenly that we wanted to leave most of our baggage behind and continue traveling as lightly as we could. So we started off with just a suitcase a piece, going down to Rome, and to Africa, and elsewhere for weeks, without any more baggage." One particular evening in Rome stood out when the couple walked around the moonlit Colosseum: "I never dreamed that beauty could be *exalted* like that." From Rome, the pair made their way to Naples and then over to Sicily. They arrived on the island at night during a storm, narrowly escaping being thrown in jail by some local villagers who did not know what to make of the young couple with papers that were not regularly signed. Ann and Leslie then moved on to Africa, where the couple soaked in the blood-red sunsets of the Sahara. As Ann recounted, "We'd go for long drives and our driver would be wrapped in a burnoose, silent as a statue even when we came to pay him. He never once mentioned a price—we knew for sure we were in uncivilized country!"[20] As much as she enjoyed the major cities of Europe, wandering about during these waning weeks of the trip was also significant, as Ann stated, "The most fun we've ever had was in the loneliest spots we visited; on board the tanker coming up the coast, in forgotten places in Africa and on unfrequented oceans."[21]

Finally, the Fentons decided the time had come to return to Los Angeles. As Ann later noted, "Twice, while we were away, we were penniless, but something always turned up to save us."[22] By February 1933, the two figured it was a good idea to end the trip while they had enough money to get home. They made their way back to Italy, and after a quick stop in Genoa, Ann and Leslie boarded the SS *Rialto* in Livorno and prepared to return to the town and industry they had turned their backs on. The journey home would take well over a month, partially because they were, according to Ann, "stopping at all sorts of unheard of places in the tropics."[23]

While the happy vagabonds were traipsing through Europe, Warner Bros. was trying to decide what to do with Ann. She had caused the studio a lot of grief, but it had already invested such a large sum of money in Ann that dropping her contract was unthinkable. To make matters worse, the terms of the Caddo contract were also presenting the studio with difficulties. If Ann had been working under a standard Warner Bros. contract, the months she had been suspended during her walkout would have been tacked on to the end of her term. This was a common practice with all the studios, and if an actor was particularly troublesome and suspended often, the life of his or her contract could be extended indefinitely. Fortunately for Ann, the lawyers at Warner Bros. determined that the wording in the Caddo contract regarding suspensions was too ambiguous. The Caddo document addressed an employee's inability to work due to illness, but did not discuss a suspension induced by a player's refusal to work. Ultimately, the studio decided not to risk any adverse legal interpretations, which meant that the nine months Ann had not worked at the studio would not have to be made up later.[24] Additionally, Warner Bros. decided to exercise her options as they came up. Notices to this effect were sent by registered mail to 3339 Troy Drive and to Ann in Europe, if the studio happened to know her whereabouts. When Ann returned to Hollywood, two options had been taken up, and she was on Warner Bros.' books as earning $325 per week. On paper, the studio seemed not to be holding any grudges toward Ann. Time would tell if this were true.

There is no doubt that Ann's actions had many Warner Bros. executives pulling their hair out, but the main person she needed to worry about was Jack L. Warner. J. L., as he was known to many around him, was the youngest of the four founding Warner brothers and hated being viewed as the baby. With the death of Sam Warner in 1927, and with the other two brothers opting to operate business dealings out of New York, Jack came to be the public face of the studio from his helm in Burbank. Having started his career in show business as a song-and-dance man, Jack Warner reveled in his position of power, but was never one to shy away from spouting an ill-timed bad joke. Despite this comedic side, Warner's credo was reportedly "Give an actor a break and he'll fuck you later," and he earned a reputation for being abrasive with his staff, particularly the talent.[25] Jack L. Warner was reviled by many of the actors on the lot, like James Cagney, whose nickname for his boss was "the Schvontz," a slang Yiddish term that was not complimentary. However, other stars, like Bette Davis, who were able to match wits with J. L., came to respect him deeply. Jack Warner was a shrewd businessman who helped his studio succeed and who stayed on top of the industry for decades. He was also incredibly ego-driven and could hold a grudge over a perceived slight for an indefinite amount of time. How he would ultimately handle Ann Dvorak's actions remained to be seen, though the press quoted him as saying, "Miss Dvorak is still under exclusive contract to us. And I'm not mad at her."[26]

The SS *Rialto*, carrying Ann and Leslie, docked at the Port of Los

Angeles in San Pedro on March 22, 1933. They had been absent from Los Angeles for almost nine months. For Ann, the importance of this trip could not be overstated. Her experiences abroad became a favorite topic of conversation, and she even admitted to one journalist, "I always talk about Europe sooner or later, so you may as well hear it now."[27] As Ann prepared to face the future, she clung tightly to the preceding months, commenting, "No matter what happens now I've got something to hold onto—the memory of this past year. People don't do enough with their lives. They sit back and wait for their hopes to materialize, instead of going ahead and doing the things they want to. That is what I was doing— waiting. I feel as if I'd wasted so much time."[28] It had been an extraordinary nine months, perhaps the most memorable period of her life. In her later years, Ann loathed talking about her past and usually avoided it. However, every so often, the one topic she would bring up from her acting years were her travels with Leslie Fenton in 1932.[29] Once she returned to Hollywood, Ann was often asked about the decision to walk out on her contract. She invariably responded that she did not regret her choice; as she told one reporter, "So much happened to me in the year before Leslie and I went away together. I had been given a chance in pictures after three years of heartbreaking disappointments. I had fallen in love and I had been married. It was just too much to ask me to go on with all of these— career, love, and marriage—at the speed they had started. I had to get away to get my life and thoughts straightened out. I'm glad I did."[30]

As soon as the couple set foot in Los Angeles, Warner Bros. became aware of its prodigal daughter's return. Ann may have been apprehensive about returning to the studio, but Jack Warner seemed willing to welcome her back. He was also ready to meet his wayward actress head-on. The day after Ann arrived back home, Warner sent a memo to his immediate staff reading:

> Should ANN DVORAK appear here at the Studio, let her come in, give her a dressing room and treat her just as though nothing ever happened.
>
> However, if she wants to talk to you on the status of her contract, refer her to me personally immediately.[31]

10

Prodigal Daughter

Ann was not sent to see Jack Warner the next day because she did not show up at the studio. Rather than reporting for work, she consulted her agents, Myron Selznick and Frank Joyce. Even in the midst of her fairy-tale honeymoon, she had come to the realization that Charles Feldman had done a less than stellar job of handling Warner Bros. during her extended vacation, and had switched agencies while still abroad. She had her new representatives feel out the studio's attitude toward her, and figuring transparency was the best route, had them turn over all the wires and correspondence she had received from Feldman. This move was presumably made to alert the execs that bad agenting had been the main cause of Ann's insolent behavior. Since it still needed to draft an official contract for Ann to replace the Caddo document, Warner Bros. mailed a formal agreement to her on March 29, which would serve in the interim. It stated that two options had been exercised and her pay had been increased to $325 a week. The agreement also declared that the studio was waiving its rights to extend Ann's contract for the period of the suspension. Warner Bros. also made it perfectly clear that if Ann subsequently took similar action, there would be no such waiver. Ann had no problems revealing to her agents that the trip had left her and Fenton cash poor, because the studio also agreed to advance her $1,000, which she would pay back through a weekly paycheck deduction of $100.[1] Myron Selznick, who was the brother of producer David O., loved to play hardball with the studio execs, but even he could see that Warner Bros. was being extremely generous toward Ann. He advised his new client to take what the studio was offering her and get back to work. She signed the document.

Now that the working relationship between Dvorak and Warner Bros. was finally squared away, the next logical step was for studio to start casting her in films. But this did not happen for months. One reason for the delay was the annual studio shutdown, which took place in the spring instead of the summer that year. Considering that Ann was officially back on the payroll as of April 1, it seems that even with the closure, Warner Bros. might have loaned her out to another studio. Instead, it paid her weekly rate, even deciding to write off the last $400 she owed from the advance.[2] It's unknown why the studio waited so long to cast Ann in a film or loan her out. Perhaps Jack Warner wanted to let her stew and prove he had the upper hand, or maybe Warner Bros. really didn't have anything suitable for her. Whatever the reasons, Ann went a full year without making a movie.

The one action the studio did take regarding Ann was to finally draft an official Warner Bros. contract for her. The agreement was for five years, and it would increase her pay to $800 a week by the end of the year and top out at $2,300 a week at the time of expiration. It was a standard agreement, with the artist forfeiting his or her right to engage in acting jobs outside the studio—or in any other occupation, for that matter. The contract also stated that if Ann was unable to work due to illness, she would be suspended and would submit to any medical examinations requested by the studio. Unlike the Caddo Company contract, this one made it very clear that any sort of suspension induced by the artist's actions would be tacked onto the end of the term.[3] According to Ann at the time, "My new contract allows me time to 'run away' each year! It's going to be the Orient next; then we're going to sail around the Grecian Islands."[4] There was actually no such provision in the contract for additional time off, but perhaps Ann and the execs had a verbal agreement. When asked if she would impetuously take off again at the whim of her husband, Ann cautiously responded, "I don't know. I've often asked myself that question—because we are both subject to that longing for far places and it *is* apt to attack us, violently at any moment. I think perhaps I might go—but not as I did before. Not so childishly, not so inconsiderately, not without explanation and asking for permission. I think every so often, both Leslie and I will have to travel. We have it in our blood." She concluded this thought, "But no, I shall never again act like a child playing hooky from school."[5] With this seemingly new devotion to Warner Bros. in place, she signed the document on May 18, 1933, and at long last, Ann Dvorak had an official Warner Bros. contract. What she didn't have was a movie role.

Ann and Leslie chat with Vince Barnett at a screening of *Another Language* at the Filmarte Theater shortly after returning from their eight-month honeymoon.

While Ann waited for an assignment, she and Leslie started getting reacquainted with the city they had left behind. They were seen around town at film screenings, boxing matches, and celebrity hangouts like the Brown Derby restaurant and the Cocoanut Grove nightclub. Ann even made a personal appearance at a joint benefit for the American Legion and the Boy Scouts.[6] When it became apparent she was not going to be getting work immediately, the couple took off to Palm Springs for a few days. After Ann and Leslie had been back a little over a month, they decided they had had enough of Hollywood nightlife and started to consider moving to a more rural setting. During this time, many industry people began moving out to the San Fernando Valley. Most of the communities in the Valley were part of the City of Los Angeles, but they provided a break from the rapid urban development that was taking place, while still being close enough to all the major studios. Al Jolson, Ruby Keeler, Edward Everett Horton, Paul Muni, Clark Gable, and Carole Lombard were just a few of the Hollywood notables who would come to call the Valley home in the 1930s, owning sprawling ranches with citrus and walnut trees. After a year and a half of being in the public eye, the Fentons were ready to claim some privacy, and the Valley seemed the perfect place to do so. Rather than taking the plunge into ranch ownership, they opted to lease an estate located at 6948 Woodman Avenue in the community of Van Nuys. The two-story Spanish-style residence was surrounded by acres of walnut trees and had the obligatory Southern California swimming pool. The pair quickly dove into ranch life, tending to the land themselves—or at least they appeared to do so for publicity photos—and raising rabbits and chickens. Hanging in the living room of their home was a large portrait of Ann by artist Edward School. For Ann, who had spent a lifetime living in numerous apartments, the spacious quarters must have been a welcome change. After establishing themselves as Valley residents, Ann and Leslie spent many evenings at home, developing a reputation as recluses. When questioned about this, Ann replied, "We very seldom go out and don't even have people in very often. We study a great deal—music and languages, art and history and other things that we began in Europe." The two also reportedly developed a secret sign language for when they were stuck in social obligations and wanted to cue each other to make an early exit.[7]

If the Fentons' diminished social calendar failed to raise eyebrows, then the hobby they feverishly threw themselves into most certainly did. The study of bacteria was an interest Leslie Fenton had more than likely picked up from director Paul [Pál] Fejös. Fejös had been a bacteriologist of note in his native Hungary and probably introduced Fenton to the subject when they worked together on two films in the 1920s. When

Of Ann and Leslie's many hobbies, bacteriology was one of their most peculiar.

asked how she had become involved in the unconventional pastime, Ann said, "I first became interested when Leslie and I spent 48 days aboard a tramp steamer on a trip around the world. Among the many books we took along was one on bacteriology. I was immediately intrigued and since then have read everything I could get on the subject." The couple set up a laboratory at the ranch in which Ann was photographed, her hair and makeup studio-perfect, intensely working with her equipment. When Fenton wanted to surprise Ann on her birthday, he bought her a higher-powered microscope. Ann could drone on about the subject, claiming that bacteriology was a cure for an inflated Hollywood ego because "in the first place, there will be no applause to reward your most strenuous efforts, such as might follow your work on the screen. For even if you were fortunate enough to make progressive discoveries, they'd be absorbed in the infinitely greater discoveries of Pasteur and Koch. Secondly, there's nothing that reduces a single life or one's screen fame to a paltry ephemeral thing as the study of these life-giving and death-dealing micro organisms. And at the same time, there's nothing more fascinating than a progressive knowledge of them."[8] The couple reportedly enrolled in classes at the University of Southern California and had plans to study at the University of Vienna, although these never came to pass. After about four years, the two got bacteriology out of their system and donated their equipment to a young doctor doing cancer research.[9]

Rumors started sprouting up that Ann was going to be cast in various films: *Shanghai Orchid* opposite Richard Barthelmess, which seems never to have started production; *Wonder Bar*, which was made but without Ann; and Fox's *The Worst Woman in Paris?* Instead, Ann continued to collect a paycheck for doing nothing, though she still did not seem to regret her actions of the previous year. "My marriage is the most important thing in my life. After that comes my career. No matter how brilliant a career might be offered, I wouldn't strive for it if I thought there was even the slightest chance of it breaking up my home."[10] She continually repeated her credo: "Everybody in Hollywood ought to 'run away' once in a while! It gives a person better perspective."[11] Ann's sentiments echoed those of her husband, who was also quick to say, "I think everybody in Hollywood ought to get away once in a while. There's too much luxury, too much softness, everything is too easy. It's healthful to go places where you don't have hot running water, to mix with real people in workaday life."[12]

In August, nearly five months after Ann returned to Los Angeles, Warner Bros. finally decided to put her to work by loaning her out to Paramount Pictures. She was to costar with Maurice Chevalier in the semi-musical *The Way to Love*, directed by Norman Taurog, who had won the 1931 Best Director Academy Award for the Jackie Cooper feature

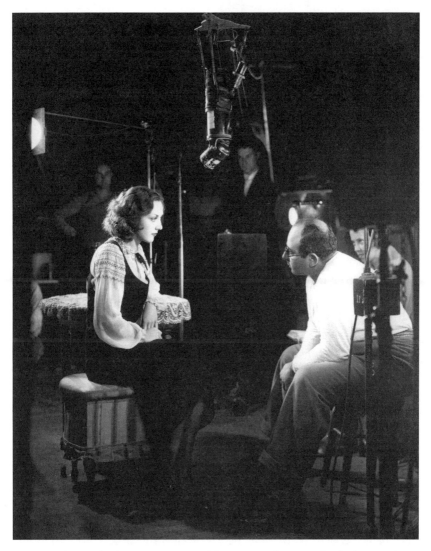

Ann confers with director Norman Taurog on the set of *The Way to Love*, Ann's first film after returning from an extended honeymoon.

Skippy. In *The Way to Love*, Chevalier plays a Parisian native who wants nothing more than to have a career as a tour guide. Along the way he encounters Madeleine, a forlorn and jaded gypsy girl essentially held captive by her abusive guardian who uses her as his assistant in his knife-throwing act. Chevalier introduces her to the joys of bohemian life and eventually gets to her closely guarded heart. Like many Paramount features of the early 1930s, *The Way to Love* is an odd and disjointed film with musical numbers that seem out of place, though it's still a lighthearted romantic story and is enjoyable enough. Sylvia Sidney was originally cast as the brooding brunette and was involved with the production long enough to sit for publicity photos, some of which ended up on sheet music. Several of these pieces made it out to the retail market, and later on Ann would be mildly amused when people would bring her this version to be autographed.[13] Sidney ended up walking off the picture over her own salary dispute with Paramount, and when Carole Lombard refused to play the part after it was assigned to her, Ann got it. The studio paid Warner Bros. $8,300 for her services. Curiously, she was not engaged to appear in the French version of the film, even though she supposedly spoke the language fluently.[14] Madeleine in *The Way to Love* was another second-tier role for Dvorak, though it's definitely more interesting than the characters she had played in *Stranger in Town* and *Crooner* over at Warner Bros. Instead of the loyal and steadfast gal behind a troubled leading man, Madeleine is high-spirited and at times aloof and surly. *The Way to Love* has some musical numbers, but Ann does not get to sing; instead she has to sit around being serenaded by Chevalier while trying to appear interested. Still, Ann looks striking in the gypsy garb, sporting slightly pointed eyebrows given to her by Paramount's makeup department. And at least she was back in front of the camera.

When Ann returned from Paramount, she finally had a role waiting for her at Warner Bros., that of Claire Gore in *College Coach*, directed by William Wellman, who had previously worked with Ann on *Love Is a Racket*. As the title implies, *College Coach* is set in the world of collegiate football where Ann plays the woefully neglected wife of Pat O'Brien, a high-profile coach. Newcomer Dick Powell is the all-around good guy/star player, and Lyle Talbot is the unscrupulous hotshot teammate who, again, steals Ann from an onscreen husband. If Warner Bros. was trying to make a statement about its disapproval of Ann's actions of the previous year, *College Coach* certainly does that. Ann's part is less than secondary, and she has minimal screen time, though one could argue that in the end her actions ultimately save the big game. Ann is clearly giving her all to the character, who spends the bulk of the film alternating between being angry and morose, but she has so little to do that Claire is not a noteworthy role in the least. However, the affectionate scenes between Dvorak and O'Brien are believable, and she looks lovely while still sporting her *Way to Love* gypsy eyebrows. Despite the secondary nature of the role, Ann received second billing onscreen below Powell and above Pat O'Brien, who plays the title character. She also appeared on the "window card" advertisement with Powell, even though they do not appear in any scenes together. Overall, the most interesting things about *College Coach* might be a blink-and-you'll-miss-him walk-on by a very young John Wayne and the realization that college football was as much of a controversial moneymaker eighty years ago as it is today. The film was a less than stellar return to Warner Bros. for Ann, but the studio now seemed poised to make up for lost time. *College Coach* would launch a two-year run of nearly nonstop work for Ann, which would prove to be the most prolific time of her career in terms of quantity, if not always of quality.

11

Warner Workhorse

College Coach marked the beginning of a productive run of filmmaking for Ann Dvorak, though the movies often left a lot to be desired, particularly in regard to the size of her roles. The main part Ann seemed to be playing in the mid-1930s was that of a Warner Bros. workhorse. No studio could churn out films quite like Warner Bros., and generally no one under contract was immune from appearing in his or her fair share of B films, made on the cheap and shot in less than a month or sometimes in a couple of weeks. As one Bette Davis biographer wrote of 1930s Warner Bros. films, "Even a screen buff could not always differentiate between an 'A' and 'B' film strictly by the players but could make the distinction within the first five minutes by counting the close-ups."[1] Later on, James Cagney summed up Warner Bros.' vast output in the 1930s: "What is usually not realized is that most of the scripts we were forced to do were acutely dreadful."[2] The number of movies one actor could appear in during the course of a year was impressive. In 1932 alone, eight Warner films had Bette Davis's name in the credits, and Joan Blondell appeared in an astounding ten movies. However, for all the throwaway quickie programmers the contract players were forced to appear in, there were usually a few choice roles thrown in to keep them happy, like *Fog over Frisco* and *Bordertown* for Davis, and *Blondie Johnson* and *Footlight Parade* for Blondell. As 1933 was winding down, Ann Dvorak officially joined the Warner ranks, and by the end of the following year had appeared in nine films. Unfortunately, the parts were usually small and the films not always memorable. Even if the movie itself was of higher quality or had an interesting story, Ann's contribution was usually minimal and saw her playing the stalwart girlfriend.

Warner Bros. seemed to have no intention of casting Ann in anything akin to *The Strange Love of Molly Louvain* or *Three on a Match*. One newspaper even reported that, following her prolonged absence, Warner Bros. had made a conscious decision not to star her in anything. There is no official documentation to back up this claim, but it did seem to be the studio's intentions. Ann downplayed it, as if the assignments she had been receiving did not bother her . "I may get another chance to become a star, and if I do I'll try hard to make good, because I don't believe anything could come between Leslie and myself now. However, I would rather wait indefinitely for a starring opportunity, happy with my husband, than to be a star now, at the possible cost of a matrimonial shipwreck."[3] On another occasion, she proclaimed, "I do not want to be starred at this point in my second career. I really would prefer to play comparatively small parts. But I'm human, and if someone urged me to star in some terrifically attractive picture, I would probably clutch at it with both hands. But, reasonably, I would rather not. I want to start all over again, near the bottom and build up slowly, substantially, growing with my own growth."[4] Ann approached this demotion of sorts with a positive attitude, but would change her mind about the repeatedly drab parts before her contract was over. As for Leslie Fenton, his reply to questions about his wife's future in film was "Ann has a right to her career."[5]

Rumors started floating around that Ann was going to be cast opposite Leslie Howard in *British Agent*, but instead she was given *Massacre* with former silent star Richard Barthelmess. *Massacre* is an interesting film for the time period, as it brings to light the hardships of reservation life and the mistreatment of Native Americans at the hands of government officials. Barthelmess plays a Native American who has escaped the reservation by becoming a noted rodeo personality, donning a "traditional" chief costume. When his family sends a distress call, he returns to the reservation, where his perceived meddling makes him the target of corrupt government employees. The ultimate theme of *Massacre* seems to be that Native American reservations are A-OK as long as the right people are running them, but even so, the subject matter of the film is still ahead of its time. The Sioux were so impressed with the film and Barthelmess's performance that he was adopted as a tribal brother, a rare honor.[6] Ann plays the weary but sympathetic secretary who aids Barthelmess in his quest for truth and justice, and eventually wins his heart. The role of Lydia is essentially not much of a departure from her recent parts at Warner Bros., but the story is stronger than *College Coach* or *Stranger in Town*. She looks lovely made up as a Native American, and producer Hal

Ann and Richard Barthelmess made up as Native Americans in *Massacre*.

Wallis commented to director Alan Crosland, "Dvorak is photographed beautifully and certainly looks the part."[7] Four days after expressing these sentiments, one scene caused Wallis to partially revise his opinion, and he requested the wardrobe department be instructed to "watch the clothes they put on Ann Dvorak because she is so terribly thin. She is sitting here in a scene in 'Massacre' with a waist on with very short sleeves coming just below her shoulders and her arms are so thin that it looks bad."[8] The scene in question remained as shot, but for the rest of her tenure with Warner Bros., Ann would usually be clothed in outfits with full, long sleeves. On the rare occasion that she wore short sleeves, they would be loose fitting to camouflage how thin she was becoming.

While filming *Massacre* on location in Calabasas, Ann was allegedly bitten by a rattlesnake on October 17. As she described the incident, "I was standing [in] back of the camera at the moment, watching a shot being taken, when I felt something strike my leg and heard several yell 'snake.' The reptile wriggled off toward the camera and everyone ran. I didn't know I had been bitten until they started to examine my leg and found the glancing puncture and scratch where the fangs struck."[9] The *Los Angeles Examiner* even ran a dramatic photo of Ann convalescing in bed with a concerned Leslie Fenton at her side. It was reported that Ann would be sidelined for a few days, but the couple was anxious to run the sample that had been retrieved from Ann's leg under the microscope. Years later, a former press agent named Tommy McLeod revealed there never was a rattlesnake bite and the whole incident was staged to garner publicity.[10] The ploy worked; the story was picked up by papers across the country. McLeod also recalled that the incident caused the three hundred extras to refuse to go near the brush where Ann was "attacked." McLeod's claims are backed up by the studio's production log, which record Ann back at work the following day and does not reference her being injured on set.[11] For Ann, and particularly Leslie Fenton, to cooperate with this sort of publicity ruse is highly out of character, but perhaps the five months she had spent waiting for Warner Bros. to put her in a film convinced Ann that she needed to cooperate with her bosses, for a while at least.

One week after principal photography on *Massacre* wrapped, Ann started work on what would be one of her better Warner Bros. films, *Heat Lightning*. Directed by Mervyn LeRoy, who had guided Ann through *Three on a Match*, *Heat Lightning* centers on two sisters operating a gas station/rest stop on the way to Las Vegas. Ann plays Myra, the younger sister who is chomping at the bit to get out of the oppressive desert and start living. Aline MacMahon is the older and wiser Olga who escaped to the desert in order to forget the living she has already done. Olga's peaceful existence is shattered when former flame Preston Foster rolls in while on the run from the law. At the same time Myra receives a brutal reality check after sneaking off for an evening with an ill-intentioned beau. The film is peppered with reliable contract players like Glenda Farrell, Ruth Donnelly, Frank McHugh, Jane Darwell, and Lyle Talbot, who add color to the intense drama, which was largely filmed on location in Victorville, California. Ann's role is limited to a supporting one, but it's still one of the strongest of her career; she is effective as the restless, dreamy-eyed teen who goes against her sister's wishes and suffers the consequences. When she realizes the man to whom she has presumably given her virtue is no longer interested, her subsequent confrontation/breakdown with her sister is a heartwrenching and unforgettable moment in Ann's career. Like Cesca Camonte, Vivian Revere, and Molly Louvain, Myra is more fleshed out than most of her other Warner Bros. characters, and she has more to do than be a backbone and voice of reason for the male star. As good as Ann's performance is in *Heat Lightning*, Aline MacMahon dominates the film as the self-sufficient, tough-as-nails Olga, and the two actresses are believable as sisters. The script was based on a play of the same name by Leon Abrams and George Abbott that began a brief run on Broadway two months before production on the film started. Given the source material, the film version of *Heat Lightning* is a dialogue-heavy precursor to the better-known *The Petrified Forest*, which would be made by Warner Bros. in 1936, featuring Bette Davis, Humphrey Bogart, and Leslie Howard. The last part of the second act of *Heat Lightning* is particularly interesting as the intense dialogue is accompanied by the distant sounds of a guitar played by a Mexican farmer who is camping at Olga's for the night. Production on *Heat Lighting* started on November 20 and wrapped two and a half weeks later. Filming probably would have been completed even sooner had it not been interrupted by the Thanksgiving holiday.[12] After eighteen months of marriage, Ann and Leslie still could not bear to be separated for even a short time, so he joined his wife on the location shoot.

Around the time *Heat Lightning* was in production, Hollywood was again under attack for its lack of self-censorship. The Legion of Decency, organized by the Catholic Church, was effectively getting a large enough chunk of the population to boycott films that the film industry had to respond. An Irish Catholic named Joseph Breen was brought on to run the Production Code Administration, and he took his job seriously. For the next thirty-plus years, American-made films would be sanitized to the point where many films made before 1934 could not even be rereleased. Because of the strictness of the PCA, many pre-Code performances, including Ann's, would be hidden until the advent of home video in the 1980s revived these strong female characterizations. *Heat Lightning* would be one of the last pre-Code films for Ann Dvorak, and she would soon find herself banished to the land of bland leading ladies for most of her remaining days at Warner Bros.

After the filming of *Heat Lightning*, the Fentons began preparing for their first Christmas in Los Angeles, which included having a Warner Bros. photographer come to their Van Nuys home to take images of the actress wrapping gifts for family members. Ann had to return to the studio the day after Christmas to shoot *Heat Lightning* retakes but was then able to take a month off to catch her breath after working nearly nonstop for the past four months.

Her next assignment was another film with Aline MacMahon tentatively titled *Fur Coats*, and later released as *Side Streets*. The film focuses on Aline as a successful furrier in San Francisco who is also a bit of an old maid. Her better judgment fails her when she falls for and marries a navy grifter played by Paul Kelly, who not only makes the moves on her niece but also has a pregnant girlfriend (Ann) on the side. *Side Streets* is a watchable film, mainly due to Aline MacMahon's performance as a smart and self-sufficient woman who resigns herself to marrying a lowlife rather than living alone (the UK title for the film was *A Woman in Her Thirties*). Aline inexplicably clutches her purse in every scene, even one in which she is wearing her night clothes, so perhaps she developed a complex backstory for this character that is never fully revealed onscreen. Ann's character as the jilted mistress is less weak than a lot of her other Warner Bros. portrayals, but the role is minuscule and her lack of screen time is a major letdown. Ann's part in *Side Streets* is so limited that she worked on the film for only six days.[13]

Friends of Mr. Sweeney offered Ann a bigger part than in *Side Streets*, but only slightly better. This yarn stars Charlie Ruggles as a former college stud turned working-class stiff whose boring life is turned on its ear when an old university pal shows up. Ann is Beulah Boyd, his loyal secretary who harbors not-so-secret feelings for Ruggles, though he is too shy to respond. *Friends of Mr. Sweeney* was another leading-lady role for Ann, but while *Crooner, Stranger in Town*, and *Massacre* saw her playing fairly serious and noble women, Beulah Boyd is flighty and flirty, a side of Ann's acting not normally seen onscreen. In one scene, told her clothing is inappropriate for the office, she proceeds to change her dress in full view. The pre-Code era was on its way out, but not yet completely dead. The *Los Angeles Evening Herald and Express* reported of her performance as Beulah, "Ann Dvorak in the inspirational role of the girl has little to do, but does it charmingly," while the *New York Times* thought Ann handled the straight part correctly, and the *Los Angeles Examiner* quipped, "Ann Dvorak gives no evidence of acquiring any weight. She is still tall and lovely looking in a lackadaisical sort of fashion."[14] The *Washington Post*'s claim that "Ann Dvorak increases in pictorial value in each picture" can only be attributed to the continued effort Ann put into the parts she was assigned, and not to the films themselves.[15] As for Ann, she referred to parts like the one in *Friends of Mr. Sweeney* as "stooge roles."[16]

Ann did not fare much better on her next assignment, *Midnight Alibi*.

She was again teamed up with Richard Barthelmess and director Alan Crosland, both of whom she had worked with on *Massacre*. In *Midnight Alibi*, based on a story by Damon Runyon, Barthelmess is a gangster who gets on a rival's extreme bad side by dating his kid sister (Ann). While on the run from his adversary, Barthelmess stumbles into the decaying estate of an elderly woman who proceeds to tell him, in flashback, her tale of lost love. By the end, he is determined to go on the straight and narrow in order to be with the woman he loves. Ann's part is another thankless one, and she has very little to do. The film itself isn't terrible, though its original title, *The Old Doll's House*, is much more appropriate, as most of the story takes place there. When the movie was released, it was bizarrely marketed as a screwball comedy, perhaps trying to capitalize on the recent success of the Clark Gable/Claudette Colbert hit *It Happened One Night*. Production on *Midnight Alibi* lasted less than three weeks, with Ann working on it for nine days.[17]

In the midst of being thrown into one Warner Bros. production after another, Ann found time to serve as a mentor to aspiring actress Helene McAdoo. Ann took a shine to McAdoo, the daughter of a retired army colonel who had acting ambitions despite her mother's wishes that she pursue a career in medicine. Ann assumed the role Joan Crawford and Karen Morley had played for her by encouraging the young woman, and she brought McAdoo to Warner Bros. as her stand-in.[18] McAdoo eventually earned an uncredited part as a hostess in the Cagney vehicle *Ceiling Zero*, but otherwise did not have any sort of career despite Ann's best efforts. Even though Ann had attained a decent level of success in Hollywood, she had remained true to her chorus girl self by not letting her ego get out of hand.

Following *Midnight Alibi*, Ann was finally given a more substantial part, the title role in *Housewife*, costarring Bette Davis and George Brent. As Nan Reynolds, Ann is once again the devoted partner of the leading man, though this time the character has more of a personality and backstory than those in her other quickie Warner Bros. films. Here, she is a housewife who revels in her day-to-day tasks, hectic though they may be, all the while providing moral support for her underachieving husband (Brent). When he finally does find success in the world of advertising, it's only because Nan is the brains and backbone behind him. This is one of the few times Ann would play a loving and attentive mother, a complete turnaround from Vivian Revere in *Three on a Match*, and she also exudes

Ann takes a break on the set of *Housewife*, one of two features she made opposite Bette Davis.

a stylish elegance that many filmgoers would come to associate her with. Bette Davis is the career girl who wants nothing more than to steal George Brent away from Ann, and she projects an aura of strength and bitchiness that would become her trademark. The casting is so on the nose that it may have actually been more interesting had the actresses switched parts. Even so, their brief screen time together is effective, and the catty standoff scene in a powder room is especially fun. Of her costar, Davis remembered she "was always impressed with Ann Dvorak's performances. She also was a smashingly nice person." As for her participation in *Housewife*, Bette could only say, "Dear God! What a horror!"[19] In a postfeminist era, the movie's message that being a devoted housewife, no matter how unmotivated or unfaithful your husband is, is the most rewarding station a woman can aspire to is dated. Ann's abrupt reconciliation with Brent is actually disappointing, as she probably would have been happier had she ended up with the wealthy cosmetic king who truly appreciates her. Despite any shortcomings the film may ultimately have, in the overall career of Ann Dvorak, it's one of her more important performances, and Ann herself thought it was one of the best roles Warner Bros. gave her during this period.[20]

Housewife also afforded Ann an opportunity to boost her culinary skills. By this point, she was able to work her way around a kitchen, though she admitted, "Since I have been married I have learned to cook a little, but I don't do it enough to accustom my husband to my cooking."[21] Ann had a natural aversion to sweets, so her knowledge of baking was nonexistent. Director Alfred Green wanted her early scenes in *Housewife* to be convincing, so he had Ann take a couple of classes in cake making. The resulting scene of Ann preparing a cake while juggling many other tasks is indeed believable, and the cast and crew were treated to a Dvorak dessert at the end of the day. When Green jokingly gave her a hard time about sharing only half the cake with everyone, she replied, "That's for somebody at home, if you must know, who won't believe I can bake a cake unless I show him."[22]

Any hopes Ann may have had of appearing in moderately challenging roles after *Housewife* were quickly dashed with her next assignment. *I Sell Anything* stars Pat O'Brien as a fast-talking, unscrupulous New York auctioneer who gets taken in a long con by a high-society dame (Claire Dodd). Ann is the down-on-her-luck good girl who passes out from starvation on O'Brien's doorstep, and is then hired on as his secretary/housekeeper. She eventually becomes O'Brien's voice of reason and, by the closing credits, his gal. Other than giving the movie a happy ending, Ann's character serves no purpose, and it seems as if it was thrown into the script as an afterthought. Her lines could have easily been assumed by any of the men working at the auction house and actually seem like they may have been transferred to her character just to give her something to say. Claire Dodd is the more interesting female character as the spoiled girl from Fifth Avenue who takes O'Brien for a ride and gives Ann a tongue lashing when she tries to get in her way. Ann's part in the film was such a throwaway that the *New York Times* didn't even bother to mention her in its review. When asked why she thought so many women's roles were in support of the main male characters, Ann curiously responded with, "Because this is a man's world. The reason women don't do big things is that so many are not capable of it. Woman's job is to inspire a man when he falls in love with her." Ann apparently realized how old-fashioned these sentiments sounded and immediately followed up with, "But, of course, these things are subject to exceptions."[23]

If Ann's role in *I Sell Anything* is completely thankless, the part in her next assignment, *Gentlemen Are Born,* is practically nonexistent. Originally titled *Just Out of College,* the film represents the socially conscious side of Warner Bros., presenting the trials and tribulations of graduates unable to land jobs during the Depression. Franchot Tone and Margaret Lindsay are the main stars of this one, with Charles Starrett, Jean Muir, and Dick Foran in support. Ann plays Foran's devoted new wife, and the character is not that far removed from Judy in *Crooner,* Joan in *Midnight Alibi,* and Barbara in *I Sell Anything.* Her scenes mainly consist of being supportive of Foran, whose luck in the job market seems to be even worse than his friends'. In an act of sheer desperation, he commits a petty theft and is shot and killed by pursuing police. After Foran's death, a patented Dvorak breakdown scene is expected. Instead, she is merely alluded to as having left town, and does not appear onscreen for the duration of the movie. Ann would find herself in many lesser roles in subpar films during her career, but *I Sell Anything* and *Gentlemen Are Born* may possibly be the lowest points.

Less than two weeks after *Gentlemen Are Born* wrapped, Ann reported to the set of *Murder in the Clouds,* where she was again teamed with Lyle Talbot. It was another leading-lady role, but at least she had more to do than in her previous two films. Talbot is a short-tempered, hotshot pilot who is employed for a top-secret delivery mission by the Feds. Ann is a flight attendant who can't decide if she is annoyed or turned on by Talbot's exploits. Robert Light is Ann's pilot brother who unexpectedly takes over the government mission and is killed in the process by sabotaging evil forces. The scene in which Ann find out her brother is dead is a classic Dvorak moment. Her expression goes from shock to horror to grief in mere seconds and is very moving. After playing so many unchallenging parts, Ann seems to have fiercely grabbed on to to any redeeming moments in these films to make them her own. This reaction shot in *Murder in the Clouds* is a fleeting moment where Ann's potential is revealed, though never fully exploited. Though still a B picture, the production value of *Murder in the Clouds* is elevated over many of Ann's preceding films, largely due to the impressive aviation photography by noted aerial cinematographer Elmer Dyer. Ann was featured prominently on the poster art for *Murder in the Clouds*, which was a rare occurrence at this point in her career.

When *Murder in the Clouds* wrapped in September 1934, Ann had been back before the cameras for a little over a year following her much-publicized walkout. In that time, she had made one film for Paramount and a staggering ten movies for Warner Bros. The studio was definitely doing what it could to make money on Dvorak, but it did not seem to have any plans of elevating her above leading lady or lower-billed roles in B films. Ann was happy to have the work and to collect a paycheck that was now amounting to $1,100 a week, but she was less than thrilled with the parts coming her way. Would Warner Bros. actually start casting Ann Dvorak in roles worthy of her talents, or was the studio just going to let her languish for the remaining three years of her contract? The next two years would find Ann and the studio asking each other that question.

12

Life Off Camera

If the mid-1930s were the most productive and stable years of Ann's career, then the same could arguably be said of her personal life as well. During this time, Ann and Leslie Fenton seemed to have found a harmony between work and home life, which still included traveling and other personal hobbies. Many in the film community would question the couple's social habits, or lack thereof, and would raise their eyebrows at the amount of influence husband had over wife, but Ann seemed genuinely happy during this time.

After only five months of living at the Van Nuys ranch, Ann and Leslie took the plunge and became property owners in October 1933. They bought a parcel of land in the developing community of Encino, just west of Van Nuys and not too far from the home owned by Ann's former costar Paul Muni. They kept purchasing adjacent property for the next six years until the ranch numbered thirty-six acres and took up most of the acreage bordered by Ventura and Magnolia boulevards and Libbit and Woodley avenues. When they acquired the property, the land was vacant of any buildings and covered in walnut trees. The Fentons began making plans for their dream home, and the initial design was a sprawling one-story Andalusian-style structure shaped like a Z, with eleven or twelve rooms. Once construction began, the couple realized that a large residence would encourage extended houseguests. Ann and Leslie were becoming less and less social, and the fear of crashers was strong enough that in the midst of construction, Leslie ordered the builders to stop and close off any open walls, leaving only three rooms. Compared to the grandiose mansions of other actors, Ann and Leslie's humble home seemed odd. When asked why they would want to reside in such small quarters, Ann replied, "Why live in three rooms? Well, because it's all we need. We've got thirty seven acres outdoors and it's more fun—and much

Ann poses in front of the fountain and main structure of the Encino walnut ranch.

healthier—to be in the open."[1] However, after only a year, they realized that three rooms really weren't enough. The living room was expanded and a master bedroom added, giving the house a ticky-tacky yet charming look.

The home had a large built-in swimming pool, which Ann used practically on a daily basis. Near one end of the pool stood a giant star-shaped fountain decorated with tile, and at the other end was a stone bench, embellished with winged creatures in statuary. A pool house included a small bathroom and bed, which could serve as guest quarters in case Ann and Leslie relented and allowed visitors. In addition to the main house, a garage with servants' quarters was constructed, where at one point a Chinese couple named Ben and Emma Kam resided while they were employed by the Fentons to help out on the ranch. In 1934 the Kams' first child, Walter, was born and joined his parents in the servants' quarters.[2] Rounding out the structures on the property was a series of cow stables, which housed Garbo Jr. and Sweetheart, who were milked every morning by a professional milker who made the rounds of the neighborhood. However, after a while, the cows went away because as Ann explained, "We went through the cow period but it didn't work out. Sweetheart was too much trouble. Sweetheart wasn't happy with us. Hugh Herbert has her now, and I am sure she is happy."[3] The main house had concrete floors and block walls to offset the extreme summer heat of the San Fernando Valley, and tiles made by local makers D&M embellished a fireplace, bay windows, and an enclosed porch. Their interior taste was simple, with Monterey furniture complementing beamed ceilings.

Members of the press would occasionally be invited to the home for an interview and would immediately take note of the bookshelves filled with volumes of the *Journal of the American Medical Association* and other books documenting the history of medicine and surgery. One reporter described the main living room as "not an uncheerful room. No, it has been too well lived in for that. There are books about, but they are not the frilly novels to divert the movie star invalid. They are Leslie's books, deep transports into philosophy and psychiatry written by the most iconoclast writers of the world. There are pipes and jars of tobacco, deep chairs that border the fireplace and comfortable pillows and footstools. There are so many windows that, in the day-time, I presume the room is flooded with sunlight. But when I saw it, late at night, the room was filled with enormous shadows. I had been there several hours before I realized there was nothing of Ann about that room."[4]

If the interior did bear the sole stamp of Leslie Fenton, the same could not be said of the outside grounds, which completely reflected Ann. A hand-painted front door that dated from the fifteenth century led to a courtyard featuring a wishing well that was reportedly imported from

Ann with her personal library at the Encino home.

Sicily. Decorative fixtures could be found all around the exterior of the structures as well as a smaller fountain covered in D&M tile. Ann's love of the outdoors had translated into her having a green thumb. Countless Bauer pots filled with various plants and flowers were placed all around the grounds in addition to other assorted flora planted around the property, including a rambling rose bush that would grow to massive proportions before having to be removed over seventy years later. After the couple had been living on the property awhile, Ann had a professional greenhouse built complete with a piped watering system. She raised countless types of plants in the greenhouse and became known locally for her black orchids, which she sold to local florists. She also entered and placed in the occasional local flower show. Of this additional pastime, Ann remarked, "They're fascinating. When you really love flowers and study them, working with them is something like—like a religious experience."[5] In addition to the greenhouse, there was also a lath house on the property for growing various types of plants. Behind the pool, where the rambling rose stood, was a small man-made creek with a very small stone bridge crossing over it. The house itself may not have been overly impressive, but the lush grounds covered in flowers and walnut trees, along with the European-inspired fixtures, birdbaths, and other assorted decor, resulted in a peaceful atmosphere of simple elegance. As of this writing, nearly eighty years later, the walnut ranch is long gone, but the heart of the property retains a picturesque and soothing atmosphere despite being surrounded by homes and sitting a block away from the 101 Freeway.

Ann was proud of the house and that she finally had a place to plant her roots, figuratively and literally. As she enthused to one interviewer, "This is the first real home Leslie or I ever had. My mother . . . was an actress and we traveled about a great deal. I was put in boarding school. Leslie left home as a boy and he, too, wandered about, living in hotels and apartments." As always, Ann was especially impressed with her husband, continuing, "Leslie is really highly practical. Though he had no experience before, he worked with the architect on the house, let all the contracts himself and oversaw all the work."[6]

The estate, with the official address 5070 Libbit Avenue, was fairly remote, as it sat in the middle of the ranch and was accessible only by a small, poorly marked road. Guests visiting for the first time would usually get lost and arrive late. This delighted Ann and Leslie, who would answer the door together and ask in unison, "Have any trouble finding the place?" They would then look knowingly at each other. However, not everyone had as much difficulty tracking them down, like the home intruder who made off with thousands of dollars worth of Ann's jewelry in 1939, or the tour bus that came ambling up the road leading to the main house one afternoon. After she got over the initial shock, Ann obliged the unexpected fans by signing autographs. The property also proved to be not so remote when broadcasts from a nearby radio tower were heard though the showerhead.

The property appealed to the couple's bucolic sense, but it was also a functioning walnut ranch, which Ann and Leslie took full advantage of. The walnuts were harvested every year, and the couple cleared an annual profit of several thousand dollars. At one point they toyed with marketing "Ann Dvorak Walnuts" complete with her face and signature on the packaging, but those plans never came to fruition. According to neighborhood lore, the couple would occasionally have "walnut parties" in which guests would arrive in evening finery and then proceed to shake the trees, causing the walnuts to fall to the ground, to the accompaniment of live

Ann in front of her greenhouse at the Encino ranch.

mariachi music. In addition to shaking tress, Ann and Leslie also had a major hand in the operations of the ranch. As Ann stated, "We're not gentlemen farmers, we work the ranch as hard as our hired hands. Whenever possible we spend most of the day planting, trimming, and plowing."[7] Even though the two would pose for photographers on their tractor, it's hard to believe Ann was actually operating the machinery in between films at Warner Bros.

Ann was an ardent animal lover who would report her bosses to the Society for the Prevention of Cruelty to Children and Animals if she suspected four-legged creatures were being mistreated on film shoots. As she put it, "I don't care how many people get killed in a picture. They know what they're up against and take the jobs voluntarily. Animals don't. What right has anyone to injure an animal just for a lousy movie?"[8] She even contributed her time to the society by attending benefits held by the organization and was reportedly not shy about battling anyone whom she suspected were mistreating their pets. Along with the cows, Garbo Jr. and Sweetheart, there were other animals on the ranch, including two cocker spaniels, a dachshund named Heinzie, rabbits, and chickens. When a coyote got into the chicken pen and the hired help was, well, too chicken to confront the predator, Ann took matters into her own hands. She marched all of her five feet, four inches and 110 pounds into the pen and dealt with the problem herself. Of all the headlines she was to feature in during her life, "Ann Dvorak Clubs Coyote" is one of the best.[9]

In addition to wayward coyotes, ranch living proved to have its own set of unique challenges with feathered creatures. When a wren abandoned her nest after being scared off by the sprinklers, Ann wrapped the orphaned eggs in cotton and placed them under an electric light until they hatched. She then hand-fed the birds a diet of milk, ants, and flies.[10] The couple was mildly amused to discover that the reason their newly planted grass had not been growing was because twelve mallard ducks had been dining on the lawn.[11] However, Ann was less taken with the mockingbirds that would perch on her roof in the evenings and burst into song, sometimes for hours on end. When the birds began imitating the mooing of Garbo Jr., Ann publicly called on the Audubon Society to get involved.[12]

When Ann wasn't tending to flowers, walnuts, and animals, she practiced the piano and pursued her love of writing. Leslie's brother Howard Fenton noted, "Ann is above all a very accomplished musician. Many evenings she sits at the piano playing for hours, her husband listening and reading her moods through her music. Here is an ideal combination. Ann composes lovely melodies and Leslie writes lyrics to fit them."[13] Ann never lost her desire to be a professional writer, and throughout her career there would be various reports of Dvorak-penned works to be published. Among those listed were books of poetry, a travelogue detailing the extended honeymoon, and a play about her parents entitled *Vaudeville*

Days. Sadly, none of these appear to ever have been published and most of Ann Dvorak's writings are lost.

In between work assignments, the Fentons also squeezed in some travel, including quick trips to Tijuana. They purchased a small yacht, *The Nymph,* from actor Ken Maynard and spent three weeks in the summer of 1935 sailing down the California coast to Del Mar, San Diego, and Ensenada before spending some time cruising around Catalina Island, where they docked and were the guests of Johnny and Lupe Weissmuller. This vacation only partially placated Ann's wanderlust, as she excitedly looked forward to their next big trip, expressing, "It just occurs to me that above all things, I'd like to visit some of the islands which seem alone to have been uninfluenced by modernisms. I not only mean far islands in the Pacific, but such primitive places as the islands off the northwestern coast of Scotland and those lying off the west coast of Ireland." She continued, "There, I am told, much can be seen which is unmodernized and primitively genuine. Some of the Scottish Islands retain much of the feudal clan spirit, and even the native costumes and customs of the colorful old Highlanders. On the Irish islands, they say, there are hundreds of natives who speak the old original Irish Gaelic and who know not a word of English. Such people, and their habits, must be singularly interesting."[14]

Ann and Leslie never expressed an interested in politics, both declining to state a party affiliation when they registered to vote.[15] They were among the first 150 actors to become members of the Screen Actors Guild (SAG) when it officially formed in 1933. For unknown reasons, they subsequently withdrew their membership, something almost unheard of in the Guild's history, but rejoined in August 1937.[16] Ann's membership in the labor union would serve her well after she retired.

As Ann and Leslie became immersed in their ranch life, they continued to maintain their reclusive reputation. Ann admitted, "I am deeply interested in bacteriology and languages. That takes a lot of time. So you see that in order to get all the things done I wish to, there are few hours for anything else. Yes, I suppose I am a hermit of sorts. But I prefer it."[17] Anna Lehr, who was one of the few guests to visit the Fenton ranch on a regular basis, had dropped out of the spotlight following Ann's honeymoon, but she was concerned about her daughter's relationship. To one reporter she said the "point that concerns me is: what will they do to each other? . . . She's always liked people, been a friendly approachable girl.

Now, in the short time they've been married, I can notice the change in her personality. She talks with Leslie's tongue and sees things through Leslie's eyes. There was a time when work and a career were the most important things in her life. Now, there isn't anything important but Leslie who has never cared anything about the things that matter to most people. I wonder where their love will lead them?"[18] When one reporter aggressively questioned their decision to lead such an isolated existence, Ann seemed to become defensive, and her response was a lengthy one:

I supposed you mean we are living foolishly, dangerously. We aren't supposed to wrap so much of ourselves into one person, are we? Marriage isn't supposed to stand such a strain. Hollywood has always said: "It won't work. It never has." Well, we know we are digging our own emotional graves with the love we have found! We are binding our lives more closely around one another everyday we live. But that is the kind of life we know and I wouldn't want anything else in the world in trade for this completeness. Don't think for a minute that we haven't spent long hours in discussion about ourselves. We know what would happen if one of us would suddenly lose the other: nothingness. That's the penalty of our love. But it is a penalty we accept freely and willingly. All we really want in the world is to be left alone. We don't want the things the others want from life. We don't see things with the same eyes. All the time we were traveling through Europe we used to thank our lucky stars that we weren't so fame-splashed that we couldn't sink into the background, tramp about in old clothes . . . yes, even sit in the pouring rain in the ruins of the Colosseum at Rome without landing on the front pages of the newspapers as movie stars indulging temperament gags. It made us so completely ourselves. Even Hollywood and the work we've done couldn't cheat us of our grand inconspicuousness. We just didn't matter, except to ourselves. Maybe ours is a selfish love. We don't share it, even with those who might be our friends. We have been rude to people we might have learned to like. Some of them have come here to see us and we haven't let them in. It is a simple matter to shake your head at the house-boy when you hear a name announced through the door. Nor have we ever cared whether our almost-guest realized our attitude or not.

She continued, almost defiantly:

I haven't much patience with loves that are compromised with a hundred other diverting interests—bridge clubs, cocktail parties, casual telephone friends, guests for dinner every night—all fed by the overwhelming fear of boredom from spending one short hour together and alone. When I was a little girl, I dreamed of the very sort of love I've found. Now that we have found one another, why should we make the usual concessions made by people who have found so much less in life and love than we have found? I am not ashamed of having a love that fills my life to the exclusion of everything else. I'm happy it is that way.

Ann summed up her sentiments on the matter with, "It isn't a gag. We haven't any friends, we've never had any—nor do we want any!"[19]

Many may have found their lifestyle questionable, but some, like Howard Fenton, viewed their relationship as a positive one. Howard, who would remain in contact with Ann until her death, admitted, "The Fentons don't enjoy being social along with the rest of the movie clan. They are wholly absorbed in each other and get the greatest pleasure from being by themselves. They do very little entertaining as their hours together are crammed with a large variety of common interests." He also stated, "When Ann and Leslie are working, even if they are at separate studios, they nearly always lunch together, meeting at some hideaway spot as though they were a newly engaged couple. While they are at work each devotes every thought to the task at hand. But when free they think only of each other." To Howard, the behavior of his brother and sister-in-law was completely normal: "There is nothing more romantic and beautiful than this marriage. Ann Dvorak and Leslie Fenton have learned the true secret to happiness in Hollywood."[20]

For all Ann and Leslie's proclamations about privacy, the press statements about their reclusive behavior, and family members throwing in their two cents, this perception that the couple barely had contact with other people in their off-hours was grossly exaggerated. Compared to many who were seen on the town nightly, the Fentons probably did seem

Ann and Leslie at the boxing matches in Hollywood, which they attended almost weekly.

hermitlike. However, there is plenty of documentation proving that Ann and Leslie did get out of the house often. They were seen at the Brown Derby, dining with other film folk like actress Isabel Jewell or Ann's old friend Karen Morley and her husband, director Charles Vidor. They attended the occasional Warner Bros. premiere, were spotted at the circus, and were among those who descended on the Hollywood Bowl for the gala performance of *A Midsummer Night's Dream*, where Olivia de Havilland would be discovered among the cast. They sometimes went to private parties at the homes of fellow actors like Dorothy Burgess and Spencer Tracy, were also seen at some public gatherings, and had season tickets for boxing matches in Hollywood. Ann also paid a visit to her alma mater, the Page School for Girls, where she received a warm reception from the student body. Even Howard Fenton contradicted his statements about their lack of entertaining when he described how Ann "has a little trick of fooling her dinner guests with her coffee. She believes real coffee to be bad for the health so she brews a coffee substitute and serves it, watching her friends' faces as they taste it. 'Isn't it good?' she will inquire impishly. The answer is always in the affirmative. Then Ann will lean forward and whisper confidentially, 'It's Sanka! I'll bet you can't tell the difference!'"[21] The Fentons may not have been out on the town every night, but they were making the social rounds far more than either admitted.

During this time of reported isolation, Ann sponsored a local baseball team, the Ann Dvorak Stars. In the mid-1930s, Los Angeles did not have a Major League team, though the Los Angeles Angels and Hollywood Stars of the Pacific Coast League were around to entertain fans. Smaller leagues sprang up in the area and were frequently sponsored by local celebrities, such as Joe E. Brown, or by movie studios, like Paramount, Universal, and Warner Bros. Ann provided uniforms for her team and even attended some of the games when they played against the Paramount Cubs, Los Angeles Cardinals, and the Merchants of Monrovia, Arcadia, and Pasadena. At one point Ann looked into purchasing land in the Cahuenga Pass to build the team a field, but those plans fell through when local residents objected.[22]

In the mid-1930s the Fentons employed business manager Bo Roos of the Beverly Management Corporation to handle their finances. Roos represented a number of Hollywood clients, including John Barrymore, George Brent, Joan Crawford, Marlene Dietrich, and Fred MacMurray. Roos's teenaged daughter Carolyn ended up working for the company, and has particularly fond memories of Ann: "Dad and I were both crazy about her. I kept a bigger scrapbook on her than any other client. She was talented and gorgeous. I always thought she never went as far as she could have, probably because of her salary demands. Talented and gorgeous women were a dime a dozen in those days."[23] She added, "My father had very 'warm' feelings for Ann and she was always sweet around me." As for Ann's husband, Carolyn admitted, "I do recall that we were not fond of Leslie . . . can't remember why."[24]

By all accounts, it seems the early years of the Fenton marriage were happy and serene for Ann, but was that really the case? The amount of influence the thirty-something Fenton had over his younger wife is undeniable, though it seems that Ann did not mind his having so much control over her. After the first few years of marriage she stated, "We have made a go of it so far. We have got over the first year, which I think should be the easiest, not the most difficult, the second year, which has been a lot of fun, and we are well into our third without a single quarrel." She continued, "We have been very happy and the fact that we are both interested in the same things helps us to have more in common than we otherwise would. We even listen to each other's lines, although I must say not often."[25]

As for Fenton's influence on her career, Ann continued to stand by her belief that marriage had only a positive effect on it, commenting, "I am happier in my work today than I have ever been. I know I have a different feeling about it now. I know that back of it all, there's Leslie. That, no matter what would happen to me in pictures, I would still have our marriage. And that's really the most important thing of all—*much* more important than pictures. Leslie had proved many times that pictures aren't the most important thing in the world to him. And I'd give up my career any day for him if I had to make that choice."[26] However, around the same time, Ann contradicted herself elsewhere: "Although I enjoy my home very much, it would never be enough to absorb all my time. I wouldn't like to stay in it, nor would I like to cook or do the housework." She continued, "Besides, I must be independent and have my own money, to be happy. Having been used to earning my own way since I was very young, I wouldn't like to have to depend on someone else."[27] This last quote sounds more like the Ann Dvorak of 1931 and is perhaps an indication that sometimes Ann did find her home life overbearing and did indeed value her career. Still, by the mid-1930s, she was pulling in a decent paycheck at Warner Bros., so she wasn't reliant on her husband financially and could have supported herself if she were unhappy enough to want to move. For all the outside debate about the nature of the Fenton marriage, Ann did seem to be happy.

Now that Ann had a secure career and home life, she focused on the one thing that was missing—her father. Ann had not seen Edwin McKim since she was a small child and admitted, "My desire to see my father is nothing new. I have wanted for years to find him and to know him." Attempts she had made to find him were futile, largely because "many things made this impractical. There was the matter of money. Searches for lost people cost a great deal of money and until I was doing well in pictures there was nothing I could do about it." She continued, "I tried every way I could outside of hiring private detectives. I wrote to people, but it was fruitless. I think a blood tie is unlike any other tie in the world. I have only one father and I simply had to know where he was, what he was doing, how he was. I believe he is around 56. I had no unpleasant memories of my father. It seems to me only human to want to know your own parent."[28] In December 1933 she turned to the press for help, and the syndicated columns ran pieces about her search, quoting Ann as saying, "I am very anxious to hear from him. I wish that he would communicate with me by wire or by letter at 9460 Wilshire Boulevard, Beverly Hills, California. I am sure that when he learns how anxious I am to get in touch with him before Christmas, he will communicate with me. I will be extremely grateful to the newspapers and news associations if they will aid me in finding my father."[29] This attempt initially resulted in countless claims from crass opportunists alleging to be Ann's father who requested cash for train fare to Los Angeles. Most of these individuals were quickly discredited after giving their surname as Dvorak, unaware that Ann had only assumed it as a stage name. Others offered their services as for-hire private detectives, and one unemployed man in Chicago said he would devote some time to the search for a mere $100. About a month and a half after the initial search, Ann's true father was finally located.

Edwin McKim's whereabouts after the divorce from Lehr and the bankruptcy of the Advanced Photo Play Corporation are a bit hazy. According to one source, he traveled down to Florida with a "troupe of midgets," though the details of this final foray in show business were not further elaborated on.[30] When the act fell apart, McKim remained in the Sunshine State and got in on the big Florida land boom of the mid-1920s. Ann had never been far from his thoughts, and around 1928 he traveled to Los Angeles to find her. Since Ann and her mother were living under Arthur Pearson's name, McKim was unable to locate his daughter and returned to Florida. By 1931 he had relocated to Philadelphia, where his brother Walter was living. After his return to Pennsylvania, he began storing his car at 1533 Parrish Street in the garage of owner William Herting, who tried to fill in some of the gaps in McKim's story. According to Herting, "He used to come to my garage once in a while and I gathered from his conversation that he was a bachelor. He often talked to me about his business connections and several times he mentioned the stock market in which I understand he lost considerable money." Herting continued, "I also heard that he had $75,000 tied up in a Philadelphia bank. He owned an orange grove at Fort Pierce, Fla., and once asked me to buy it from him. He was always interested in some kind of business and often talked about regaining his lost fortune. Some of the Philadelphia papers maintained that he was a CWA [Civil Works Administration] worker, but he denied that. He appeared to be well-to-do—always paid his garage rent on time."[31]

When Vincent Norwood, a Philadelphia resident and friend of Walter McKim, came across an article that mentioned Ann's real last name, he

Ann and Leslie meet Edwin McKim at the Pasadena train station. Father and daughter had not seen each other in more than ten years.

showed the paper to his friend. Walter had a sneaking suspicion the actress was indeed his niece, and wrote a letter to Ann. Despite his brother's former film career, Walter was not a movie fan and had no clue who Ann Dvorak was. This was probably what caused his letter to stand out from the hundreds of others Ann had received. When further proof was requested, Edwin shipped a strip of film he had taken of Ann when the family was in Cuba in 1913. The film was shown to an anxious Ann and Leslie in one of the Warner Bros. screening rooms, and when the tot frolicking on the screen matched a snapshot she had from the same trip, Ann Dvorak knew she had finally found her father.

Ann was ecstatic to have made contact, and McKim was equally thrilled. When reporters questioned McKim on how he could have been so ignorant of the fact that this famous film actress was his next of kin, he admitted, "I have not been to many movies since I left the business, and I did not recognize her as the child of eight from whom I was parted after her mother, Anna Lehr, and I were divorced."[32] Of the last day he saw his daughter, McKim wistfully recalled, "I remember her as a little girl of eight, with curls hanging down her back." Even though he had never seen any of his daughter's films, McKim stated, "I remember seeing Ann's pictures in the paper often." He added, sadly, "But I never recognized her."[33] Regarding Fenton and Lehr's reaction to the news, Ann noted, "Leslie is as happy as I am that we have found father." She added, "We have no idea what he'll be like and we don't know what to expect. We want a long visit with him so that we can fill up those vacant years and learn to know each other." Ann also stated, "My mother does not relish any publicity in the matter. Mother, of course, has been happily married for years so there is no question of reconciliation. She has expressed a wish to see father when he comes West but she wishes her name left out of the news stories as my stepfather is in business and it might all prove embarrassing to him and to her."[34] For once, Anna Lehr was avoiding the spotlight.

Ann was eager for her father to come out to Los Angeles and offered to pay his train ticket for the journey. McKim, however, was insistent that he pay his own way, though he admitted he would need some time to save up the money. Six months later, McKim notified Ann that he was finally ready to come out, and when he arrived at the train station in Pasadena on August 20, 1934, Ann and Leslie were there to greet him. When McKim emerged from the train, he hugged his long-lost daughter, proclaiming, "Well I'm here at last. I've been a long time getting here."[35] After he shook hands with his son-in-law, the trio posed for pictures, though in many of the photos Ann, who was wearing a dress from *Gentlemen Are Born,* which had just wrapped filming, seems to be uncomfortable sharing this very private moment with the press. The resemblance between father and daughter was undeniable, as they shared the same strong chin and close-mouthed smile.

Following the photo op, the couple quickly whisked McKim away to Encino where he stayed for a couple of months, presumably sleeping in the pool house bed. Over the next few days, Ann was spotted around town showing her dad the sights, and he accompanied her to look at land in the Cahuenga Pass for the baseball team. By all accounts, the visit was a successful one, and at one point Ann and Leslie reportedly journeyed back east to rehabilitate a farm McKim owned near Syracuse. The reunion between Ann and her dad had been very public, but any sort of relationship they fostered after this initial meeting was between the two of them.

It appears Ann did maintain contact with Edwin McKim until his death in Philadelphia in 1942, though she was out of the country when he passed.

By the mid-1930s, Ann Dvorak had a solid if not sterling career with Warner Bros., a secure if sometimes questionable relationship with her husband, and an idyllic home in the San Fernando Valley. She had renewed ties with her long-lost father, and was the image of youth, health, and beauty. Her early chance at potential superstardom had been jeopardized, but Ann was still young and it seemed that her career could only go up. Unless, of course, she continued to irritate her bosses at the studio.

13

Suspended Contract Player

•

It appears that Jack Warner never fully got over Ann's walkout and harsh statements to the press, though he was never outwardly nasty to her, nor did he speak ill of her publicly. In fact, he seemed to be quite fond of her, yet he possessed the type of personality and ego that did not allow him to completely let go of any perceived slight. Ann had been working nonstop since fall 1933, yet the parts tended to be minuscule and the movies mediocre. While she had once graced the posters advertising her films, she was no longer treated as a movie's selling point. Still, as 1934 rolled into 1935, it looked as though Warner's position was softening and Ann's career began to take an upswing. However, by the end of the year, she would once again find herself locking horns with her employer.

While Ann was traveling the globe in 1932 and 1933, Warner Bros. had launched a revival of the movie musical, which had become passé during Ann's chorus days. This new breed of musical, set against the backdrop of live theater, made the song and dance numbers more realistic, as opposed to having the characters randomly break into song. However, the realism of the musical sequences themselves was completely discarded under the choreography of Busby Berkeley, whose over-the-top visions were executed in a way only film could achieve. These lavish numbers, with dozens of dancers carrying bizarre props filmed from overhead, were a huge hit with audiences looking for a distraction from Depression woes. Films like *42nd Street*, *Dames*, and *Gold Diggers of 1933* featured all-star casts and gave Warner contract players the opportunity to show off their musical talents.

Given her background as a chorus dancer, Ann would have likely been cast in at least one of these films had she been in the country. *Footlight*

Parade started production shortly after her return, but Warner Bros. was not ready to cast her in much of anything, let alone this sure-fire hit starring James Cagney, Ruby Keeler, and Dick Powell. Ann felt as if she had missed out by not being around for the musicals, and when she caught wind of an upcoming project directed by Alfred Green and featuring crooner Rudy Vallee, she actively lobbied the studio bosses to appear in the film, titled *Sweet Music*. Ann had a hard time landing the role; as she explained, "It's funny, though I started out as a dancer and singer I had a terrific time convincing Alfred Green out at Warners that I could do either. I worked like mad practicing for two weeks and were my muscles sore."[1] This was one of the few roles Ann actively pursued at Warner Bros., and she "certainly 'went out' to get this part. I've never been very shy about trying for what I want and I all but bullied them into making a test of me for this. I think they did it only to shut me up—but they did do it."[2]

Ann was beyond thrilled to land the role, and she thoroughly enjoyed the experience, remarking, "Before this picture I had sort of trained myself to be calm and unexcited when I heard music. Now I'm having a wonderful time, just letting myself go."[3] In *Sweet Music* Ann and Vallee star as rival performers vying for top billing in various venues. They verbally spar, fall in love, fall out over a misunderstanding, and by the closing credits are reconciled in a big splashy number. It's not the best of the 1930s Warner musicals, but is one of the bigger-budget productions of Ann's career, and took almost two months to complete, not including retakes.[4] The film features Al Shean, vaudevillian uncle of the Marx Brothers, and a cameo by torch singer Helen Morgan along with contract players like Allen Jenkins, Ned Sparks, and Alice White. As Bonnie Haydon, Ann is self-driven, and for once her character is at odds with her leading man instead of propping him up. The reaction to this change of role was largely positive, with critics noting, "Ann Dvorak dances as well as sings, displaying stellar abilities which won her the chance in pictures" and "Ann Dvorak is charming and resourceful in this so different a role for her."[5] Louella Parsons was also impressed with Ann, reporting, "I have never liked Ann Dvorak as well as I do with Vallee. Her characterization of the hoofer and the singer is excellent. She does some really good dancing and she sings too, if not like a Jeritza, at least in a pleasing manner. She does some real trooping."[6] Overall, the experience of making *Sweet Music* was one of the most positive of Ann's tenure at Warner Bros. However, one morning production was held up because Ann was two hours late getting to the set,

though the reason is unknown.[7] This was one of the only times any production would be delayed by Ann, who was a consummate professional
and generally respected by her fellow actors.

In preparation for the film, Ann brushed up on her dance steps with
instructor John Boyle, admitting, "I began in the chorus. I learned to
dance that way. Until lately, I never had a dancing lesson." She was thrilled
to be involved with the film and was even happy to retrace her early roots:
"I have gone back to the chorus, so to speak. In this picture, I sing and
dance and the numbers are gorgeous."[8] Ann does get a couple of song
and dance numbers, including one where she is clad in a ridiculous costume made of large white feathers. However, the musical emphasis is
clearly on Vallee, a major crooning radio star at the time, who performs
multiple songs. For the sake of plot, Bonnie Haydon's singing voice is
criticized as flat, but Ann's deep tone is pleasant enough and preferable to
the dancing, which tends to be lead footed and slightly awkward. Despite
some rumors that Dvorak and Vallee did not get along, the pair apparently liked each other just fine, or at least acted that way for publicity's
sake, with Vallee naming Ann as one of the ten most beautiful women in
Hollywood, and Ann reporting, "He is likely to take himself seriously
because he thinks his job as a radio star and screen calls for it. But this new
picture, I believe, comes nearest his secret charm. And that is the ability to
take kidding in the spirit of fun. I kid him all through the picture and I
think you'll like him in the role."[9] *Sweet Music* received an advertising
push not seen with Ann's previous Warner Bros. films, including pictorials
splashed across the pages of numerous movie magazines, interviews on
radio programs, and an appearance by Dvorak and Vallee at the Women's
Western Golf Tournament. After a year of Ann's appearances in largely
lackluster films, it looked as if her career at Warner Bros. had some renewed
promise.

By this time Ann had been married for well over two years, and for all
her talk of marriage being the focus of her existence, she also began
reflecting on the path her acting career had taken since she met her husband and what lay down the road. When one interviewer brought up
Cesca in *Scarface*, Ann was quick to reply, "It was an actor-proof part. Of
course I liked it. Who wouldn't? It was drama, melodrama, and tragedy
and it brought both George Raft and myself to the attention of producers
and audiences all over the country. Paul Muni was already established, but
Raft and myself were fairly new." She continued, "It should have been the

beginning of a career of starring parts for me, but it wasn't. I have played many good roles since, but I didn't leap into the top brackets as Raft or almost anybody would have done during similar circumstances. That is why I believe we are following a pattern. I wasn't ready for stardom and I didn't get it. When I am ready, I will be given a chance."[10] The first part of this statement almost sounds as if she were blaming Hollywood for somehow failing her, even though Cesca did set her on a path toward stardom—her own actions put the brakes on her career. She does conclude with the admission that she was not ready to cope with the trappings of film fame, but still doesn't completely own up to how much of a role she played in dictating her own fate.

But that was the past, and now she was looking toward the future. As much as she may have enjoyed the change of pace in *Sweet Music*, her strength lay in drama, as she knew. "This picture [*Sweet Music*] is right up my alley, but I don't want to be typed. I want to do all sorts of things, especially a costume drama. When I was a child, I used to do *Hamlet* before the mirror every night before I went to sleep. I loved [Shakespeare] and read him over and over. I can quote whole passages from him—and sometimes do, to my husband's annoyance. I would rather do *Marie Antoinette* than anything in the world. I understand another studio is going to do it, so that will let me out, but just the same I shall do it sometime, if I have to wait 15 years."[11] MGM was in fact the studio that would produce *Marie Antoinette*, starring Norma Shearer, so Ann never stood a chance of getting that role. She would likewise never have the opportunity to play Shakespeare, but at least her prospects at Warner Bros. were looking rosier.

Retakes on *Sweet Music* wrapped up in late December 1934, and when the studio, for no apparent reason, changed its mind about casting her in *King of the Ritz* (aka *A Night at the Ritz*), Ann had some time off over the holidays. She and Leslie took the opportunity to make an abbreviated trip to Hawaii. They sailed for the islands on Christmas Eve of 1934 and returned on January 6, which meant the bulk of the trip was spent cruising the Pacific. Rather than hitting the regular tourist spots during their short stay in Honolulu, the couple visited the U.S. Experiment Station for sugarcane and met with station director Hamilton P. Agee, even dining with him in the evening.[12] The visit to the islands may have been short, but the impression Hawaii made on Ann Dvorak would be strong and lasting.

After returning from her tropical trip, Ann started off 1935 on Warner Bros.' bad side when a deal she had made with one producer came to the attention of Hal Wallis, the head of production at the studio. Under the standard Warner contract, the studio had the right to lay off an actor for four-week periods if nothing was lined up and it wanted the talent temporarily off the payroll. As *Sweet Music* was wrapping, Ann had appealed to producer William Koenig to reduce her layoff period to two weeks instead of four because she was in need of money.[13] Koenig agreed. When Wallis got wind of this in early February, he blew a gasket, calling it "the most ridiculous arrangement I have ever heard of." He reprimanded Koenig: "I don't understand how you could have possibly made a deal with DVORAK, whereby we would lay her off for two weeks and put her on for two weeks, during anytime she was idle. There certainly is no advantage to us in this kind of deal." He bemoaned having to "put the girl back on salary for no reason at all" and demanded that Koenig get Dvorak to abandon the "unworkable arrangement" and go back to the four-week periods.[14] Ann would not agree to the old terms, and the two-week layoffs stayed in place for the remainder of her contract. Warner Bros. made do with the arrangement by engaging her in publicity for *Sweet Music* while it figured out what film to cast her in next.

As February was drawing to a close, Ann, who had been named one of the previous year's forty-six busiest actors by the Association of Motion Picture Arts and Sciences (AMPAS), was finally assigned to her first role of 1935. The character Jean Morgan in *"G" Men* was another second-tier role for Ann, but it was an A picture and she would be appearing alongside James Cagney. The pro-FBI film finds Cagney as a kid from the wrong side of the tracks who rises above the ranks with the help of a local crime lord, who supports Cagney's decision to become a federal agent despite the conflict of interest. Ann is the local chorine with a crush on Cagney, but after he takes off for Washington, DC, she marries a thug in defeat. Margaret Lindsay is Cagney's main love interest and the primary female character, but Ann's role is the prized one, even though she has far less screen time. There is a genuine affection between Cagney and Dvorak that is readily apparent in her introductory scene at a nightclub when she performs the song "You Bother Me an Awful Lot," with a full orchestra and chorus backing her up. The number is, in fact, more polished and fun than any of the ones in *Sweet Music,* and the interaction between Ann and Cagney during the song adds to its appeal.

Interestingly, producer Hal Wallis objected to the glitziness of the nightclub scene, noting that the club "should have been one of those low ceiling places, with sketchy lighting and more of a 'joint' instead of a high class night club." He felt this dingier design would have conveyed "a menace of these gorillas who run them." Wallis also found fault in the subsequent scene between Ann and Barton MacLane, who plays the hoodlum she marries and who ultimately kills her when she betrays him in order to aid Cagney. In this backstage setting, Ann playfully spars with MacLane whereas Wallis felt the scene called for Ann to openly show disgust for her future husband. He noted, "I feel the scene between COLLINS [MacLane's character] and DVORAK is all wrong. She calls him 'Darling' and chucks him under the chin, and what we were trying to establish and as I read it in the script, he was a definite menace." Wallis continued, "We definitely want to do this last scene over—with DVORAK and COLLINS."[15] Apparently there was no budget for reshoots or else Wallis was not taken too seriously by director William Keighley, for the objectionable parts in "*G*" *Men* remain as originally filmed. Ann's death scene comes quickly and unexpectedly; MacLane shoots her down in cold blood in a phone booth. By the time Cagney arrives at the scene of the crime, Ann is on her way out and the final moments between them are extremely moving. When Cagney tenderly says, "I'll be seeing you later," Ann's response of "I won't be here" is both bitter and sorrowful. "*G*" *Men* stands as a high-water mark in Ann's career at Warner Bros.

Warner Bros. planned to have some of the cast of "*G*" *Men* attend the San Francisco premiere to promote the film. Ann initially agreed to go as long as costar Margaret Lindsay would also be attending. When she found out that Lindsay, who was on a routine layoff, would not be available to appear, Ann changed her mind and told the Warner publicity department that she too was off salary. Although she would have been off the books had she been subject to the four-week layoff, under her new deal, she was indeed on salary when the premiere was scheduled. After Ed Selzer in the publicity department confirmed this, he immediately contacted Jack Warner, stating, "I have tried to get her back on the phone all yesterday afternoon, evening and again this morning, and get the answer that she is out and don't know when she will be back, which convinces me that she is purposely avoiding coming to the phone." He concluded, "I think a wire should be sent her, ordering her to attend the opening of '*G*' *Men*."[16] Jack Warner heeded Selzer's advice, and when the train from Los Angeles

Ann arrives in San Francisco for the city's *"G" Men* premiere.

pulled into San Francisco in late April, Ann was all smiles as she was handed a large bouquet of roses and had her picture snapped for the *San Francisco Examiner*. She stayed in Northern California for four days, and reportedly her personal appearances broke box-office records.[17]

Following *"G" Men*, Ann's casting luck continued when she was given the opportunity to costar opposite comedian Joe E. Brown in the Busby Berkeley–directed *Bright Lights*. In this light comedy, Brown and Dvorak play a husband and wife vaudeville team whose marriage is threatened by his newfound success on Broadway. The film is not as high budget as *Sweet Music* or *"G" Men*, and does not contain any of the signature Berkeley dance routines, but it's enjoyable enough. Dvorak's limited screen time is equal to if not less than that of Patricia Ellis as the heiress turned actress who threatens the couple's marital bliss. Joe E. Brown's schtick can wear thin at times, and the film is most watchable when Dvorak shares the screen with him. They play off each other well and are convincing as a couple, especially in one scene where Brown walks past a sleeping Ann during rehearsal and casually wakes her by pulling her up by her necktie. Ann performs a partial dance routine, though the spotlight is really on Brown for the entire film. Ann considered it "a good part, but I think I'm miscast. There are others who could have done better with it," an interesting comment considering how often she had played the supportive wife/girlfriend role, and how hard she had lobbied to appear in a musical film the last time. Perhaps she was tired of being the sympathetic leading lady and was attempting to distance herself from it. However, Ann also admitted that perhaps she wasn't always the best judge of scripts, noting, "I used to think I could tell about a picture, how good or bad it was going to be before it was made. But now—I don't believe anybody can pick a winner in advance." Without giving any specifics, she continued that some films that "I knew were terrible, just from a reading of the script, turned out to be pictures that got good notices. I still thought they were bad pictures—one in particular stands out as my candidate for the world's worst movie—but the box office didn't think so. And when I see what happens to a really fine picture at the box office—I'm thinking of a certain film I'd have given anything to have a part in—I'm sure that nobody can tell."[18] Despite these sentiments, Ann would develop some very strong opinions of her assigned films before the year was over.

After Ann's hectic pace of the previous year, her career commitments had been reeled in considerably for 1935. When she started filming *Dr. Socrates* in June, it was only her third feature of the year. *Dr. Socrates* was another higher-quality picture, teaming her with *Scarface* costar Paul Muni, who had become one of the most respected screen stars in Hollywood. *Dr. Socrates* is also about gangsters, though this time the gang is terrorizing a small town instead of a large city. Muni is a doctor running from his past and trying to establish a private practice, and Dvorak is a hitchhiker trying to put her past behind her by thumbing her way to California. The two develop a mutual respect and attraction for each other, and when they inadvertently become mixed up with the local gang, led by Barton MacLane, they must use their wiles to thwart the bad guys. Directed by William Dieterle, the film wasn't anywhere near the caliber of Muni and Dvorak's first pairing, but it was a slightly better role for Ann than the majority of parts Warner Bros. had cast her in since her return in 1933, and in *Dr. Socrates*, she receives a couple of beautifully shot close-ups.

For her next film, Ann was loaned out for a musical at the newly formed 20th Century-Fox. In 1933 Warner Bros. whiz Darryl Zanuck had left the studio, where he had gotten his start as a *Rin-Tin-Tin* sce-

Ann takes a break from her hectic schedule to visit with *Scarface* costars Paul Muni and Karen Morley on the set of *Black Fury*.

nario writer, to become an executive at Twentieth Century Films. When the studio bought Fox in 1935 and became 20th Century-Fox, Zanuck's first production, *Metropolitan*, was a hit with critics and a dud with audiences. His next film had to be a winner, and Zanuck initially developed the story for *Sing, Governor, Sing!* himself, under the pseudonym Melville Grossman. The final script, centering around a traveling crooner who boosts his public persona by running for the state's highest office with the help of his road show crew, was completed by Nunnally Johnson. The popular Dick Powell was cast in the title role with comedians Fred Allen and Patsy Kelly in support. For the part of the faithful and supportive girlfriend, Zanuck thought of Ann, who had played that role countless times for his old employer. Jack Warner was feeling generous enough toward his former protégé to loan Ann out, though he charged Zanuck's studio over $20,000 for her services in addition to Ann's $1,100 per week pay.[19] Released as *Thanks a Million*, the film's initial preview in Santa Monica was an utter disaster, which devastated Zanuck. As he later recalled, "I was just sick that night. Before I ran it again, I remember going into the toilet and thinking, how could I make this? How could I do it? Then I went back to the projection room and worked on it. I ran it reel by reel, stopping after each reel, making notes. Suddenly, I found the weakness. I cut twelve minutes, that's all, and rearranged the rest. I previewed it in Santa Barbara to an absolute ovation."[20] The film proved to be the hit Zanuck was looking for; he claimed, "More than anything else, the success of that movie saved my first year at Fox from disaster."[21] Zanuck and audiences may have been enthusiastic about *Thanks a Million*, but Ann did not share in their excitement. When she returned to Warner Bros., Ann complained to casting director Max Arnow that the picture gave her "no chance whatsoever" and that "Sugar Plum," one of two song and dance numbers she had with Patsy Kelly, was "silly and ridiculous."[22] The musical numbers were largely geared toward Dick Powell and, to add insult to injury, the limited singing accorded to Ann was partially dubbed by Marjorie Lane.[23] For Ann, *Thanks a Million* was a huge step in the wrong direction.

Upon Ann's return to Warner Bros. from her loan out, the plan was to reteam her with James Cagney and director Howard Hawks in the aviation drama *Ceiling Zero*. However, the part they had pegged her for was not as leading lady opposite Cagney, but rather a much lower-billed role as Pat O'Brien's wife. The thought of playing such a second-tier part on the heels of the Fox musical was more than Ann was willing to endure. For two years she had played whatever role was given to her without too much complaint, but *Thanks a Million* and *Ceiling Zero* seemed to have been the tipping point. She was fairly vocal in her objection to appearing in the Cagney film, expressing her frustrations to Pat O'Brien and crew members. Finally, Ann directed her ire toward her boss. However, while someone like Bette Davis had no problem marching into Jack Warner's office to tell him she thought an assigned part stank, this was not Ann's style. As was evidenced in her 1932 walkout, she was not confrontational, preferring to take a more passive approach. So instead of reporting to work on September 30, for her first scheduled day on *Ceiling Zero*, Ann called in sick and wrote a letter to Jack Warner objecting to the film. "I must insist that you place me in productions of dramatic merit, in which my artistry, personality, intelligence and experience may be displayed. Failure to do so will be considered a breach of contract on your part."[24] Warner responded four days later by putting her on suspension without pay and replacing her in *Ceiling Zero* with Martha Tibbetts. Since Ann was claiming ill health, Warner Bros. was within its rights to take this action. Under the terms of her contract, an inability to work due to poor health was reason for the studio to suspend her rather than risk any financial losses by casting her in a movie she could not complete. The suspension was lifted on October 15, and both parties were positioned for their next standoff.

Ann was genuinely unhappy with the minuscule part in *Ceiling Zero*, but at the same time, her overall health was in fact starting to become a major concern. She was naturally very slender, but by the latter half of 1935, Ann had become painfully thin. Publicity stills from *Thanks a Million* show Ann looking gaunt and tired, and her normally lustrous hair looks flat and fine. She had even reportedly collapsed two different times on the set of an unspecified production earlier in the year.[25] Her increasingly drawn appearance made the Warner front office take notice. The studio became fearful that her health, along with her progressively negative attitude, would become a financial liability to any picture she was cast in. After the *Ceiling Zero* suspension, the studio's doctor examined Ann and reported back, "It is my opinion that in her present state of health, she could not pursue her duties as a contract player without greatly endangering her health, and there is a strong possibility that she would not be able to complete a picture should you undertake to have her do so at this time." He further advised it was "necessary for her to take a complete rest and be under the supervision of her physician."[26] For Warner Bros., the next logical step was to suspend Ann for a longer period of time until her health and appearance returned. However, Ann was claiming she had fully recovered from the illness that had prohibited her from appearing in *Ceiling Zero*, so the studio felt it needed additional proof she was unable to maintain the rigors of a full production. Even with the doctor's report, executives at Warner Bros. suspected the subject of her health could be interpreted as their word against hers and did not want to leave themselves open for a potential lawsuit. They decided to cast her in *Backfire*, later changed to *Boulder Dam*, in which she would play a chorus girl with a few musical numbers. They figured Ann would never make it past the rehearsal period, leaving sufficient grounds to suspend her. As it turned out, they were right.

Preliminary production for *Backfire* began in late October, and while Ann was able to make it to the studio for wardrobe fittings, she did indeed call in sick the first couple days of rehearsals, telling dance instructor Bobby Connolly, "I feel like hell." When the studio called the Fenton home on October 30 to check in on her, Leslie responded that Ann was feeling "pretty badly," had been in bed since the previous day, and was waiting for the doctor to arrive.[27] That was all Warner Bros. needed. The studio replaced Ann on *Backfire* with Patricia Ellis and sent a letter later that day notifying Ann that she was suspended on account of her present illness incapacitating her from performing under the terms of her contract.[28] The studio felt even more confident about its actions when Ann's own doctor admitted via a telephone conversation that he could not guarantee she would be able to finish a picture, would need six months' to a year's rest, and added, "It's unfortunate people had to ruin their health to pay off yachts and homes."[29] Ann, disagreeing with all of them, arrived at the studio on November 1, whereupon Max Arnow promptly sent her to the office of executive Roy J. Obringer, who did not see Ann but merely relayed a message through his secretary that Jack Warner would be advised. Incensed, Ann returned home and drafted a letter to her bosses stating she had reported for duty and was ready, willing, and able to work but had been turned away. Warner, who was not in the mood "to be forced to have to pay Dvorak when she is actually sick just because she reports back to the studio and pretends that she is able to work," refused to budge on the suspension.[30] The studio responded with its own letter, which attempted to be sympathetic in asserting that Ann's "incapacity is, of course, not a matter of mere will-power or desire on your part" but nonetheless firm in insisting that the suspension would remain until she became "capable of rendering those services in the spirit and to the extent to which it is necessary in picture work."[31] The battle of wills between actress and studio had officially begun.

What was wrong with Ann in the fall of 1935 that caused Warner

Bros. to suspend her is unclear. Some newspapers reported she had suffered a nervous breakdown, while others attributed her condition to overwork. If sheer exhaustion was the culprit, it seems this would have manifested the previous year when she had been assigned to nearly ten films, as opposed to 1935 when her film output had been scaled back considerably. Or maybe the workload of the previous two years had finally caught up with her. Was she, as some suspected, in a stifling marriage that was fraying her nerves? On the surface the Fenton union seemed as strong as ever, and it's impossible to know what was going on behind closed doors. Perhaps her weight loss and exhaustion were caused by some sort of medical condition. Rumors started going around that the actress was tubercular. Whatever was ailing her, Warner Bros. felt it was severe enough to keep her off the payroll indefinitely. Ann, however, continued to deny there was anything wrong and she and the studio locked horns, with Warner Bros. denying her numerous requests to resume employment unless she received a clean bill of health from both her doctor and the studio's, and Ann continually refusing to submit to an examination. When the holidays rolled around and the suspension still had not been lifted, she had had enough and turned to the courts for help. Ann Dvorak was going to war with Warner Bros.

14

Legal Eagle

The year 1936 would prove to be a litigious one for Warner Bros. James Cagney made good on his numerous threats of legal action and filed a lawsuit against the studio in early March. The actor claimed Warner Bros. had breached his contract by assigning him to more than four pictures a year and by failing to give him top billing in one of those films. The judge saw it Cagney's way and he was released from studio servitude. In the fall of the same year, Bette Davis faced off against Jack Warner himself in the British courts. Her counsel claimed that studio contracts rendered the actors "chattel in the hands of the producer," but this was a thinly veiled protest against the thankless parts she felt were beneath her talent.[1] Davis lost her suit but gained the respect of her employer and went on to have a phenomenal career with Warner Bros. for the next thirteen years. What most don't realize is that before these two now-legendary stars gave their studio battles a very public face, Ann Dvorak paved the way for both and was one of the earliest actors to use the legal system to rebel against her studio.

While Ann waited for Warner Bros. to let her return to work, she focused her energies on her home life, even serving a Thanksgiving dinner comprised solely of food raised on the ranch.[2] As November came to a close and the studio still had not budged from its position, Ann felt she had no other choice but to hire an attorney. Leslie Fenton no doubt played a role in this decision, though how much of this was driven by him is unclear. Fenton had been engaged in steady freelance work for Universal, RKO, Columbia, and Paramount, but the parts were small—along with the paychecks—and the loss of Ann's income of $1,500 a week was starting to take its toll. The couple was becoming desperate for some sort of resolution, but didn't want to find it on Warner Bros.' terms. The two decided using the legal system to press for a release from the contract was the best route to take.

In early December the Warner Bros. legal department met with Ann's attorney, Louis B. Stanton. The studio reps became concerned the actress might actually have a case against Warner Bros. Stanton claimed that immediately after the suspension, Ann had been examined by three reputable physicians who "pronounced her in satisfactory physical condition for any practical purpose." He also asserted that Warner's doctor had made a "most superficial" examination that did not prove any physical incapacity. Additionally, Ann's own doctor was now stating that the verbal assessment he had provided to the studio confirming her poor health had been misinterpreted, and he would testify to that effect. Ann's doctor was also concerned that rumors of her being tubercular had been circulated by Warner Bros. as a way to scare off any outside studios that might be considering the use of her services. In light of these developments, Ann's counsel stated that her contract had been breached when the suspension was issued on October 30 and demanded Ann's immediate release from all studio obligations. As a bargaining chip Ann was offering to appear in a few more films, if a mutual agreement to terminate the contract was established. Warner's lawyers were impressed enough with Ann's impending case that they advised the studio to consider settling with her.[3] Jack Warner was not about to agree to any terms proposed by an actress. He decided to call Ann's bluff and take his chances, noting that even if she did manage to get out of her contract, he was "not going to worry about losing her."[4]

On December 17, 1935, the official complaint for declaration relief was filed at the Los Angeles Superior Court by "LESLIE C. FENTON and ANN D. FENTON, husband and wife vs WARNER BROTHERS PICTURES, INC., a corporation." The complaint charged that Ann's contract had been breached as the studio had "repeatedly refused to permit said actress to further perform any services whatsoever" and had "wholly failed, neglected and refused to pay said artist any sums whatsoever."[5] The complaint also argued that during this time, Ann's contract with Warner Bros. had prevented her from earning a living elsewhere in that it prohibited her from seeking employment at other studios. Ann sought financial compensation for the time she was not allowed to work, the termination of her contract, and all legal costs incurred. The court date was set for February 14, 1936.

To take Ann's mind off the upcoming battle, the Fentons sailed from Los Angeles down to Panama, where they spent Christmas and the New Year. Upon returning they made one of their limited public appearances at the Hollywood Brown Derby where friends eagerly greeted them, with a few no doubt anxious to get details of the lawsuit. Throughout January Ann and her bosses exchanged correspondence in an attempt to reach an amicable agreement, but to no avail. The studio continued to insist that Ann agree to a full physical examination by one of its doctors and she continued to refuse. As the court date drew closer, Ann finally submitted to the medical examination by two doctors approved by the studio. The reports were sent to Warner Bros. which found them "not at all reassuring." The studio informed Ann, "We are unable to see how you can, in justice either to yourself or to us, perform under your contract." However, interested in avoiding court, the studio added, "While we are less than hopeful, we are anxious now, as we were when we lifted your former suspension, to have you back at work. We have decided again to give you the benefit of the doubt."[6] Warner Bros. officially lifted her suspension on January 27, directing Ann to report to the Burbank studio on February 3 at 10:00 a.m. Dvorak's attorney was irked by the studio contacting his client directly, and became even more incensed when Warner Bros. began repeatedly calling Ann's home after she did not report for work at the designated time. He requested that Warner Bros. communicate with Ann only through him, and sent a very clear message that the litigation would indeed continue. Since Ann was finally off suspension, the studio was once again generating her much-needed paychecks, though she was required to come in person to pick them up. Plus, the edict was to pay her only by check, not in cash. Under the advice of her attorney, Ann continued to stay away from the studio, even though it meant not getting paid.[7]

On Friday, February 14, 1936, Ann showed up at the Superior Court of the State of California in and for Los Angeles County, where Judge Harry R. Archibald would be presiding over her case. She looked flawless, clad in fur with a black hat and black leather gloves—she could have been ready to step onto a film set rather than a witness stand. Ann was sworn in, and the case of *Ann D. Fenton & Leslie C. Fenton vs. Warner Bros.* officially began.

The entirety of the first day's proceedings found Ann on the stand with Warner Bros.' lawyers, who tried to portray her as temperamental and physically unfit for her job. The initial line of questioning focused on *Ceiling Zero*, as they sought to prove Ann had used false claims of ill heath to get out of playing the part. She had reportedly complained to Pat O'Brien that the part in *Ceiling Zero* was "lousy," but when asked about

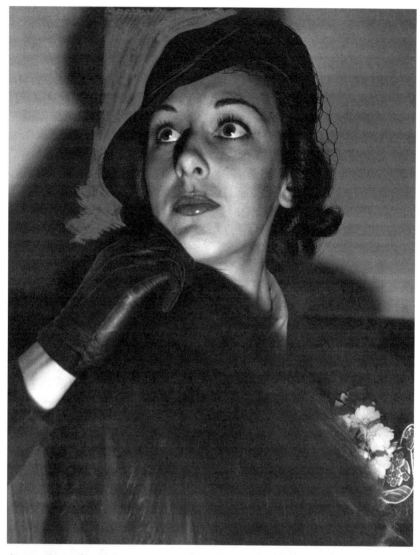

Ann makes a dramatic entrance at the Los Angeles County courthouse to face off against Warner Bros. (Courtesy of the *Los Angeles Herald Examiner* Collection/Los Angeles Public Library)

the comment, Ann responded, "No, I made no such remark, but I did tell him I thought it was only a fair part. I didn't accept it because I was ill just at that time."[8] In regard to the quality of the roles Warner Bros. had been assigning her, Ann admitted, "I told Mr. Warner if I was not worth my salary for him to release me," and when asked if she thought the parts the studio had placed her in were unsuitable, she replied, "Yes, somewhat." However, when asked if this dissatisfaction was her reason for not appearing in *Backfire,* Ann was quick to respond, "Not at all. I wanted very much to take the part."[9] The line of questioning then turned to Ann's health as Warner lawyer Robert J. Files inquired, "For some time, have you not been conscious that you were growing thinner?" Ann replied, "I have not. I was laid up with the flu for a short time, but I was soon well and ready to go to work. The studio doctor examined me, and though they claimed I was not in condition to work, I knew better. As an actress, I am qualified to do anything in my line of work, singing or dancing."[10] She did agree that "my physician advised me not to work while I was ill and to take it easy afterward," but claimed she had soon recovered.[11] She added that as of November 1, 1935, "I have been ready to work at all times. . . . On that day I offered my services but they were refused."[12] Warner's lawyer then submitted photographs of Ann in *Bright Lights, Dr. Socrates,* and *Thanks a Million* as proof that she had grown increasingly thinner as a result of her illness. After Ann's testimony, R. J. Files made a motion for a nonsuit, which the court denied.[13] Since Judge Archibald was scheduled to be in Ventura the following Monday, the case was postponed until Tuesday, February 18, and Ann and Leslie went home to spend their Valentine's Day evening together.

When the case resumed on February 18, it proved to be a day of doctors: six physicians were called to the stand to testify in Dvorak's favor. When Dr. Rolla Karshner produced X-rays of Ann for the court to view, the actress jumped up from her seat in order to get a closer look. With the X-rays displayed, Karshner dispelled the rumors of tuberculosis. "The photographs reveal that Miss Dvorak was in excellent physical condition at the time they were taken. They show no abnormalities of the chest and no lung affliction whatever."[14] When Dr. Frank G. Nolan took the stand, he introduced a new angle to Dvorak's perceived health problems by testifying that Ann's habit of drinking ten cups of coffee a day had caused her weight loss. He further commented, "Had I known she was a heavy coffee drinker, I would not have become alarmed and ordered a thorough examination." Apparently Ann was no longer serving Sanka at her home. When Warner attorney Files asked, "You think she could go to work now, and play an important role in an important film production?" Nolan was quick to respond, "Yes, I believe she is in good condition to work."[15]

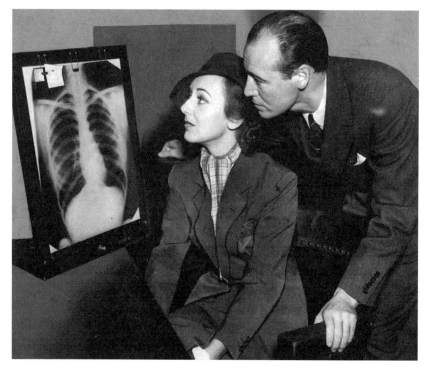

Ann and Leslie Fenton examine X-rays of Ann's chest that were presented in court. (Courtesy of the University of Southern California, on behalf of the USC Special Collections)

Following the testimony of the doctors, the court adjourned for the day, although the proceedings were to continue for two more days.

Ann was no doubt on pins and needles for the next week and a half as Judge Archibald deliberated her case. On March 2, he issued a preliminary decision stating, "I am forced to the conclusion that plaintiff Ann D. Fenton was, on October 30, 1935, physically incapacitated by reason of sickness from performing the work required of her under her contract with defendant, and that said incapacity continued for a considerable time after November 1st, 1935." He added, "I am further convinced that even on January 27, 1936, when she was examined by certain physicians, that she was not yet fully over the effects of her sickness, and that it is doubtful, if she had been put to work much before that date, if she would have been able to complete any picture requiring sustained physical effort on her part."[16] Despite the testimony of multiple doctors vouching for Ann's good health, the judge saw otherwise and concluded that no breach of contract had occurred, though the exact nature of her illness was never made clear. Ann Dvorak would remain the property of Warner Bros. until her contract was set to expire in 1938, though the studio no doubt had every intention of extending the contract to include the suspension time. The judge did state that Warner Bros. was to pay Ann $7,000, which would cover the time since the suspension had been lifted on January 27. Archibald also declared that Ann was entitled to "the further sum of $1,500.00 on Wednesday of each week she is required to work under such contract, providing she immediately reports for duty and performs the duties required of her under said contract."[17] Jack Warner had gambled on the courts and won. As for Ann, she made no public comments about the defeat, but later grumbled to her bosses that she "did not believe the conclusion of the court is correct."[18]

Before the judge had yet issued the final signed judgment, Warner Bros. was ready to put the whole episode behind it and figured Ann would as well. Nearly a week after the judge's initial ruling, the studio sent a letter to her home stating, "We have been expecting you to report to our studio for work under the terms of our contract with you. In checking the various departments we find that you have not reported to us."[19] The studio requested that she report for work at the Burbank studio immediately, and when Ann failed to respond, issued a telegram on March 11 demanding it. The wire got Ann's attention, and she arrived at the studio the following day with business manager Bo Roos to meet with executive Roy Obringer and casting director Tenny C. Wright. Since Ann still considered the litigation pending, she agreed to go back to work if the studio provided "a written agreement or stipulation to the effect that she would return to work without prejudice."[20] Obringer refused to issue any sort of notice, and she later complained in a letter to Jack Warner, "Your representative refused to permit me to work without imposing upon me conditions which he did not have a legal or moral right to."[21] Ann claimed that Obringer repeatedly stated during their meeting that Warner Bros. did not consider itself bound to the court's decision and that if Ann returned as requested, the studio would consider the still-pending litigation forfeit.[22] Obringer vehemently denied these claims, stating that the decision to return to work lay solely with Ann and her lawyer.[23] Ann soon returned home to Leslie Fenton without any sort of resolution and planned her next move. The judge may have given his verdict, but the battle wasn't over.

Ann awaits the judge's verdict in this previously unpublished photo. (Courtesy of UCLA Charles E. Young Research Department of Special Collections/*Los Angeles Times* Photographic Archives)

Less than a month later, on April 4, Ann once again appeared before Judge Archibald. She was now requesting that the judge specify an exact date the court believed she had been ready to work. She added that if this date occurred prior to January 27, when the suspension was lifted, Warner

Bros. would have breached the contract, which would therefore be considered null and void. Additionally, Ann claimed the contract should be voided on the grounds that it was in restraint of trade and therefore unconstitutional. Ann was also requesting that in light of these claims, the minutes from the March decision be recalled. Before appearing in the courtroom, Ann took a few minutes to meet with Mary Jane Viall, a young fan who happened to be the daughter of one of the jury clerks. Ann put on a brave face for the child and the press photographers, but she must have been disappointed when Judge Archibald responded merely that he would take the matter under consideration.[24]

The case would drag on for another three months as Judge Archibald continued to have cases assigned to him by the Master Calendar Department, which prevented him from reviewing Ann's most recent grievance. Warner lawyers believed that "if the court wishes to take a very technical view of the contract, there might be some ground for concern; however, we have always considered the opinions of this judge to be well founded and he is not one to go off tangent."[25] In the meantime, Ann and Leslie's finances continued to suffer. Even though Ann's agents had advised her to claim the $7,000, she had not picked up the check for fear it would bring the litigation to a close. Since Warner Bros. held the opinion that Ann had not reported for work, she was still not receiving a salary. In order to stay afloat, the Fentons sold a piece of property they owned at the corner of Burbank Boulevard and Fulton Avenue in Van Nuys.

On July 1 Judge Archibald denied Ann's recall request, stating he did not have sufficient facts to determine what had occurred between Ann and Warner Bros. after January 27. The circumstances surrounding Ann's reporting for work in early March was her word against the studio's, and the judge was no longer willing to play referee between the two parties. As far as he was concerned, the matter was closed, and "any controversy between the parties as to salary after said January 27th must be settled outside of the present controversy."[26] Once again, the court had ruled in Warner Bros.' favor, but the war was far from over.

Ann acknowledged this latest defeat and showed up at Warner Bros. the next morning with her agent. Rumor had it she would be cast opposite the studio's newest star, Errol Flynn, in *The Green Light* or in *God's Country and the Woman* with her *Housewife* costar George Brent. Instead, Warner Bros. gave her no assignment and then laid her off for two weeks. The studio was in no hurry to put her back in front of the cameras, but it was concerned about the increase in pay Ann was set to receive when her next option came up in September. In order to skirt the scheduled raise, Warner Bros. decided to extend the life of the current option with the time Ann was on suspension. The studio estimated this to be 225 days, which included the initial suspension after Ann called in sick on *Ceiling Zero*, the time covering October 30 through January 27, and the post-court period of February 26 through July 1. Under these adjusted terms, Ann would not be receiving her next raise until April 1937.[27]

The studio sent Ann a letter on July 22 stating these intended terms and requesting her signature agreeing to them. As guided by Leslie Fenton, Ann refused to sign the letter. Warner Bros. responded with another letter on July 31 bluntly stating the option would be extended, and while the studio did not come out and say that her signature was unnecessary, the implication was there.[28] Ann and Leslie had been defeated twice in court, yet they felt the need to continue fighting the studio, perhaps in hopes her bosses would tire of her actions and just release her. This time around, Ann was arguing that she was entitled to pay for the dates spanning early March through July, and that the time frame should not be considered a period of suspension. She had reported to work in early March and the studio had not availed itself of her services. According to Ann, "That was the choice of Warner Bros. and was not my choice. I am not responsible for actions and decisions of your managers; and I do not believe that I could fairly be penalized because your representatives did not choose to permit me to work." Ann went on to state, "I respectfully decline to accept your conclusion that you are not obliged to pay me compensation for that period; and I decline to accept your conclusion that you are entitled to add 126 days to the term of my present contract." Ann probably figured going the legal route was no longer a viable option, as she added, "I do not, however, desire to open litigation again in the courtroom. I would like to avoid a public record of differences of opinion with my employing studio." Ann was now suggesting that both sides select arbitrators who would then decide if the 126 days in question should be recorded as a period of unpaid suspension. Ann continued, "Both of us should agree to be bound by the decision of the majority of the arbitrators; and both of us should accept that decision as final and conclusive, without the right or privilege to go to court." Ann concluded that this proposal, sent directly to Jack Warner, was being submitted "for your calm consideration. With assurance of my personal respect."[29] Warner

Bros. had its lawyers notify Ann that given the court's decision, she was in no position to make any sort of requests or demands.[30]

While actress and studio continued haggling over the finer points of their disagreement, they were able to reach enough of a compromise for Ann to be loaned out to RKO in late July for *We Who Are About to Die.* Warner Bros. would receive $3,000 for Ann to appear in this prison drama starring John Beal as a man wrongly accused of murder and sentenced to hang.[31] Preston Foster is the local detective who aids in Beal's conviction, then crusades to set him free when he becomes convinced he has the wrong man. Ann plays Connie, Beal's steadfast girlfriend who maintains his innocence. The film is a quickie programmer, coming in at eighty-one minutes, but its commentary on capital punishment makes for an interesting watch, particularly in the scenes between the death-row inmates. Unfortunately for Ann, her part in the film as the noble and devoted girlfriend was exactly what she had spent the better part of a year rebelling against. Different studio, same role. Ann tried to give the casting a positive spin, remarking, "Yes, it's another 'leading lady' role, but at least it has some character, some drama to it."[32]

The day after Ann completed production on *We Who Are About to Die,* Warner Bros. laid her off for two weeks and began negotiating with RKO for her to appear in another picture on loan. This probably suited Ann just fine, as Leslie Fenton had recently been cast in an upcoming Broadway production of the Elmer Harris play *Inner Silence* and was needed in New York for rehearsals. Ann used the time off to accompany her husband to New York, where she was offered the lead female role in the play.[33] The Fentons had not acted opposite each other since *The Strange Love of Molly Louvain,* and previous plans to appear onstage together at the Pasadena Playhouse had not been realized.[34] Ann no doubt relished this chance not only to perform live theater with her husband but to do so on Broadway, something her mother came close to achieving but never quite did. However, there was one stumbling block for Ann, and that was Warner Bros. The situation over the terms of her current option had not been resolved, and the studio was not receptive to her suggestion of using arbitrators. Perhaps, Ann thought, if she finally made amends with the studio, it would be more amenable to her appearing onstage. On September 22 Ann finally signed a document agreeing to the terms of her next option, which mirrored the previous letter she had refused to sign and which included the full 225 days of suspension added on.[35] The gesture was too little too late, and Warner Bros. had no intention of allowing Ann time off for a Broadway show. The studio was adamant: "On account of picture production plans and so forth, will be unable to grant Miss Dvorak the right to appear in New York in this play."[36] Once it was established that Ann would not be appearing, Leslie Fenton dropped out and *Inner Silence* did not move forward. Elmer Harris would rework the play, which finally appeared on Broadway under the title *Johnny Belinda* in 1940. When the story was adapted for the screen, Jane Wyman would win a Best Actress Oscar as a deaf mute who becomes pregnant after being raped. Had Ann been allowed to appear in this role, it would have been unlike anything she had ever attempted, and in retrospect, is as much a lost opportunity as the Sadie Thompson part in *Rain*. It would be another twelve years before Ann had the chance to appear on Broadway.

Instead of appearing onstage in an acclaimed drama, Ann went back to RKO for the low-budget *Racing Lady*. Based on two short stories, Damon Runyon's "All Scarlet" and "Odds Are Even," by J. Robert Bren and Norman Houston, *Racing Lady* was a rare starring role for Ann. As Ruth Martin, Ann is a thoroughbred trainer whose sportsmanship is put to the test after she is employed by a wealthy businessman who uses her celebrity to sell cars. *Racing Lady* may be short, with a thin plot, but at least it was a departure from most of the supporting parts Ann had been appearing in at Warner Bros., and she is in the majority of the scenes. As Ann's love interest, Smith Ballew, known more for singing than acting, is awkward and wooden, and there's only so much Ann can do to make their interactions interesting. At least Ballew proved to have more personality offscreen. Early on in the filming, the cast and crew became jittery when they began hearing eerie offstage voices that did not seem to belong to anyone. Turns out, Ballew was a trained ventriloquist who was purposely throwing his voice as a practical joke.[37] However, the scenes between Dvorak and veteran actor Harry Carey, as her father, are especially effective and demonstrate how Ann's performances could be elevated when working opposite a seasoned professional. Ann genuinely seems to have enjoyed making the film, and her love of animals is apparent whenever she interacts with the horses onscreen. She even reportedly purchased the colt used in the film for the Fenton ranch.[38] However, when comparisons between Ann and the character she was playing were brought up, she was quick to point out, "It's not exactly what you'd call a real life role however. In the first place we raise walnuts instead of horses on our farm. And even most of our work is done by tractor."[39]

After a full year without appearing in a Warner Bros. film, the dust between Ann and her employer was finally settling, and the studio was ready to put her in one of its own productions. Ann's health seemed to have improved considerably, and she gained a much-needed ten pounds in two weeks' time, something she achieved by sleeping eleven hours a night.[40] The film she was set to appear in was *Midnight Court* opposite John Litel as a washed-up former district attorney who finds renewed success circumventing the law for a gangster running an auto theft ring. Ann plays a night court reporter who also happens to be Litel's ex-wife and his conscience. It was a standard Warner role for Ann as the tried-and-true backup for the male lead, but at least this time she was given top billing and a fair amount of screen time. Another plus was the presence of family friend Herbert Rawlinson in a small role. Ann was also featured prominently on the advertising art for the film, though the title card and half sheet featured recycled art from the Bette Davis vehicle *The Girl from 10th Avenue* with Ann's likeness slapped on over Bette's.

Midnight Court also featured one of the most unflattering costumes of Ann's career. According to one report, this "exciting dress," designed by Milo Anderson, was "patterned after the costume of a knight of old. The dress, with its long slim skirt is powder blue and silver metal cloth. Sleeves are wrist length, but long enough to be crushed all the way to the shoulder. A sleeveless tunic made of silver petals simulates a coat of mail. The full-length shoulder cape of powder blue velvet to wear with the gown is attached with epaulettes in the manner of a Crusader."[41] The tunic actually looks like it's made from the scales of a skinned fish, and the Juliet cap and hair, modeled after Norma Shearer's headgear from *Romeo and Juliet*, released the previous year, do not suit Ann well.

With *Midnight Court*, it appeared to be business as usual for the Warner Bros. casting department, but Ann was willing to put on her best face, commenting, "The story deals with big-city night courts, crooked politics, the car stealing racket and so on and is called 'Justice After Dark' [the title was later changed]. It is a remarkable story, really—I've just read the script. The author is Don Ryan, scenarist, novelist and newspaper man."[42] To a journalist visiting the set of *Midnight Court*, Ann exclaimed, "See that lady and gentleman over there—the pair who do not look like actors? They are Judges Irving Taplan and Oda Faulconer, who often pre-

Wearing a dress that looks as if it's made of fish scales, Ann converses with John Litel in *Midnight Court*.

side at the Los Angeles night court. They're here because they are interested in how we're putting on the story."[43] In an effort to evoke a realistic performance as a court reporter, Ann reportedly began attending night court.[44] She was enthusiastic about her leading man, who was two decades older than she, and backtracked on a comment she had previously made about being able to share screen kisses more effectively with actors she did not know, commenting, "Well, this will have to be different, so I'll just conveniently abandon that theory. Mr. Litel and I have many other scenes together before there's one in which a kiss is exchanged. And we're well acquainted by this time, so perhaps you'd better strike that statement of mine—which I thought had been forgotten long ago—from the records. Your readers will agree that a woman has the right to change her mind."[45] She also noted, "Kissing for the screen is as impersonal as ordering a ham sandwich."[46]

Of her lost litigation and ongoing issues with the studio, Ann would comment only that she was "just back at the Warner Brothers lot after an extended absence." However, she took the opportunity to compliment her bosses by recounting the story of the last time she had returned to the studio after a lengthy time away, referring to her honeymoon trip of nearly four years earlier: "Instead of breaking my contract we discovered at the end of our long journey that Warners were going to be very considerate."[47] It seemed that Ann had finally conceded complete defeat and had every intention of making the remaining two and a half years of her contract as pleasant as possible.

In late November 1936, a little over a year since the battle royale had begun, Warner Bros. decided two things: Ann would be cast as Perry Mason's loyal secretary Della Street in *The Case of the Stuttering Bishop*, the latest installment in the popular series, and it would be her last film at the studio. Della Street was not a stretch for Ann at this point, as it was the type of character she had played countless times during her tenure with Warner Bros. Donald Woods was enlisted to play the beloved lawyer, following in the footsteps of Ann's former costar Warren William, who had been Mason in four previous films, and Ricardo Cortez, who had played the role once. As far as Ann Dvorak films at Warner Bros. go, this one had a higher budget than most and Della Street was a more generous role than one would have expected from the studio at this time. Ann genuinely seems to be enjoying herself in the film, especially when she's exchanging quips with Donald Woods, and her wardrobe, designed by Howard Shoup, is extremely stylish, making up for the unflattering attire she wore in *Midnight Court*. Despite the events of the past year, Ann would be leaving Warner Bros. on a high note.

There are no existing records documenting why Warner Bros. chose to finally release Ann at this point. It had been a rocky relationship that lasted nearly five years, and it seems the studio had finally had enough of Ann Dvorak. She had been trying to get out of her contract for over a year, but Jack Warner would never have given in to any actor on that actor's terms. After a lengthy and futile litigation followed by a couple of loan-outs and two Warner productions, perhaps Jack Warner felt he had proven his point and that he was letting her go on his own terms. After the failed court case, Ann had fired the Selznick agency, apparently unhappy with the advice it had given her during the proceedings, and moved over to William Morris. She was now being represented by Johnny Hyde, a legendary agent and future mentor of Marilyn Monroe, and Warner Bros. made sure Ann's termination papers arrived in his office early enough so that all the paperwork could be completed as soon as the cameras stopped rolling on *The Case of the Stuttering Bishop*. On December 19 filming wrapped and Ann was handed her final $1,500 paycheck. After a year of practically nonstop battling, Ann was finally free of her contract. The day ended like any other working day, except this time, Ann would not be returning to the place that had been her home away from home since late 1931. Louella Parsons, one of the first to report the parting, remarked, "Too bad, really, that Ann and Warners had to have that trouble at the time of her marriage to Leslie Fenton. She was one of the biggest bets on the screen when she chose to kick up her heels and walk out on one of the best opportunities any young player ever had."[48]

For all the headaches Ann caused Jack Warner and his studio, the mogul bore amazingly little resentment toward her, considering his ability to hold lifelong grudges against people he felt had wronged him. When he penned his memoirs thirty years later, he would omit any mention of ace producer Hal Wallis, with whom he had a falling-out in the 1940s, and would fail to acknowledge the existence of his own son or first wife. For Ann Dvorak he reserved a couple of paragraphs filled with praise for her talents and tinged with regret about how their relationship had played out. He recalled her as "a beautiful girl," declaring, "I had seen her in *Scarface*, and she had a dainty, unworldly quality that was rare in the actresses around Hollywood at that time." He remembered that "almost inevitably, she came down with the temperament disease, and when agents Myron Selznick and Charlie Feldman began double-crossing each other in a fight to get her, Ann ran away and took a slow boat to New York through the Panama Canal." Thirty years after the fact, Warner had his timeline mixed up, because he recalled Leslie Fenton entering the picture "some years later" instead of being directly responsible for many of Ann's actions. Warner's sentiments still seemed bittersweet when he somewhat inaccurately wrote, "I put her under suspension, and she never came back to the Burbank lot, which is too bad because she had a dazzling future until her quarreling agents snuffed it out."[49] If Ann had only played by the rules for a couple of years, who knows what she and Warner Bros. could have accomplished together?

But it was over and done, and the early promise of 1932 had been severely compromised. If Ann learned anything from her experiences at Caddo and Warner Bros., it was that long-term contracts were not the way to go, and studio servitude was something she would never succumb to again. Instead she would assume the role of the freelancer, which in theory would give her more control over her personal life as well as her onscreen roles. Only time would tell if her freedom from Warner Bros. would translate into success elsewhere in Hollywood.

15

Freelance Artist

After nearly eight years of working under the control of MGM, the Caddo Company, and Warner Bros., Ann Dvorak finally had the career freedom that her husband had been enjoying all along. Leslie Fenton had found steady work as a freelancer throughout the 1930s, with his acting career culminating in 1938 with a role in the much-heralded *Boys Town*. The Fentons were about to enter a new phase in both their careers, with Ann choosing where she would work and Fenton giving up acting in favor of directing. Other actresses, most notably Barbara Stanwyck and Carole Lombard, had successfully maneuvered careers without the aid of the studio machine, and Ann's reputation—both as a competent actress and as a troublemaker—would soon be tested as she ventured out on her own.

Of her new status as a freelancer, Ann reflected, "Long-term contracts are fine for beginners. It means an assured income at least until the next option time. It's fine when the producer has time to be interested in individual careers. But for a player who is beginning to be well known, it's not so good. One had to take any part that's offered, the studio gets too used to one and does not note the possible versatilities, and, of course, one doesn't make so much money." As for her personal issues with long-term studio contracts, Ann continued, "My concern wasn't money so much as the types of parts. I'd rather play a smaller role with dramatic opportunity, than a larger but inane one."[1] Little could Ann know how prophetic this sentiment was.

One of the first things Ann did to promote this chapter of her career was to book some photography sessions with famed portrait artist George Hurrell. The renowned photographer had started his employment at MGM right around the time Ann left for Caddo, but by 1937 he was operating out of his own studio in Hollywood. Hurrell was known for his striking portraits featuring dramatic lighting that epitomized Hollywood

183

Ann poses for master photographer George Hurrell after becoming a freelancer.

glamour, and Ann no doubt hoped the photographer could produce some portraits that would help entice movie studios into hiring her. Leslie Fenton sat in for a more traditional husband/wife portrait. One of Hurrell's photos of Ann would even run in an issue of *Esquire*, but could sophisticated portraiture help the studios forget about the troubles Ann Dvorak had caused Warner Bros.?

Before Ann could kick-start her freelance career, she suffered a few setbacks that delayed her post-Warner comeback. On December 5, 1936, at 7:20 in the morning while driving her 1936 Chrysler coupe, Ann collided with a Willys sedan at the corner of Riverside and Cahuenga, causing the sedan to overturn and be pushed off the highway. John J. Kelly, the driver of the other car, filed a lawsuit the following March asserting that Ann's "negligent, careless, unskillful, reckless, and unlawful" driving caused the accident. He was asking $26,625 in damages and personal injuries.[2] Ann disputed Kelly's claim, stating that the accident was unavoidable.[3] Four months later Ann was absolved when the court dismissed the case.[4]

Around the same time the lawsuit was filed, Ann also found herself preoccupied when Leslie Fenton underwent a major abdominal surgery at Cedars of Lebanon Hospital. Ann held her husband's hand until he lost consciousness, and reportedly was allowed to remain in the operating room during the eighty-minute surgery.[5] Leslie was confined to bed for a couple of months, with Ann constantly tending to him and spending large sums of cash on mystery novels to keep him occupied.[6] In between the real-life high drama, the Fentons found time to squeeze in some social activities, which included attending a soirée at the Trocadero, hosted by Ann's mentor Joan Crawford and her second husband, Franchot Tone, and showing up at a midnight Red Cross event at the Chinese Theatre to benefit midwestern flood victims.

Rumors started spreading that Ann was a serious contender for a role in *Dead End,* based on a popular Broadway show, which was to be directed by William Wyler and star Joel McCrea, Humphrey Bogart, and the "Dead End Kids." *Dead End* would have been an impressive start to Ann's career as a freelancer, but Sylvia Sidney landed the part. Instead, B. P. Shulberg at Paramount was the first to take a chance on the rebellious actress by casting her in the light comedy *She's No Lady,* directed by Charles Vidor, who at the time was married to Ann's old pal Karen Morley. *She's No Lady* was Ann's first opportunity to appear in a sheer comedic role and it was a far cry from the characters she had so effectively played in *Scarface, Three on a Match,* and *Heat Lightning.* Playing against type may have been an interesting choice if the film had actually been any good, but it wasn't, and for the first time Ann Dvorak gave a mediocre performance. *She's No Lady* is a would-be screwball comedy featuring Ann as one of a trio of jewel thieves. She comes to see the error of her ways when she falls in love with John Trent, an innocent bystander she uses to gain access to one of her targets. Ann spends a great deal of the picture ineffectively mugging, and the *New York Sun* summed up Ann's freelance debut by remarking, "Why any one should have bothered to produce 'She's No Lady' will probably remain one of Hollywood's out-standing mysteries, for the picture has nothing whatsoever to recommend it. Its plot is threadbare. It has some of the silliest dialogue ever heard by this reporter. And for sweet charity's sake it is best to skip all mention of the performance of the cast." The *New York Times* wasn't any more kind: "The picture . . . is eligible to compete for the Academy annual booby awards (if any)."[7] Ann had battled Warner Bros. tooth and nail in large part because she was frustrated by the roles the studio had been giving her, yet *She's No Lady* is arguably worse than anything she did in five years for Jack Warner.

The one positive thing *She's No Lady* accorded Ann was the opportu-nity to show off the results of her latest hobby: millinery. Ann has started making her own hats, largely because she disapproved of the headwear being put out by the fashion industry, remarking, "Nobody would dare to wear such hats in pictures. They look ridiculous. And that's one good thing the movies are doing. Nearly always they display sane clothes and that is a good influence on the audiences."[8] Ann figured she was as good a hat designer as any working at the studios, and she was allowed to don her creations onscreen.[9]

Despite reports that she had signed a long-term contract with Paramount, *She's No Lady* was the only film Ann made with the studio at the time, and next she decided to try her luck elsewhere. The result was a gig at Republic Pictures in *Manhattan Merry-Go-Round*. Loosely inspired by a weekly radio revue program of the same name, *Manhattan Merry-Go-Round* stars Leo Carrillo as a gangster who inexplicably takes over a record company and starts strong-arming talent like Cab Calloway, Gene Autry, and Kay Thompson to record with him. Ann plays the company's secretary who also happens to be romancing one of the recording artists (Phil Regan). The usually frugal Republic reportedly spent $400,000 on the film, which was directed by Charles Reisner, with whom Ann had worked multiple times back in the MGM days. The higher budget may have helped the film snag an Academy Award nomination for Best Art Direction, but it couldn't do anything to salvage the weak plot and going-through-the-motions performances from the cast, including Ann. Her

Ann and Leslie on the town in 1939 at the Brown Derby.

role is not unlike the many dull parts she had been dished out at Warner Bros., and she disappears for a large chunk of the film. The one worthwhile thing in *Manhattan Merry-Go-Round* is the unexpected cameo by future baseball legend Joe DiMaggio, who is forced at gunpoint by the gangsters to sing, awkwardly, "Have You Ever Been Lonely?" If Ann was hoping to gain parts of greater substance and screen time, it clearly wasn't going to be at Republic.

After *Manhattan Merry-Go-Round*, Ann either decided she needed to recover from the two mediocre films she had just made, or the studios didn't have any more mediocre films for her to appear in. Also, she reportedly was asking $10,000 a picture, which may have been more than any studio was willing to pay for her services.[10] *She's No Lady* and *Manhattan Merry-Go-Round* turned out to be the only two titles she worked on in 1937 until the end of the year. Instead she devoted much of her time to her horticulture skills. She swept the potted plant division at a Van Nuys flower show and dazzled Brown Derby patrons one evening by donning Brazilian tiger orchids. Apparently, the money Leslie Fenton had started

Ann and Brian Aherne clown around on the set of *Merrily We Live.*

to pull in directing *Crime Doesn't Pay* shorts at MGM gave Ann the opportunity to spend some time off the screen.

In December 1937 Ann finally went back to work, this time for the Hal Roach Studios, run by the man her mother had unsuccessfully begged for work nearly twenty years earlier. The film *Merrily We Live* stars Brian Aherne as a millionaire mistaken for a hobo and hired as a butler for a nutty but lovable family headed by Billie Burke and Clarence Kolb. Constance Bennett is the eldest daughter who spars with the newly hired help before falling for him, and Ann plays a senator's daughter who sets her sights on Aherne. The film is more or less an inferior knockoff of MGM's *My Man Godfrey*, but it's still a lot of fun and earned Billie Burke her only Oscar nomination. *Merrily We Live* gives Ann her best character name, Minerva Harlan, and another chance at a purely comedic role, in which she fared much better than in *She's No Lady*. It's also one of the smallest roles Ann played over the course of her career. She was definitely putting her theory of quality over quantity to the test with the film, but it still was a step up from her first two freelance attempts. For *Merrily We Live* Ann was paid $2,500 a week, only $200 more than what she would have been making at Warner Bros. had she stayed.[11] A year after rebelling against the Burbank studio, Ann had found neither stronger roles nor much more money. She wrapped up her first full year as a freelancer by playing opposite Tyrone Power in a radio drama called *Never See Snow Again.*

The year 1938 would prove to be even less prolific for Ann than the previous year as she appeared in only one film, a crime drama for Republic Pictures called *Gangs of New York.* The part may have been bigger than in *Manhattan Merry-Go-Round,* but it wasn't much better and neither was the film. Inspired by a small portion of a book by Herbert Asbury of the same name (which would also be the loose inspiration for the 2002 Martin Scorsese film), *Gangs of New* York is notable today as being one of the earliest Samuel Fuller screenplays to be produced. As Fuller later recalled, "I wrote it in a day-and-a-half, just a story," which is reflected in the final product.[12] In one of moviedom's most contrived plot devices, Charles Bickford plays two unrelated men who happen to be identical. One is a known criminal, the other a police officer trying to catch the crook and his gang. Ann is a nightclub singer who aids good guy Bickford because her younger brother has gotten mixed up with the gang. We never actually get to see Ann perform in the nightclub, and her costumes, hair, and makeup are not flattering. The promise in publicity stills of a physical showdown between Ann and Wynne Gibson is missing from the actual film. The movie was directed by James Cruze, who had worked with Anna Lehr in *Ruggles of Red Gap.* For Ann, making *Gangs of New York* was not a happy experience. This would be one of the few times she exhibited temperament on a movie set, resulting in an anonymous sign posted on her dressing room mirror: "Patience is a virtue."[13] Fellow actors, such as Jane Wyatt and Hugh O'Brian, were typically quick to describe Ann as "very professional," so for her to illicit a negative response from her colleagues on *Gangs of New York* was unusual. Despite its shortcomings, the film was fairly well received by critics as "a bit improbable but none the less a good yarn."[14]

With Ann's career in a holding pattern, she and Leslie turned to what they enjoyed most, traveling. Fenton was able to take some time off from his busy directing schedule at MGM, and the couple sailed abroad for roughly three months. With the climate in Europe becoming more and more hostile under the shadow of Nazi Germany, the Fentons probably realized it would be the last time they would be able to freely travel on the continent for the foreseeable future.

Upon their return, Leslie went back to MGM, and Ann signed a three-picture deal with Columbia. The first film she made for the studio was a psychological drama called *Blind Alley*, costarring Chester Morris and Ralph Bellamy. Ann was again working under the direction of Charles Vidor, and the results were far better than their previous pairing in *She's No Lady*. Based on a play by James Warwick, the film is primarily set at the lakeside residence of a psychology professor whose dinner party goes horribly wrong when an escaped convict and his gang crash it while waiting for a boat that will take them to Canada. The ride is delayed and the wily professor (Bellamy) uses his powers of psychology to drive a murderous Chester Morris insane. Originally optioned by MGM in 1935, the film was not made at that time because Joseph Breen at the Production Code Administration found that "the whole story is so thoroughly unacceptable that we ask and urge that you dismiss it entirely from any further consideration."[15] The story then went to Fox before winding up at Columbia, which managed to get the script to adhere to the Code. Ann plays Morris's trustworthy moll. The part is actually just a variation on the supportive leading-lady roles she usually played, but this time she had the opportunity to play a bad girl, brandishing a gun while snarling and locking the hired help in the basement. She effectively alternates between a hard-as-nails dame with the hostages and a concerned nurturer to Chester Morris. Plus she looks stunning, with a subtle maturity starting to appear in her features. The original play ended with Chester Morris's character reaching a breaking point that causes him to shoot his gal and turn the gun on himself, but this was too intense for the PCA, so censorship robbed Ann of another spectacular death scene. Columbia films may not have been as highly regarded as those from Warner Bros., Paramount, or MGM, but *Blind Alley* was the strongest film and best character Ann had been given since she became a freelancer.

Ann took a brief break from the Columbia deal and returned to her original home studio, MGM, to be directed for the first time by her husband. She had first set foot inside the Culver City gates nearly a decade before as a spunky but naive teenager, trying to get work as a dancer, and now she returned as a respected, if not quite A-list, actress. Leslie Fenton would be directing his wife in *Stronger Than Desire,* a melodrama starring

Ann shares a laugh with Gary Cooper at the Pirate's Den nightclub, circa 1940.

Walter Pidgeon as a high-profile attorney who defends a working-class woman (Ann) on charges that she murdered her cad of a husband (Lee Bowman). Virginia Bruce plays Pidgeon's wife, who may actually be the guilty party. A remake of 1934's *Evelyn Prentice* starring William Powell and Myrna Loy, *Stronger Than Desire* provided Ann with another supporting role but gave her a chance to demonstrate her dramatic abilities, especially when she breaks down on the witness stand. Many of Ann's previous roles saw her playing women who were confident and self-possessed, but as Eva McLain, Ann is nervous, beaten down by a bad marriage, and self-conscious, traits she was seldom required to convey onscreen. MGM's ability to create and present Hollywood glamour was unequaled and under the expert eye of cinematographer William H. Daniels, *Stronger Than Desire* is arguably the most beautiful Ann ever looked onscreen. Leslie Fenton was proving himself as a director, and in *Stronger Than Desire* he capably guides his wife.

With their work schedules less hectic and with their more offbeat personal interests having mellowed, the couple was becoming more social and appearing at events around town. The two were spotted at an annual holiday benefit Basil Rathbone held for the Hollywood Guild, at Ciro's for a birthday bash for Mrs. Fred MacMurray, and at Mrs. Ray Milland's Brown Derby baby shower as well as at various movie screenings. It seems that after seven years of marriage, Ann and Leslie were finally tiring of their somewhat reclusive ways.

The year 1939 is frequently heralded as the high-water mark of Hollywood's golden age, with films like *Gone with the Wind*, *The Wizard of Oz*, *Stagecoach*, *Ninotchka*, *Mr. Smith Goes to Washington*, *Dark Victory*, and *The Women* all being released. It would also prove to be Ann's strongest year after departing from Warner Bros., even if she was still on the fringe of A-list Hollywood. At one point, David O. Selznick mentioned Ann as a possibility for the role of Melanie Hamilton Wilkes in *Gone with the Wind*, although he called it "a very remote possibility indeed."[16] Ann's nervous energy, which had served her so well in pre-Code roles and even in *Stronger Than Desire*, may not have lent itself so well to the part of the gentle, generous Melanie. In light of some of her acting that was to come in the mid-1940s, particularly in *Abilene Town*, a more appropriate role for Ann may have been Belle Watling, the madam with a heart of gold. However, Ann missed out on the chance for screen immortality at the Selznick studio when Olivia de Havilland was cast, and instead she went back to Columbia to make her second film.

Cafe Hostess found Ann sharing the screen with Preston Foster for a third time. In this drama she is a nightclub "hostess" who hustles male customers for drinks and lifts their wallets when prompted by the club's owner. Foster is the wise sailor who stumbles into the club, wins Ann's heart, and is more than happy to fulfill her dreams of escape, much to the chagrin of her abusive and murderous boss. At around an hour running time, *Cafe Hostess* is a B picture all the way, but it's Ann's B picture and she makes the most of this rare starring role. Her scenes with Wynne Gibson, as a former hostess who failed at going straight, are especially worthwhile. Columbia may have been considered a lower-tier studio, but its films at least gave Ann more challenging parts than the bulk of what she had been given at Warner Bros.

Following the filming of *Cafe Hostess*, Ann took the rest of 1939 off, returning to Columbia in May 1940 to make her third and final film with the studio. *Girls of the Road* was another quickie programmer running at a little over an hour, and tackled the issue of female hitchhikers and hobos. Ann plays the daughter of a governor who is compelled to infiltrate the world of women vagabonds after witnessing the state politicians' lack of empathy to their plight. With a primarily female cast, featuring Helen Mack as the world-weary Connie, Lola Lane as Ellie, a tough cookie with a heart, and Ann Doran as bad egg Jerry, the film delivers everything one would expect from a movie titled *Girls of the Road*. In preparation for the film, Ann and Helen Mack went to Saugus, a community some thirty miles north of Los Angeles, to interview female drifters. The experience affected both actresses; as Ann explained, "We found the girls to be good girls but in most cases they were so undernourished and frightened of outsiders, it was difficult to get them to talk to us."[17] *Girls of the Road* does have some over-the-top moments, such as Ann attempting to be "one of them" in a full-length white coat and expensive suitcase, along with the dilemma of Irene (Marjorie Cooley), who must make a financial choice between a wedding dress or train fare to meet her fiancé. She chooses the dress. However, the film is still admirable in its attempt to present a legitimate social issue of the time.

After nearly three years away from Warner Bros., Ann's career finally seemed to be gaining steam once again. Freelancing had started out rocky, and while the three films at Columbia weren't exactly award winners, they were solid parts for Ann with decent scripts that would hopefully pave the way to bigger and better pictures. As it turned out, *Girls of the Road* would be the last film Ann Dvorak would make in Hollywood for four years.

In 1935, as the possibility of a European war began to loom, a reporter asked Ann what that would mean for Leslie Fenton, who had retained his British citizenship. Ann was quick to respond, "If there's a war, we're going immediately to the South Seas. I wouldn't allow Leslie to go to war. I love him too much, so it's unthinkable. But I'm sure we could surely find a safe refuge in one of those little islands."[18] Five years later, these plans would turn out far different.

16

War

War had officially broken out in September 1939 when Hitler invaded Poland, and England was quickly drawn into the conflict. To many English actors residing in Hollywood, this would prove to be a call home to enlist in the service or to be near loved ones. Others remained in the United States, choosing to participate remotely through war-bond tours or by appearing in morale-boosting films. For Ann Dvorak, the wife of a British-born citizen, war would come to her doorstep much sooner than for most Americans. No matter how she may have felt about the situation, Leslie Fenton was still an Englishman at heart, even though he had lived longer in America than his homeland. Despite the very domestic existence he had been living for over eight years, Fenton had not lost his strong sense of adventure, and the opportunity to fight overseas was too alluring to resist. Any doubts about Ann's love and loyalty to Leslie Fenton were put to rest in 1940 when she literally put her life on the line for him. As it was for so many others, World War II was a time of extreme sacrifice for Ann Dvorak, yet she never behaved as if she were enduring more than anyone else. During the course of the conflict, Ann would experience adventures beyond her wildest childhood dreams as well as horrors beyond comprehension. She would also obtain a level of independence previously unknown to her. She would once again stifle her film career just as it was picking up momentum, and by the end of it all, would sacrifice something that had previously seemed enduring—her marriage.

In early June 1940 reports emerged that the Fentons were planning to buy a schooner and head for the South Seas.[1] Apparently, they did seriously consider hiding from war as Ann had predicted they would five years prior. However, less than two weeks after their schooner shopping began, Paris fell under Nazi occupation. The attack on one of their favorite cities seemed to be enough to jolt them back to reality, and in a wave of patriotic fervor, the couple penned a song entitled "Remember Paris," with Leslie writing the words and Ann composing the music. The song would eventually be arranged for radio and performed by singer Jane Froman on Chicago's WGN station.[2] Immediately following the occupation of Paris, Leslie Fenton began making plans to return to his native country and enlist in the Royal Navy.

By September 1940 all the arrangements had been made, and Fenton traveled from Hollywood to New York. From there he journeyed to Montreal, his departure point for England, and Ann was able to join him briefly before he crossed the Atlantic. The separation was excruciating for Ann, who admitted, "I'm terribly lonely. I miss him so much." It is unknown if Ann had initially intended to stay behind, but she soon began making her own plans to enter a war zone in order to be near her husband. She could not be deterred, commenting, "The danger doesn't disturb me. All that bothers me is the efforts of friends to dissuade me from going because there is danger." She added, "But I think I should be with him. I've written over 70 or 80 letters since he went over and volunteered and I've received only four—the mail is so uncertain."[3] For Ann, the decision was simple: "Les and I have never been separated. I don't think they'll let me grow a beard and join the Navy, but we'll be in the same country. And most important of all, there are lots of things I can do to help. If I'm lucky, I'll also see Les."[4] Joining her husband was no easy task, as the United States was not eager to allow its civilians to travel through dangerous waters, and a transatlantic passage was harder and harder to come by. Ann confessed, "I tried several times to go to him but the United States State Department refused me a passport through the war zone. But I obtained a British passport because while I am American by birth, I found I could be English by marriage."[5] It took Ann three months to finally secure her British passport and gain entry onto a boat that would take her away from the safety of a still uninvolved United States.

As Ann awaited her mid-December departure date, she tried her hand at live performing, traveling around the Midwest and East appearing onstage with Edmund Lowe. The veteran actor had worked out a routine for the two of them, which they performed in cities such as Chicago, Milwaukee, Indianapolis, and Hartford, whose *Courant* paper reported of Ann's performance, "As she warms up, she sends her wise-cracking lines well over the floodlights and adopts a let-her-go manner which changes the crowd's attitude toward her. Starting as simply another glamour girl, she really does (in a small way of necessity) some acting."[6] It seems Ann preferred to live out of a suitcase rather than be at home without Leslie, and care of the walnut ranch was handed over to his mother. Leslie's American-born brother Howard would visit the ranch while on leave from the military during the war, referring to it as a "paradise to escape to," adding, "My mother kept it secure."[7]

On December 15, 1940, Ann finally boarded the American Export liner SS *Exeter* in New Jersey. The ship carried only fifty-six passengers, but was loaded down with three thousand bags of mail and fourteen hundred tons of cargo.[8] Ann's ultimate destination was London, where Leslie was stationed, but the *Exeter* would be taking her first to Lisbon via Bermuda. Once in Lisbon, there was no guarantee she would be able to gain transport to London, so she ran the risk of being stranded in Portugal indefinitely. The journey across the Atlantic took eleven days and unlike trips she had taken in the past, Ann observed, "It doesn't resemble a pleasure trip in any sense of the phrase. There is a definite atmosphere aboard that is unlike anything I have ever known. We joke and try to keep as cheerful as possible, but in all our conversation, there is an undercurrent of tenseness that fades in and out, with cables, wireless messages, and the ship's news day by day. It is not a visible tenseness, but it is felt by everyone aboard this ship."[9]

As the ship traveled through enemy waters, Ann recorded, "Last night there was a report by radio that a ship of undetermined nationality was being torpedoed and was sinking within a few miles of us. We all felt strongly that we would like to go to the rescue of the survivors. But the *Exeter* continued straight on her course. I wondered whether there were tiny lifeboats being lashed about in this sea. It is so rough that we can hardly stand upright on deck for more than a minute at a time." As the journey progressed, Ann chronicled, "We are in submarine waters now and floating mines are also a topic of conversation. As I understand it, these mines break away from the moorings and drift great distances. We have one Italian woman who cries and leaves the room when we discuss the possibility of hitting a floating 'devil.' Otherwise, no one seems visibly worried over it." Ann continued, "I confess that I kept a sharp eye out for a small round object for an hour or so. But what I thought was a mine turned out to be a turtle, floating peacefully by with two bedraggled little birds on its back. Nevertheless, we have had two boat drills in eight days. I have never seen passengers ready to take a drill seriously until now."[10]

The fifty-six passengers on board represented sixteen nationalities, and Ann thought of the group as "a small floating nation of our own," noting, "And so the evenings go aboard the Exeter, Lisbon-bound. Listening to French and English spoken in Italian, Portuguese and Hungarian dialects has not only gone a long way towards ruining my French but has done a good job of ruining my English, such as it was." Of her fellow passengers, she recorded, "When we reach shore we will soon be scattered over the face of Europe, but for a brief period of 11 days we have a revealing glimpse into one another's lives and thoughts." On the ship were "four American boys in the diplomatic service" who were "all enthusiastic over the prospect of seeing Europe under war conditions and are just now in the stage between the glamour and the reality." The main topic of conversation among the passengers was politics, though Ann noted, "The only ones who don't appear to take an interest in political discussions are the Japanese, who have a table to themselves and are the only passengers who order wine with dinner." When the passengers weren't discussing politics, "common topic of conversation among us is how soon we will be able to get out of Lisbon. We have heard there is a waiting list of over 200 for the plane to London."[11] Christmas on the liner came and went, though Ann did not record how, or if, the holiday was celebrated.

Ann landed in Lisbon in time for New Year's Eve. For the first time in her life, she was completely on her own and facing an uncertain future. The rumors of being delayed in Portugal proved to be correct and Ann remained in Lisbon a little over a month. As she waited to obtain passage on a plane that would take her to London, and Leslie Fenton, Ann fulfilled a lifelong dream of newspaper reporting. She penned an article describing her transatlantic crossing that was distributed by the North American Newspaper Alliance and picked up by newspapers in the States, carrying the byline "Ann Dvorak Fenton." She was reportedly also going to be writing pieces about refugees stranded in Lisbon, but if she did produce these articles, they have yet to surface.

Ann was finally able to get on a plane to London in late January 1941. She arrived after midnight in an airfield outside the city, which was in the midst of the Blitz. Leslie Fenton had been temporarily relieved of his naval duties to direct *The Saint's Vacation*, starring Hugh Sinclair, and was filming at the Denham Film Studios, roughly twenty miles outside of London. With air-raid sirens blaring, Ann successfully used a £5 note to bribe a cab

A portrait of Ann during the war years.

driver to make the harrowing trip to the studio. When they reached Ann's destination, the cabby refused the extra tip, commenting he had "never seen a better raid in my life. Worth the price of admission."[12] Ann and the driver were quickly pulled behind the studio gates, which were blocked with sandbags, and Leslie Fenton was notified via telephone that his wife had finally made it to England. He arrived at the studio as soon as possible, wearing pajamas and an overcoat. Ann, Leslie, the cab driver, and the studio gatekeeper shared some tea, brewed in the gatekeeper's office, and enjoyed the Christmas decorations that were still hanging up, awaiting Ann's arrival. The Fentons then retreated to Leslie's nearby quarters while the cab driver was set up in a star dressing room to spend the rest of the night.[13] After five months of separation, the Fentons were finally together again.

The reunion was short-lived, as Leslie soon returned to service and Ann turned her attentions to helping with the war effort. Almost immediately after arriving in England, the weekly news periodical *Illustrated* recruited Ann as a reporter. She jumped at the chance to continue the journalistic pursuits she had begun in Lisbon and eagerly departed for her first assignment, to the East Anglia region of the country to write about the day-to-day lives of residents in a locale known as "Invasion Village." Ann was accompanied by photographer Haywood Magee, who was initially apprehensive, noting, "Decidedly the whole idea was an experiment. Here was an American girl, and a film star at that, setting out on what was anything but a 'boudoir' assignment." However, Ann quickly won the cameraman over. "Any other girl, I believe, would have taken the two-day option, boarded a train and waved me a relieved 'goodbye'—but not Ann Dvorak. She stayed on, just refused to surrender to the difficulties and discomforts of reporting 'out in the blue' of an England at war and during a week got close to the hearts of those strange quiet men and women of the sea. I like to think that Ann got closer to us English folk than any American has during these haunting days." Ann enjoyed meeting with the "people who speak with a lilt and a twang, and men who walk with the roll of a ship." It took the locals a little while to warm up to the "smart-looking young lady and a man without a hat carrying a tripod upon which a camera might possibly be erected." As Ann wrote, "Ferreting them out was the hardest job I think I ever had. In the first place, suspicion is the keynote of the village. Everyone suspects the stranger in town. You're a foreigner if you've lived there for less than twenty-five years, anyway."[14] However, they eventually came around and Ann got her story about the remote village.

For her second *Illustrated* assignment, Ann was sent on the road with the King's Lynn Follies, a group of amateur actors comprised of hairdressers, photographers, secretaries, and grocers, among others, who were, in Ann's estimation, "actors in the true sense, bringing gaiety and laughter to thousands of boys stationed in deserted Tommy towns; in isolated units where nothing breaks the lonely monotony of duty." Despite the fact that "sometimes the show is stopped during raids when they can hardly hear themselves over the din of bombs," Ann seemed to genuinely enjoy traveling with the troupe. She was especially taken with one member of the group: "Billy Bray traveling grocer and female impersonator in the show reminds me vividly of a great American comedian, Chic Sale. Whether Billy likes it or not, he is the star of the Follies. I hope that after the war Billy will entertain again with his song 'Blackout Bella, the whitest girl in town.' It's one of the funniest routines I've ever seen put across on the stage."[15]

During this time Ann was befriended by a young man named Charles Foster, who later went on to become an entertainment publicist. As he recalled:

I met Ann Dvorak in 1941 when I was only 18. I met her several weeks before I joined the Royal Air Force but had no idea at first she was anyone other than Ann McKim, the name on the mail box in the apartment she had rented in Walton-On-Thames, Surrey. She must have been about 28 and was surely the most beautiful person I had ever met. I was living at 75 Hersham Road in a huge apartment lent to me by my uncle Tommy (Sir Thomas Beecham the London Symphony conductor). The other half of the house was a separate luxury apartment that Uncle Tommy's agents rented out to "appropriate people" from time to time. Other show-business people in from the United States had rented the apartment before, it was very beautiful. I spotted her walking around the grounds of the house and made that a good enough excuse to go out and see who this gorgeous new arrival might be. I introduced myself and she introduced herself as Ann McKim! We soon became good friends and walked along Hersham Road to the centre of Walton on a number of occasions to see movies. I noticed people looking at her intently but had no idea that she was really Ann Dvorak. She accompanied me to three musical shows in London and I remember at the Prince of Wales Theatre a man came over and asked for her autograph. She shook her

head and said, "I think you are mistaking me for someone else."
We walked away with several people gazing at her. I recall telling
her she was beautiful enough to be a film star.[16]

After her *Illustrated* assignments, Ann became a member of the
Mechanised Transport Corps (MTC), a uniformed female civilian organization operating with the support of the Ministry of Transport. As a
recruit of the MTC, Ann would be driving an ambulance around London.
She was required to undergo three weeks of intensive training, which
included vehicle maintenance, map reading, and first aid.[17] Ann's fellow
ambulance drivers were initially wary of her. "Because I was the only
American in the corps and the only actress, my co-workers regarded me a
bit skeptically at first. But they soon learned that neither an American nor
an actress was so different from themselves—frightened when they were,
tired when they were, eager to work with them."[18] After completing the
training, Ann dove into the work and enthusiastically wrote to a friend in
the States, "I drive ambulances and trucks up the wrong side of the street,
and can change a tire in ten minutes flat! And I'm my own mechanic and
grease monkey—mostly grease!"[19] Ann and the other women in the MTC
faced some outside hurdles; as Ann recounted, "In the beginning,
Londoners—particularly the men—were inclined to laugh at the ladies in
fancy uniforms, driving 'lorries' about the streets." However, as the Blitz
intensified, "they were grateful when these same ladies arrived with ambulances to rush the wounded to medical care." The work was grueling.
"Our corps schedule was on a 48-hour basis. We were on duty or on call
for 48 hours, then off for 48 hours. And I could be proud of my sex in
general. For the corps was only one among many women's services."[20]
Ann became such an adept mechanic that reports later popped up claiming she was going to compose a driving guide for women with mechanical
advice and tips such as "Engine oil cleans off as easily as cold cream and
won't harm the complexion."[21] Sadly, the Ann Dvorak guide to automo-
tive mechanics never became a reality.

When she wasn't working for the MTC, Ann lived like other
Londoners, which meant coping with frequent bombardments from the
German Luftwaffe. She quickly came to admire the resilience of the British
people, commenting, "Somehow it's not the obvious things that keep
impressing you in London. The destruction is vaguely familiar—like
newspaper pictures of earthquake damage suddenly come to life. That

Ann (right) in uniform for the Mechanised Transit Corps.

catch in your throat for those lovely old London landmarks gets you sometimes. But somehow it isn't the scarred edges of a crater. It isn't the gaping hole piled high with twisted girders. It's the little sign you find tacked to a mass of debris—'Cottwitts regrets to have moved around the corner.'" She continued, "It's the quick flutter of a ragged dusty Union

Jack hanging somewhere in the wreckage. The fleeting expression on the grimy face of a boy in a demolition gang, or the red-rimmed eyes of a fire fighter." Ann was clearly proud to be among "the passing parade of Piccadilly growing more cheerfully shabby everyday," and was constantly aware of her surroundings. "An old station master I know feeds the birds at tea time and keeps a gun by his side in case of invasion. There is an ever growing heap of rubble in the park, carted there from the ruins of many an Englishman's home. Cigarette machines are marked Empty, tobacco stores Closed. Woolworth's windows display huge sacks of potatoes and little signs say No Hairpins." In the midst of the ruin, Ann marveled at the locals' ability to maintain a sense of humor: "A famous dinner club's orchestra has an alert signature song. When the siren goes it plays Here We Go, and for the all-clear Happy Days Are Here Again." She also recorded, "A voice I shall always remember was that of a lady in curlers who in the midst of the thunder and deafening noise of a bad blitz, leaned out her window and shouted to a group of us standing in the street, 'Please don't talk so loudly—I'm trying to sleep.'"[22]

Ann may have been trying to hold her head high during these times, but she admitted that an air-raid alert "came to mean only fear and hope that you would survive this one too. No plans were made for more than an hour ahead. You walked in darkness every night. Yet the bleakness of that life was brightened by England's undying courage and will to win." Ann described being "bombed out of a London flat and left with make-shift quarters in what Londoners call a 'mews'—an alley, that is."[23] Once she was back in the States, Ann tried to give some perspective to her fellow countrymen, explaining, "In America, you can't imagine what it is really like. We civilians are not in a state of war here. In England, it is different. It is death not only for those in the Service, but for old people, children, everyone."[24] During the raids Ann would find comfort listening to the song "Jalousie" by Jacob Gade, which was the lone recording in her possession. After she returned to the United States, Ann suffered a serious flashback when pianist Phil Ohman performed the song at the Mocambo nightclub. As soon as Ann heard the first few notes, she ran into the powder room, where she was discovered shaking like a leaf as the memories of her months in London came rushing back. Out of respect for the shell-shocked actress, Ohman dropped the song from his repertoire.[25]

As grueling as the constant air raids were, Ann discovered one little thing that stood out for her when she wrote to the Ray Millands: "War or no war, the thing I miss the most is silk stockings. Not that I particularly care—but believe it or not, the boys in the service actually want the girls who drive ambulances to wear good-looking hose!"[26] The silk stocking shortage had become such an issue that when Ann first left the States, she was advised to bring plenty of pairs of the precious commodity with her to London because, as she explained, "There are many women there who are going without hose. And . . . there is a movement among certain classes to advocate the prohibition of silk stockings entirely so that those who can't afford them will not feel conspicuous."[27]

Despite Ann's obligations to *Illustrated* and the MTC, it did not take long for her to resume her previous occupation. In early May 1941, roughly three months after arriving in England, Ann went to work for, of all companies, Warner Bros. Apparently, in the face of a real war, Ann and her former employer were able to put their differences behind them, and she headed to the company's studio in the Teddington area of London. *This Was Paris* stars Ann as an American fashion designer in France who is suspected of working for a German fifth column within Paris. Griffith Jones is a British intelligence officer investigating Ann who falls in love with her, and Ben Lyon is the drunken, ornery Australian newspaper reporter observing it all. This propaganda film, which seems to be addressing fears of a divergent faction operating in Britain, is an interesting look at English film production during the height of the Blitz, even if it wasn't exactly a showcase role for Ann. In a case of art imitating life, Ann's character ditches her primary occupation in order to drive an ambulance. Ann donated the money she made from the film to the MTC.[28] During production Ann even took time to correspond with Jack Warner, writing, "We are working here with a very short crew, as you know, and it would do your heart good to see how everyone carried on in the face of difficulties that seem positively insurmountable. One man was working rather late one night and his home was bombed. When he got to the ruins all he could find was his wife's arm. See what I mean? What they don't realize in Hollywood is that it is very important to keep the film business going in England. The money it brings into the country buys all sorts of fighting planes." She continued, "We have a sign at the studio gate which says: 'Act victory, think victory, or damn well shut up.'" Warner Bros. had been the first American movie studio to openly oppose the Third Reich, with its 1939 release *Confessions of a Nazi Spy*, and Jack Warner no doubt admired Ann's decision to go to England, admitting, "I read Ann Dvorak's letters myself many times, and I read them to others on the lot."[29] Despite the newfound respect that seems to have developed between Ann and Jack Warner, *This Was Paris* was the last film she would make bearing the Warner Bros. shield.

After completing *This Was Paris*, Ann resumed her duties with the Mechanised Transport Corps. The work proved to be a godsend on one particular night when the Greenwich district was severely bombed while Leslie Fenton was stationed there. Despite being sick with worry, Ann worked unceasingly for twenty-four hours. She later admitted that she and "the people of England could never have survived the terrible bombings if it hadn't been that they were so well organized, that they all had work to do."[30] Much to Ann's relief, Leslie survived the attack unscathed. Little did she know that the worst was yet to come for her husband.

17

Ann of All Trades

In the spring of 1941, Leslie Fenton received the rank of lieutenant in the Royal Naval Volunteer Reserve (RNVR). One year later he was commanding a ship in the now-legendary raid on St. Nazaire, known as Operation Chariot. St. Nazaire was a port town in German-occupied France that provided the Nazis with a dry dock for repairing their ships. In January 1942 the imposing battleship *Tirpitz* was docked at St. Nazaire, and the Royal Navy and British commandos immediately launched a plan to prevent the battleship from entering Atlantic waters and to put the dry dock out of commission once and for all. On March 28, 1942, the raid was launched, with Leslie Fenton commanding one of the smaller ships, *Motor Launch (ML) 156*. The operation would prove successful, though it came at a high cost, with a large percentage of the men involved being killed, wounded, or taken prisoner by the Germans. Fenton joined the ranks of the wounded when early on in the action a shell "transferred part of the bridge and some shrapnel into my left leg and the leg of Captain Hooper, the Commando officer who was on the bridge with me."[1] After the events, word was sent to Ann that her husband had been severely injured in the raid, though it would take time for Leslie to be transferred to a hospital close enough for her to see him.

Ann resigned her post with the MTC and made the journey to see Fenton.

Leslie had been wounded and had been in the hospital for two months. I traveled from London to see him. Traveling in war time is like being on a boat with Russian refugees. People were lying in the aisles. The trains were jammed. When I got to the town, it was jammed too. I walked the streets, went from door to door looking for a place to stay. I finally slept all night in an old summer house off the country road.

The next morning I visited my husband. He was on his back on a fracture board. He couldn't move. That night the blitz began. It was the night of the Bath raid, and it was worse than Coventry. It lasted all night. I knew the hospital was being bombed. I saw fires. It had been hit several times. Some of the patients could walk; others could be moved. But Leslie was help-less. I remembered that other night when I had been on duty when I thought Leslie was in the flames of Greenwich, and I prayed to God for work. Because of work, I lived through that first night. I died through this second one.

Morning came at last. I was able to telephone him. He was safe. He was as glad to hear my voice and I was to hear his. For he had spent the night in desperation too. The town was pulver-ized, and he didn't know if I had found shelter.[2]

Ann was not going to take any more chances if she could help it; she wrote to an acquaintance back home, "I've made friends with the head nurse. She lets me sleep by the floor of his bed." Despite the gruesome events of the preceding months, being reunited with Leslie seemed to be rejuvenating for Ann. She lightheartedly reported, "Les is badly hurt. His hip and pelvis have been smashed. They've got him all wrapped up like a mummy, but he's still laughing. Yesterday I threatened to shave him. He refused hotly, said it was the first time his beard has been long enough to lie back and enjoy it."[3]

Leslie was eventually transported to a hospital in London, but when it was determined that his injuries would take considerable time to heal, Ann reported, "They've moved Les to one of the provincial hospitals where he can get specialized care." Ann wasn't able to accompany him on the trip, but soon made plans to be with him at the hospital, which was located in Devon, a county in southwestern England. The journey from London, over two hundred miles, was far from comfortable, and Ann relayed, "There are no reserved seats on the trains anymore. In fact, there are no seats. I ate, slept and squatted on the floor in the aisle. I said slept a sentence back. I didn't sleep, but my body did. I prickled and twinged the whole trip and wished I knew more about untying knots. When the train pulled in I was one endless chain of Double Bolans [bowlines]."[4]

Once Leslie was settled into his new quarters, Ann discovered yet another way to be useful to the war effort by joining the Women's Land Army. The WLA was a civilian organization whose vast numbers worked the fields in order to harvest enough crops to keep the nation fed. The work Ann engaged in turned out to be very different from tending to a walnut ranch in the San Fernando Valley; as she wrote to a friend, "I'm doing farm work for Navy Aid. You'd never know me. I'm quite frightening. We farm from four in the morning until it's too dark to see, and it is the truth that these early morning hour mists are real soupers!" She continued, "I'm living with an elderly woman, and the two of us have ploughed and planted three acres of carrots and beets without the benefit of a horse—unless you want to call me the horse. She steers while I pull. Everything we raise is given to the destitute families of Navy men and to hospitals. You never see a man in the fields!"[5] Even though the WLA was a civilian group, Ann called it "a real military unit which campaigns for food as systematically as the armed forces campaign for victory. In harvest times school children and all others who can aid are called out, but the regularly drafted Land Army works steadily at its job, under orders." Ann was awed by how the WLA "has turned an island which never dreamed of feeding itself into a place which produces an astonishing amount of food." As she continued working the land, Ann eagerly wrote to friends in the States requesting they send fruit and vegetable seeds because "there is a terrible shortage here. Also, flower seeds of all kinds. Sounds crazy, but it will be fun to think some day of California wild flowers growing between English daisies and blue bells."[6]

After a year and a half of experiencing abject horrors, Ann seemed to settle into her new life in Devon and actually enjoyed working the fields with her husband nearby. She wrote to a friend, "It's wonderful having Les so near me now, though he is in great pain, and the bones are taking forever to mend. You'll think me awful saying this, but as much as I want him to hurry and get well, I still wish it would take a long time. The minute he's well, he'll go back and I'll lose him again. I know it's what he has to do, but sometimes you can't help wishing it weren't." Exhibiting typical Dvorak spunk, Ann followed up these melancholy sentiments with, "Yesterday while I was ploughing, a funny thought struck me. Who would have imagined five years ago, that I would be married to Les who wanted to be a director and who now was a Lieutenant on a British war ship? And who would have thought that I—a girl who wanted to be an actress, would now be a war-time farmerette!"[7] She also marveled how programs like the WLA were "resulting in a remarkable back-to-the-farm movement. Typists and office workers who always lived in the city are working on farms and loving it. Some of the farmers' families whom they are helping want to adopt them. Some of the girls marry farmers. And when the war is over they're going to remain in the country, bringing a new type of woman to the farm."[8]

Eventually, Leslie Fenton recovered enough to be released from the hospital and return to the city. However, the navy still considered him an invalid, and much to Ann's relief, he would not be reporting back to active duty. "Les is on his feet again, but they won't let him go back to sea. He's grumbling in an office in the War Department. I've moved to London to be with him." Shortly after returning to the city, Ann received an offer to appear in motion pictures once again, and as she responded, "Of course I was delighted. Only one drawback—have to wear gloves saturated with hand cream night and day." After working the fields in Devon for a few months, "my hands are better fitted to hold rakes than rings. But in a way, I hope I never lose the stains from the rich red loam of Devon. Next to my own ground in the San Fernando Valley, it is the most beautiful soil on earth!"[9]

The film, *Squadron Leader X*, is an espionage thriller starring Eric Portman as a Nazi flying ace masquerading as an English airman in Belgium on a mission to distribute anti-British propaganda. When he inadvertently ends up in Britain, he attempts to get back to Germany by blackmailing his ex-fiancée (Ann) into assisting him. Based on a story by Emeric Pressburger, who would later gain acclaim for writing the screenplay for *The Red Shoes*, and directed by Lance Comfort, the film was produced by RKO Radio British Productions (which was also responsible for Leslie Fenton's *The Saint's Vacation*) and distributed in the United States by RKO Radio Pictures. For this higher-budget production, Ann returned to the Denham studios, where she had spent her first night in England. *Squadron Leader X* was well received by critics as well as the public.[10]

During the production, Ann was able to renew her friendship with Charles Foster, the young RAF pilot who had befriended her without realizing who she was. Foster later recalled that after he completed his initial drill training "I was astonished to hear that 10 of us had been loaned by the RAF to take walk-on roles in an RKO film. The first day we arrived at the studio I was astonished to see 'Ann McKim' rehearsing for

Ann and Eric Portman from the "lost" film *Squadron Leader X*.

her starring role in *Squadron Leader X*. When she saw me she rushed over. 'Sorry I didn't tell you who I really was,' she said. 'We were having such a great time and you liked me as Ann McKim not Ann Dvorak. That is a rare thing for me.'" He continued, "I explained why I and nine other very new airmen were present. None of us had lines of course and we spent most of our time watching Ann. Everyone else was jealous that Ann and I ate our lunches together."[11] During Ann's remaining time in England, she would spend quite a bit of time with Foster whenever his RAF schedule permitted.

Squadron Leader X proved to be such a positive experience that shortly after its British release in November 1942, Ann returned to the Denham studios to make *Escape to Danger*, another large-scale production starring Eric Portman and again directed, at least in part, by Lance Comfort.[12] This time around, Ann plays the spy, who has a day job as a schoolteacher, and *Escape to Danger* afforded her another opportunity to perish onscreen. This film was also produced by RKO, which again distributed the film to theaters in Britain and the United States. Curiously, no prints for either title are known to exist; *Escape to Danger* and *Squadron Leader X* are both considered "lost" films. Of the two, *Squadron Leader X* seems to have been the better received, and in 2010 the British Film Institute named it as one of its seventy-five most wanted films that are missing, believed lost.

Ann would make one other film during her time in England; a short feature directed by Leslie Fenton. After being denied active service in the Royal Navy, Fenton turned his attention to the Ministry of Information and had become interested in adapting the short stories of author H. E. Bates for the screen. As Bates later recalled, Fenton was "contacting the Ministry of Information on some propaganda project or other [when] he came across the stories of Flying Officer X, for which he at once evinced an enormous admiration. As a result he made it his business to get to know me and then when we met declared, and in no uncertain terms, that the stories were not only admirable in themselves but that unquestionably they ought to be filmed."[13] Fenton would end up directing two of Bates's short stories as films: *It's Just the Way It Is* and *There's a Future in It*. The latter co-stars Ann and Barry Morse, who would later find fame on the television show *The Fugitive*. *There's a Future in It* centers on Morse as an ace flying pilot, risking life and limb for his country as well as his girl, played by Ann. She in turn must endure the constant threat of losing him in battle along with the ridicule of her well-to-do parents, who do not approve of her dating a man they see as common. The film runs only a little over twenty minutes, but gets across the point that everyone should support the country's brave boys rather than passing judgment on them. Ann's performance is uneven, but considering the conditions in which the film was made, she does an adequate job. In her early thirties at the time, she has some difficulty pulling off a character who is supposed to be ten or so years younger. At times she affects a slight British accent, which may have been the result of living in England for a couple of years rather than a conscious effort. In some scenes Ann looks worn out, which could be attributed to the lower quality of production than her Hollywood films or to the sheer strain of living in wartime conditions. Ann herself identified the limitations an actor could experience under the circumstances. "To give a truly good performance, an actor ought to be free from pressure and apprehension. A writer or a painter may thrive on physical hardship, but an actor shrivels up inside when he's deprived of light, heat, food, transportation and laundry." However, she felt she was able to overcome the harsh conditions of her environment: "I managed to do my job only because I'd been trained to surmount physical discomforts by life on tramp steamers and in primitive places."[14] Whatever shortcomings Ann's performance in *There's a Future in It* may have, her final scene in the film, in which she looks, teary-eyed, up to the British skies, is classic Dvorak.

By early 1943 Leslie Fenton was sufficiently recovered and busy with the Ministry of Information and Ann had completed production on *Escape to Danger,* so she felt comfortable accepting an invitation from fellow actress Bebe Daniels to join a traveling show performing for the troops. Daniels, who was married to Ann's *This Was Paris* costar, Ben Lyon, had also recruited composer and banjo player Freddy Morgan along with brothers Len and Bill Lowe. The show, which also included dancers and a seven-piece orchestra, was rehearsed for about a week, and the troop hit the road in mid-February 1943.[15] The company's first stops were in Northern Ireland, where the group performed at Red Cross clubs and military hospitals. The early performances were a bit bumpy, as Ann later admitted: "Some of the first shows that went out to the camps and the hospitals actually did more harm than good because of the way they were put together and the subject material." She continued, "But don't get me wrong. Those early shows, most of them filled a definite, pressing need for morale boosting. It's just that entertaining the troops on this new, mass worldwide basis was something on which there were no rules and few guides."[16] One of the bits included the performers throwing vegetables, chicken, and beer to the members of the audience who sang along the loudest. The crowd ate these "prizes" up both figuratively and literally, and also enjoyed participating in a live version of the popular American program *Truth or Consequences.*[17] The group traveled around Ireland and parts of England, and Williams B. Dover, the head of the U.S. Army's Special Services Section, included Ann and Bebe Daniels on a short list of "trailblazers" in the USO Camp Show movement.[18] When they weren't onstage, Dvorak and Daniels could be found visiting wounded soldiers in hospitals, looking like the film stars that they were. In full hair and makeup, clad in a fur coat, Ann was a far cry from the self-described grease monkey and farmerette she had been during the preceding two years. The pair performed together for over three months, and then, "After the first tour, Bebe and I split up, each heading our own company, so that we might entertain twice as many soldiers."[19]

In May 1943 Ann developed her own camp show, called *Hi De Ho,*

Ann and Bebe Daniels outside a hospital in Belfast during their camp show tour. Pictured with them are Major S. Vogel, Major J. Franklin, Andre Van Zandt, Major L. Charney, and First Lieutenant George P. Kelly. On the staircase are fellow camp show performers Freddie Morgan, Len and Bill Lowe, and Matty Heft.

which included dancers, singers, comedians, and musicians.[20] As she recorded, "After the American troops landed, I worked for the USO, entertaining all over England, Ireland, and Scotland. You've heard that our men overseas find more than entertainment in the USO shows. In my case, the situation was reversed. I don't know what my work did for the morale of those troops. I do know what it did for my own morale. You can imagine what it meant to me, an American girl, to stand up before my compatriots over there. It was a poignant reminder of home."[21] Ann toured relentlessly with *Hi De Ho* into the summer months, but she and Leslie Fenton had begun to feel a strong call to return home. Leslie had received the Distinguished Service Cross for his participation in the St. Nazaire raid, and had also been invalided out of the Royal Navy. Closing in on their third year in a war-torn country, the two decided they had had enough. They soon began making arrangements to return to Los Angeles.

Ann chats with Private Joseph D'Onofrio at a hospital in Belfast as nurses L. Carpenter and Andre Van Zandt look on.

The couple's plans were temporarily postponed when Ann was asked to fill in at the last minute in a London Red Cross production of *The Eve of St. Mark,* which had previously enjoyed a successful run on Broadway.[22] Virginia Chew, the Red Cross nurse who had been playing one of the main roles, had been stricken with jaundice and the play was in danger of closing. The cast and crew collectively agreed that Ann Dvorak was the only hope for the show. Ann's immediate response was, "I'm war weary. I've had three years of war and need a rest." When she was informed that the play would therefore need to close, she replied, "If that's the alternative, just forget what I said. I'll do it."[23] Roughly forty-eight hours later, Ann entered the theater to apply the makeup and grease paint that would make her appear twenty years older. She took the stage to loud cheers from the soldiers, sailors, and WACs (members of the Women's Army Corps) in the audience.

In two and a half years in Europe, Ann had served as war correspondent, ambulance driver, farmer, film actress, and camp show performer. In later years, she would also list among her war duties "shortwave broadcast to US & ships at sea from BBC London." Bizarrely, she would also claim to have performed confidential services for Tomas Garrigue Masaryk, the president of Czechoslovakia.[24] However, the Czech president had died in September 1937, a full three years before Ann arrived in Europe. It's possible that instead Ann was in contact with Masaryk's son, Jan, who was exiled in London but serving as a foreign minister to the Czech government. The younger Masaryk had famously struck up a friendship with actress Myrna Loy, which so infuriated Adolph Hitler that he banned her films in Germany. Given this relationship, it's not out of the question that Jan Masaryk would have interacted with Ann while she was in London. If this were the case, the relationship was not given the public exposure that Loy's support received.

On August 27, 1943, a week or so after finishing the run of *The Eve of St Mark*, Ann and Leslie boarded the RMS *Mauretania*. The trip home proved to be much easier for Ann than the passage she had taken in 1940, as the ship departed from Liverpool and arrived in New York six days later. When the Fentons boarded, Leslie identified himself as a "film director," the same occupation he had listed before the war. Ann, however, listed herself not as an actress but rather as a "journalist," a post she had first strived for when she was fifteen. The Fentons had spent almost three years with the war directly on their doorstep, and the experience had been transformative. For the first time in her life, Ann had experienced true independence and learned to be self-sufficient. Now, as they looked west toward the lives they had left behind, only time would tell if Leslie Fenton and Ann Dvorak would be able to pick up where they had left off.

18

Shell Shocked

After nearly three years of being submerged in the day-to-day trials of war, Ann Dvorak and Leslie Fenton were finally back in the United States. The experience of being on soil untouched by bombs was initially surreal for Ann; after arriving in New York, she "walked around just looking and wondering for four days. I was astonished to discover how completely I had forgotten the plenty and warmth of America." She continued, "When I came west on the train, I was excited again by the spaciousness and richness of our country."[1] Even though the country was fully engaged in war production in terms of manufacturing and manpower, the Fentons could not help but observe, "It's almost like the war is over, coming back here after living in England, and we don't mean this as any criticism, merely observation." They continued, "Besides, the war is so close in England. For a long time it was right overhead and at your front door. No one knew what would happen next. That put a strain on every one that has never, fortunately, been experienced here and makes the way of life easier and less nerve-racking."[2] Ann was also quick to note, "You don't know what America is until you leave it. You miss the little things—sunshine, gay shop windows, the corner drug store and the hamburger stand. There's a symbol of America."[3]

As happy as the Fentons were to be back in the United States, Ann still noted some key differences between English people and Americans, and she was not shy to criticize her compatriots: "There would be no paper shortages in America if we were half as earnest and systematic as the English. There it is against the law to throw away even a transfer or a bus check. Paper saving and grease saving are not left to voluntary effort. Grease and paper are systematically collected, from door to door. Here I offer grease to a butcher and he doesn't want to bother with it. Many things like that show the differences between the war effort there and here."⁴ Ann also had stern words for her countrywomen when she spoke to the Hollywood Women's Press Club. She strongly believed that not enough women were volunteering for work in war plants and that a draft for women was a possible solution, noting, "American women don't seem to realize they're needed. I've heard all kinds of excuses."⁵ Another key difference Ann noticed between women in the two countries was the American emphasis on glamour, observing, "English girls are charming, but America is a woman's country while England is a man's. American men have faith in a woman's world so American women, to live up to that faith constantly make the most of themselves with individual personalities and flawless appearances. For instance, when I knew Leslie was coming home on leave I spent hours prettying up for him, hunting out my most attractive clothes. The English girls in the ambulance corps couldn't understand me. 'Why bother when you're married to him?' they'd say, amazed. You can see why American boys are homesick for ankle bracelets, high heels, flattering dresses, flowers in their hair, bright lipstick and perfume."⁶

The couple also noticed a great deal of positive change in their American friends, commenting, "People here may not be aware of it, but after being away we see it." The two, who had never shown any religious preference, elaborated: "People seem to pray more. More people go to church. They've gotten closer to the land, too, which is a good thing for both the people and the land. Everyone has a garden. When people can't get help they learn to do things for themselves. Many people we know who never lifted a finger when we went away are doing their own house-work, mending, cleaning. All this is good." Ann and Leslie had also expe-rienced a great deal of change themselves. The two, who once upon a time had declared they did not have nor need any friends, now stated that the key to becoming reacclimated was to "get yourself a circle of friends, either old ones if you return home or new ones, if you settle into a new place. But get a community group around you."⁷

Leslie Fenton was eager to get back behind the movie camera, but the resumption of their film careers was put temporarily on hold. As he explained, "When we returned, I wanted to get right back to work. But Ann's first thought was to get ourselves into proper shape. We went back to the San Fernando Valley ranch. She got our old cook back, and the first thing we did was to see that the land was in order. We planted a victory garden. Now all the fruit and vegetables we use come off our own land."

Ann and Leslie at home shortly after returning from war-torn Europe.

Ann was equally proud of how the Fentons were utilizing the land on the walnut ranch, explaining, "Everyone in England grows his own produce. There is so little land for growing there, and when we got back I realized there is so much here. It was our duty, to ourselves and to the country, to be as self-sustaining as possible. It may be a little hard to understand here, but it's not in England, where an orange, a carrot, or an onion is worth its weight in gold."[8] Ann and Leslie eagerly posed for press photographers at their home, performing various tasks around the ranch—hoeing, riding a tractor—or just enjoying each other's company.

On the surface it seemed that Ann had easily slid back into her prewar life, but this was far from the truth. She fell into a deep depression. As she later admitted, "I was like many of the soldiers who are returning from the war. I had to get my perspective again. After all, when people live through a violation of everything that is normal for four years, it takes a year or two getting used to the normal again."[9] One of the main reasons she had been hesitant to resume her film career was that she was self-conscious about her appearance and thought audiences had forgotten about her: "I came back tired, naturally, but I wasn't prepared to be greeted like a rather well-preserved survivor from another generation. I'd meet people at parties and they'd fairly gasp as they exclaimed over how well I looked, just as they might if they'd seen Whistler's Mother with a face-lift." She also half-jokingly said, "When I came back, I discovered that I was a hag, at least 99 years old and ready for characters." After receiving this response more than a few times, "I began looking into my mirror, wondering. It wasn't good for me and I had to snap out of it."[10] On another occasion, Ann noted, "It was a painful thing to come home to Hollywood, for it's still largely untouched by any of the things going on in Europe. Hollywood stands blessedly in the middle of a productive area where foodstuffs are plentiful. Film making goes on very much as usual. They make war films and go to see them, but they still don't realize. It won't be until the return of the men who have been through the war and know Europe and Asia, that Hollywood really will find out about the war."[11]

One thing Ann did to pull herself out of the doldrums was visit army hospitals, which, she said, "made me happy as a schoolgirl."[12] She also began lending her expertise to the preparation of USO camp shows because "during those three awful years in England, I got a pretty good impression about what the boys wanted."[13] Ann turned down an offer to go on a lecture tour, but agreed to a brief Red Cross tour, and she continued to do little things for the British war effort like sending dried lemon peels to her friends in England and collecting toys to send to British children for the holidays. There were reports she would continue her role as a journalist for a London publication, with assignments comparing America and Britain in such areas as women in war work and conditions in mining industries, but it's unclear if these were ever published. There were other reports about her progress on the ill-fated auto-repair manual for women as well as a manuscript detailing her wartime experiences in Europe. As with the project to document her world travels in 1932, nothing ever came of these. She did pen a couple of articles for movie magazines, but it seems as though her career as a journalist was fairly short-lived once she returned home.

When Ann finally gained enough confidence to again tackle her film career, rumors started popping up that Paramount and RKO were both vying for her services, with the latter wanting to reteam her with Dick Powell in an adaptation of the Raymond Chandler novel *Farewell, My Lovely*, ultimately released as *Murder, My Sweet*.[14] Ann's contemporary

Ann at her Encino ranch in 1943.

Claire Trevor played opposite Powell's Philip Marlowe instead. British film mogul Arthur Rank was also reported to have offered Ann a five-year deal to make British productions, though it's hard to imagine she would have been willing to return overseas.[15]

Nine months after returning to the States, Ann finally signed a three-picture, nonexclusive deal with Republic.[16] In her first film, she would be costarring with John Wayne and Joseph Schildkraut in the period drama

Flame of Barbary Coast. Republic was not, and would never be, an A-list studio, but *Flame of Barbary Coast* was a major production for the company, and this marked the first time Ann would have the opportunity to appear in a costume film. It also provided her with a rare opportunity to play a starring role and she received top billing alongside Wayne, whose star had been on the rise since 1939's *Stagecoach* and was still rising. *Flame* presents Wayne as a green cowhand who encounters hostile casino owners (led by Schildkraut) on the notorious Barbary Coast. Schildkraut becomes even more hostile when Wayne wins the affections of a sassy saloon singer named Ann "Flaxen" Tarry.[17] *Flame of Barbary Coast* would mark the first time Ann performed multiple full-blown song and dance numbers. She had sung briefly onscreen in *Scarface, Molly Louvain, "G" Men,* and *Bright Lights,* but *Flame* really gave her the opportunity to showcase her talents in numbers like "Love, Here Is My Heart" and "That Man (Is Always on My Mind)." Virginia Grey provides additional sassiness as the new babe in town and shares a delightfully catty scene with Ann who, upon meeting Grey, chimes, "We're not going to like each other very much, are we?" The film culminates in a fairly impressive re-creation of the 1906 San Francisco earthquake, giving Wayne an excuse to carry Ann through piles of rubble. As Flaxen Tarry, Ann's signature dark tresses were lightened and she sports some of the most elaborate hairstyles and costumes of her career. There were rumors that legendary designer Adrian was going to be creating the costumes, but credit ended up going to longtime Republic costumer Adele Palmer.[18] *Flame of Barbary Coast* may not have been the most significant film for John Wayne or Republic, but it was one of Ann's higher-profile roles. It also marked her postwar comeback, though Ann disagreed with this view, remarking, "You couldn't really call it a comeback 'cause I never got very far before. But this time I will—just wait and see."[19]

Leslie Fenton resumed his career as a director and was soon signed to do *Tomorrow, the World!* starring Fredric March and Betty Field. Ann and Leslie were both happy to be working again, noting, "People without work get discontented, scattered, prone to fears and phobias. There will be enough of these without sitting and waiting for them to come up and grab you." Compared to their service in England, the two's current contributions may have seemed slight to them, but of their reentrance into the film industry, they enthused, "If any of the pictures we make cheer up the troops or provide entertainment for the people actually in the war

Candid shot of Ann on the town in the 1940s.

effort we feel we're doing something. And the money we earn buys bonds."[20]

By all appearances the couple seemed to have weathered the war years and were forging ahead as strong as ever. However, when Ann was asked if it were advisable for other women to follow their enlisted husbands overseas, she hesitated in answering. "It's a tremendous question, depending for its answer on the individuals. If two people are strong, facing adverse conditions strengthens them, brings them closer. But suppose they aren't strong enough? Would it not be better for her to stay home? A man wants to know his home is there waiting for him when he's through fighting."[21] Columnist Hedda Hopper thought the Fentons were the strong sort when, in August 1944, she ran a lengthy article on the couple, noting the two "are providing a pattern for thousands of other couples who will shortly be returning to pick up the threads of their personal lives which they dropped when they heard the call to duty."[22] A month after the article appeared in print, Ann publicly announced that after twelve years of marriage, she and Leslie were separating and the walnut ranch was going on the market.

Ann Dvorak and Leslie Fenton had developed a reputation as one of Hollywood's odder but most devoted couples, so news of the separation came as a shock to the film community. Ann broke the news to Hedda Hopper. "Yes, it's true that Leslie and I have separated. Our marriage can be classed as a war casualty. It's so very unpleasant that I'd rather not discuss it anymore."[23] To another reporter she elaborated, "We just couldn't get along. Our unhappiness started in England while we were working on the war effort. Neither of us plans an immediate divorce."[24] Leslie Fenton made no public comments and moved to an apartment in Beverly Hills. When later questioned why the seemingly indestructible union had fallen apart, Ann responded, "Thousands of reasons," without specifying one.[25] Ann and Leslie had been a practically inseparable unit for over a decade, but their time spent apart during the war gave Ann a level of independence she had never experienced and that allowed her to come into her own. She was very young when she fell in love with Fenton and had gone directly from the watchful eye of her mother to living under the influence of her husband. From the time Fenton left for Europe in September 1940 until they both returned three years later, Ann had frequently been responsible for only herself under the most trying of circumstances and had thrived. Charles Foster, the young RAF soldier who spent a fair amount of time with Ann in England while he was on leave at various intervals, revealed, "If there was a husband, Leslie Fenton or someone else, I never met him, didn't even see him. At 18 I was head over heels in love with Ann and didn't care who knew it."[26] Perhaps when the couple returned to their former lives, Ann realized she no longer wanted the life she had led before. After some time had passed, she reflected, "When we got back home we had a little time to think about ourselves instead of the buzz bombs, and we discovered we weren't in love anymore, so we called it quits."[27] One reporter summed up the demise of Ann's marriage by describing how they "began to grow apart as they grew older. Neither one of them can explain it. It is one of those evanescent things that leave the two people, who have lost what they had together, the most puzzled of all."[28] Whatever the specific reasons may have been, the couple appears to have split amicably, and for the time being, there were no immediate plans for divorce. Their frequent appearances together in public constantly fueled rumors that a reconciliation was just around the corner.

The ultimate fate of the Fenton marriage was unknown for the foreseeable future, but Ann's days as a walnut farmer were officially coming to an end. Rather than sell the walnut ranch as a whole, Ann immediately started subdividing the land; she ultimately made a profit of approximately $50,000.[29] The area would be subdivided even further by subsequent owners, and by the end of the decade, the once prosperous walnut ranch would fall to postwar suburban growth and be taken over by dozens of single-family homes. In June 1945 the portion of the property containing the house, pool, stables, greenhouse, and garage was sold to crooner Andy Russell and his wife, Della. They christened their new home Rancho Amour in honor of his hit song, and turned Ann's beloved greenhouse into a rumpus room. After a dozen years of living in the San Fernando Valley, Ann moved to the other side of town into a house at 12319 Nineteenth Helena in Brentwood. This was the first time Ann had ever lived by herself, though she was joined by her two cocker spaniels and Heinzie the dachshund. The acreage in Brentwood didn't compare to the amount of land Ann had been tending to in Encino, but the new home was much larger and decorated with Ann's simple taste. Of course, the landscaped backyard bore the mark of her green thumb, and while she did not have a pool, she had ample room for sunbathing.

If there was one marked difference from Ann's life with Fenton, it was her more frequent appearances on the social scene, though she still claimed to enjoy time alone. "I don't have to have people underfoot all the time. When you work in pictures, you are around so many people all day long, it is a wonderful relief to just be alone. I like to read—I go on reading sprees as enthusiastically as Ray Milland went on liquid ones in *The Lost Weekend*."[30] On the nights she did hit the town, her unique

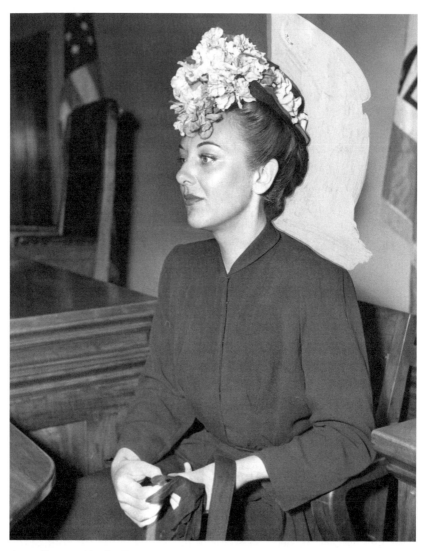

Ann divorces Leslie Fenton in 1946. (Courtesy of the *Los Angeles Herald Examiner* Collection/Los Angeles Public Library)

clothing style received some attention, with columnists pointing out accessories like shoes with a pattern of red toenails painted on the outside, and her personally designed "curfew bracelet," which contained a dozen tiny bells that the wearer tinkled at midnight.[31] A jewelry manufacturer apparently shelled out a tidy sum to Ann for that idea.[32] Ironically, her frequent dining partner on many evenings out was Leslie Fenton, though Ann continually denied that a reconciliation was on the horizon: "We're great friends but I've observed that reconciliations between people like us seldom work out."[33] Just to keep the gossip columnists on their toes, Ann was also spotted around town in the company of Mexican actor Arturo de Cordova.[34]

In October 1945 Ann filed for divorce in Los Angeles. She asserted that Leslie Fenton had deserted her and was asking the court to approve a property settlement the pair had agreed upon.[35] Less then two months later, the proceedings were postponed because, as Ann explained, "We were married a long time, and we went through a lot together in England during the war. There's no one in my life and no one in Leslie's. We both hated to break up our marriage, and we sat down and talked it over."[36] When the couple was spotted together at the Hollywood Beach Hotel in Florida, it was believed that a reconciliation had occurred.[37] But the reunion proved to be short-lived, and after a two-year separation, amid unrelenting reconciliation rumors, Ann appeared at the Superior Court on August 1, 1946, a day before her thirty-fifth birthday, and was granted a divorce from Leslie Fenton. Looking appropriately forlorn, she answered yes to five questions, affirming that "Fenton had deserted her on September 1, 1944; that this was against her wish and without her consent; that they had not lived together since; that there had been several attempts at a reconciliation and that these had failed."[38] The claims of desertion were probably agreed to by Ann and Leslie beforehand to appease the court, which at the time would have required concrete grounds to end a marriage. The final decree would take another year to come through, but overall the proceedings were smooth, and the couple never seemed to bear any ill will toward each other. For the first time in over fourteen years, Ann Dvorak was a single woman, once again focused on being an actress.

19

Career Girl

Without a marriage to concentrate on, Ann finally turned her attention to her film career. Now that she had some perspective over what had transpired during her Warner Bros. years, Ann's outlook was much different than it had been in 1932 when, she admitted, "I was Mrs. Fenton first and Ann Dvorak second. When he wanted to take a trip around the world, we took a trip around the word. And to heck with the movie business." She continued, "The only thing wrong with that was that I wasn't an actress so much as I was a wife."[1] To another reporter she continued this line of thought: "Then I got married. I found out I really didn't have time for a career and the family and I decided it was better to neglect the career than neglect my husband. Oh, I did a few pictures, but my heart wasn't in it." Now, she was ready to tackle her career head-on, claiming, "When I came back to Hollywood I was a new woman. I lightened my hair, talked to an agent, threw out my chest and said 'Here I come.'"[2] Her new agent was Zeppo Marx, and she seemed determined to put him to work. "I'm going to give my career a chance this time. No pulling out across the world again. I'm going to pull all the stops and give it everything!"[3]

Ann's next film, *Masquerade in Mexico*, was to be a showcase vehicle for Paramount star Dorothy Lamour, with Ann in a supporting role. Directed by former costume designer Mitchell Leisen, the film was a loose remake of the 1939 classic *Midnight* starring Claudette Colbert, Mary Astor, John Barrymore, and Don Ameche, which Leisen had also directed. In order to avoid working with Paramount's reigning and unreinable star Betty Hutton, Leisen was inspired to update *Midnight* because of the studio's desire to pair Lamour and Arturo de Cordova and find employment for a large Mexican hacienda set that had been built for another film but not used.[4] Lamour plays a dancer stranded in Mexico who is paid off by wealthy Patric Knowles to masquerade as a countess in order to divert the attentions of matador de Cordova away from his wife, played by Ann. Lamour thought the script was good and welcomed the opportunity to show off her singing voice, and it was one of the higher-budget productions of Ann's career.[5] Zeppo Marx was able to negotiate nearly $25,000 for Ann's work on the film, second only to Lamour, who was paid $60,000.[6] *Masquerade in Mexico* also gave Ann the opportunity to play an unsympathetic and conniving character, a rare turn for her, and she seems to have relished her snarky dialogue and multiple scenes slapping people. For the film, Ann's tresses were turned blonde so her hair would contrast with Lamour's signature dark locks, and in many scenes Ann sports outrageous hairdos.[7] Some of her costumes were also over the top, and even though Edith Head received credit, Leisen himself had a major hand in designing the gowns for Dvorak and Lamour. Ann was supposedly so enamored with the wardrobe that she made arrangements to purchase some of the outfits for her personal collection.[8]

One of the more interesting aspects of *Masquerade in Mexico* is an elaborate ballet scene late in the film depicting the history of Mexico. The presentation was watered down, largely to avoid offending the Mexican government by depicting unsavory moments from the country's past. Leisen was especially disappointed about one sequence where "Maximilian and Carlotta were supposed to dance on a platform supported by the oppressed Mexican people. Juarez comes out from under the scaffold, shoots Maximilian and Carlotta goes insane. She finishes the ballet completely non compos mentis. Ann Dvorak would have been brilliant in that, one of the reasons we chose her was that she could dance, but the Mexican government wouldn't allow it."[9] In the final cut, the number is barely alluded to with a scene in which Ann is dressed up like the empress of Mexico, a role Bette Davis had undertaken dramatically in the 1939 Warner Bros. feature *Juarez.*

Following *Masquerade in Mexico,* Ann was rumored to be resuming her deal with Republic in a film called *No Other Gods,* costarring Fred MacMurray and directed by Leslie Fenton, which would include a $12,000 costume budget.[10] During this time, director Frank Capra was also considering Ann for the role of Mary Bailey in the perennial favorite *It's a Wonderful Life.*[11] Instead, Ann was cast in the independently produced *Abilene Town,* starring Randolph Scott and released through United Artists. *Abilene Town* was one of the few westerns Ann would appear in during the course of her career. Here, Scott is the marshal of the

Ann makes a personal appearance in Abilene, Kansas, for the premiere of
Abilene Town.

post–Civil War town of Abilene, trying to maintain peace between the
cattlemen and newly arrived homesteaders. Ann is Rita, a local showgirl
and savvy businesswoman who has a hard time hiding her true feelings for
the marshal. Producer Jules Levey handpicked Ann for the role after seeing her in *Masquerade in Mexico*, noting, "In that she played second fiddle
to Lamour, but in my picture she will be the top woman and it's a big
role."[12] Rita is a less polished version of Flaxen Tarry from *Flame of
Barbary Coast*, but the musical numbers are livelier and Ann was enthusiastic about the role. "It's in *Abilene* that I show my stuff as a song and
dance queen. There's some life in the old girl yet."[13] A bonus to the filming of *Abilene Town* was the presence of Ann's former mentor at MGM,
Sammy Lee. The dance director had returned to Hollywood in the early
1930s and had worked steadily as a choreographer and short-film director
ever since. It's unknown if Ann had anything to do with Lee being
brought in for *Abilene Town*, one of his last Hollywood projects. In mid-
January 1946 Ann and the rest of the cast traveled to Abilene, Kansas, for

a gala premiere of the film. There they were greeted by resident Ida Eisenhower, mother of the future president, and rode in a parade where they were cheered on by thousands of Abilene locals.[14]

When Republic failed to come up with anything to her liking, Ann again opted for an independently produced film released by United Artists. It's anyone's guess if the major studios were purposely staying away from Ann or if she were deliberately favoring smaller production companies during this time. If she hoped to find better-quality roles by engaging with the smaller fishes, then her next film, *The Bachelor's Daughters*, must have been a letdown. Starring a solid cast, including Adolphe Menjou, Billie Burke, Gail Russell, Claire Trevor, and Jane Wyatt, *The Bachelor's Daughters* is about four shop girls who rent a mansion and pose as sophisticated sisters in order to meet wealthy men. Ann is an aspiring vocalist attempting to land an audition from their next-door neighbor, who happens to be a major stage producer. The film, a light comedy with a heavy-handed climax, is enjoyable enough, if not exactly a showcase for Ann's talents. She had demonstrated in *Flame of Barbary Coast* and *Abilene Town* that she was capable of carrying a tune, but in *The Bachelor's Daughters* her singing voice is dubbed, which had not happened since *Thanks a Million*. As a minor consolation, she does get to dance in a fairly elaborate number, which would prove to be influential in her personal life.

Ann was unimpressed with the films Republic had proposed and had reportedly turned down fourteen scripts they had sent her.[15] When she spotted a good opportunity elsewhere, Ann decided being indebted to the studio for two more pictures wasn't worth it. She sold some investment property in Brentwood and used $25,000 to buy out her Republic contract.[16] The project that prompted Ann to spend such a large sum was an independently produced period piece, *The Private Affairs of Bel Ami*. Based on a novel by Guy de Maupassant, the film stars legendary scoundrel extraordinaire George Sanders as a social-climbing cad who sleeps his way up the ranks of 1880s Parisian society. The film also featured Marie Wilson, John Carradine, a young Angela Lansbury, and Warren William, who had played Ann's much-maligned husband fifteen years earlier in *Three on a Match*. The film may be a bit dry and stagy under Albert Lewin's direction, but Ann looks stunning in the well-designed nineteenth-century Parisian costumes, set against the complex and elaborately constructed sets. Her character, Madeleine Forestier, has a level of depth and intelligence not seen in many of Ann's roles, and is one of the strongest and most admirable women Ann would play over the course of her career. In many ways, Madeleine is an early feminist trapped by the social mores of her time; as one film historian points out, "Madeleine, it turns out, is a journalist and politician, but she is forced to take cover behind her men and to act through them."[17] For the film, Ann's hair color was once again changed, this time to red, and she expressed, "I think I feel better as a titian. Maybe I'll keep it this way."[18] George Sanders is his usual delightful self and Ann's scenes with him are entertaining. While not a large-scale production at a major studio, *The Private Affairs of Bel Ami* demonstrates how maturity and a war had helped Ann grow as an actress. The film received some advance publicity when Albert Lewin dreamed up an art competition wherein the winner would have his or her version of the *Temptation of St. Anthony* prominently featured in the black-and-white film, in Technicolor no less. Artist Max Ernst's painting was selected over the eleven other entries, which included a submission by Salvador Dali.[19]

Over the years, Ann had kept in touch with Anna Swensen, the teenager she had briefly taken under her wing when they were both in the MGM chorus. Swensen had long left the film industry, and around this time visited Ann over the course of a few days with her family. The visit made a lasting impression on Swensen's son, Dick Peterson, who decades later recalled, "We spent the first afternoon with Ann, and most of the second day, and lastly only lunched together before we started on our return trip. During those times I vividly remember a tall, thin lady that had an effervescent nature. Always active, smiling, leading conversations and such. Even today (sixty-four years later) she still stands out in my mind. I can still see her genuine and fascinating smile, wide-open eyes that looked right into you, and a personality that was really something." He continues, "The second day I saw Ann in those late 1940s days (I suspect it was in early summer of 1947) we went to a park with my mom, dad, I, and two other families that were also friends of Ann's. Ann was everywhere during that time. She was so involved and active that her mood rubbed off on everyone there. I wish I could better describe the scene; but I can say that Ann Dvorak was a very, very energetic person. There was just something about her." He concludes, "I'm sure she wasn't the most exotic actress, nor the absolutely most beautiful or talented (although quite close in all categories), but she had a real, genuine personality that came through to everyone, especially those in her audiences."[20]

Even before her divorce from Leslie Fenton was final, Ann was spotted around town in the company of Igor Dega, a professional dancer who made his living mainly performing at nightclubs, but occasionally picked up film work when the script called for a dancer. He was born Igor De Navrotsky in Russia in 1916, but was educated in France.[21] He enlisted in the army in 1943, before he was a U.S. citizen, but this gesture seemed to have sped up the process, as he attained citizenship a few months later. He appeared in a handful of films throughout the 1940s, most notably in Anatole Litvak's classic thriller *Sorry, Wrong Number*, starring Barbara Stanwyck. Ann had first met Dega years before, either in Paris or London, and they became reacquainted when he was cast as Ann's dancing partner in *The Bachelor's Daughters*.[22] Ann admitted that when they first met, "we never dreamed it would turn into a romance until he came to Hollywood and I met him again." Igor Dega was the polar opposite of Leslie Fenton in many respects. He was five years younger than Ann, whereas Fenton had been a full decade older. Fenton was slightly built, balding, and thin lipped, but Dega had a robust dancer's form, an impressive full head of hair, and bore a slight resemblance to actor Victor Mature. Both men had chosen entertainment as a career, but after Fenton put in a day's work, he retreated to his isolated ranch in the evenings; Dega usually spent his evening hours at a nightclub. Whereas Fenton was a serious and brooding sort, Ann describe Igor as "very sweet, and sunny tempered."[23] The couple was seen at Hollywood hot spots like Ciro's and Sardi's, and one evening at the Florentine Gardens, Ann took the stage with Igor to fill in for his regular partner, who had fallen ill.[24] After more than a decade of being a studious and dutiful wife at the walnut ranch, Ann was ready to take a whirl at being a party girl, and Igor was the man to show her how. The ink on her divorce papers wasn't even dry, but it was looking like wedding bells were about to ring again for Ann Dvorak.

In the meantime, Ann signed on with Select Productions, Inc., to appear in the RKO-distributed *The Long Night* with Henry Fonda, Vincent Price, and Barbara Bel Geddes in her film debut. This film noir, directed by Anatole Litvak, is a remake of the 1939 French feature *Le jour se lève*. Set in a factory town, the story focuses on a war veteran (Fonda) driven to murder by a conniving traveling magician (Price) who has been romantically linked to the vet's young girlfriend. Ann plays Price's cynical assistant, Charlene, who falls for Fonda even though she knows their relationship is just a temporary distraction for him. The role is a small one for

Ann on the town with her new beau, dancer Igor Dega.

Ann, but she embraces it and shows how her dramatic capabilities allowed her to easily transition from the sophisticated Madeleine Forestier to the rough-around-the-edges Charlene.

After the filming of *The Long Night*, Ann's plans for a second go at marital bliss were put in doubt when Igor's roving eye allegedly landed on actress Abigail "Tommye" Adams.[25] Ann immediately picked up and sailed down to Acapulco, whence she made her way over to Mexico City, where she was reportedly seen on the arm of Tyrone Power, who was simultaneously carrying on a fling with Lana Turner.[26] After this brief but no doubt pleasant diversion, Ann returned to Los Angeles, patched things up with Igor, and resumed wedding planning.

Ann's next role was in the Eagle-Lion production *Out of the Blue*, based on a short story by author Vera Caspary, who is best known for her novel *Laura*, later made into a classic film starring Gene Tierney. Caspary also had a hand in the screenplay of *Out of the Blue*, which gave Ann a rare opportunity in a purely comedic role. Director Leigh Jason seems to have purposely selected some of his cast to play against type. Turhan Bey, who normally played "exotic" types opposite the likes of Maria Montez and Sabu, portrays a carefree playboy, and the usually sultry Carole Landis is a stern shrew. Ann plays Olive Jensen, an eccentric but lovable drunk who gets under George Brent's collar and ultimately on his nerves when she overstays her welcome at his apartment while his wife (Landis) is out of town. Unlike her first turn at a predominately comedic role in *She's No Lady*, Ann is effective in *Out of the Blue*, the bright spot in what costar Virginia Mayo admitted "wasn't much of a picture."[27] Ann's early scenes with George Brent at a bar and then his apartment are delightful, showing a side of Ann's abilities rarely seen. She admitted the role was challenging: "Timing is so important in such a portrayal that it keeps you on your toes all the time." As the film drags on, Ann's over-the-top performance begins to wear thin, but overall *Out of the Blue* is watchable because of Ann more than the film itself. She enjoyed this change of pace. "I play a humorous drunk who goes on a week's binge. It's done for comedy, and between you and me we probably got away with murder. That is, none of the performance was censored, saved by the comedy angle no doubt."[28] Ann was now playing supporting parts regularly, but claimed she was happy with that, commenting, "I like those kind of parts, character roles. I've played several drunken ladies in my life, but I never stayed under the influence of the bottle all through an entire picture until *Out of the Blue*. Quite an experience, I must say."[29]

Caspary was so pleased with Ann's performance that the author was reportedly inspired to write a follow-up just for Ann entitled *Out of the Red*. Ann was enthusiastic about the prospective project: "In it I'll play a gal who goes to Las Vegas and in a moment of imbibing rather freely, cleans up at the tables." She excitedly continued, "Miss Caspary and I. A. Goldsmith, who produces her murder mysteries, might even work in

Ann steps off the ship after landing in Acapulco in 1947.

something about the celebrated Bugsy Siegel slaying. Miss Caspary is something of an expert on murders, you know; her stories 'Laura' and 'Bedelia' proved that."[30] Nothing ever came of *Out of the Red* and Ann soon went back to dramas.

Ann and Igor are married at Ann's Brentwood home in August 1947.

In between *Out of the Blue* and her next project, *The Walls of Jericho* at 20th Century-Fox, Ann and Igor were finally wed on August 7, 1947, at her Brentwood home. On the marriage certificate, Ann shaved three years off her age while adding three years onto Igor's, so she appeared to be younger than her groom. On the eve of the ceremony, Ann revealed to Louella Parsons, "Frankly, I never expected to marry again after I divorced

Leslie Fenton. I really thought he was the one love of my life. You remember, Louella, that we called off our divorce plans several times and tried to make a go of our marriage again, but it just wouldn't work, much as we regretted it." When Parsons brought up the subject of the war, Ann continued, "Well, I honestly think that's where our trouble started. Everything was so nerve wracking that when the letdown came after all the excitement, we just couldn't seem to get along. We're still friends, however, and he was one of the first to send me a telegram wishing me happiness in my new marriage." Parsons also recalled the negative reaction Anna Lehr had to Ann's first marriage, to which Ann responded, "Mother is wonderful. She likes Igor, and this time I have her blessing. Naturally, that adds to my happiness."[31]

The couple immediately took off for a brief, low-key honeymoon in Boston, but Ann was soon back in Los Angeles and reporting to Fox for *The Walls of Jericho*. Ann was impressed with the project, commenting, "I'm in some pretty stellar company, what with Cornel Wilde, Linda Darnell, Anne Baxter and Kirk Douglas. 20th Century-Fox decided to load this one for sure."[32] In this ragtime soap opera, Ann, billed fifth, again plays a woman with a severe drinking problem. Unlike *Out of the Blue*'s Olive Jensen, whose drunkenness is played for pure comedy, Belle Connors in *The Walls of Jericho* is a bitter and caustic drunk whose addiction seems to be fueled by crippling insecurities. Ann plays the character convincingly, and even gets to shoot Cornel Wilde, but she has limited screen time. However, the standout in *The Walls of Jericho* is Linda Darnell as Algeria Wedge, a ruthless social climber who easily manipulates husband Kirk Douglas.

After the split from Leslie Fenton, Ann had loudly proclaimed she was really going to give her career a chance this time. She had been getting steady work at some of the major studios and smaller production companies, but it had become apparent she was beyond being cast in A-list starring roles. By the end of 1947 Ann had a new marriage and an exciting social life, and her commitment to her film career would once again begin to waiver. As had happened during her first marriage, Ann would disappear from movie screens for over a year, though this time she would be abandoning Hollywood partially for the hot lights of Broadway.

20

Broadway Bound

Ann Dvorak's career took a different turn in the late 1940s. In fact, 1948 would find her completely missing from cinema productions. She had appeared in forty-seven feature films in sixteen years, and had recently turned in strong supporting performances in *Out of the Blue*, *The Long Night*, and *The Walls of Jericho*. Some gossip columnists claimed Ann was in demand, though it's hard to tell if this was actually true as her film roles suddenly evaporated. Whether or not she actively sought a career change, Ann was about to start performing on the airwaves and for live theater crowds.

Ann had made the occasional radio appearance over the years, usually in promotion of a recently released film, but had rarely engaged in scripted dramas, with the exception of *Never See Snow Again* with Tyrone Power in 1937. Now radio was becoming a more viable option for Ann, who tried her hand at broadcast dramas a few times in the late 1940s. She appeared before the microphones in "Sunday Punch," a *Your Movietown Radio Theater* program costarring Jeff Chandler as a down-on-his-luck boxer who finds himself being trained by a hard-nosed dame (Ann) who ultimately falls for him. Not earth-shattering storytelling by any stretch of the imagination, but it's still nice to hear Ann's clear and distinct voice being put to good use. The program also featured Ann's childhood hero Herbert Rawlinson, who had continued working over the years, getting bit parts in serials and westerns. This would be the third time in almost thirty years that Ann and Rawlinson had acted together; first back in 1920 in *The Five Dollar Plate*, followed seventeen years later with *Midnight Court*. It is unknown if Ann arranged for her old family friend to join her on air, or vice versa, or if the casting was just a nice coincidence. Briefly interviewed by host Les Mitchell at the end of the drama, Ann talked about her love of gardening.

Ann soon starred in two more *Your Movietown Radio Theater* programs: "The Other Side of the Moon" and "Under the Big Top." In the first, Ann plays an Annie Oakley–type character who is reunited with her estranged husband and former rodeo performing partner whose outlaw past comes back to haunt him. This twenty-minute drama costarring Robert Holton and Jim Hayward is actually quite compelling and a welcome addition to Ann's body of work. Less impressive is "Under the Big Top," a tale of mayhem and betrayal in the mad, mad world of circus performers. Ann is the circus publicist who plays a witness to all the drama, and her role is about as crucial as most of the thankless parts she had played at Warner Bros. At least for her mere four and a half hours of work she received $500.[1]

After these radio appearances, there was some talk of Ann venturing into the infant world of television with Igor to star in a Mr. & Mrs. show, which would be produced by Larry Finley and scripted by Ann and Igor. However, this intriguing project never moved past the planning stages.[2] The couple later resurrected the idea for a five-day-a-week radio program titled *At Home with Ann and Igor,* but this venture never got any further than the cutting of an "audition platter."[3] Ann was also slated to perform twelve dramatic readings for Standard Transcriptions' *Moments for Meditation* series, though this also seems to have fallen through.[4] Another radio program Ann later became involved in was with the short-lived Progressive Broadcasting System, also operated by Larry Finley.[5] The thirty-minute, five-day-a-week audience participation program, called *My Secret Desire,* actually went live on the air in January 1951 from the ABC studios at 1539 North Vine Street in Hollywood.[6] However, when the Progressive Broadcasting System went belly-up a couple of weeks later, that was the end of *My Secret Desire.*[7]

In the late summer of 1948, Ann finally made it to Broadway. An earlier attempt to act onstage in New York had been thwarted by Warner Bros. in the mid-1930s, and she had not pursued East Coast theater since. She had cut her stage chops during the war with the traveling camp shows and a last-minute appearance in the Red Cross production of *The Eve of St. Mark,* and was now ready to make her debut as a "legitimate" actress. The play Ann would be appearing in was Jean-Paul Sartre's *The Respectful Prostitute,* a controversial commentary on racism in the southern United States that at one point caused the French playwright to be accused of anti-Americanism.[8] The production made its American debut in April

Ann onstage as Lizzie McKay in *The Respectful Prostitute*.

1948 with Meg Mundy in the title role of Lizzie McKaye, but when Mundy's contract was up in early September, she left the play to pursue other roles. A replacement was sought by the producers, who initially approached Ann's former costar Joan Blondell to portray the small-town prostitute who, after witnessing the murder of a black man, must decide if she will choose truth over racial prejudice.[9] When Blondell declined the role, Ann was officially announced as Mundy's replacement on August

11. She arrived in New York about a week and a half later to begin rehears-als. The play, staged at the Cort Theatre on West Forty-eighth Street, opened with Ann as the star on September 1, 1948, and ran through December 18. Ann's reviews were positive, if not raving, and her appear-ance injected life into the box-office receipts.[10]

During the play's run, Janet Grayson had the opportunity to meet Ann backstage at the Cort Theatre. As Janet remembered,

> I was just a teenager (probably about fourteen) and had put together an Alan Ladd fan club. Always in need of material to fill the pages of our club magazine, I wrote her to ask for a backstage interview. I'm sure she was amused by it all, but movie stars were very accommodating in those days, and she very graciously invited my friend and me into her dressing room before the mati-nee performance. Probably it was a Wednesday—matinee day. . . . We entered, sat down, and asked a few questions about the play. She was seated in front of the dressing table, I remember the big mirror behind her, and stayed in her chair. She was very attrac-tive, not a great beauty like the big stars, but very attractive: olive skin tone, brown hair pushed straight back, distinctive eyes and brows, absolutely recognizable as Ann Dvorak. By that I mean she looked exactly in person as she looked onscreen. I also recall that she wore a white, or pale pink, sateen dressing gown, full length, embroidered in places down the front. We spoke for a bit, and she said nice things about being onstage. Then we said our good-byes and left. She had been friendly, patient, and warm. We could feel it even in the brief half hour or so we were there.

As far as getting tickets to see the show, Janet added, "No, we didn't stay for the performance. . . . I have a vague memory that Ann said something about seeing the play and that my friend and I were a little too young."[11]

Ann enjoyed performing live enough that, after taking a few months off following the run in *The Respectful Prostitute*, she joined a summer-stock company in a production of *Anna Lucasta*. Ann's participation in the production was jeopardized when she broke her foot after dropping a milk bottle on it.[12] But she limped along and made all her appearances in the play, which went on a brief tour in New Jersey, Connecticut, and Pennsylvania.[13]

The marquee at the Cort Theatre advertises Ann in *The Respectful Prostitute*.

After *The Respectful Prostitute* and *Anna Lucasta*, Ann received an offer to return to the screen in the adoption drama *Our Very Own*, produced by the Goldwyn Company. Shortly after signing with Goldwyn, Ann was also chosen for the lead in *People Like Us*, scheduled to open on Broadway in the fall of 1949. Goldwyn agreed to film around Ann's theater schedule so she could do both. *Our Very Own*, starring Ann Blyth,

Farley Granger, Jane Wyatt, and a preadolescent Natalie Wood is a rare film that tackles how a family is affected when a child inadvertently discovers she is adopted. Blyth plays the adoptee, and Ann is her birth mother who is tracked down against her wishes. The part seems to have cemented Ann's status as a supporting actress, which may not have been a bad thing, as it is a stronger and more haunting performance than many of her leading roles. In the character of Gert, Ann conveys a sadness over the choices she has made and also expresses insecurity over her appearance and station in life when adoptive mother Jane Wyatt and daughter come to visit. For the role, Ann wore padding and a curly blonde flyaway wig, giving her a less sleek and more working-class look. Ann seemed pleased with the role: "I'm a real character in this. I'm such a character I think I'll be afraid to see myself. The padding makes me look 30 pounds heavier." However, after the filmmakers viewed the rushes, Ann said, "They tell me that it looks sexy. But it's not supposed to be."[14] Jane Wyatt, who had also worked with Ann on *The Bachelor's Daughters*, remembered Ann as "very professional" and "a lot of fun" to work with.[15] The part may have been considerably smaller than those Ann had been used to, but it's still a noteworthy appearance. Ann's reviews for the film were largely positive, with the *Chicago Daily Tribune* declaring her work on the film "superb," remarking, "Miss Dvorak as the adopted girl's real mother projects with consummate art, the fidgety, harried, deteriorated personality the part calls for. Aside from the producer and director themselves, nobody contributes more importantly than she to the picture's quality."[16] Once filming was completed, Ann looked forward to resuming a top-billed role on Broadway.

People Like Us was a controversial play with the makings of a strong show, but instead it became a mismanaged mess that would sour Ann on the stage permanently. Originally titled *Spellbound*, the play was written by Frank Vosper and inspired by the notorious London murder trial of Edith Thompson and Frederick Bywaters. The sensational production was initially prohibited on public stages in Britain, but it made its way to New York for a brief run in 1927.[17] The play was reworked as *People Like Us* in 1929 and revived nearly two decades later in London's West End. It was to be brought to American stages by novice producer William Taub. Margaret Sullavan initially committed to the lead role but quickly dropped out after discovering *People Like Us* was a revival of the ill-fated *Spellbound*, even though the producers claimed the work had been so

Ann donned a wig and padding for the role of Gert in *Our Very Own*.

heavily rewritten that it constituted a new play.[18] Maureen O'Sullivan was also offered the role, but decided to stay in Hollywood with her six children.[19] Finally, Ann was selected for the lead. She would be joined onstage by Sidney Blackmer for preview runs in Toronto, Detroit, and Montreal, with an official Broadway debut set for the end of October. Igor Dega arranged a dancing engagement in New York for the same time, and the couple traveled east together, making a quick stop in Chicago for sightseeing.[20]

Ann arrived in New York on September 7 to begin rehearsals before heading to Toronto for previews beginning on October 4. By this time, Ann had switched agencies and was now being represented by Bill Brighton at Manning O'Connor. She kept him abreast of what was going on with the production, and the news was seldom sunny. Upon arriving in Toronto, Ann was unimpressed. "There are only three newspapers and *one* theater in this hick town. So, I guess two critics are enough to cover one show a week." She recorded, "We still have a lot of editing and re-arranging to do—*real* re-arranging," including "omitting lines and business that cause laughs in the wrong places." She also mentioned, "We had a half full Wed. Matinee house today—which is really unusually good for *any* town—let alone this square jerk village." Despite the shortcomings Ann thought the play had, she exhibited her old Dvorak spunk: "We have a chance, I think in the next two weeks of breaking in, to bring something a bit different to Broadway. A great deal depends on me. Two weeks is not a long time to break in a play of this caliber—we are gradually modern-izing it—it won't be too hard to do—but carefully & with audience reac-tion, I think we can. Well—we will try." She still had some doubts, concluding, "That is not to say we won't come in for stinking reviews regardless. Oh well."[21]

Before the troupe had even made it to Toronto, the booking in Montreal had been canceled because of expense, so Detroit would be the last preview city. As it turned out, the Motor City would be the last place this incarnation of *People Like Us* would play. As Ann relayed to her agent in mid-October, "The whole true story of our friend Taub is now a very fantastic tale. Lies, misrepresentation, borrowing—he has left bills every-where—the company is going broke and Equity has stepped in to pay the transportation of the cost back to N.Y. when we fold this Sat. night. Meanwhile Taub himself disappeared to New York—leaving all of us to face the music alone. *Two* directors—neither of which has been paid—and *each* of whom has a contract with him as *sole* producer-director of the play." She continued, "Now it comes out also that the guy has been in jail twice and hasn't a cent of his own. Left a hotel bill here & in Toronto— IOU's everywhere, and including one IOU with which he paid *me*. There is no doubt now in my mind but that our hotel suite in N.Y. was also not paid and that I will have to sue for it." Ann went on to explain that producer William Taub had spent most of the box-office receipts before disappearing, but the cast and crew had made valiant efforts to keep the show afloat. Unfortunately, the Detroit preview proved disastrous. As Ann explained,

> Due to the *drastic* & sudden changes our *2nd* director made here 24 hours before opening, no one knew (including crew) what in God's name they were all on—curtains came down in the middle of scenes—bells were clanging instead of door knocks, lights blacked out instead of going on—it was without a doubt the most hysterical fiasco ever seen on an opening night *after* one week of playing a totally different play—with totally different stage directions. I had sudden changes to make that were completely impossible—no work lights on stage for rise of a curtain blacked out—we all fell down getting into the set—the special effects didn't work— pin spots failed to douse, leaving me at the end of a dramatic prologue standing at the procession right stage, for five horrible seconds when I had finished speaking—& having to *crawl* out through *the* wings over *two* frantic crew members trying vainly to pull the curtain ropes. I came so near going out with the curtains, that no one will ever know. . . . You have *never* seen such Madness. The cast was completely distracted. Everyone ran around anxiously wondering what horrible thing could happen next. Then— in the final scene—just as the tragic wind up in prison finds the heroine hysterical over her denial of appeal, & sentenced to death the guy backstage drops the clang bell—this being the signal for the curtain—it came down suddenly half way through the scene. God almighty. What did I do to deserve this?—which is line *from* the play. The critics have thought we were all mad. *All all* Taub's fault. *We were* all nearly in tears that night.

She concluded, "We are planning on chipping in to buy the handcuffs used in the play to send to Mr. Taub with our compliments. His two counts in jail were embezzlement and morals charges with a young boy. Well—it's been just 'grand' I have knocked myself out for nothing. But the experience was good. The hell with it. Hope you are well—and my God how I miss the Pacific Ocean—I feel like retiring and opening a sea food joint in Topanga Canyon. With special shrimp effects. Fried."[22]

Ann and Sidney Blackmer in the ill-fated stage production *People Like Us*.

After the failure of *People Like Us*, Ann went to Florida for a much-needed rest and to spend time with Igor, who was playing a long-term engagement with dancing partner Grace Poggi.[23] After arriving, Ann reported to her agent, "Well—we are here—and it's hot as hell—and I love it. Having the first real rest in a long time. Just not working doesn't always mean resting." She added, "In less than 48 hours I am already getting to look like an Indian." She continued to receive offers to appear on Broadway, but the experience on *People Like Us* had permanently scarred Ann. "I will *not* undertake another theater piece unless I really believe in it. It's just complete & utter madness. Kill yourself for nothing."[24]

Ann stayed in Florida through the holidays, then made an unexpected announcement; after two years of marriage, she and Igor were separating. Ann returned to Hollywood, pronouncing, "We just couldn't live each others' lives. Igor is in Florida and I have come back to Hollywood to resume my screen career. My life for a long time has been connected with pictures. Igor's dancing engagements take him most of the time to night clubs. I tried but I just can't go night after night sitting in these cafes." Ann had traded in her relatively reclusive life with Leslie Fenton for a more glamorous existence with a professional dancer, which turned out to be more of a social commitment than she was able to handle. The main thing she took away from the relationship was a taste for alcohol that would eventually spiral out of control. On January 24, 1950, Ann posted a classified ad in the *Los Angeles Times* stating, "I am not responsible for any debts but my own."[25] One month later, she filed for divorce from Igor Dega, charging extreme cruelty. Her only request was that she be permitted to resume her maiden name.[26] Like her divorce from Leslie Fenton, the separation from Dega would be on-again, off-again, taking well over a year to officially end. With her personal life in a shambles, Ann again turned attention to her film career—though, as it turned out, her days on movie screens were numbered.

21

Seasoned Professional

At the dawn of the 1950s, Ann Dvorak had been making movies for more than twenty years. She had demonstrated the depths of her talents as an actress early on in her career with performances in *Scarface* and *Three on a Match*, and in the postwar era had been establishing herself as a reliable supporting player. With television becoming more and more prominent in American homes, Ann would also begin testing these waters as another avenue of employment. Ann Dvorak seemed to be in a good position to advance her career in supporting roles and perhaps establish herself as a TV commodity. However, only a couple of years into the new decade she would be off screens, both big and small, forever.

Following the *People Like Us* fiasco, Ann's next professional assignment was for Lippert Pictures in the low-budget *The Return of Jesse James.* The film stars John Ireland as a Jesse James look-alike who assumes the late gunslinger's identity. Ann's character, introduced "dealing cards to no one in particular in a saloon," seems to fall in love with Ireland, but ultimately betrays him for personal gain.[1] It was an inauspicious return for Ann, who looks tired and worn out onscreen, appearing considerably older than Ireland though she was less than three years his senior in real life. *The Return of Jesse James* was an early film for actor Hugh O'Brian, who would later star in the television series *The Life and Legend of Wyatt Earp*. O'Brian had limited screen time with Ann and did not interact with her much, but recalled the actress as "lovely" and "very professional."[2] If there was anything positive about *The Return of Jesse James* for Ann, it's that Sue Ellen Younger is one of the few villainous roles of her career and her death scene, in which she clutches a horse while sinking to the ground, is eerie and memorable.

After working for the lower-tiered Lippert Pictures, Ann returned to an A studio when MGM signed her for two pictures. The first was *Mrs.*

O'Malley and Mr. Malone, which reunited her with director Norman Taurog, with whom she had worked on 1933's *The Way to Love.* This slight comedy stars James Whitmore and Marjorie Main as an unlikely duo trying to solve a murder, or two, on a train. Ann plays a client of lawyer Whitmore who is along for the ride. The part is once again supporting and she does not have a lot to do, but at least she gets to catch the killer, literally, with a fur stole. Under the expert care of MGM's makeup department and cinematographers, she looks beautiful. But this is otherwise an unimpressive role, and it is unsettling to compare Ann's career at this point with that of her contemporary Bette Davis—the year Dvorak appeared in *Mrs. O'Malley and Mr. Malone,* Davis was attaining a new level of screen immortality in *All about Eve.*

Ann's next MGM film would be her last at the studio that had first employed her as a teenage hoofer back in 1929. The movie, *A Life of Her Own,* would also prove to be one of the crowning acting achievements of her long career. Directed by George Cukor, *A Life of Her Own* was to be a comeback vehicle for Lana Turner, who had been away from the cameras for two years following a lengthy suspension. The story is set in the cutthroat world of New York modeling, with Turner as the young hopeful right off the bus. Ann plays Mary Ashlon, a washed-up, aging glamour girl who squandered her opportunities and serves as a ghost of Lana's modeling future if she doesn't keep herself in check. Ann's screen time clocks in at around ten minutes, but the performance resonates throughout the entire film, which turns into a melodramatic mess after Mary Ashlon hurls herself out the window of a high-rise. Despite Ann's limited screen time in *A Life of Her Own,* it is one of the most unforgettable performances of her career, for which she arguably deserved an Oscar nomination. As Mary, Ann runs the gambit of emotions—venomous one moment, pathetic the next. She dominates the screen during her first entrance with a slick yet worn sophistication that quickly melts into childish insecurity as she tries to convince agent Tom Ewell to find her work, promising, "I'll be good this time." It's downhill from there as Ann alternates between mentoring Lana's Lily James and jealously lashing out at the younger model with a promising future. In 2010, Turner Classic Movies listed Ann's Mary Ashlon in *A Life of Her Own* as one of ten great overlooked performances, placing her alongside such film luminaries as Marilyn Monroe and Montgomery Clift.[3] Ann almost always gave solid performances, no matter the quality of the script, and *A Life of Her Own*

Ann and Lana Turner confer with director George Cukor on the set of *A Life of Her Own*.

reinforces what dizzying heights she could rise to when working with a high-caliber director like George Cukor, Mervyn LeRoy, or Howard Hawks.

A Life of Her Own should have been a high-profile part for Ann, leading to stronger supporting roles than the ones in *The Return of Jesse James* and *Mrs. O'Malley and Mr. Malone*. Unfortunately, the film was a box-office dud that came and went with little notice given to Ann's performance. Filmmaker François Truffaut said of *A Life of Her Own*, "Here, beauty enters straight off from the first image; the beauty of Lana Turner, the beauty of the story, and finally the beauty of Cukor's work," but Cukor agreed with indifferent audiences and loathed the film.[4] The director later remarked, "All I can remember about that one is that I hated it. It was an awful story. When we went to the first story conference, I could not believe my ears. It was terrible."[5]

After her work in *A Life of Her Own*, Ann decided to try her hand again at the small screen, where contemporaries like Joan Blondell, Sylvia

Sidney, and Glenda Farrell were now finding steady employment. Television in the early 1950s largely consisted of anthology programs, and Ann's limited body of TV work would consist of this type of content. Her first foray reunited her with Donald Woods, who had played Perry Mason to her Della Street in *The Case of the Stuttering Bishop*. The teleplay, "Close Up," was part of *The Silver Theater*, and she received $300 for her services.[6] Ann again appeared on the small screen for a *Gruen Guild Theater* production called "Ballerina," in which she was appropriately cast as a hard-nosed dance instructor, which gave her another chance to play a heavy. Her next small-screen venture was "Flowers for John," a *Bigelow Theater* production. The half-hour drama costars Joan Leslie as a wealthy wheelchair-bound young woman who discovers that the auto accident that killed her father and disabled her was actually caused by her seemingly loving stepmother (Ann), who had hoped to knock off the pair in order to get the inheritance. John Howard is the doctor who falls for Leslie and becomes her protector. "Flowers for John" was not the most original storytelling, but it gave Ann the opportunity to play a bad girl, something she usually did not have the opportunity to do, and she appeared to especially enjoy the scene in which she attempts to throw Joan Leslie off a cliff.

Ann soon returned to the big screen, this time for Allied Artists, a sort of prestige arm of Monogram Pictures. The studio signed her up for a rare starring role in a film titled *I Was an American Spy*. The movie was based on the real-life adventures of Claire Phillips, a native of Portland, Oregon, who was living in the Philippines when the war in the Pacific broke out. After the death of her husband, a GI stationed in the area whom she had known only briefly, Phillips began running a nightclub under an assumed name. She soon established a covert espionage operation, providing the Allies with valuable information that sometimes came in the form of messages she hid in her brassiere, earning her the code name "High Pockets." Phillips was ultimately captured and tortured by Japanese forces, though the camp she was held at for ten months was liberated by the Allies before her death sentence could be carried out. Her fantastic exploits were first presented as a serial in *Reader's Digest* and eventually compiled as the book *Manila Espionage*. For her efforts, Claire Phillips earned the Presidential Medal of Freedom, as recommended by General Douglas MacArthur in 1948.[7] Phillips's story was not produced by one of the major studios, but it would still be a plum role for the actress who was cast to portray the "Manila Mata Hari."

Ann was thrilled to be playing one of the war's female heroes, commenting, "I consider it the greatest possible honor to portray Claire Phillips, one of America's honored spies. No work of fiction could equal the story of this plucky American woman who braved capture, torture and even the death sentence from the Japanese in order to help our troops. . . . My hat is off to the lady, the only feminine holder of the coveted Medal of Freedom." Claire Phillips was hired as a consultant for the film, and she and Ann became fast friends, no doubt brought closer by their shared war adventures. Phillips was impressed with the actress's dedication to the film, noting, "She told me that this was my story and that she wanted to do it in accordance with the facts." Despite limitations of the film's budget, Phillips was happy with the progress of the production as well as the performance of her onscreen counterpart, remarking, "Naturally, we cannot be too arbitrary in a picture. I could not duplicate certain settings as they actually were in the Philippines, but we approximate them. They give the right impression and contribute to the right atmosphere. That is as much as one can ask for or expect." She continued, "It's funny though, if I seem to question anything that is done, Miss Dvorak immediately will want to know my opinion."[8] Ann was so dedicated to the film that when additional retakes were needed after the initial production was complete, she agreed to do them without being paid her rate of $3,500 a week.[9]

The production value of the picture isn't as high as works produced by the likes of MGM or Paramount, but the story is moderately compelling and Ann is clearly giving the part her all in trying to do Phillips's story justice. She is appropriately glamorous during the nightclub scenes and alternately looks like hell in the prison camp. One of the highlights of Phillips's story centers around a makeshift Sally Rand–type fan dance for a Japanese commander that leads to the sinking of an Axis submarine fleet. The incident is played to dramatic effect in the film, but unfortunately the final print of the movie includes only Ann's entrance wearing the large fans, even though existing still photos indicate that more of the dance was actually filmed. The spotlight does shine brightly on Ann when she performs the song "Because of You," later made a popular standard by Tony Bennett. Ann's heartfelt rendition of the song is a highlight of the film. The critics were underwhelmed by *I Was an American Spy*, the *New York Times* calling it a "seemingly earnest account" that "isn't especially stimulating either as a narrative or as a tribute to personal courage."[10] The *Washington Post* agreed, calling the film "second hand" and

Ann Dvorak

Ann and Claire Phillips (left) bonded during the production of *I Was an American Spy*, in which Ann portrayed the "Manila Mata Hari." (Courtesy of the *Los Angeles Herald Examiner* Collection/Los Angeles Public Library)

noting, "Unfortunately, the general level of the movie is completely undistinguished."[11] Despite what the critics thought, *I Was an American Spy* was one of Ann's favorite roles.[12]

January 1951 proved to be an extremely busy month for Ann. *I Was an American Spy* began production on January 4 and wrapped up in time for Ann to appear in a supporting part in the 20th Century-Fox western/noir *The Secret of Convict Lake*, which commenced on January 30. The film featured an impressive cast headed by Glenn Ford and Gene Tierney, with Ethel Barrymore, Zachary Scott, and Ruth Donnelly in support. In the film, Ford leads a group of escaped convicts who demand refuge in a small outpost occupied by an enclave of women who are alone while their men are on an extended hunting expedition. Ann plays the slightly paranoid and extremely distrustful Rachel Schaeffer whose loneliness is exploited by Zachary Scott. For the role, Ann was given an unglamorous and weatherworn appearance that makes her sudden passion for Scott unexpected. After their liaison, Ann looks up at him in a subtle yet pleading manner that poignantly conveys her knowledge that rejection is right around the corner. It's a quick and simple scene, yet it sums up Ann's talent for acting with her eyes and a small gesture. Over forty-five of Ann's contemporaries were considered for the part of Rachel, including Miriam Hopkins, Agnes Moorehead, Audrey Totter, Una Merkel, Sylvia Sidney, Mercedes McCambridge, Ruth Hussey, Claire Trevor, and Patricia Neal.[13]

When production on *The Secret of Convict Lake* finished, Ann probably did not realize it would be the last time she would set foot in front of movie cameras. For her work on the film, she received $2,500 per week, only $200 more than she would have been making fifteen years earlier had she stayed with Warner Bros.[14] Not counting her early work as a child actress, she had been employed in the film industry for over twenty-two years and had appeared in more than eighty features or short films, fifty-five under the name Ann Dvorak. Despite columnist Hedda Hopper's claims that Ann's "stock is zooming" following her strong performances in *I Was an American Spy* and *The Secret of Convict Lake*, as of 1951 Ann Dvorak's film career was effectively over.[15]

Less than a month after completing her work on *The Secret of Convict Lake*, Ann went on an extended tour of Europe, her first transatlantic visit since the war. She had not yet gone through with the divorce from Igor and was now vehemently denying that there was anything wrong with the marriage. "It's true that I have been so busy in pictures that we hardly see each other, but we're still happily married."[16] Ann's actions seemed to contradict her words when she traveled abroad with her stand-in, Margaret Spahr, rather than with her husband. Ann justified this, "Igor has just gone into the agency business and he can't leave at this time. My trip will combine business with pleasure. I'm going to try to buy up some old English films to sell to television over here. If things work out, I also may make a picture in England."[17] The fiction that the Dega marriage was stable was even less convincing when Ann signed over power of attorney to an E. S. Blum before sailing.[18] Why Ann took this action is unknown, though it may have been a safeguard in case she wanted to file for divorce from across an ocean. Igor did briefly join Ann in an attempt to save the marriage and squelch divorce rumors, but the reunion was brief, and he flew back to the States alone at the end of April.[19]

During the extended trip, Ann visited Italy, France, England, Sweden, Germany, and the Netherlands. Any hopes she may have had to make pictures abroad were quickly dashed, as she reported to agent Bill Brighton, "Everything in Europe is pretty bad, from all I can gather. Although opinions differ as to possibilities of pictures here. Apparently, there may be still a lot of American money frozen in England—but the Board of England considers it all 'dead money.' And in order to use it, pictures should be made with a great deal of British talent, which fouls things up for American concerns." With plans for working put on the back burner, Ann settled in for a leisurely vacation. She had not been to Paris since before the war, and now observed, "Paris is so full of fruits that you can barely turn around (no cracks please) and real pretty ones too. With hair like Igor." Ann, just shy of her fortieth birthday, seemed to be developing a wry cynicism not previously evident. While in Paris, she also complained, "Americans (so few) pounce on each other like long lost bosom pals. Every American service man stops us everywhere—in bars, in cafes—in clubs. With the battlecry—'Say—you're not American by any chance?'"[20] Ann's annoyance with her compatriots would continue to grow in the ensuing years.

As much as Ann may have wanted to detach herself from life back home while she was in Europe, one bit of domestic business popped up that she could not ignore. She had sold the house in Brentwood and had been dividing her time between a beach house located at 18722 West Topanga Beach Road in Malibu and a large Spanish-style residence at 1514 Schuyler Road in Beverly Hills. As Ann began spending most of her time at the beach, she rented out the Beverly Hills property. Shortly after she left the country, the house on Schuyler Road was raided by police, who arrested ten people, mostly women, on vice charges, including Berrie Bensen Lazes, whom police named as "the first serious aspirant to the mantle of the notorious Brenda Allen, panderess."[21] Local newspapers ate

Ann with former stand-in Margaret Spahr (right) after obtaining a California divorce from Igor Dega. (Courtesy of the University of Southern California, on behalf of the USC Special Collections)

up the story, running photos of the house, including shots of "the purple room," where unspecified "business" took place. Curiously, none of the reporters covering the raid made the connection to Ann, though she became well aware of what had occurred and joked to her agent from Paris, "How did you like the Schuyler Road whorehouse episode? It was a good house for that purpose. Had all the makings (no cracks please). Den of Vice Incorporated. I particularly liked the 'Purple Room.' $150 for a 'double header'—man & two women. Please tell me Bill how they manage that?" The police were more than likely aware that Ann was the landlord of the property, but must have been able to quickly absolve her of any guilt without needing to interview her. She closed a letter from Paris to her agent with, "And don't tell anyone where I am—Do you get the message?"[22] However, it's not clear if "anyone" meant Igor or someone wanting to connect her to the Schuyler Road raid.

Since she was out of the country, she called upon her old friend Leona Cary to take care of the house for her. Leona's husband, George, had been employed at one of the studios as a police officer, and at times Ann hired Leona as a personal secretary. Of the incident, Leona later recalled to Ann, "I laugh to myself when I think of the time you called me and said you wanted me to arrange your moving from the Schuyler Road house in a hurry. Boy! Did I have 15 rooms of furniture. . . . I did a good job, I think."[23]

After a three-month vacation, Ann returned to Los Angeles in July 1951 and promptly announced that her marriage to Igor was over. This was the second time in less than two years that the couple had made this proclamation, but this time, Igor confirmed that Ann would immediately be filing for divorce, adding, "We talked it over and decided it was no use to go on. This has been coming for a long time."[24] On August 7, 1951, which happened to be the couple's fourth wedding anniversary, Ann appeared at the Superior Court to end her second marriage on the grounds of extreme cruelty, which may have been an overstatement used to meet the state's divorce requirements. She testified that Igor was "sullen and morose and frequently stayed out until four or five a.m. in the morning."[25] The judge granted the decree though, as with the split from Leslie Fenton, the California divorce would take a full year to be finalized. Less than two weeks after the proceedings, Ann and Igor started showing up together at various local hot spots like Ciro's and the Mocambo, though Ann denied there was anything to it, commenting, "We're better friends since our divorce, but we're not thinking about a reconciliation." She added, "When you've been together a long time, it's perfectly natural that you want to have dinner together and find out how things are going. Lots of divorced people have dinner together."[26] And indeed, reconciliation with Igor was the furthest thing from Ann's mind. In fact, the divorce was going to take too long for her liking. Never one to be deterred from love for long, Ann was already prepared to tackle marriage number three. Not wanting to wait for the ink to dry on her California divorce papers, Ann soon found herself on the train to Reno.

22

Enter Nick Wade

Of Ann Dvorak's three husbands, Nicholas Wade was the most enigmatic. A Hungarian native, he was born Nicholai Harry Weiss in 1909 to Morris Weiss and Hermina Fried.[1] Wade's father came alone to the United States in 1914, settled in Allentown, Pennsylvania, and opened a tailor shop. The rest of the family, which included an eldest son named George and a daughter, Juliet, joined him around 1920. A second daughter, Irene, was born in 1922.[2] Even though Nick, as most people called him, was not the eldest son, he was looked upon by his parents as the shining star of the family and was given the most privileges and opportunities to excel.[3] Expressing an interest in design, art, and architecture, he earned a BA from Columbia University and won a $10,000 competition for a design of the eleventh floor of a Rockefeller Center structure sometime in the early 1930s.[4]

Working under the professional name Nicholas H. Weiss, he launched a career as an architect, briefly working with Thomas W. Lamb, one of New York's most prolific theater designers. Together with Donald Deskey, they designed the International Casino, a mammoth three-story night-club that opened in September 1937.[5] Located at the corner of Forty-fourth and Broadway in Times Square, the International Casino could accommodate twenty-five hundred guests and featured a "spiral" bar that ran the length of the staircase between the first and second stories, allow-ing the venue to skirt a requirement of the New York State Liquor Authority that allowed for only one stand-up bar per establishment.[6] During the late 1930s, Wade was involved in a number of projects, includ-ing design work on apartment buildings in Linden, New Jersey, and nightclubs in New York, including the Monseigneur on Forty-second Street and La Marquis on Fifty-sixth Street.[7] In the fall of 1938 he helped redesign an establishment called the Hollywood Restaurant, which he also operated once it reopened.⁸ Five months later, Wade was arrested for failing to pay a pastry cook's wages and for bouncing a check with a local liquor supplier.⁹ In what would be one of many legal run-ins, Wade was fined $1,000 after pleading guilty.¹⁰

Nick Wade was thin, tall, and balding, with a Hungarian accent. He and his first wife, Katherine, maintained an active nightlife in New York City, living out of hotels and leaving their son, Richard, to be raised by bellboys.¹¹ By 1940, Wade found himself without work, which would be a common theme for the rest of his life. He joined the U.S. Naval Reserve in 1942, and after the war gained American citizenship, changing his surname from Weiss to Wade, as did his brother George. Wade's niece suspects that the pair made the name change to avoid anti-Semitism, though it does seem odd Nick would choose to do this when he was almost forty and had already made a professional name for himself.¹² Nick moved his family to Southern California in the late 1940s, seemingly having abandoned his career as an architect, and started a company called Panawade, which made cabinets for televisions.¹³

Impressions of Nicholas Wade vary wildly. An acquaintance of his in the 1970s uses words like "eccentric," "mischievous," "clown," and "character" to describe him, while his niece, Ann Weiss, prefers "manipulative," "untrustworthy," "nutcase," and "psychopath."¹⁴ To illustrate her opinion, Weiss recalls how Nick's first wife, Katherine, told her mother he was trying to "gaslight" her, a reference to a popular 1944 film of the same name, in which Ingrid Bergman is slowly driven insane by her husband, played by Charles Boyer.

Whatever the truth of Nicholas Wade's character, Ann was instantly smitten with him. They were most likely introduced by Igor Dega sometime in 1951, and any hopes of salvaging that marriage evaporated as soon as Wade entered the picture.¹⁵ After obtaining her interlocutory divorce from Dega in California, Ann decided to go to Reno and establish residency, enabling her to obtain a Nevada divorce, which took weeks instead of a year. Nick was still married to Katherine, but he quickly ended his own union. Both newly divorced, the pair was married in Las Vegas on November 17, 1951. After the quickie wedding, Ann took a bit of time off, presumably to go on a honeymoon with her groom. By this time, Ann's star was officially waning and the Hollywood gossip columnists no longer reported her whereabouts.

After taking the winter off to settle into her third marriage, Ann returned to television and landed a couple of strong roles. At the beginning of April 1952, she starred in an adaptation of Elmer Rice's 1929 Pulitzer Prize–winning play *Street Scene,* opposite her *Side Streets* costar Paul Kelly. Presented by the *Celanese Theatre,* this staging of the play, about the complex lives of everyday people living in a New York brownstone, was well received, with *Billboard* noting, "Ann Dvorak gave a fine performance of the love-starved, erring wife and Paul Kelly came thru most effectively in his final scene as the husband who killed her in a jealous rage."[16] This continued television work seemed to indicate that maybe her future lay with the medium, which was rapidly gaining in popularity; even stars like Bette Davis and Joan Crawford were testing its waters.

Immediately following "Street Scene," Ann was hired to participate in a television experiment of sorts. As TV was finding its place in the world, programs were frequently broadcast live and ran only once. In order to give viewers multiple chances to catch a particular show, WOR-TV in New York devised *Broadway Television Theatre,* wherein a cast would perform the same show on air and before a live audience for five consecutive nights. This brainchild of producer Warren Wade (no relation to Nick) was cheap to produce and would present, according to the producer, "plays to entertain people. We keep away from plays that don't entertain. . . . The trouble with television is that too many people are putting on things they believe have a great message. All we want is a good piece of theater."[17] Actor Christopher Plummer, who costarred with Sylvia Sidney in the *Broadway Television Theatre* versions of "Dark Victory" and "Kind Lady," described it as a "weekly marathon" that "was like doing summer stock with cameras," adding, "It was really quite bizarre." He also distastefully recalled, "At the end of each show, which was sponsored by General Motors, the three leading cast members were obliged to stand beside the latest car, usually a Ford, and in a few choice words, extol its praises. It was humiliating and awful, particularly for important stars like Sylvia, but we gritted our teeth and did it."[18]

The inaugural episode of *Broadway Television Theatre* was "The Trial of Mary Dugan," a popular courtroom drama that had debuted on Broadway in 1927 with Ann Harding in the title role, and had been a moderately successful early MGM talkie starring Norma Shearer. Ann Dvorak was brought on to play Mary Dugan opposite Vinton Hayworth and Richard Derr. The ninety-minute drama provided Ann with one of the most substantial and dramatic roles of her career. Arthur Vergara, who was fifteen years old at the time, accompanied his parents to one of the live airings of "The Trial of Mary Dugan." He admits, "My head was too much elsewhere to have retained much besides a recollection of Ann's imparting a really dramatic sense of the character's pathos," adding, "In this respect her face is engraved on my memory—the 'mask of tragedy.'"[19] The *New York Times* partially agreed, reporting, "In the title role, Ann Dvorak offered a convincing portrayal of the woman wrongly accused of murdering her paramour, but in the second-act climax, she seemed noticeably unsteady in the detailing of the mistress' philosophy on love, the best scene in the play."[20] *Broadway Television Theatre* was successful enough that it ran for a couple of years. In retrospect, one major drawback of this model is that the show was not filmed, so no record of Ann's performance survives.

With the strength of these two appearances in the spring of 1952, Ann seemed to be making the transition from the big to the small screen with little difficulty. Her next appearance was as a guest on *The Ken Murray Show*, whose namesake she had costarred with twenty years before in *Crooner*. Inexplicably, this would be her last appearance on television. Other than a couple of radio performances in 1953 on the *Pepsi-Cola Playhouse* and *Radio Playhouse*, Ann Dvorak's acting career was officially over. It's not clear if she stopped acting by choice or if Nick Wade pressured her to quit. Ann's new husband seemed to like having money he didn't have to work too hard for, so it's difficult to fathom why he would want his wife to stop earning a paycheck. The other possibility is that parts were simply no longer being offered to her. She had terminated her contract with the Manning O'Connor Agency in December 1951 "as a result of my not being employed as an actress in motion pictures."[21] However, the back-to-back jobs in "Street Scene" and "The Trial of Mary Dugan" demonstrated that while film roles might now be harder to come by, television was still an open playing field for an older actress. Ann Sothern, Eve Arden, Joan Davis, and of course Lucille Ball all carried successful episodic series in the 1950s, and while comedy was not Ann's strongest suit, she could easily have hosted an anthology series as Loretta Young did. Even if she wasn't able to get her own show, guest spots were readily available and continued to be in the succeeding decades, as Ida Lupino and Miriam Hopkins proved with memorable appearances on *The Twilight Zone* and *Alfred Hitchcock Presents*. Had Ann continued a career in television, it's possible she would have been introduced to a new generation and could have made a more lasting impression than she did in film. However, like

Ann and friends at her home in Malibu during happier times. (Courtesy of Temple University)

many other times in her career when she was on the cusp of potential greatness, Ann Dvorak walked away. Her retirement from acting became official when she suspended her Screen Actors Guild membership in January 1954.[22]

Ann's days before the camera may have been over, but Nicholas Wade now fancied himself a television producer and had access to his wife's industry contacts along with her bank account and real estate holdings. Ann agreed to the venture, and together they launched a production company called Annik Television and Recording Co., Inc., subsequently changed to Annik Productions, Inc.[23] They were focused primarily on producing documentary-type programming, and as was the case with most endeavors that interested Ann, she threw herself into the work. After a prolonged absence from the public eye, she updated Louella Parsons in 1954, writing, "For two years I have been working on a vast project, concentrating every ounce of my energy on a show for TV titled 'This is God's Country,' which is designed to show America to Americans—and the world. It will tell the story of our great industries and natural wealth—to mention just a few of the subjects covered are the stories of Anaconda Copper, Plymouth Cordage, Heinz, the pickle king, and many more." She added, "I have spent $200,000 to date. I am doing it alone. To keep my project going I'm producing two commercial shows, 'Song and Story' and "Anna McKim, M.D.,' the latter having the backing of the American Medical Association. Everything earned by these shows will go towards finishing 'This is God's Country.'"[24] *Anna McKim, M.D.* doesn't seem to have ever actually gotten off the ground, and *This Is God's Country* never saw the light of day either. The Wades continued working on *Song and Story,* which was to be six short films in color, for an additional two years. At one point the couple claimed that production was delayed because actor Bert Kalmer Jr. and Ann were both injured in separate accidents, which indicates she may have been involved with the project as an actress as well as producer.[25] These failed ventures did not stop the couple from continuing to purchase large amounts of expensive equipment, including film cameras and editing docks. In 1955 they continued to self-finance their projects, obtaining a $10,800 chattel mortgage from Southwest Bank and using the equipment as collateral.[26]

In addition to the production company, the Wades also began advertising themselves as music publishers under the business name Annik Music Corp., which was copyright protected by BMI.[27] However, it does not appear that they actually ever published anything, though they did register a couple of Ann's compositions with the U.S. Copyright Office.[28] During this time, Wade had also become friends with music promoter and producer Fabor Robison, who ran the music label Abbott Records. At some point in the mid-1950s, Robison utilized the Wades' setup to make some short films of his recording artists. Country singer Ginny Wright recalled that the filming took place on a Sunday and that Ann opened her closet and offered Wright the choice of any of her dresses to wear before the camera.[29]

Like many entertainers in Los Angeles, Ann had continued to invest in real estate. In addition to the beach house she was now permanently residing in, Ann owned adjacent properties in Malibu, a sleepy beachside community in the 1950s that had not yet attained its high-end status. Ann rented out one of the properties and set her mother up in the other. She had been supporting Anna Lehr financially ever since the final split from Arthur Pearson in the late 1930s, and as well as the house, she had also purchased a car for her mother's use. But once Nick Wade entered the picture, he set his sights on the Malibu properties as a production and recording space and wanted his mother-in-law out. His influence over Ann was immediate and strong, and he was not as tolerant of her mother as Leslie Fenton had been. As Lehr later described, "I gave back the house she bought for me (in cash) and even the Austin Car she bought me . . . Her murderous husband asked for it, and like a fool I gave it all back . . . I regret it now."[30] Mother and daughter became estranged for well over a decade. In the mid-1960s, Lehr complained in a rambling letter to a family member, "Poor sweet annie dvorak has abandoned me 15 years ago Her anguish will be *terrible*, after I am gone!!!!!!"[31]

As the Wades poured more and more money into their unsuccessful production company, their finances began to slide sharply downward. Wade brought virtually no personal assets to the relationship. Once he married Ann, whatever random employment he may have been engaged in halted altogether. Additionally, he was discharged in bankruptcy in 1953 and brought in no income afterward.[32] As their fortunes worsened, the couple sold the Malibu home they had been living in and relocated to the smaller property in which Anna Lehr had previously resided. They became more and more reclusive, hiding inside the confines of the Malibu house and hitting their liquor cabinet with greater frequency. When they did see anyone, it tended to be at their home rather than in public. Impressions of the couple from outsiders vary. Wade's attorney Marvin Kapelus spent some time with the two in the late 1950s and recalled Nick describing their situation as being "on the bottom, hiding out." He told his lawyer, "We're hibernating." Despite their extreme change in fortunes, Kapelus remembers Ann and Nick as happily married and very devoted to each other. He also noted that although the Wades engaged in

A weary Ann poses for the camera, circa 1951.

social drinking, he "never saw them get boozed."[33] He also recalled that Ann often liked to talk about art and that the portrait of herself from the early 1930s was displayed in the home.

Nick's brother, George, was also an occasional guest, though he usually visited the Malibu home alone rather than with his family because his wife, Mary, disliked the couple and the "trauma drama" they seemed to create. As George's daughter Ann Weiss explained, "Dad acted like a different person when he was around Uncle Nick. He was the older brother, but when he was around Uncle Nick, he acted subservient and my mother didn't like to see that." Ann Weiss admits that her childhood impressions of Dvorak and Wade were probably heavily influenced by her mother's feelings toward them, but her own memories are also unfavorable. She vividly recalls visiting her aunt and uncle for Christmas in the mid-1950s: their house "had giant floodlights, like a Hollywood set," and when she and her parents arrived, Ann and Nick had already both been drinking. "There was a huge piano in the room and Ann was drunk and slumped over it. She motioned me to come over to her and asked me what my favorite Christmas song was. I didn't know what to say and blurted out 'Rudolph the Red-Nosed Reindeer,' which she then started banging out on the piano." She also recalled Dvorak looking "haggard, drawn, with bags under her eyes and sloppy speech. She was the type that would fawn over you in an uncomfortable way, and seemed to be putting on a show. Ann and Nick seemed very insincere and always acted like they were playing to the camera."[34]

One person who tried to visit the couple with little success was Nick's son, Richard, from his first marriage. Father and son had always had a strained relationship, but it deteriorated even further after Nick and Ann were married. According to Richard's daughter, he was so desperate to gain Nick's approval that when his wife, Nola, was recovering from the birth of their first child, he took it upon himself to name the baby in honor of Ann. The name, Ramona Dian, came from Ann's first movie and the name of Claire Phillips's daughter in *I Was an American Spy*. He also later commandeered the birth certificate of another daughter, whom he called Rachel, possibly after Ann's character in *The Secret of Convict Lake*. Nola spoke of one visit to the Wades shortly after Ramona was born. She remembered the visit being pleasant, if not exactly homey, and that when Ann laid eyes on the baby she jokingly exclaimed, "Why, Nick, she looks just like you. No hair!" Nola also remembers Ann repeatedly expressing an admiration of Jackie Gleason, regretting that he wasn't making any more episodes of *The Honeymooners*. This visit from Richard was an anomaly, as he was usually shut out and on at least one occasion he was shocked to discover a charged fence the couple had erected around the property. The estrangement from his father was only part of the troubles for Richard Wade, who also suffered ill effects from his service in the Korean War and later joined a motorcycle gang. His wife, coming to fear for the safety of herself and the couple's three daughters, took the children and left in the middle of the night, flying from Los Angeles to Michigan. Richard never saw his family again, and it does not appear that he was able to maintain much contact with his father either.[35]

Along with the dwindling finances, another reason Ann preferred to remain behind closed doors is that she was facing her own obscurity. After witnessing the indifferent treatment of her mother at the *Hollywood Revue* premiere in 1929, Ann was very much aware of how quickly someone could become a has-been in the entertainment industry. According to attorney Marvin Kapelus, Ann was very sensitive to the fact that the same thing was happening to her.[36] Rather than face anonymity in a town filled with film stars, it was easier just to remain hidden. However, if Ann was so concerned about being forgotten, and with the couple's failed projects throwing them deeper into debt, why Ann didn't make herself available for film and television work is as much a mystery as why she stopped acting in the first place.

One possible explanation for Ann's reluctance to return to acting was her health. Early rumors of tuberculosis had been dispelled during the 1936 Warner Bros. lawsuit, but by the 1950s Ann had actually contracted the disease. Her suffering was so acute that she spent time convalescing at La Vina Sanitorium in Altadena, a suburb of Los Angeles. San Gabriel Valley resident Lisa Smith's father also suffered from the disease in the mid-1950s and was treated at La Vina. She remembers her dad being extremely excited to be recovering alongside the former movie star, and recounted that he would frequently spend the summer hours sitting on a patio, chatting with Ann. Smith, who was a mere youth at the time, had never heard of Ann Dvorak and therefore did not press him for details about his conversations with her.[37] Marvin Kapelus and Ann Weiss both confirm that Ann was ill with the disease during this time.

In addition to her health problems and troubled finances, Ann's life with Nicholas Wade had become a nightmarish hell of emotional and physical abuse. On May 24, 1957, she vacated their Malibu home and moved in with Margaret Spahr, her former stand-in, at 2822 Waverly Drive.[38] Five days later she filed for divorce on the grounds of extreme cruelty. Ann was represented by husband and wife attorneys Milton M. Cohen and Patti Sacks Karger, who stated in the divorce filing, "Defendant [Nick] has physically attacked plaintiff [Ann], pulled her hair, beat her in the face and body, thrown her across the room, and on one occasion about 2 years ago tore all the ligaments in plaintiff's leg; the last time defendant beat and attacked plaintiff was on or about April 25, 1957." The statement continued, "Defendant had threatened to sell plaintiff's separate property, threatened to burn down her home, and to dispose of various items of personal property contained therein, although they are subject to a chattel mortgage executed by the parties." The complaint revealed that Ann's real estate holdings, which at one time had included multiple parcels, now consisted only of the two adjacent properties in Malibu and some unimproved land in Maryland.[39] Ann claimed she did not have sufficient funds to support herself or pay the attorney fees, and that Nick was able-bodied and capable of providing financial assistance in the form of alimony.

Regarding the assets Ann still had in her possession, she stated that everything belonged to her and that there was no community property, an assessment that even Nick's lawyer agreed with. In recent years she had started acquiring rare books and manuscripts and had amassed an impressive collection that included a 1717 edition of the La Saint Bible and a thesaurus published in 1585. Clearly concerned about the collection, Ann had an itemized list included in the divorce filing along with an inventory of all the production equipment. She also included a 1954 Packard automobile, stating that Wade had been hiding the keys from her. She requested that her husband be restrained from entering the property at 18708 West Topanga Beach Road and be barred from using or disposing of any of her property. She was also asking for the restoration of her maiden name. Nicholas Wade denied each and every charge and refused to leave the Malibu house. On June 7, a week after the divorce filing, the court issued an order evicting him from the property on or before June 15, though it did give him exclusive use of the 1954 Packard.[40]

Southwest Bank, made aware of the divorce filing, became concerned that something adverse might happen to the production equipment, which was still tied to the loan the couple had taken out two years earlier. The note had been renewed twice and was payable by September 4, 1957, or on demand. The bank now opted for "on demand" and when Wade informed it he did not have the money, Southwest was within its rights to foreclose on the equipment. Southwest instead decided to be more accommodating, offering to have the equipment placed in storage, remaining subject to the loan. According to the bank, both Ann and Nick were agreeable to this arrangement and a date was set for the transfer, which Nick postponed multiple times. The bank finally insisted it be allowed to remove the items on June 15, which happened to be the day Nick was supposed to leave the premises. Even though he had known about the impending move for weeks, Wade had done nothing to prepare the expensive equipment for transport, and the removal, which began around 9:30 in the morning, took around seven hours to complete. Ann arrived at the scene with her attorney at 10:30 to sign a written consent for the bank to remove the property. When she saw the consent, she reportedly said to her husband, "You are doing it to me again," to which he replied, "Annie, I didn't write this letter; I didn't have anything to do with it." Ann was on the verge of going back into treatment for what she called a "throat and lung infection," most likely a euphemism for tuberculosis, and planned to rent out the Malibu house. She had the written consent altered so that the bank agreed to leave enough furniture for the place to be rentable and then signed it. When Nick was asked to add his signature to the document, he refused, snapping at Ann, "According to your claim it is all your property anyway; that's what you claim. You claim that you own it and I am just here as a spectator. I am watching what goes on and am not signing anything."[41] Even though he was also supposed to be out of the house by day's end, he remained on the property.

On June 26, 1957, Ann entered the hospital for what turned out to be a prolonged stay of four to six months, during which she was heavily sedated most of the time. By now, Nick had finally left the Malibu home, and Ann had turned over management of the property to Gabriel and Lucinda Cotta, a real estate broker and licensed real estate agent, respectively. They were supposed to rent the house while Ann was convalescing, but in August they informed Ann that the property would need to be sold to prevent the note and chattel mortgage from being foreclosed on. The couple also told Ann that Nick had agreed to the sale, and although she was not in a clear state of mind, Ann signed the paperwork to authorize the sale of the Malibu property. When she was finally discharged from the hospital, Ann no longer had a home, and all the production equipment along with the film projects and her book collection remained in storage. Ann presumably went back to Margaret Spahr's Waverly Drive residence. It is unknown where Nick Wade was living.

In May 1958, Ann was informed that the bank had in fact not been in the process of foreclosing on her home and personal property—the

Cottas had defrauded her. That same month, she unexpectedly reconciled with Nick Wade, and their divorce went off the record before it was finalized. Nick was more than likely the source of the fraud information, and whether it was true or not, it was enough to convince Ann that her husband was on her side and looking out for her. Within months, Ann filed a lawsuit against the Cottas and her former lawyers, claiming the parties were guilty of "fraud, oppression, and malice" and asking for over $100,000 in damages. Nick filed his own lawsuit against the Southwest Bank and Benkins Storage for unlawfully removing the production equipment from the Malibu property. His claim against the two companies was for over $2 million. Neither suit was successful, though Nick appealed his case up to the state level, where the judge declared, "There has been no miscarriage of justice here."[42]

With the decade winding down, Ann and Nick began weighing their options. Their venture into production had been a bust, and bad business decisions had caused Ann to lose nearly all her assets. Her marriage to an abusive and manipulative man was hanging by a thread, and her relationship with her mother was so severely strained that they barely had contact with each other. Either by choice or by circumstance, Ann's career as an entertainer was completely dead, so she saw little reason to maintain any ties to Hollywood geographically. One brief highlight for Ann came in the late 1950s when she was asked to participate in the annual Hollywood Christmas Parade. According to attorney Marvin Kapelus, Ann was delighted to be invited to the festivities. Aside from this small ego boost, Los Angeles, which had been Ann's hometown for nearly forty years, held little glamour for her. The Wades decided to plant their roots elsewhere.

23

Hawaiian Hopeful

Under the guidance of Nicholas Wade, Ann's finances had been seriously depleted, but the couple apparently had enough left over from the sale of the Malibu property to consider moving far away from Southern California. Whatever difficulties their marriage had been facing in the mid-1950s seem to have been resolved, at least temporarily, and they looked forward to a fresh start. Nick leaned toward moving to Italy, but Ann had other ideas. She had first visited Hawaii in 1935 with Leslie Fenton, and the tropical paradise was appealing to her on many levels. The warm climate and numerous beaches were a huge draw to her, a life-long sun worshipper, and she knew they would also benefit her continuing bouts with tuberculosis. The lush landscapes of the islands were also perfect for Ann, who had always had a remarkable green thumb. Ann asked Nick to spend a couple of weeks in Hawaii before committing to Europe, and as he put it in 1965, "So we came here for two weeks and we've been here for six years now."[1]

In 1959 the Wades formally bade Hollywood adieu and relocated to the island of Oahu. They moved into a house at 5362 Uhi Uhi Street, one of at least five residences the couple would occupy over the next fifteen years. With a fresh start, the two became more social than they had been on the mainland, with Nick becoming a member of the local Elks lodge and Ann gaining lifetime membership to the Outdoor Circle, a nonprofit organization whose mission was to protect the natural beauty of the islands from the blight of overconstruction and billboards.[2]

After relocating, the couple launched business ventures that were far removed from entertainment. First the two were involved with United Suppliers, an import-export wholesale company where Wade served as vice president and secretary, and "A. D. McKim" was listed as president.[3] Shortly after they took out a $25,000 loan from the company's treasurer,

Morris H. Gold. They were somehow able to use the production equipment and rare book collection, still in the Santa Monica storage unit and still tied to Southwest Bank, as collateral.[4] By 1965 they finally got the loans settled, and Ann was reunited with her book and manuscript collection, though it's not clear if they maintained possession of the film and equipment. In the mid-1960s, the Wades established an entity called Ken-Tech Chemicals that manufactured some sort of solvent used in wood preservation. There's not a lot known about United Suppliers or Ken-Tech, but it appears the latter was successful enough to put the couple back in the black financially for a time.

With the infusion of income, Ann continued building her collection of books and manuscripts, which now included a complete set of works by horticulturist Luther Burbank. Ann was particularly proud of this set: "I've always been sorry that Luther Burbank did not come to Hawaii. If he had, he would have changed our flowers. We'd have double hibiscus and double papayas." The collection also contained a large tome of engravings documenting Captain James Cook's travels from New Zealand to Alaska. Of this volume Ann admitted, "Nick thinks I should give this to the Bishop Museum. But I love it so much I cannot part with it. I always say they can borrow it anytime. But give it up . . . not yet."[5] Every addition to the library was a thrill for Ann, who remarked to a friend,

> I have some new books to study . . . Greece and Rome . . . as well as some very special books Nick got for me on all the recipes from all over the world . . . the last one was on Italy . . . it includes the history of cooking in all the separate cities and territories of Italy . . . the next one coming will be France. They are fascinating. And I also have some new books on Leonardo Da Vinci . . . the newest of the man is so wonderful. The prints involved are beautiful and very revealing. Did you know that Leonardo always wrote his notes backwards so that the only way you could read them was in a mirror??? Even Nick didn't know this (or else he forgot it).[6]

One of Ann's more unusual holdings was a replica of the Rosetta Stone, cast from the original. Wade claimed he earned the honor of being allowed to copy the stone when he won a Paris Architecture Prize while studying at Columbia. He could not afford to have the copy made at that time, but apparently it was a long-standing offer that he cashed in once he married Ann. He explained, "My wife had always wanted the Rosetta Stone, so I finally gave her a copy for her birthday." He presented the gift to his wife with a letter that read, "As a fit companion to your exquisite library."[7] In addition to book collecting, Ann was also able to reengage her passion for traveling, and the Wades took trips to Europe and the Orient, including Japan, where the Ken-Tech manufacturing plant was located.

Ann remained an ardent animal lover until the end of her days. After she had been in Hawaii for a handful of years, she acquired a cat named Omar whom she doted on, gushing, "Omar is certainly a person. He is the most profound animal I have ever known. I love him more everyday. I just adore this pusseycat. He has me roped and tied."[8] Ann would frequently cook for her cat:

He understands every word I say. I cook this Mahi Mahi (fish) for him . . . which has almost no bones . . . and I show it to him . . . then I place him on the kitchen chair . . . and he stays there until he begins to smell the fish cooking . . . and he starts yelling . . . to find me no matter where I am here . . . he starts running to find me to tell me that the fish is cooking . . . He runs into the bedroom . . . he runs into the library . . . he runs all over the place until he finds me to tell me that his fish is cooked. And he really talks, he tries to talk English.

Ann didn't mind that Omar cut visits to a neighbor short:

He just stands on the doorstep and howls. He wants his mama to get out of there. He thinks I am in danger when I am out of his sight. Have you ever heard a Siamese howling? It sounds like someone is murdering a cat. You can hear him two blocks away. And the lady next door laughs and I laugh . . . but I still have to cut short my visit . . . Omar has us by the balls. There is nothing we can do about this howling. He sounds like a werewolf. And any minute Dracula and Frankenstein will enter the picture.

Age had not mellowed the woman who used to report her studio bosses to the ASPCA; she proclaimed, "In this neighborhood where we live you will never see any stinking little bastards throwing stones at cats." Ann recalled how a friend's cat in a nearby neighborhood was stoned to death. "If it were not for Nick, who is always against any public display . . . I would have gone over there and . . . (Nick Knows Me) . . . I would have beaten the holy be-Jesus out of all of them." She continued, "I got myself in this same type of trouble in Spain. And in Mexico. These are also the worst people with animals. I also got into trouble in the Canary Islands. On the same count, I nearly ended up in more jails than you can count. I was even trying to save a bull from the ring. What else can one do to get in jail?"[9] In addition to the very spoiled Omar, Ann also kept carp, which she named. She enjoyed demonstrating how the fish would respond to their names and eat out of her hand.[10] As for Omar, Ann reported, "He will not touch the carp in the pond. He thinks these fish are 'his property' . . . and that no one should touch them. He watches them by the hour."[11]

The tropical surroundings allowed Ann to exercise her horticultural skills. Rudy Grau, an acquaintance of the couple in Hawaii, recalls being impressed with the amount of foliage in the Wades' yard at 4690 Kolohala Street. Ann was quick to point out, "I plant everything from seeds."[12] However, in the battle of cat versus nature, the feline won out: "We had to get rid of six cocoanut trees. This killed me. But, they are very dangerous. Only last week, a nut fell and nearly killed Omar. It landed two inches from his head. And not only dangerous . . . but they are a continuous maintenance . . . it costs a fortune to keep them trimmed so that you don't have people sueing you for getting hit in the head with cocoanuts."[13]

In the late 1960s Ann resumed her dreams of being a writer and launched the impressively ambitious project of penning an eighteen-volume history of the world and recording herself reading it. She titled the work "Historical Digest" and planned to market it to universities. According to Ann, "In 50 hours a student can get a concept of History, Art, Architecture & Religion—they can even do it in Summer School." Ann felt her innovative instruction was necessary because, as she wrote to a friend, "They [professors] cannot teach the way I am teaching. They have *not* put it *together*—the students get it in all bits and pieces and they come out knowing nothing." She added, "I know exactly what I am doing." Ann was convinced there was a market for "Historical Digest," noting, "This new set-up in the Washington Educational Department will be the thing. They have this entirely new revised Department which they are actually begging for new educational methods and I have it right in

Ann with actress Jobyna Phillips in Hawaii, circa 1970.

my hands. However, the professors may fight each other over this."[14] Ann was incredibly enthusiastic about "Historical Digest"; when she received the occasional letter from a film fan, she was quick to respond with a return letter focused almost exclusively on the project. Since moving to Hawaii, she had renewed contact with her mother, and Ann's enthusiasm for the project rubbed off on Anna Lehr, who relayed to a relative, "Ann D. has started something vital to the general youth . . . NOT fiction . . . But, data . . . Important, wait and read it. May take her two years to finish."[15]

While Ann was working on "Historical Digest," she was contacted by Dr. Arnold "Arne" Scheibel, a professor of neurology at the University of California, Los Angeles, and his wife, Mila, who in 1959 had purchased

Ann's former Encino ranch home. Ann was thrilled hear from the couple, though this probably had more to do with Arne's ties to the world of academia than the connection to her previous life. If there was a common theme among people who encountered Ann Dvorak in her later years, it was that she lived in the present and never dwelt in the past. She took to sending Arne cartoons cut out of *Playboy* magazine, including one of a negligee-clad woman seated in front of a college class, which she captioned, "Ann teaching Historical Digest." Once she had a rough manuscript of "Historical Digest," she sent it to Arne to review and share with his colleagues, who apparently gave some constructive criticism, though the specifics are unknown. She then began shopping it to various academic institutions. The feedback was not positive, but exhibiting the old Dvorak spunk, she wrote to the Scheibels,

> As to Historical Digest . . . it all turned out in a very strange way. I don't mean that it is completely dead . . . it will have its use . . . but of all the reasons for instance given by your friends . . . and many similar ones from people everywhere . . . against it . . . you would never guess in a million years what it came down to. The real reason for its failure (temporary at least) are two . . . *Number One* . . . *PEOPLE DON'T UNDERSTAND IT. And Number Two:* The university professors are against anything new in form and will have nothing to do with it. None of the reasons your kind friends gave were the answers . . . to my own amazement. Because I was thinking along the lines of every answer they gave . . . and I thought they were honestly good probabilities. But how could I imagine in my wildest moments that it could be because people could not understand it? . . . It only means that it is the greatest living proof of the lack of knowledge of History there is in this country.[16]

Unfortunately, no manuscripts or recordings of "Historical Digest" seem to exist, so there is no way of knowing if Ann Dvorak's history of the world was truly awful or had some merit. Over the years, Ann had continued to claim that she had attended Occidental College and she always appeared insecure about her lack of formal education. With "Historical Digest" she seemed to be attempting to integrate herself in the academic world, and it must have been crushing to have her labor of love unanimously rejected by a community she was trying to impress.

Initially, the move to Hawaii seemed to have breathed life into Ann and Nick's troubled marriage. Even George Wade and his wife, Mary, who usually stayed away from the couple, agreed to visit Oahu and, according to their daughter, had a fine time.[17] However, as the decade wore on, old patterns reemerged and the union began to deteriorate again. Acquaintance Rudy Grau admitted to seeing Ann drink enough to be tipsy, though never saw her get out of hand. He also remembered that during the time he spent with the two, he never saw them being affectionate with each other. Grau recalled Ann and Nick as polar opposites, with Wade being an eccentric type who would go out to dinner in shorts and bare feet and grab food off other people's plates when the waiter walked by. He also remembers that Nick would walk around the house with Omar the cat around his neck just to irritate his wife. Ann, on the other hand, Grau recalls, was very sweet and nice, though exceptionally serious and seemingly very well educated.[18] The Wades may have been able to hide their domestic problems from friends on the island, but there was one person Ann was not afraid to confide in.

As her marriage became strained, Ann began repairing her relationship with her mother, which had been in tatters for well over a decade. After Anna Lehr was kicked out of the Malibu cottage, she found a small apartment at 1235 Fifth Street in Santa Monica and began receiving government assistance to survive. She also began contacting distant family members and asking for money, insisting that she would be winning the Irish Sweepstakes or making a big comeback in films any day. Of her current station she commented, "I am a loner. I don't mix at all. NOT bitter, just aloof, from it all . . . Don't get me wrong while I try to live like a holy woman, NOT a prude. NOR am I an angel, yet. BOTH are vastly different. I love to attend the *Races*. My only recreation."[19] Lehr had attained a certain level of spirituality. "I am not a churchy-person, every day I ask God, to, 'help me to believe,' and to 'show me the way' it is a part of my short daily prayer. In reverence. In humanity." By this time, Anna had given up on lying about her age and now proudly admitted that at seventy-six she had "NO false teeth, no operations. Fine hands, fine feet, fine complexion, no polish, no make-up, *none* . . . Long hair, braided simply around my head."[20]

As for her formerly famous daughter, Lehr did not shy away from discussing Ann's situation and her problems. "There is an alcoholic in my life. Do you know of my daughter??????? ANN DVORAK," she wrote once, and another time, "If it wasnt for that fact that she is emotionally-sick from boozing . . . she would not abandon me as she had thru the many many years."²¹ On another occasion she quipped, "Ann D is also doing some 'writing' if she will stay 'on the wagon.' Poor Annie D." Time had not mellowed Lehr's animosity toward her son-in-law. "She is married to a monster. I am sure he connivingly wishes her dead! A sad story."²² Anna Lehr also revealed, "Every cent she has in the world is tied up, in *her* property, with *his* signature. This was accomplished during a dringing [drinking]—orgy. She explained."²³ Of this latest development, Lehr added, "And he is just waiting to fly the coop. To Europe, with every cent of cash!"²⁴

Despite her criticism and her words of pity for her troubled daughter, Anna Lehr also seemed proud of Ann, even impressed by her: "She is a great lady, refined, speaks many languages, fluently. Beautiful serene. Poised. A posture, a regal manner." Despite her own personal and financial problems, Lehr was also constantly worried about her daughter. "Poor girl. With her name on the street in the GOLD Star, to think she has allowed that demon, to let her get soooo lost," Lehr reflected, referencing Ann's inclusion in the inaugural list of fifteen hundred industry personalities whose names launched the Hollywood Walk of Fame. By 1968 Lehr expressed hopes of being able to get Ann off the island and deal with her alcohol issues by having "her committed for 90 days. This is nothing to be ashamed of."²⁵ Lehr was convinced Ann would be able to restart her career. "Show business would pay her $250 a month," which is what she had been making every week nearly forty years before.²⁶ She also believed that Mervyn LeRoy or Howard Hughes would help get Ann back on her feet, though this was delusional, as LeRoy's career had wound down by this point, and Hughes was battling his own demons.

Ann visited her mother a couple of times in 1968 and seemed to be considering leaving Wade again. However, in January 1969, Nick suffered a heart attack, and any plans for separation quickly vanished. During his recuperation at the hospital, Ann noted, "I was there everyday for over three weeks." She recounted how two days after being moved from the special care unit, "he was giving all the nurses trouble. He pushed his bed out on the lanai and took a sun bath. This was something which created a riot in the whole hospital. The rooms facing his in another building were filled with old dames (wealthy type) who were amazed, astonished and shocked at seeing a naked man in a bed on his lanai. Well, he wasn't naked

. . . he was only stripped to the waist . . . but this shocked their poor sensibilities." During her daily visits, Ann, who had never expressed much interest in children, described how "I watched the 'Baby room' everyday there in the hospital. Some mornings there were as many as ten new babies, all marked and tagged." In the months after his release, Ann threw herself into taking care of her husband and keeping him on a special diet. He lost twenty pounds and Ann was pleased with the results, remarking, "He looks better now than he has for years. All his pants fit him and he is his old kidding self. He looks wonderful now. In fact now what shall I do with him? He is raring to go all over the place." Three months after the heart attack, Nick celebrated a milestone: "He had his 60th birthday and he could not believe it. And I don't believe it. And let us say that I am 56 [she was actually fifty-seven] and do not feel a day older. There are only a few days when I do not feel a day older."[27]

The positive effects the heart attack had on the marriage quickly wore off, and by May 1969, Anna Lehr informed a family member, "I am flying to Honolulu Saturday. I'll write you from there. Ann D. pleads that I fly and bring her back here. Poor Annie D. What a mess she had made of her life!"[28] Lehr, who was deathly afraid of flying, did not make it out to the island; she stated in July, "Lots of news. And yet none at all. I was going to fly to Honolulu Monday. But it is off. (I'm glad) She goes to Italy for six months, on a fine writing job."[29] Ann did not go to Italy, but instead flew to Los Angeles in early August. Her marriage had reached a tipping point and she was now turning to her mother for help.

After settling into Lehr's cramped Santa Monica apartment, Ann connected with Arne and Mila Scheibel. The couple made arrangements to dine with Ann and her mother, and as Arne recalled nearly forty years later,

They did not want us to see the apartment they were living in, so they asked to be picked up at a nearby hotel. As I made my way to the hotel lobby, I heard a raised voice which turned out to be Ann, who was causing some sort of minor scene. She was not particularly dressed-up for an evening out and I could tell that she had already been drinking. Anna Lehr, on the other hand, was a very handsome woman. She was dressed all in black and her face was covered in white powder. No other make-up, just white powder.

They piled into the Scheibels' Cadillac, with Ann sitting in the backseat with Mila and Anna Lehr riding in front. As they made their way to the San Fernando Valley, Scheibel recounted, "Anna Lehr began sliding over next to me in the front seat making comments like, 'I can tell we are going to be really good friends.' I had to drive with my right elbow sticking out, just to keep her at a safe distance!" When the party arrived at an El Torito restaurant in Encino, Arne remembers that no one in the restaurant paid any attention to Ann, but heads turned as Anna Lehr walked through the room. Even though she had ceased acting decades ago and had never been a huge star, she still carried herself like one. Arne was also impressed with Anna Lehr's ability to down mugs of beer in a single gulp. While Scheibel does not recall what Ann Dvorak's drink of choice was, he does remember that whatever it was, she consumed a lot of it. "At one point, a flamenco guitarist started performing and whenever he finished a song and the applause was not sufficient enough for Ann's taste, she would stand up with arms flailing and yell, 'Why don't you all clap? Can't you see this man's breaking his heart for us?'"[30]

After the awkward dinner, the couple drove Ann and her mother to the house in Encino that Ann had built and called home for ten years. The Scheibels were the fourth owners of the property. Despite multiple possessors and the passage of nearly twenty-five years, the property remained remarkably like it had been in the days when Ann and Leslie Fenton lived there. The greenhouse was no longer functioning, now housing the Scheibels' ping-pong table, but it still stood. The garage had been converted into a seminar room, where Scheibel met with his graduate students, and the horse and cow stables were being used as storage. However, the pool and pool house were still intact, as were most of the fixtures around the property. Even the Bauer flowers pots with which Ann had populated the grounds were still there. The Scheibels were eager for Ann to visit the house and became extremely puzzled when, as Arne remembers, "She came into the house and there was no sign of recognition on her face. Nothing. It was very odd." It was as if the decade she had lived on the property had been washed away. Were the years with Leslie Fenton so stifling, as some suspected, that she just chose to block out what was left of the tangible evidence of their life together? Or was it the opposite— in the midst of her troubles with Nicholas Wade, did the Encino estate represent a bright period of her life that was now too painful to recall? As it turned out, not only did Ann have no recollection of her former home, but likewise retained little memory of that evening in general. When she returned to Hawaii, she wrote the couple a letter. "I don't know how you can still love me . . . frankly I have great blank spots . . . but my mother filled in a few for me. She was very understanding. I should never have gone out at all. It was soon after that I collapsed. It was in a great portion due to overwork and a certain type of disagreement. It was coming on a very very long time, several years." Arne Scheibel diplomatically summed up his time with Ann: "It was obvious that she was a deeply troubled woman at the time."[31]

Over twenty years later, Howard Fenton, who always remained in contact with Ann, wrote to one of the Scheibels' neighbors, "Both mother and daughter, later had alcoholic problems, as Arne knows only too well. He was wonderful to receive them at the 'Ranch' during the bad times for Ann, and her Mother. I wish he had known the Ann I knew, and I loved."[32]

Following the ill-fated evening in Encino, Ann took to writing to the Scheibels nearly every night for over a week. The letters she handwrote during this time were markedly different from those she had typed from Hawaii both in tone and coherency. This correspondence usually began with "It's 3am, the witching hour," were more than likely written under the influence of something, and confirm that Ann Dvorak was indeed a troubled woman during this period. In one letter she wrote, "The more I think the more of a mess I get into. If I could just stop thinking—If I could only stop thinking."[33] In another she recorded, "I have to get my mind off of myself—& on to other things. I simply have to forget. This break-up was almost too much. But I am recovering—slowly—not as fast as I would like to."[34] She closed the last letter she wrote them during this time with, "Truthfully speaking—the only thing that is saving my life is my sense of humor—And Mama's sense of humor."[35]

Ann's return to Southern California was not made under the most ideal circumstances, but at least it enabled her to repair the damaged relationship with Anna Lehr. However, after spending so much time together in relatively cramped quarters, tensions could run high, especially on Lehr's part. As Ann admitted, "We seem to get along best when we are both asleep. She gets so mad at me—I certainly am right back to 16 again." Ann also said, "She may be watching me like a 16 year old, 24 hours a day, but I am watching *her* also & she does listen to me. But I have a little trouble with her. She has a temper out of Solomon's Temple— when she gets mad at such petty things—it is the Holy end of the World.

So here I am—the Devil in the Deep Blue Sea. It will be alright eventually. I have to take care of her as much as I can in any case." Lehr could at times have a nasty streak and Ann confessed, "But once in a while she makes these cracks—that floor me, like, 'Hello my drunken daughter.'" Despite Lehr's temperamental flare-ups, Ann delighted in watching her mother cook every night, an activity in which Anna maintained a running dialogue with the food. "Whatever she cooks she talks to. She talks to the oven and the burners & the pots & pans. And if she burns her finger she yells at the stove—& I lose two of my stomachs listening to her, & laughing. She puts on an entire show when she is cooking. Billy Rose & Ziegfeld couldn't do any better. I could sell her as an act into Las Vegas & make money with Mama cooking dinner."[36] As much as Ann enjoyed the nightly dinner show, it was the late-night hours she tended to prefer, commenting, "I like to see her sleep—she sleeps like an angel and she generally hears nothing—I believe that if she rests enough, she will be alright. And she has enough common sense to do it. She *has a lot* of common sense. A lot more than I have."[37]

Whatever issues that may have arisen between the pair over the years were quickly put aside as Ann turned to her mother for help in leaving Nicholas Wade once and for all. Ann could have simply remained in Santa Monica and never returned to Hawaii. However, there were too many ties and loose ends in Honolulu that needed to be resolved. At the time, Ann was still working on "Historical Digest" and was loath to leave it behind, remarking, "I have so much to do with Historical Digest—to polish about 8 of the books." She continued, "The question is to get it off the ground— And I am going to get this thing off the ground—but I have to go back for the tapes—all my scripts are there—I cannot work from here—I really wish I could—but it's impossible—all my work is there in the library— about 18 volumes—& I don't have it—I have nothing but one small suitcase which I didn't even unpack. How can I handle this project if I don't go and get it?"[38] There was also the matter of Omar the cat, whom Ann could not bear to permanently leave behind. "I am so worried about my pusseycat who is looking for his Mama—& sleeping on my bed every night. My heart is breaking for my beautiful Siamese pusseycat—I can't even talk about it—it breaks my heart."[39]

As much as Ann needed to return to her home in Hawaii, she could not bring herself to do it alone, and she was counting on Anna Lehr to see her through this troubled time. As Ann recorded, "I want her to help me with my domestic problems—and *she is the only one who can do it*—She is the only one—he should *touch her* and it will be the biggest scandal in the history of Honolulu. So of course he won't. He wouldn't dream of it. There would be no trouble."⁴⁰ On another occasion Ann pronounced, "I wouldn't cross the line with Mama—and there's *someone else who wouldn't cross the line with Mama*—He wouldn't dare." Unfortunately, Lehr's fear of flying persisted, so she kept delaying the trip, and Ann remarked, "I am getting her off the ground on Sunday or Monday—(I hope)." She added, "It is just imperative that she comes with me. I won't go back alone." Despite her mother's phobia, Ann felt there was no alternative, noting, "I actually would go by boat in order for her to feel better—but I don't have time—an arrangement for boat passage would take far too long—& time is of an essence right now—after all it is only 4½ hours to Honolulu. *We just have to make it.* She doesn't quite understand how much is involved—but she is getting it—*little by little*—& she *is* helping me as much as she knows how—She is a wonderful person."⁴¹

As for Lehr, she was no doubt happy to have her daughter back in her life, but could have done without the drama surrounding the return. As she exclaimed in a letter to the Scheibels, "My whole world of serenity, peace, solitude, has collapsed! The place is in chaos, disorder, nothing will ever be the same!! Nor will I ever be the same . . . I could collapse!!! Poor annie dvorak. Poor wonderful person. *How sick* . . . We have only been reconciled lately after ten yrs. Or more of 'kind estrangement.'" She continued, "Ann D. has no money of her own, but she will have when I get to Honolulu . . . And they will divorce. DEFINITELY . . . I have called him a 'deseased rat' with maggots for a conscience!!!" Lehr also admitted, "I love ann d. and would die for her, BUT not to 'go down the drain' because of any vile living." She followed these sentiments with a plea: "If there is any cash you can spare and will send it to me. Even fifty dollars will help a humiliating situation . . . I may inherit an oil-well and even an Irish Sweepsteaks."⁴²

Ann finally did get her mother over to the islands, but when Lehr returned to the mainland, she was alone; Ann had decided to stay with Nicholas Wade. If nothing else, one of the darkest times in Ann's life had brought her and her mother closer together than they had been in years. As eccentric and sometimes meddling as Anna Lehr may have been, Ann always adored the mother who had been such a huge influence on her. When Lehr was diagnosed with colon cancer in the early 1970s, Ann

Anna Lehr and Ann Dvorak in Hawaii, circa 1969.

cared for her. Anna Lehr succumbed to the disease on January 22, 1974, at the age of eighty-three, and Ann was right by her mother's side.

After her mother's death, Ann remained in Santa Monica and did not return to Nick Wade. In the end, Anna Lehr did enable Ann to escape from her abusive third husband. She struggled financially and relied on food stamps to survive, but at least she was responsible only for herself.[43] When Nicholas Wade died in January 1975, presumably of another heart attack, his wife of twenty-four years was not with him. With Nick gone, Ann started making plans to return to Hawaii. After the passing of her husband, Ann reflected on her life in a poem she titled "The Rainbow Sunset."

I had to reach 62 to finally become free.
A career and 3 marriages. 2 divorces.
A life of fire and brimstone.
Adventure? Yes—lots of it.
In many ways.[44]

For the first time in her life, Ann Dvorak was completely alone.

24

The End of Everything

After Ann Dvorak died in the winter of 1979, the *National Enquirer,* a notorious tabloid magazine, ran a scathing article about her final days. The magazine depicted a desperate, paranoid, impoverished woman living in squalor, a moment away from landing on the streets. For those who had never heard of Ann Dvorak, this article was a sad introduction to her. For those who did recall Ann from her days as a film actress, the piece made a lasting impression. The question remains: How accurate was the *National Enquirer's* portrayal of the former actress? As with many articles published within the pages of the scandal sheet, the finished piece seems to have a foundation in truth with some exaggeration.

After the deaths of Nick Wade and her mother, Ann was more or less alone in the world. She never had children, did not have siblings, and had never maintained close ties with any other relatives. Additionally, she was usually not one to foster close friendships, instead preferring the company of her husbands, all of whom she outlived, as Igor Dega passed in July 1976, followed by Leslie Fenton in March 1978.

After Nick Wade died in 1975, Ann came to realize just how dire their finances were. The Revered Jack Stump, a neighbor who was the informant on Ann's death certificate, reported, "Ann had been left virtually penniless by her husband. She made millions in the movies and she was reduced to this because of her husband's handling of their businesses. She used to complain that he 'virtually stole my money—he didn't use the funds properly.'" Another friend was quoted as saying "It was quite a comedown. She'd been one of Hollywood's wealthiest women. Now she was living on her Social Security and her Screen Actors Guild pension."[1] Ann had pulled in a decent salary at times in her career, but had never risen above the tier of leading lady or B picture star, so to say that she made millions or was one of Hollywood's wealthiest women was an overstatement. Even with her former real estate holdings, she was never worth as much as the *National Enquirer* claimed.

Two months after Nick Wade died, Ann was back in Hawaii, living in a house at 190 Nenue Street. A year later she moved to 682 Paopua Loop.[2] It is not clear why she relocated so often, but by the fall of 1977 she had moved again and was renting what she described as "a little white house about the size inside of a small apartment. Garden all around" in the Kaimuki neighborhood near Diamond Head. The rent was fairly high, at $250 per month, so Ann needed to apply for rent subsidy. She was no longer living the life of a movie star, and had not for decades, but she claimed, "This little place is just fine for me" and "Financially I am ok at present."[3]

Despite the downgraded lifestyle, it seems that Ann found a certain amount of peace at this time: "I am calm and collected, and live alone with my pusseycat—'Frosty.' He is pure white with yellow eyes. I no longer have any interest in large money. I was 66 this year—and all I want to do is get straightened out—get my legs well—and write." Her physical health had recently taken a downturn and she had undergone surgery on her left hip. After nearly a month in the hospital, she relied on a walker and wheelchair, as her leg was still in a cast, and she was in a great deal of pain. Still, she remained optimistic, noting, "I am making this a transitional period—a lot of thinking and planning." Proof that the movie star in Ann was not completely gone, she added, "I am due for a complete overhaul, mentally and physically. I plan on a facelift—so I must save as much money as possible."[4] Ann also reclaimed herself by reverting to her maiden name, going by Ann Wade McKim.

From the late 1950s through the 1970s, there was a small enclave in the Waikiki Beach area known as "the jungle." The neighborhood was filled with small apartment buildings and rooming houses that catered to a bohemian set, along with surfers and transients. In March 1978 Ann relocated to this area, moving into an apartment unit at 2144 Lauula Street. This is where she would spend her final years. The degree of unpleasantness Ann found in these surroundings is open to some interpretation, although Ann herself called the alley next to the building "Garbage Alley. . . . Here the garbage and trash are right at the door—the whole street is garbage. But . . . I am on the 2nd floor—it doesn't bother me. At least there is hardly a dull moment—the police are here about 3 or 4 times a week. But not in my place of course." Usually a private person,

Always the animal lover, Ann cradles her orange tabby in July 1979, five months before her death.

Ann now allowed herself to become acquainted with some of her neighbors. As she wrote to a friend, "I am fortunate here in having a few friends in the building. I have other friends here and there but they wouldn't understand where I am living."[5]

Ann seemed to be making the best of her situation, concentrating on keeping herself healthy. "My main physical concern is walking—on a cane—but I walk twice a day and a lot around the apartment here. And sometimes I even dance—if it's the right music—like Lawrence Welk when they really 'go.'" Ann also exhibited some of the old Dvorak innovation by concocting some sort of mystery formula that would benefit cotton farmers. She even put together a brochure for her product and tried to get a firm to help with the marketing, but nothing came of these plans.[6] She was also interested in writing once again, and came up with the idea of becoming a self-styled TV critic, commenting on everything from commercials and soap operas to sports and network shows. She thought of contacting *TV Guide* with the idea, but it's not clear if she followed through. Most important, Ann had stopped abusing alcohol. As she recorded in her journal, "I am not drinking like a fish any more."[7]

While living on Lauula Street, Ann reconnected with her childhood friend Leona Cary with whom she had lost touch shortly after marrying Nick Wade. Cary was also widowed and had retired to Grass Valley, a small community in Northern California. The two were thrilled to rediscover each other and exchanged letters often, reminiscing about their days at the Elliott School for Girls and commiserating about the hard knocks each had endured over the years. Cary even hinted that Ann should revive her former career, writing, "I'll make a bet you could do some good character roles of older women."[8]

Cary started saving money to visit Ann. She finally made in out in July 1979 and stayed with her old friend for three weeks. After the visit, Cary began looking into selling her mobile home in Grass Valley and moving to Hawaii to be near Ann. "I couldn't help but think . . . how silly it is that you and I are both so alone and so far apart." Unfortunately, those plans did not come to fruition before Ann passed away. Cary, tracked down by the *Enquirer* after Ann's death, was quoted as saying, "I was shocked to discover her real condition. She was living in poverty in a rundown apartment house in an area full of drug addicts and alcoholics. She didn't even turn off the lights because she was afraid."[9] Cary's letters to Ann clearly demonstrate a genuine love and affection between the two women, and it seems unlikely she would have deliberately aimed to portray her friend in a negative light. While Ann herself had admitted that the location of her apartment left a lot to be desired, it's more than likely Cary also made positive comments that the *Enquirer* chose not to include.

Not long after relocating to this part of the island, Ann was befriended by Rudi Polt, an Austrian native and avid surfer who had moved to Hawaii to take advantage of the legendary island waves. An extremely likable fellow with a Peter Pan nature, Rudi was also starstruck and had become friends with former actress Dorothy Mackaill, who held court at the Royal Hawaiian Hotel. When Rudi discovered where Ann Dvorak was living, he had no qualms about knocking on her door and introducing himself. Though Ann was still very private, she took to Polt and was happy to accept his company. She even cooked him French onion soup on at least one occasion. Rudi recalls the apartment house as a charming deco-style building in which Ann occupied a fairly roomy corner unit. Her living quarters were tidy, and he remembers that the large portrait of Ann done in the 1930s was on display.[10] Rudy Grau, who had known Ann and Nick around 1970 but had lost touch when he relocated to the mainland, moved back to Honolulu shortly after Ann's death and, by sheer coincidence, was the next occupant of the apartment. He also confirms that the unit and building were not at all what the *National Enquirer* had described and that the apartment was perfectly livable.[11] Photos taken inside the apartment months before Ann died confirm that while the unit was on the small side, it received a lot of natural light and, typical of Ann, was filled with potted plants. Unfortunately, the building has been replaced with a parking lot, so it's the word of the two Rudies versus the tabloid.

Rudi Polt frequently stopped by Ann's place unannounced and would often find her napping on the couch with the television on. Contrary to the *Enquirer*'s report that Ann left the lights on at night because she was afraid of her surroundings, Polt is quick to point out that had she been in fear, she would not have left her door unlocked as she often did, and she did not object when he entered without knocking. Polt does admit that Ann was uncomfortable being sought out by fans, and was loath to be contacted by fellow Americans who, according to Ann, would ask "stupid, silly questions." She also said, "Americans are so crazy. Some guy might come and shoot me so he gets his name in the paper because he killed Ann Dvorak." However, she was more than happy to invite some of Polt's Viennese friends into her home because she felt she could trust Europeans. She also enjoyed it when Rudi brought a young neighborhood boy named Devon to visit. The Reverend Stump had mentioned, "She refused to talk about her movie career—she would become upset if you brought it up. It reminded her of when she was rich."[12] But this attitude of living in the present, not the past, was nothing new for Ann—she had adhered to it since the 1950s. Polt does recall that the one time she brought up her past, it was to talk about her 1932 honeymoon with Leslie Fenton and how all the women fawned over Hans Albers, the star of the German-language version of *F.P.1*.

Polt claims he never saw Ann exhibiting any trace of a drinking problem, which backs up Ann's own claims that she had quit abusing alcohol. Leona Cary exclaimed to her friend, "You Annie dear made my day when you told me about being off liquor. I had some heartaches over that," and on another occasion she wrote, "Words can't tell you how happy I am about the drinking problem. You won! I'm so proud of you."[13] After her death, Rudi connected with a woman who had lived in Ann's building who told him, "Annie used to come down here because I never talked about her and show business. We were the same age and talked about things that happened today. So, she would come down with a bottle of wine and a glass. And so we'd sit in the room and she would pour herself a glass of wine and drink maybe half. And then at the end, she'd go back with the glass and have the rest with her supper." Polt reasons that the other tenants may have observed Ann with her bottle and glass and assumed she had a severe drinking problem. After the publication of the *Enquirer* article, the neighbor was reportedly so upset she declared she would have sued them if she had the money. "Why did they call her the alcoholic? I'm the one who's the alcoholic, not her!"[14] The *Enquirer* article quoted Leona Cary as stating that Ann "drank heavily," and while she certainly had had issues in the preceding years, all evidence points to Ann having kicked the habit after the deaths of Nick Wade and Anna Lehr. Her letters and journal entries from the time are much more coherent than the letters she wrote to the Scheibels in the late 1960s, when she was clearly under the influence. It's quite possible that when Cary spoke of Ann's drinking, she was referring to her past, but the *Enquirer* manipulated her words to suit its purpose of relating a more scandalous story.

The tabloid had also contacted Ann's former brother-in-law, Howard Fenton, who was quoted as saying, "In her last letter to me, she talked about making a trip to Europe to see Pompeii—a trip I know now she could have never afforded."[15] Rudi Polt, who frequently traveled between Europe and Hawaii, claims that he and Ann were indeed planning to take a trip in early 1980. With Ann's finances in worse shape than they should have been, she definitely was living on a very fixed income after Wade's death. In addition to Social Security and a SAG pension, some sort of government assistance would not have been out of the question. However, despite reports that Ann was virtually penniless at the time of her death, she had $1,111.63 in the bank.[16] This may have been a pittance for a woman who at one time had earned $2,500 a week making films, but it was enough to cover rent and trips to the corner grocery store, and perhaps a trip to Europe. And, after a lifetime of being under the thumb of her mother and three successive husbands, at the very least Ann had something she valued a great deal—freedom and independence.

Polt had long made a habit of going back to Austria for an extended stay during the holidays, and when he left in the fall of 1979, he fully expected to come back to Hawaii and resume making plans with Ann for the two to travel abroad. Upon his return, he was shocked to learn that Ann had suddenly passed away. She had gone to the Straub Clinic and Hospital in early December complaining of stomach pains and was immediately diagnosed with cancer. Leona Cary later stated, "I think she knew she had cancer, but she told me: 'I can't go to the hospital—I'll never come out.'"[17] Ann was scheduled for surgery, but the medical team discovered that the cancer had spread too much to save her. After less than two weeks in the hospital, she passed away on December 10, 1979, age sixty-eight. The official cause of death was cancer of the appendix. Because she was living under the name Ann McKim, it took nearly two weeks for the mainstream media to be alerted to the death of Ann Dvorak. The Reverend Jack Stump knew so little about Ann that her parents were listed as "unknown" on the death certificate and she was identified as being also known as "Ann McKin Dvoray."[18] Without any close relatives, Ann instead listed Leona Cary as the beneficiary of her SAG pension.[19] Ann's body was cremated three days after she died, and a small group of acquaintances who had known her in those final years spread her ashes off Waikiki Beach. Despite the *Enquirer*'s declaration that the state had to pay for the cremation, the money in Ann's bank account was ultimately used to cover this cost along with all the funeral and medical expenses.[20] In the end, Ann Dvorak truly took care of herself.

As for her belongings, the Reverend Stump more than likely took charge of the contents of her apartment, and while some of these personal items have surfaced, including canceled checks and photos from Leona Cary's visit, it is unknown what happened to her rare book collection, which may have been sold long before she died, and the portrait painting, which was in her possession until the end. She also had a storage unit, the contents of which ended up in the hands of an antique dealer a year or two after her death. Sadly, most of the items from the unit were destroyed in a hurricane on Kauai at some point, but the dealer, who for years has operated a shop called the Only Show in Town on the North Shore, recalls there being "a great deal of sheet music and maybe soundtracks from her movies."[21] Was the sheet music possibly Ann's own composi-

Among Ann's possessions at the time of her death was a scrapbook contain-
ing countless photos from her travels with Leslie Fenton, like this one of the
couple vacationing in 1938.

tions, of which she claimed to have published many? Since Ann's films
never had soundtracks, perhaps the records in the storage unit were
recordings Ann made of herself reading from her beloved project
"Historical Digest."

What have survived are photographs from Ann Dvorak's heyday as a
glamorous film actress. She had held on to a handful of publicity stills
from movies throughout her career, such as *Three on a Match*, *Merrily We
Live*, *Our Very Own*, and *I Was an American Spy*. She had also kept three
photos of herself in *The Respectful Prostitute*, three of the images taken by
George Hurrell in 1937, and a tall stack of duplicate 8 x 10s that she

would have used for the occasional request from a fan. By the 1970s, these inquiries must have been so rare that Ann did not feel the need to keep the photos on hand and had put them in the storage unit. There was also a glamour shot from the late 1940s inscribed simply, "With all my love—To Mama."

Among the items Ann kept with her in the apartment was a scrapbook of over one hundred photos from her honeymoon with Leslie Fenton in 1932 and some of their later travels, and a journal from 1977, whose lone entry closed with: "When I think back on my life I am ashamed of myself. I didn't study my profession well enough. I was too busy with studying science and literature. Collecting and reading my library—and growing plants and 'keeping touch with the soil'—made me a tragically disinterested figure of an actress. Also getting married in too much of a hurry without really knowing the man. I threw my life and my career out of the window."[22]

Despite Ann's frequent claims to the press in the 1930s that she never regretted walking out on her Warner Bros. contract and that marriage was the central concern in her life, she was clearly conflicted by how her profession suffered. She deeply regretted the lost potential of her acting career, yet at the end of her life one of her most prized possessions was a scrapbook from decades earlier, documenting the events that had adversely affected that career. Ultimately, we are left with an unresolved and unresolvable "What if?" about the life and career of an extraordinary woman who nearly rose to the highest heights of Hollywood, but instead followed her heart to obscurity in a small Hawaiian apartment.

Epilogue

After her retirement in 1952, Ann Dvorak was worried her contribution to cinema would be quickly forgotten. To a certain degree this did happen in the ensuing years as she fell into the ranks of actors whose names would elicit a blank stare or only the vaguest hint of recollection. Part of the reason this happened no doubt can be attributed to the "What have you done lately?" attitude of the film industry, which was prevalent even back when Ann's mother was making films. Another possible reason for Ann's quick fade into obscurity was her own reclusiveness and ultimate relocation to Hawaii, which caused her to be out of sight and mind. The unavailability of her films is yet another culprit. Some of Ann's most potent performances came during the pre-Code era. The enforcement of the Code starting in 1934 not only watered down the types of roles available to actresses of the era but also caused many films to be hidden for decades. Editing movies like *Three on a Match* and *The Strange Love of Molly Louvain* to gain PCA approval for reissues was an impossible task, so titles like these were left to collect dust in studio vaults indefinitely. The emerging field of film scholarship in the 1960s fostered a strong interest in the films of Howard Hawks, which could have shone a bit of a light on Ann Dvorak as Cesca in *Scarface,* arguably her most important film and performance. However, the classic gangster film not only faced ongoing censorship issues, it was also a victim of its producer, Howard Hughes. The millionaire had grown increasingly eccentric as the years wore on, and at one point he pulled *Scarface* completely out of circulation. The film remained unavailable until it was officially rereleased in 1979—ironically, the year of Ann's death. However, even if film scholars had been introduced to Ann via *Scarface* in the 1960s and 1970s, it's difficult to tell how receptive she would have been had anyone sought her out in Hawaii for comment.

But although Ann did become relatively obscure, she was not completely forgotten. For comedian Lenny Bruce, she was "the woman across the water" in a routine about Warner Bros. films, and author Gore Vidal paid homage to Ann in his novel *Myra Breckenridge*; he writes of a character, "She was thrilling, every inch of her a great actress on the order of Frances Dee or Ann Dvorak."[1] Occasionally, a film writer would scratch the surface of Ann's story, like Doug McClelland in his piece "Ann Dvorak: The Underground Goddess" for *Film Fan Monthly* magazine in 1969 or James Robert Parish's chapter on Ann in his 1978 volume *Hollywood Players: The Thirties*. More recently, Ann Dvorak received a closer look from Laura Wagner in the 2004 book *Killer Tomatoes: Fifteen Tough Film Dames*. Aside from these few writers, however, it seemed likely that Ann Dvorak would eventually fade away permanently, known only to the most ardent classic film fan.

Then home video came about, and with it an accessibility to films never before seen by audiences born long after Hollywood's golden age. Starting in the 1990s, pre-Code films, which had been buried in studio vaults for decades, began being released for home consumption, and new generations of fans have been discovering Ann Dvorak. *Three on a Match,* ignored in its day, has become a quintessential pre-Code film, and Vivian Revere is recognized as an emblematic character of this era. Ann's performances in early gems like *Scarface, Heat Lightning,* and *"G" Men* have garnered her a steady stream of new admirers, and later roles in titles like *A Life of Her Own* and *Our Very Own* still make viewers take notice. The year 2002 saw the launching of a website devoted exclusively to Ann, and Turner Classic Movies honored her in 2011 with twenty-four hours of programming in its annual "Summer under the Stars" festival. Ann Dvorak will never be a household name, like her contemporary Bette Davis, but she has developed a devoted following in recent years that continues to grow as more of her films become available and word about her spreads online.

The question that remains is could Ann Dvorak have risen to the star caliber of fellow Warner Bros. player Bette Davis had she played the studio game, if only for a little while? There is probably no real answer to this. Ann was definitely in a better position than most Hollywood hopefuls in 1932, though no one can guess if the public would have declared her a box-office draw. Giving her meaty roles in *Three on a Match* and *The Strange Love of Molly Louvain,* Warner Bros. seemed to be positioning her for stardom, yet casting her in inconsequential parts in *Crooner* and *Stranger in Town* indicates that the studio was not going to treat her differently than most of its contract players. The fact remains that Ann Dvorak walked out on her career before the public had an opportunity to

Ann poses with a portrait of herself in 1933. She would keep this painting her entire life and had it on display in her last apartment.

voice its opinion about her, and Warner Bros. had no intention of giving her a real chance after that. One might point out that Bette Davis also had to endure her fair share of mediocre roles, but the difference is that she tolerated it for a few years, doing what she was told. When it came time to fight the studio legally, Davis did it in such a way that Jack Warner could not help but respect her. Ann Dvorak, on the other hand, came off as an ungrateful and insolent child, first by making comments to the press about her bosses being slave drivers, and then by suing them instead of getting medical approval to be cleared of a suspension. Bette Davis had no problem marching into Jack Warner's office to complain about her roles face-to-face, but Ann took a more passive approach of complaining to her colleagues and then writing a letter to Jack Warner about her dissatisfaction, rather than go toe-to-toe with the mogul. When she did go public with her disparaging comments, the studio brass was caught off guard because they were not aware of her unhappiness. In short, Bette Davis was focused on a prosperous career as an actress and could have never been swayed or influenced by any outside force that would have jeopardized that goal. Ann Dvorak threw her priorities toward her marriage, which in turn dictated the path of her career. While she should not be faulted for following her heart, it's hard not to imagine what heights Ann could have risen to as an actress if her husband and agent had not been whispering questionable career advice in her ear.

In retrospect, Ann stands out as one of the quintessential pre-Code dames, for that was the era in which she truly shone, with high-wire performances in *Scarface, The Strange Love of Molly Louvain, Three on a Match*, and *Heat Lightning*. Her postwar career may have been filled with supporting roles, but she was almost always the standout in films like *A Life of Her Own, Out of the Blue*, and *Our Very Own*. As long as her films are still available, there will always be new viewers discovering her and wondering, "Why wasn't Ann Dvorak a bigger star?"

Her battles with Warner Bros. were not always well thought out, but she still merits recognition for bucking the studio system at a time when most actors would not dream of doing so. Ann was one of the first to take legal action against a major studio, which no doubt gave James Cagney and Bette Davis the will to follow in her footsteps. She became a freelance performer early on, and while this move did not benefit her as greatly as, say, it did Barbara Stanwyck, no one could accuse Ann of yielding to the "slave drivers" of the movie industry.

One part of Ann seems to have wanted a successful acting career, while another part wanted to abandon that career. Unfortunately for film fans, the latter usually won out, and we are left with the fractured filmography of an actress who always seemed to be on the brink of stardom but never quite made it. Still, Ann Dvorak left us with some memorable characters who remind us not to discount the talents of Hollywood's forgotten rebel.

Acknowledgments

When I first conceived of writing a biography on Ann Dvorak in 1997, I was a naive college senior who had no clue what I was getting myself into. Other than her body of film work, Ann left very little of herself behind, and unearthing her story was an incredible challenge. Since first undertaking this seemingly impossibly task, I finished college and graduate school, embarked on a career as a librarian, got married, started a family, battled thyroid cancer, and bought a house. Through all of this, there was Ann Dvorak. There were also a lot of other people along the way who aided in this project with information or moral support, and to them I would like to express my sincere thanks and appreciation.

First are the movie memorabilia dealers whose goods kicked off this amazing journey, and who were always happy to fuel my obsession for all things Ann. This bunch includes Roy Windham of Baby Jane of Hollywood, Danny Schwartz of Baseball Cards & Movie Collectibles, Mike Hawks of Larry Edmunds, Dollie Banner of Jerry Ohlinger's Movie Materials, Claire and Donovan of Eddie Brandt's Saturday Matinee, and especially the late Bob Colman and his wife, Janet, of the Hollywood Poster Exchange, where I purchased my first lobby card from an Ann-D film.

While the Internet is an ever-growing source of information, there are still amazing offline resources at archives around the world, cared for by equally amazing people. Special thanks to Sandra Joy Aguilar and Laura LaPlaca of the Warner Bros. Archives at the University of Southern California as well as Ned Comstock and Dace Taub of USC Special Collections. Additional thanks go to Marc Wanamaker of the Bison Archives, Jenny Romero of the Margaret Herrick Library's Special Collections, Valerie Yaros of the Screen Actors Guild, Ann Mosher at Temple University, Bronwen Solyom at the University of Hawaii at Manoa Library, and the various staff I interacted with at the University of California, Los Angeles, the New York Public Library, the Honolulu Public Library, and the Honolulu State Archives.

Acknowledgments

Much of the research conducted for this book was done at the Los Angeles Public Library's Central Library, where I am fortunate enough to work. The collections provided a wealth of information, but I could have not completed this book without the research assistance and cheerleading of many colleagues, past and present: Emma Roberts, Glen Creason, Michael Kirley, Cindy McNaughton, Carolyn Kozo Cole, Glenna Dunning, Lisa Falk, Terri Garst, Fernando Saucedo, Shannon O'Neill, Linda Rudell-Betts, Greg Reynolds, Robin Moon, Bob Timmermann, Millie Chong-Dillon, Sheila Nash, Jim Sherman, David Kelly, Pam Quon, Dan Dupill, Judith Strawser, Kelly Wallace, Matthew Mattson, and Heawon Paick. Extra special thanks to Mary McCoy and Kimberly Creighton, who assumed the roles of proofreader and indexer without my asking them. I owe you both dinner at Yamashiro!

In the course of my research, I encountered countless people who provided information about the elusive actress and offered encouragement: Scott Anderson, Dick Peterson, Rudi Polt, Rudy Grau, Arthur and Christine Vergara, Ann Weiss, Michael Theodore, Ramona Wade Guerra, Marvin Kapelus, Hugh O'Brian, Virginia Mayo, Jane Wyatt, Janet Grayson, Lisa Smith, Carolyn Roos Olsen, Elinor McKim, Richard Finegan, Cliff Aliperti, Gary Morris, Lisa Burks, David Kipen, Marc Chevalier, and Todd McCarthy. Added thanks to Chris Nichols of *Los Angeles Magazine,* Movie Morlock Richard Harland Smith, and Andre Soares of the Alternative Film Guide for shining a spotlight on Ann and myself. Special thanks to Anne Dean Watkins, Bailey Johnson, Robin DuBlanc, and Patrick McGilligan at the University Press of Kentucky; they not only believed in this project but were always ready to offer advice and encouragement along the way.

I am fortunate to be surrounded by loving family and friends who now know more about Ann Dvorak than they ever cared to! Much love to the Rices, including my parents, Louise and Fran; my siblings, Cory, C. J., Casey, Carly, and Susan "Soupcan" Bansmer; Uncle Al; my step-mom, Yvonne Joyce, along with the Tokar clan; my stepdad, Rick, and the rest of the Bansmers; my wonderful in-laws Maureen and Jeremy and all the other Fialkovs. Even though my grandparents, Mary, Betty "Nonnie," and Al are no longer around, they were always an inspiration to me and I know they would be proud. Hugs to my friends Nova Meza, Erik Larson, Tony Pinizzotto, Garland Testa, Tanya Whitehouse, Stephen Lewis, Michelle Morgan, Sherri Snyder, Mark Vieira, Joan Renner, Amy Inouye,

Acknowledgments

David Davis, Tom Zimmerman, Jim McCann, Michael Laroisa, Chris and Heidi Ryder, Tony Fleecs, Eric Reid, Lisa Hogg, Nena Jimenez, Nancy Davison, Ken Gehrig, and Jim Ratay.

I extend my extreme gratitude to Dr. Arnold Scheibel and his wife, Dr. Marion Diamond. Not only did they provide me with insight into Ann's later years, they opened their home to me, which was also Ann's home, without reserve, and they allowed my husband and me to be married there.

Extra special thanks to Laura Wagner, whose battle cry of "Take your time!" proved to be spot-on, and who shared in my frustration through years of trying to track down anyone who knew Ann. Laura, you're *my* hero.

Finally, this book would not exist without the following three people:

Darin Barnes, who started me on this crazy journey in 1997 with a scene still from *Three on a Match*. He has been along for the ride ever since, from the cat-pissy basement of a memorabilia shop in Brussels to the basement of the registrar recorder's office in Norwalk.

My husband, Joshua Hale Fialkov, who has willingly shared me with Ann Dvorak since the day we met, and who has cheered me on for six long years. I love you with all my heart, and my evenings are finally yours again!

My fabulous daughter, Gable, whose birth inspired me to finally get the damn book written. If it weren't for you, my dearest, darling, girl, I would still be stuck on chapter 5.

And, or course, thank you, Ann Dvorak. In my efforts to pry into your life, you helped me to become the person I always wanted to be.

Filmography

Films

Ramona (1916)
Clune Film Producing Company. Directed by Donald Crisp. Ann Dvorak as Ramona, age four, credited as Baby Anna Lehr. Cast: Adda Gleason, Monroe Salisbury, Nigel De Brulier, Richard Sterling.

The Man Hater (1917)
Triangle Film Corporation. Directed by Albert Parker. Ann Dvorak as Phemie's little sister, credited as Baby Anna Lehr. Cast: Winifred Allen, Jack Meredith, Harry Neville, Jessie Shirley.

The Five Dollar Plate (1920 short)
Oliver Films Incorporated. Directed by J. Gordon Cooper and Carl Harbaugh. Ann Dvorak credited as Baby Anna Lehr. Cast: Herbert Rawlinson.

The Hollywood Revue of 1929 (1929)
Metro-Goldwyn-Mayer. Directed by Charles Reisner. Ann Dvorak as member of the chorus, uncredited. Cast: Conrad Nagel, Jack Benny, Cliff Edwards, Joan Crawford, John Gilbert, Norma Shearer, Buster Keaton.

So This Is College (1929)
Metro-Goldwyn-Mayer. Directed by Sam Wood. Ann Dvorak as student, uncredited. Cast: Robert Montgomery, Cliff Edwards, Sally Starr, Elliott Nugent.

The Doll Shop (1929 short)
Metro-Goldwyn-Mayer. Directed by Sammy Lee. Ann Dvorak as member of the chorus, uncredited. Cast: Lionel Belmore, Cy Kahn, Buster Dees.

Filmography

Chasing Rainbows (shot 1929; released 1930)
Metro-Goldwyn-Mayer. Directed by Charles Reisner. Ann Dvorak as member of the chorus, uncredited. Cast: Jack Benny, Bessie Love, Charles King, Polly Moran, Marie Dressler, Gwen Lee.

Devil-May-Care (1929)
Metro-Goldwyn-Mayer. Directed by Sidney Franklin. Ann Dvorak as member of the chorus, uncredited (unconfirmed). Cast: Ramon Novarro, Dorothy Jordan, Marion Harris, William Humphrey.

It's a Great Life (1929)
Metro-Goldwyn-Mayer. Directed by Sam Wood. Ann Dvorak as member of the chorus, uncredited. Cast: Rosetta Duncan, Vivian Duncan, Lawrence Gray, Benny Rubin.

Manhattan Serenade (1929 short)
Metro-Goldwyn-Mayer. Directed by Sammy Lee. Ann Dvorak as member of the chorus, uncredited. Cast: Raymond Hackett, Mary Doran, the Brox Sisters.

Pirates (1930 short)
Metro-Goldwyn-Mayer. Directed by Marty Brooks. Ann Dvorak as member of the chorus, uncredited. Cast: Benny Rubin, the O'Connor Sisters, Jack Randall and Company, Arthur Lange and his orchestra.

The Flower Garden (1930 short)
Metro-Goldwyn-Mayer. Directed by Marty Brooks. Ann Dvorak as member of the chorus, uncredited. Cast: Cliff Edwards, Lottice Howell, the Five Locust Sisters.

The Song Writers' Revue (1930 short)
Metro-Goldwyn-Mayer. Directed by Sammy Lee. Ann Dvorak as member of the chorus, uncredited. Cast: Jack Benny, Gus Edwards, Dave Dreyer, Nacio Herb Brown, Arthur Freed.

The Woman Racket (1930)
Metro-Goldwyn-Mayer. Directed by Albert H. Kelley and Robert Ober. Ann Dvorak as member of the chorus, uncredited. Cast: Blanche Sweet, Tom Moore, Sally Starr.

Filmography

Lord Byron of Broadway (1930)
Metro-Goldwyn-Mayer. Directed by Harry Beaumont and William Nigh. Ann Dvorak as member of the chorus, uncredited. Cast: Charles Kaley, Ethelind Terry, Marion Shilling, Cliff Edwards, Gwen Lee, Benny Rubin.

Free and Easy (1930)
Metro-Goldwyn-Mayer. Directed by Edward Sedgwick. Ann Dvorak as member of the chorus, uncredited. Cast: Buster Keaton, Anita Page, Robert Montgomery, Fred Niblo, Lionel Barrymore, William Haines.

Children of Pleasure (1930)
Metro-Goldwyn-Mayer. Directed by Harry Beaumont. Ann Dvorak as member of the chorus, uncredited. Cast: Lawrence Gray, Wynne Gibson, Helen Johnson, Benny Rubin.

Our Blushing Brides (1930)
Metro-Goldwyn-Mayer. Directed by Harry Beaumont. Ann Dvorak as party guest, uncredited. Cast: Joan Crawford, Robert Montgomery, Anita Page, Dorothy Sebastian, Hedda Hopper.

Way Out West (1930)
Metro-Goldwyn-Mayer. Directed by Fred Niblo. Ann Dvorak as member of the chorus, uncredited. Cast: William Haines, Leila Hyams, Polly Moran, Cliff Edwards, Francis X. Bushman Jr.

Good News (1930)
Metro-Goldwyn-Mayer. Directed by Nick Grinde. Ann Dvorak as student, uncredited. Cast: Bessie Love, Cliff Edwards, Gus Shy, Lola Lane, Mary Lawlor, Stanley Smith, Dorothy McNulty (aka Penny Singleton).

Love in the Rough (1930)
Metro-Goldwyn-Mayer. Directed by Charles Reisner. Ann Dvorak as member of the chorus, uncredited. Cast: Robert Montgomery, Dorothy Jordan, Benny Rubin, Dorothy McNulty (Penny Singleton).

The March of Time (1930)
Metro-Goldwyn-Mayer. Ann Dvorak as member of the chorus, uncredited. This film was never released. Musical excerpts from it were later used in *Broadway to Hollywood* (1933), *Nertsery Rhymes* (1933), and *Roast-Beef and Movies* (1934). "The Lock Step" was later used in *That's Entertainment! III* (1994).

Filmography

The Snappy Caballero (1930 short)
Metro-Goldwyn-Mayer. Ann Dvorak as member of the chorus, uncredited. Cast: Benny Rubin.

Devil's Cabaret (1930)
Metro-Goldwyn-Mayer. Directed by Nick Grinde. Ann Dvorak as member of the chorus, uncredited (unconfirmed). Cast: Eddie Buzzell, Charles Middleton, Mary Carlisle, Nelson McDowell, the Albertina Rasch Girls.

Dance, Fools, Dance (1931)
Metro-Goldwyn-Mayer. Directed by Harry Beaumont. Ann Dvorak as member of the chorus, uncredited (unconfirmed). Cast: Joan Crawford, Clark Gable, Cliff Edwards, William Bakewell.

Just a Gigolo (1931)
Metro-Goldwyn-Mayer. Directed by Jack Conway. Ann Dvorak as restaurant customer, uncredited. Cast: William Haines, Irene Purcell, C. Aubrey Smith, Charlotte Granville.

Politics (1931)
Metro-Goldwyn-Mayer. Directed by Charles Reisner. Ann Dvorak as member of political rally, uncredited. Cast: Marie Dressler, Polly Moran, Karen Morley, William Bakewell.

This Modern Age (1931)
Metro-Goldwyn-Mayer: Directed by Nick Grinde. Ann Dvorak as party crasher, uncredited. Cast: Joan Crawford, Neil Hamilton, Pauline Frederick, Monroe Owsley, Hobart Bosworth.

The Guardsman (1931)
Metro-Goldwyn-Mayer. Directed by Sidney Franklin. Ann Dvorak as autograph seeker, uncredited. Cast: Alfred Lunt, Lynn Fontanne, Roland Young, Zasu Pitts.

A Tailor Made Man (1931)
Metro-Goldwyn-Mayer. Directed by Sam Wood. Ann Dvorak as an extra, uncredited (unconfirmed). Cast: William Haines, Dorothy Jordan, Joseph Cawthorn, Marjorie Rambeau.

Son of India (1931)
Metro-Goldwyn-Mayer. Directed by Jacques Feyder. Ann Dvorak as a

dancer, uncredited. Cast: Ramon Novarro, Conrad Nagel, Marjorie Rambeau, Madge Evans, C. Aubrey Smith.

Scarface (1932)
Caddo Company. Directed by Howard Hawks. Ann Dvorak as Cesca Camonte. Cast: Paul Muni, George Raft, Karen Morley, Osgood Perkins, Boris Karloff.

Sky Devils (1932)
Caddo Company. Directed by A. Edward Sutherland. Ann Dvorak as Mary Way. Cast: Spencer Tracy, William "Stage" Boyd, George Cooper.

The Crowd Roars (1932)
First National/Vitaphone (Warner Bros.). Directed by Howard Hawks. Ann Dvorak as Lee Merrick. Cast: James Cagney, Joan Blondell, Eric Linden, Guy Kibbee, Frank McHugh.

The Strange Love of Molly Louvain (1932)
First National/Vitaphone (Warner Bros.). Directed by Michael Curtiz. Ann Dvorak as Madeleine Maude "Molly" Louvain. Cast: Lee Tracy, Leslie Fenton, Richard Cromwell, Guy Kibbee, Frank McHugh.

Love Is a Racket (1932)
First National/Vitaphone (Warner Bros.). Directed by William Wellman. Ann Dvorak as Sally Condon. Cast: Douglas Fairbanks Jr., Lee Tracy, Frances Dee, Lyle Talbot.

Stranger in Town (1932)
First National/Vitaphone (Warner Bros.). Directed by Erle C. Kenton. Ann Dvorak as Marian Crickle. Cast: Chic Sale, David Manners, Noah Beery, Lyle Talbot.

Crooner (1932)
First National/Vitaphone (Warner Bros.). Directed by Lloyd Bacon. Ann Dvorak as Judy Mason. Cast: David Manners, Ken Murray, Claire Dodd, Guy Kibbee.

Three on a Match (1932)
First National/Vitaphone (Warner Bros.). Directed by Mervyn LeRoy. Ann Dvorak as Vivian Revere. Cast: Joan Blondell, Bette Davis, Lyle Talbot, Warren William, Edward Arnold, Humphrey Bogart, Allen Jenkins, Jack La Rue.

Filmography

The Way to Love (1933)
Paramount Pictures. Directed by Norman Taurog. Ann Dvorak as Madeleine. Cast: Maurice Chevalier, Edward Everett Horton, Minna Gombell, Arthur Pierson.

College Coach (1933)
First National/Vitaphone (Warner Bros.). Directed by William Wellman. Ann Dvorak as Claire Gore. Cast: Pat O'Brien, Dick Powell, Lyle Talbot, Arthur Byron, Hugh Herbert.

Massacre (1934)
First National/Vitaphone (Warner Bros.). Directed by Alan Crosland. Ann Dvorak as Lydia. Cast: Richard Barthelmess, Dudley Digges, Robert Barrat, Claire Dodd.

Heat Lightning (1934)
First National/Vitaphone (Warner Bros.). Directed by Mervyn LeRoy. Ann Dvorak as Myra. Cast: Aline MacMahon, Preston Foster, Lyle Talbot, Glenda Farrell, Ruth Donnelly, Frank McHugh.

Side Streets (1934)
First National/Vitaphone (Warner Bros.). Directed by Alfred E. Green. Ann Dvorak as Marguerite Gilbert. Cast: Aline MacMahon, Paul Kelly, Dorothy Tree, Helen Lowell, Henry O'Neill.

Friends of Mr. Sweeney (1934)
First National/Vitaphone (Warner Bros.). Directed by Edward Ludwig. Ann Dvorak as Beulah Boyd. Cast: Charles Ruggles, Eugene Pallette, Robert Barrat, Dorothy Burgess, Dorothy Tree.

Midnight Alibi (1934)
First National/Vitaphone (Warner Bros.). Directed by Alan Crosland. Ann Dvorak as Joan Morley. Cast: Richard Barthelmess, Helen Chandler, Helen Lowell, Robert Barrat, Henry O'Neill.

Housewife (1934)
First National/Vitaphone (Warner Bros.). Directed by Alfred E. Green. Ann Dvorak as Nan Reynolds. Cast: Bette Davis, George Brent, John Halliday, Ruth Donnelly, Hobart Cavanaugh, Robert Barrat.

Filmography

I Sell Anything (1934)
First National/Vitaphone (Warner Bros.). Directed by Robert Florey. Ann Dvorak as Barbara. Cast: Pat O'Brien, Claire Dodd, Roscoe Karns.

Gentlemen Are Born (1934)
First National/Vitaphone (Warner Bros.). Directed by Alfred E. Green. Ann Dvorak as Susan Merrill. Cast: Franchot Tone, Margaret Lindsay, Jean Muir, Ross Alexander, Dick Foran.

Murder in the Clouds (1934)
First National/Vitaphone (Warner Bros.). Directed by D. Ross Lederman. Ann Dvorak as Judy Wagner. Cast: Lyle Talbot, Gordon Westcott, Robert Light, George Cooper, Henry O'Neill.

A Trip thru a Hollywood Studio (1935 short)
Warner Bros. Directed by Ralph Staub. Ann Dvorak as herself. Cast: James Cagney, Pat O'Brien, Busby Berkeley, Rudy Vallee, Dolores del Rio.

Sweet Music (1935)
Warner Bros. Directed by Alfred E. Green. Ann Dvorak as Bonnie Haydon. Cast: Rudy Vallee, Ned Sparks, Allen Jenkins, Alice White, Robert Armstrong, Al Shean, Helen Morgan.

"G" Men (1935)
Warner Bros. Directed by William Keighley. Ann Dvorak as Jean Morgan. Cast: James Cagney, Margaret Lindsay, Robert Armstrong, Barton MacLane.

Bright Lights (1935)
Warner Bros. Directed by Busby Berkeley. Ann Dvorak as Fay Wilson. Cast: Joe E. Brown, Patricia Ellis, William Gargan, Joseph Cawthorn, Henry O'Neill, Arthur Treacher.

Dr. Socrates (1935)
Warner Bros. Directed by William Dieterle. Ann Dvorak as Josephine Gray. Cast: Paul Muni, Barton MacLane, Robert Barrat, John Eldredge, Hobart Cavanaugh, Helen Lowell, Mayo Methot.

Thanks a Million (1935)
20th Century-Fox. Directed by Roy Del Ruth. Ann Dvorak as Sally Mason. Cast: Dick Powell, Fred Allen, Patsy Kelly, Raymond Walburn, David Rubinoff.

Filmography

We Who Are About to Die (1936)
RKO Pictures. Directed by Christy Cabanne. Ann Dvorak as Connie Stewart. Cast: Preston Foster, John Beal, Ray Mayer, Gordon Jones.

Racing Lady (1936)
RKO Pictures. Directed by Wallace Fox. Ann Dvorak as Ruth Martin. Cast: Smith Ballew, Harry Carey, Hattie McDaniel. Berton Churchill, Frank M. Thomas, Ray Mayer.

Midnight Court (1937)
Warner Bros. Directed by Frank McDonald. Ann Dvorak as Carol O'Neill. Cast: John Litel, Carlyle Moore Jr., Joseph Crehan, William B. Davidson.

The Case of the Stuttering Bishop (1937)
Warner Bros. Directed by William Clemens. Ann Dvorak as Della Street. Cast: Donald Woods, Anne Nagel, Linda Perry, Craig Reynolds, Gordon Oliver, Joseph Crehan.

She's No Lady (1937)
Paramount Pictures. Directed by Charles Vidor. Ann Dvorak as Jerry. Cast: John Trent, Harry Beresford, Guinn Williams, Aileen Pringle.

Manhattan Merry-Go-Round (1937)
Republic Pictures. Directed by Charles Reisner. Ann Dvorak as Ann Rogers. Cast: Phil Regan, Leo Carrillo, Tamara Geva, James Gleason, Ted Lewis, Cab Calloway, Kay Thompson, Joe DiMaggio.

Merrily We Live (1938)
Hal Roach Productions. Directed by Norman Z. McLeod. Ann Dvorak as Minerva Harlan. Cast: Constance Bennett, Brian Aherne, Billie Burke, Clarence Kolb, Bonita Granville, Patsy Kelly.

Gangs of New York (1938)
Republic Pictures. Directed by James Cruze. Ann Dvorak as Connie Benson. Cast: Charles Bickford, Wynne Gibson, Alan Baxter, Harold Huber.

Blind Alley (1939)
Columbia Pictures. Directed by Charles Vidor. Ann Dvorak as Mary. Cast: Chester Morris, Ralph Bellamy, Rose Stradner, Joan Perry, Melville Cooper, John Eldredge, Ann Doran.

Filmography

Stronger Than Desire (1939)
Metro-Goldwyn-Mayer. Directed by Leslie Fenton. Ann Dvorak as Eva McLain. Cast: Walter Pidgeon, Virginia Bruce, Lee Bowman, Ilka Chase.

Cafe Hostess (1940)
Columbia Pictures. Directed by Sidney Salkow. Ann Dvorak as Jo. Cast: Preston Foster, Wynne Gibson, Douglas Fowley, Arthur Loft, Bruce Bennett.

Girls of the Road (1940)
Columbia Pictures. Directed by Nick Grinde. Ann Dvorak as Kay Warren. Cast: Helen Mack, Lola Lane, Ann Doran, Marjorie Cooley, Bruce Bennett.

This Was Paris (1942)
Warner Bros. Directed by John Harlow. Ann Dvorak as Ann Morgan. Cast: Ben Lyon, Griffith Jones, Robert Morley.

Squadron Leader X (1943)
RKO Radio Pictures. Directed by Lance Comfort. Ann Dvorak as Barbara Lucas. Cast: Eric Portman, Walter Fitzgerald, Martin Miller, Beatrice Varley.

Escape to Danger (1943)
RKO Radio Pictures. Directed by Lance Comfort and Victor Hanbury. Ann Dvorak as Joan Grahame. Cast: Eric Portman, Karel Stepanek, Ronald Ward, Ronald Adam.

There's a Future in It (1944)
British Ministry of Information. Directed by Leslie Fenton. Ann Dvorak as Kitty. Cast: Barry Morse, John Turnbull, Beatrice Varley.

Flame of Barbary Coast (1945)
Republic Pictures. Directed by Joseph Kane. Ann Dvorak as Ann "Flaxen" Tarry. Cast: John Wayne, Joseph Schildkraut, William Frawley, Virginia Grey.

Masquerade in Mexico (1945)
Paramount Pictures. Directed by Mitchell Leisen. Ann Dvorak as Helen Grant. Cast: Dorothy Lamour, Arturo de Cordova, Patric Knowles, Natalie Schafer.

Filmography

Abilene Town (1946)
Guild Productions, Inc. Directed by Edwin L. Marin. Ann Dvorak as Rita. Cast: Randolph Scott, Rhonda Fleming, Edgar Buchanan, Lloyd Bridges.

The Bachelor's Daughters (1946)
Andrew L. Stone Productions. Directed by Andrew L. Stone. Ann Dvorak as Terry Wilson. Cast: Adolphe Menjou, Billie Burke, Claire Trevor, Gail Russell, Jane Wyatt.

The Private Affairs of Bel Ami (1947)
Loew-Lewin, Inc. Directed by Albert Lewin. Ann Dvorak as Madeleine Forestier. Cast: George Sanders, Angela Lansbury, John Carradine, Warren William, Frances Dee, Marie Wilson, Katherine Emery.

The Long Night (1947)
Select Productions, Inc. Directed by Anatole Litvak. Ann Dvorak as Charlene. Cast: Henry Fonda, Vincent Price, Barbara Bel Geddes.

Out of the Blue (1947)
Eagle-Lion Films. Directed by Leigh Jason. Ann Dvorak as Olive Jensen. Cast: George Brent, Virginia Mayo, Turhan Bey, Carole Landis.

The Walls of Jericho (1948)
20th Century-Fox. Directed by John M. Stahl. Ann Dvorak as Belle Connors. Cast: Cornel Wilde, Anne Baxter, Linda Darnell, Kirk Douglas, Marjorie Rambeau.

Our Very Own (1950)
Samuel Goldwyn Productions. Directed by David Miller. Ann Dvorak as Gert Lynch. Cast: Ann Blyth, Farley Granger, Jane Wyatt, Joan Evans, Donald Cook, Natalie Wood, Phyllis Kirk.

The Return of Jesse James (1950)
Lippert Pictures. Directed by Arthur David Hilton. Ann Dvorak as Sue Ellen Younger. Cast: John Ireland, Henry Hull, Reed Hadley, Hugh O'Brian.

Mrs. O'Malley and Mr. Malone (1950)
Metro-Goldwyn-Mayer. Directed by Norman Taurog. Ann Dvorak as Connie Kepplar. Cast: James Whitmore, Marjorie Main, Phyllis Kirk, Dorothy Malone.

Filmography

A Life of Her Own (1950)
Metro-Goldwyn-Mayer. Directed by George Cukor. Ann Dvorak as Mary Ashlon. Cast: Lana Turner, Ray Milland, Tom Ewell, Louis Calhern, Barry Sullivan, Jean Hagen, Phyllis Kirk.

I Was an American Spy (1951)
Allied Artists Productions. Directed by Lesley Selander. Ann Dvorak as Claire "High Pockets" Phillips. Cast: Gene Evans, Douglas Kennedy, Richard Loo, Lisa Ferraday, Freddie Revelala, Nadine Ashdown.

The Secret of Convict Lake (1951)
20th Century-Fox. Directed by Michael Gordon. Ann Dvorak as Rachel Schaeffer. Cast: Glenn Ford, Gene Tierney, Ethel Barrymore, Zachary Scott, Ruth Donnelly.

Television

"Close Up "(1950)
Silver Theater. Directed by Frank Woodruff. Ann Dvorak as Shirley. Cast: Conrad Nagel (host), Donald Woods.

"Ballerina" (1951)
Gruen Guild Theater. Cast: Ann Dvorak, David Ahdar, Kathleen Case.

"Flowers for John" (1951)
Bigelow Theater. Directed by Frank Woodruff. Ann Dvorak as Karen Fletcher. Cast: Joan Leslie, John Howard.

"Street Scene" (1952)
Celanese Theatre. Directed by Alex Segal. Ann Dvorak as Anna Maurrant. Cast: Paul Kelly, Coleen Gray, Michael Wagner.

"The Trial of Mary Dugan" (1952)
Broadway Television Theatre. Ann Dvorak as Mary Dugan. Cast: Vinton Hayworth, Richard Derr.

The Ken Murray Show (1952)
Ann Dvorak as herself. Cast: Ken Murray (host).

Radio

"Never See Snow Again" (1937)
Jergens' Hollywood Playhouse. Cast: Ann Dvorak, Tyrone Power.

"Sunday Punch" (1948)
Your Movietown Radio Theater. Ann Dvorak as Katie Murphy. Cast: Les Mitchell (host), Jeff Chandler, Herbert Rawlinson.

"Under the Big Top" (1948)
Your Movietown Radio Theater. Ann Dvorak as Toni. Cast: Les Mitchell (host), Marvin Miller, Jean Young, Ira Grossel (aka Jeff Chandler)

"The Other Side of the Moon" (1948)
Your Movietown Radio Theater. Ann Dvorak as Mary Clemens. Cast: Les Mitchell (host), Robert Holton, Jim Hayward.

Notes

1. Vaudeville Days

1. "An Amateur Theatrical Success," *Pittsburgh Post Gazette*, November 16, 1889.
2. "Pittsburgh's Many Players," *Pittsburgh Post*, December 3, 1908.
3. "At the Grand," *Perry Daily Chief*, December 9, 1904.
4. "When the World Sleeps," *New York Dramatic Mirror*, 1905.
5. Lehr and Ramsey, "What I Know about Ann Dvorak," pt. 1, 31.
6. Ibid.
7. Arthur Vergara (Lehr family member), in discussion with author, 2004.
8. "From the Mimic World—Behind the Scenes and in the Green Room of Plays and Players," *National Police*, March 25, 1905.
9. Unidentified Washington newspaper clipping, May 7, 1907.
10. "Well Acted Play at the Bijou," *Pittsburgh Leader*, January 7, 1908.
11. "Pittsburgh's Many Players," *Pittsburgh Post*, December 3, 1908.
12. "Vaudeville at Ten Cents," *Philadelphia Inquirer*, March 21, 1909.
13. "New Acts, Next Week: Anna Lehr Songs," *Weekly Variety*, June 3, 1911, 19.

2. Child Actress

1. Lehr and Ramsey, "What I Know about Ann Dvorak," pt. 1, 32.
2. "Movie Stars Coming to Pittsburgh," *Pittsburgh Gazette Times*, February 8, 1920.
3. "Players' Personalities," 91.
4. "Ann Dvorak and Chic Sale at Warner Renew Old Acquaintance," *Syracuse Herald*, August 5, 1932.
5. Advertisement, *Gloversville Morning Herald*, January 20, 1915, 8.
6. "Ramona Had Tremendous Appeal," *Los Angeles Evening Herald*, February 8, 1916.
7. "Anna Lehr Great Hit in Ramona," *Los Angeles Express*, February 24, 1916.

8. "Movie Gossip," *Lima Sunday News*, August 19, 1917.
9. Lehr and Ramsey, "What I Know about Ann Dvorak," pt. 1, 32.
10. de Kolty, "Wide-awake Ann," 19, 62.
11. Charles Foster, e-mail to Laura Wagner, February 2, 2004.
12. Vergara, discussion.
13. Lehr and Ramsey, "What I Know about Ann Dvorak," pt. 1, 33.
14. Ibid., pt. 1, 93.
15. "Snap Shots from Silent Drama," *Cedar Rapids Republican*, June 4, 1916.
16. "The Advanced Photo Play Corporation," *Pittsburgh Gazette Times*, May 30, 1920.
17. "Public Sees Making of Cinema Films," *Pittsburgh Press*, July 2, 1920.
18. Lehr and Ramsey, "What I Know about Ann Dvorak," pt. 1, 94.
19. "Wants Husband Protected," *Los Angeles Times*, July 23, 1921.

3. Schoolgirl

1. Lehr and Ramsey, "What I Know about Ann Dvorak," pt. 1, 94.
2. Ibid.
3. "Where Girls Go to School," *Los Angeles Times*, August 31, 1924.
4. Leona Cary to Ann Dvorak, March 26, 1979, author's collection.
5. Ibid.
6. "Where Girls Go to School."
7. "Noted Actresses Make Pageant Surprise Visit," *Highland Park News-Herald*, June 24, 1927.
8. de Kolty, "Wide-awake Ann," 18.
9. Lehr and Ramsey, "What I Know about Ann Dvorak," pt. 1, 95.
10. de Kolty, "Wide-awake Ann," 19.
11. Costello, "The Newest Girl to Hit the Heights," 13.
12. Ibid., 64.
13. de Kolty, "Wide-awake Ann," 19.
14. Anna Lehr to Hal Roach, September 16, 1927, author's collection.
15. Jean Paule (Occidental College), e-mail to author, January 26, 2006.
16. Edwin Martin, "Cinemania," *Hollywood Citizen-News*, April 26, 1937.
17. Jamison, "Keep Your Eye on Ann Dvorak . . . !" 41.

4. Chorus Cutie

1. Lloyd, "An Extra Girl's Diary," 74.
2. Ibid.
3. Strauss, "They All Laughed at Her," 72.

4. Lloyd, "An Extra Girl's Diary," 74.

5. de Kolty, "Wide-awake Ann," 19.

6. Biery, "Ann Dvorak," 14–15.

7. Ries, "Sammy Lee," 147–48.

8. Speed Kendell, "Talkie Chorus Work Difficult," *Los Angeles Times*, August 18, 1929.

9. de Kolty, "Wide-awake Ann," 62.

10. Lloyd, "An Extra Girl's Diary," 113.

11. Ibid.

12. Ibid.

13. Ibid.

14. Ibid.

15. In the Matter of the Contract between Metro-Goldwyn-Mayer Corporation and Anna Lehr, a minor, 1929, no. 293, 334, Los Angeles County Superior Court records, Los Angeles, CA.

16. Mary Carlisle, in discussion with Darin Barnes, January 2012.

17. Ries, "Sammy Lee," 162.

18. Costello, "The Newest Girl to Hit the Heights," 64.

19. Lloyd, "An Extra Girl's Diary," 113.

20. Lehr and Ramsey, "What I Know about Ann Dvorak," pt. 2, 62.

21. Richard Peterson, e-mail to author, May 17, 2011.

22. Mary Carlisle, in discussion with Darin Barnes, September 2, 2012.

23. Lloyd, "An Extra Girl's Diary," 113.

24. Costello, "The Newest Girl to Hit the Heights," 64.

25. "Most Chorines Stay in Ranks," *Charleston Gazette*, April 29, 1934.

26. Lloyd, "An Extra Girl's Diary," 113.

27. Lehr and Ramsey, "What I Know about Ann Dvorak," pt. 2, 63.

28. "Career of New Studio 'Find' Threatens to Get out of Hand," *Charleston Gazette*, May 1, 1932.

29. Ibid.

5. *Scarface*

1. Costello, "The Newest Girl to Hit the Heights," 64.

2. Lehr and Ramsey, "What I Know about Ann Dvorak," pt. 2, 64.

3. McBride, *Hawks on Hawks*, 45.

4. Colonel Jason S. Joy, "Resume," March 7, 1931, *Scarface* file, Production Code Administration papers, MPAA Collection, Margaret Herrick Library, Center for Motion Picture Study, Academy of Motion Picture Arts and Sciences, Beverly Hills, CA.

5. Michael Sragow, "Karen Morley, Still Sexy After All These Blacklisted

Years," *San Francisco Weekly*, April 21, 1999, http://www.sfweekly.com/1999–04–21/film/karen-morley-still-sexy-after-all-these-blacklisted-years/ (accessed October 8, 2012).

6. Yablonsky, *George Raft*, 65.

7. Katherine T. Von Blon, "Ann Dvorak Runs Cycle in Varied Career in Cinema," *Los Angeles Times*, February 25, 1935.

8. Lloyd, "An Extra Girl's Diary," 114.

9. Von Blon, "Ann Dvorak Runs Cycle in Varied Career in Cinema."

10. McBride, *Hawks on Hawks*, 48.

11. Lehr and Ramsey, "What I Know about Ann Dvorak," pt. 2, 104.

12. Agreement between the Caddo Company and Ann Dvorak, signed by Ann Dvorak, August 29, 1931, Ann Dvorak files, Warner Bros. Archives, University of Southern California, Los Angeles (hereafter cited as WB/USC).

13. "Juvenile Players Contracts Sealed," *Los Angeles Times*, September 12, 1931.

14. Lloyd, "An Extra Girl's Diary," 114.

15. Costello, "The Newest Girl to Hit the Heights," 65.

16. "Career of New Studio 'Find' Threatens to Get Out of Hand."

17. Sragow, "Karen Morley."

18. Yablonsky, *George Raft*, 68.

19. Smith, "Chorus Cutie to Star," 44.

20. Yablonsky, *George Raft*, 66.

21. Leibowitz, "The Idol Maker," 103.

22. Hall, "The Public Never Forgets, Says Ann Dvorak," 88.

23. Lehr and Ramsey, "What I Know about Ann Dvorak," pt. 2, 104.

24. Muriel Babcock, "Successors to Swanson, Garbo, Dietrich Named," *Los Angeles Times*, February 21, 1932.

25. Strauss, "They All Laughed at Her," 72.

26. Smith, "Chorus Cutie to Star," 44.

27. Colonel Jason S. Joy, "Resume," September 22, 1931, *Scarface* file, Production Code Administration papers, MPAA Collection, Margaret Herrick Library, Center for Motion Picture Study, Academy of Motion Picture Arts and Sciences, Beverly Hills.

28. "Memorandum for Mr. Hays," March 5, 1932, *Scarface* file, Production Code Administration papers, MPAA Collection, Margaret Herrick Library, Center for Motion Picture Study, Academy of Motion Picture Arts and Sciences, Beverly Hills.

29. Lehr and Ramsey, "What I Know about Ann Dvorak," pt. 2, 104.

30. Todd McCarthy, in discussion with author, 2005.

31. Strauss, "They All Laughed at Her," 72.

6. Hollywood's New Cinderella

1. Agreement between the Caddo Company, Inc. and First National Studios, December 4, 1931, Ann Dvorak files, WB/USC.

2. McCarthy, *Howard Hawks,* 161.

3. Ibid., 164.

4. McGilligan, *Backstory,* 95.

5. McBride, *Hawks on Hawks,* 55.

6. E.Y., "*Crowd Roars* Begins Run at Warners," *Hollywood Citizen-News,* April 28, 1932; John Rosenfeld Jr., "The New Motion Pictures," *Dallas Morning News,* April 16, 1932.

7. Costello, "The Newest Girl to Hit the Heights," 65.

8. Agreement between the Caddo Company and Ann Dvorak, December 6, 1931, Ann Dvorak files, WB/USC.

9. Agreement between the Caddo Company and Warner Bros., January 26, 1932, Ann Dvorak files, WB/USC.

10. Ibid.

11. Newquist, *Conversations with Joan Crawford,* 76.

12. Agreement between Warner Bros. and Ann Dvorak, February 5, 1932, Ann Dvorak files, WB/USC.

13. Various papers, *Strange Love of Molly Louvain* file, Production Code Administration papers, MPAA Collection, Margaret Herrick Library, Center for Motion Picture Study, Academy of Motion Picture Arts and Sciences, Beverly Hills.

14. Jacquie Lyn to Richard Finegan, February 14, 1995, Collection of Richard Finegan.

15. Katherine Lipke, "A Living Dreiser Hero?" *Los Angeles Times,* January 2, 1927.

16. Robbin Coons, "Fentons Seek Happiness in Life on Farm," *Hollywood Citizen-News,* June 22, 1933.

17. Albert, "Why Leslie Fenton Came Back," 135.

18. "She Knows Her Vegetables," *Oakland Tribune,* November 15, 1936.

19. Jones, "Dreams Come Through," 56.

20. Lehr and Ramsey, "What I Know about Ann Dvorak," pt. 2, 104.

21. Lee, "Three Slants on the Ann Dvorak," 56.

22. Lehr and Ramsey, "What I Know about Ann Dvorak," pt. 1, 32, pt. 2, 104.

23. Howard Fenton to "Pinky and Bettie," March 12, 1993, author's collection.

24. Lehr and Ramsey, "What I Know about Ann Dvorak," pt. 2, 104.

25. Ibid.

26. Ibid.

27. Fairbanks, *Salad Days*, 172–73.

28. Finler, *The Hollywood Story*, 243.

7. Mrs. Leslie Fenton

1. Jones, "Dreams Come Through," 56.

2. "Ann Dvorak Weds Fenton," *Los Angeles Examiner*, March 18, 1932.

3. Lee, "Three Slants on the Ann Dvorak," 84.

4. Ibid., 57.

5. Ibid., 87.

6. Grace Kingsley, "Hobnobbing in Hollywood," *Los Angeles Times*, August 16, 1933.

7. Lee, "Three Slants on the Ann Dvorak," 84.

8. Hall, "The Public Never Forgets, Says Ann Dvorak," 89.

9. Smith, "Chorus Cutie to Star," 44.

10. Kingsley, "Hobnobbing in Hollywood."

11. "Girl Names Fenton in Balm Plea," *Los Angeles Times*, March 22, 1932.

12. Louella O. Parsons, "Movie-Go-Round," *Los Angeles Examiner*, March 27, 1932.

13. Lee, "Three Slants on the Ann Dvorak," 56.

14. Lehr and Ramsey, "What I Know about Ann Dvorak," pt. 2, 106.

15. Ibid.

16. Edward Martin, "Cinemania," *Hollywood Citizen-News*, May 26, 1932.

17. John Scott, "Short Film Life Looked Forward To," *Los Angeles Times*, April 24, 1932.

18. Lehr and Ramsey, "What I Know about Ann Dvorak," pt. 2, 106.

19. Warner Bros. to Caddo Company, March 21, 1932, Ann Dvorak files, WB/USC.

20. Warner Bros. to Caddo Company, April 4, 1932, Ann Dvorak files, WB/USC.

21. Davis, *The Lonely Life*, 166.

22. Eleanor Barnes, "Ann Dvorak Gets First Hand Dope on Radio Singing," *Los Angeles Independent Daily News*, August 11, 1932.

23. Capt. Roscoe Fawcett, "Screen Oddities," *Los Angeles Independent Daily News*, August 5, 1932.

24. Davis, *The Lonely Life*, 166.

25. "3 on a Match," *Daily Variety*, November 1, 1932.

26. Lehr and Ramsey, "What I Know about Ann Dvorak," pt. 2, 104.

27. Jason S. Joy to Vincent Hart, September 2, 1932, *Three on a Match* file, Production Code Administration papers, MPAA Collection, Margaret Herrick Library, Center for Motion Picture Study, Academy of Motion Picture Arts and Sciences, Beverly Hills.

28. LeRoy, *Mervyn LeRoy*, 115–16.

29. Warner Bros. to Jefferson Pictures, Pathe Studios, June 16, 1932, Ann Dvorak file, WB/USC.

8. Sold Down the River

1. Davis, *The Lonely Life*, 170.

2. Ergenbright, "Hollywood's 'Love Runaways' Write Home," 17.

3. Read Kendall, "Ann Dvorak Insists on Right Roles," *Los Angeles Times*, February 6, 1937.

4. Costello, "The Newest Girl to Hit the Heights," 13.

5. Lane, "Danger Ahead for Ann Dvorak?" 51.

6. Ann Dvorak to Warner Bros. Accounting Department, July 3, 1932, Ann Dvorak file, WB/USC.

7. Ann Dvorak & Leslie Fenton to Charles Feldman, telegram, July 4, 1932, Ann Dvorak file, WB/USC.

8. Lehr and Ramsey, "What I Know about Ann Dvorak," pt. 1, 31.

9. Chester B. Bahn, "Speaking Very Candidly," *Syracuse Herald*, July 24, 1932.

10. "Sold Down the River, Declares Ann Dvorak," *Los Angeles Times*, July 19, 1932.

11. Elizabeth Yeaman, "'Fu Manchu' Movie to Be Produced by M-G-M," *Hollywood Citizen-News*, July 25, 1932.

12. Relman Morin, "Cinematters," *Los Angeles Record*, July 28, 1932.

13. Evans, "Watch Your Step, Ann Dvorak!" 14–15.

14. Hall, "The Public Never Forgets, Says Ann Dvorak," 88.

15. Lane, "Danger Ahead for Ann Dvorak?" 51.

16. Lehr and Ramsey, "What I Know about Ann Dvorak," pt. 2, 106.

9. Happy Vagabonds

1. Elizabeth Yeaman, "Ann Dvorak Gets Film Contract in England," *Hollywood Citizen-News*, August 12, 1932.

2. Ergenbright, "Hollywood's 'Love Runaways' Write Home," 78.

3. Robert Schless to Abel Cary Thomas, September 20, 1932, Ann Dvorak file, WB/USC.

4. Ergenbright, "Hollywood's 'Love Runaways' Write Home," 78.

5. Lane, "Danger Ahead for Ann Dvorak?" 79.

6. Ergenbright, "Hollywood's 'Love Runaways' Write Home," 78.

7. Ibid.

8. Ibid.

9. Goldbeck, "The Mad but Happy Fentons," 67.

10. Hall, "The Public Never Forgets Says Ann Dvorak," 88.

11. Ergenbright, "Hollywood's 'Love Runaways' Write Home," 79.

12. Ibid., 78.

13. Goldbeck, "The Mad but Happy Fentons," 67.

14. Ergenbright, "Hollywood's 'Love Runaways' Write Home," 79.

15. Ibid.

16. "Romance That Cost Stardom Has No Regrets," *Washington Post*, December 4, 1933.

17. Ergenbright, "Hollywood's 'Love Runaways' Write Home," 17, 78, 79.

18. *Hollywood Reporter*, January 20, 1933.

19. Reine Davies, "Hollywood Parade," *Los Angeles Examiner*, January 28, 1937.

20. Lane, "Danger Ahead for Ann Dvorak?" 79, 80.

21. "Stars Like Quiet Life on Ranch," *Lima Sunday News*, May 28, 1933.

22. Lane, "Danger Ahead for Ann Dvorak?" 67.

23. Goldbeck, "The Mad but Happy Fentons," 67.

24. Ralph Lewis to R. J. Obringer, August 20, 1932, Ann Dvorak file, WB/USC.

25. Thomas, *Clown Prince of Hollywood*, 143.

26. Nelson B. Bell, "About the Showshops," *Washington Post*, January 3, 1933.

27. Goldbeck, "The Mad but Happy Fentons," 67.

28. Lane, "Danger Ahead for Ann Dvorak?" 80.

29. Rudi Polt, in discussion with author, December 2003.

30. Irene Cavanaugh, "Ann Dvorak Does Not Regret Year Lost in Career," *Los Angeles Illustrated Daily News*, April 21, 1934.

31. Jack Warner to William Dover, Roy Obringer, William Koenig, Max Arnow, memo, March 23, 1933, Ann Dvorak files, WB/USC.

10. Prodigal Daughter

1. Warner Bros./Paul A. Chase to Ann Dvorak, March 29, 1933, Ann Dvorak file, WB/USC.

2. Roy Obringer to Paul A. Chase, memo, May 12, 1933, Ann Dvorak file, WB/USC.

3. Agreement between Warner Bros. Pictures and Ann Dvorak, May 18, 1933, Ann Dvorak file, WB/USC.
4. Lane, "Danger Ahead for Ann Dvorak?" 80.
5. Hall, "The Public Never Forgets, Says Ann Dvorak," 88.
6. "Opening of Pageant to Be Tonight," *Los Angeles Times*, July 20, 1933.
7. Goldbeck, "The Mad but Happy Fentons," 77.
8. Reine Davies, "Hollywood Parade," *Los Angeles Examiner*, March 4, 1935.
9. Edwin Martin, "Cinemania," *Hollywood Citizen-News*, January 16, 1937.
10. Dan Thomas, "Home, Husband above Career, Says Beautiful Ann Dvorak," *Lowell Sun*, January 3, 1934.
11. Lane, "Danger Ahead for Ann Dvorak?" 80.
12. Coons, "Fentons Seek Happiness in Life on Farm."
13. Polt, discussion.
14. Agreement between Warner Bros. and Paramount Pictures, August 11, 1933, Ann Dvorak file, WB/USC.

11. Warner Workhorse

1. Stine, *Mother Goddam*, 35.
2. Cagney, *Cagney by Cagney*, 52.
3. Thomas, "Home, Husband above Career, Says Beautiful Ann Dvorak."
4. Hall, "The Public Never Forgets, Says Ann Dvorak," 88.
5. Coons, "Fentons Seek Happiness in Life on Farm."
6. "Film Star Paid Honor by Indians," *Los Angeles Times*, January 23, 1934.
7. Hal Wallis to Alan Crosland, memo, October 12, 1933, *Massacre* file, WB/USC.
8. Hal Wallis to William Koenig, memo, *Massacre* file, WB/USC.
9. "Snake Bites Ann Dvorak," *Los Angeles Examiner*, October 18, 1933.
10. "Hollywood Press Agent Stunts Often 'Kick' Back," *Long Beach Independent*, November 1, 1952.
11. Massacre Production Log, *Massacre* file, WB/USC.
12. Heat Lightning Production Log, *Heat Lightning* file, WB/USC.
13. Side Streets Production Log, *Side Streets* file, WB/USC.
14. W. E. Oliver, "Worm Turns at Warners to Rites of Laughter," *Los Angeles Evening Herald and Express*, July 27, 1934; "The Screen," *New York Times*, July 31, 1934; Muriel Babcock, "Charlie Ruggles in 'Tough' Role," *Los Angeles Examiner*, July 27, 1934.

15. "Metropolitan," *Washington Post*, August 25, 1934.
16. W. E. Oliver, "Quit Hollywood to Learn Living, Says Ann Dvorak," *Los Angeles Evening Herald and Express*, July 28, 1934.
17. Midnight Alibi Production Log, *Midnight Alibi* file, WB/USC.
18. Read Kendall, "Around and about in Hollywood," *Los Angeles Times*, June 4, 1935.
19. Stine, *Mother Goddam*, 55.
20. Oliver, "Quit Hollywood to Learn Living, Says Ann Dvorak."
21. Molly March, "Ann Dvorak—A Portrait of Glamour," *Oakland Tribune, Screen and Radio Weekly*, January 27, 1935.
22. Reine Davies, "Hollywood Parade," *Los Angeles Examiner*, April 20, 1934.
23. Ibid.

12. Life Off Camera

1. "Fenton Upsets Hollywood Plan," *Charleston Gazette*, September 9, 1934.
2. Bill Daniels, "Talkie Topics," *Advance News*, July 23, 1935.
3. Robbin Coons, "Bucolic Life Praise Sung by Film Pair," *Hollywood Citizen-News*, August 17, 1937.
4. Ramsey, "In Sickness and in Health," 76.
5. Coons, "Bucolic Life Praise Sung by Film Pair."
6. Rosalind Shaffer, "Dvorak Hides from Crowd," *Chicago Daily Tribune*, January 27, 1935.
7. "Farm Life Lures Ann Dvorak and Leslie Fenton," *Los Angeles Times*, April 27, 1935.
8. Paul Harrison, "Ann Will Talk Movies Now—After Almost Anything Else," *Piqua Daily Call*, July 12, 1937.
9. "Ann Dvorak Clubs Coyote Chicken Killer to Death," *Los Angeles Evening Herald and Express*, March 20, 1935.
10. Dan Thomas, "Hollywood Gossip," *Burlington (NC) Daily Times-News*, August 21, 1933.
11. Read Kendall, "Around and about in Hollywood," *Los Angeles Times*, February 12, 1935.
12. Tip Poff, "That Certain Party," *Los Angeles Times*, April 21, 1935.
13. Fenton, "Against All Odds," 60.
14. "Hollywood Divided into Two Camps on Vacations," *Los Angeles Times*, May 28, 1935.
15. California Voter Registration, 1900–1968, www.ancestry.com (accessed November 3, 2008).
16. Ann Dvorak file, Screen Actors Guild records, Los Angeles.

17. "Farm Life Lures Ann Dvorak and Leslie Fenton."

18. Ramsey, "In Sickness and in Health," 84.

19. Ibid.

20. Fenton, "Against All Odds," 60.

21. Ibid.

22. "Talkie-Topics," *Advance News*, December 8, 1934.

23. Olsen and Hudson, *Hollywood's Man Who Worried for the Stars*, 235.

24. Carolyn Roos Olsen, e-mail to author, July 12, 2009.

25. Marsh, "Ann Dvorak—A Portrait of Glamour," 12.

26. Goldbeck, "The Mad but Happy Fentons," 67.

27. Marsh, "Ann Dvorak—A Portrait of Glamour," 12.

28. Ruth Reynolds, "Problem Play Plot: Film Star to Meet Long Lost Father," *Sunday News*, February 11, 1934.

29. Eleanor Barnes, "'Alice in Wonderland' Due," *Los Angeles Illustrated Daily News*, December 16, 1933.

30. Reynolds, "Problem Play Plot."

31. Ibid.

32. "Ann Dvorak Finds Father After 14 Years' Silence," *New York Times*, February 5, 1934.

33. "Hasn't Seen Her Since Actress Was 8 Years Old in Philadelphia," *Lewiston Daily Sun*, February 5, 1934.

34. Reynolds, "Problem Play Plot."

35. "Ann Dvorak Meets Father," *Los Angeles Examiner*, August 21, 1934.

13. Suspended Contract Player

1. Von Blon, "Ann Dvorak Runs Cycle in Varied Career in Cinema."

2. Hall, "The Public Never Forgets, Says Ann Dvorak," 89.

3. Von Blon, "Ann Dvorak Runs Cycle in Varied Career in Cinema."

4. Sweet Music Production Log, *Sweet Music* file, WB/USC.

5. "Vallee Star of Musicals," *Los Angeles Times*, February 19, 1935; Mae Tinne, "Vallee Scores in Film with Ann Dvorak," *Chicago Daily Tribune*, February 26, 1935.

6. Louella O. Parsons, "'Sweet Music' Tuneful Treat for Vallee Fans," *Los Angeles Examiner*, February 23, 1935.

7. Sweet Music Production Log.

8. Marsh, "Ann Dvorak—A Portrait of Glamour."

9. W. E. Oliver, "Garbo Element A in Star Chemistry, Says Ann Dvorak," *Los Angeles Evening Herald and Express*, February 23, 1935.

10. Marsh, "Ann Dvorak—A Portrait of Glamour."

11. Ibid.

12. "Screen Stars Study Hawaiian Sugar Cane," *Syracuse Herald*, January 6, 1935.

13. William Koenig to Roy Obringer, memo, December 4, 1934, Ann Dvorak file, WB/USC.

14. Hal Wallis to William Koenig, memo, February 1, 1935, Ann Dvorak file, WB/USC.

15. Hal Wallis to William Keighly, memo, March 18, 1935, *"G" Men* file, WB/USC.

16. Ed Selzer to Jack Warner, memo, Ann Dvorak file, WB/USC.

17. Lloyd Pantages, "I Cover Hollywood," *Los Angeles Examiner*, May 1, 1935.

18. Robbin Coons, "Hollywood Sights and Sounds," *Kingston Daily Freeman*, July 30, 1935.

19. Agreement between Warner Bros. and Twentieth Century Pictures, June 21, 1935, Ann Dvorak file, WB/USC.

20. Gussow, *Don't Say Yes until I Finish Talking*, 69.

21. Mosley, *Zanuck*, 161.

22. Roy Obringer to Arthur Freston, January 29, 1936, Ann Dvorak file, WB/USC.

23. Sidney Skolsky, "Hollywood," *Washington Post*, February 28, 1936.

24. Wagner and Hagen, *Killer Tomatoes*, 56.

25. Roy Obringer to Hal Wallis, memo, December 26, 1935, Ann Dvorak file, WB/USC.

26. Carl E. Conn, M.D., to Warner Bros., October 15, 1935, Ann Dvorak file, WB/USC.

27. Arthur Freston to Roy Obringer, January 2, 1936, Ann Dvorak file, WB/USC.

28. Warner Bros. to Ann Dvorak, October 30, 1935, Ann Dvorak file, WB/USC.

29. *Fenton (Dvorak) vs. Warner Bros.*, n.d., Ann Dvorak file, WB/USC.

30. Roy J. Obringer to Ralph Lewis, November 4, 1935, Ann Dvorak file, WB/USC.

31. Paul A. Chase to Ann Dvorak, November 5, 1935, Ann Dvorak file, WB/USC.

14. Legal Eagle

1. "Bette Davis Called Chattel in the Hands of Producers," *Los Angeles Times*, October 13, 1936.

2. Mary Hobart, "Wide Variety of Thanksgiving Festivities Planned by Film Celebrities," *Hollywood Citizen-News*, November 27, 1935.

3. Ralph S. Lewis to Roy J. Obringer, December 4, 1935, Ann Dvorak file, WB/USC.

4. Roy J. Obringer to Hal Wallis, memo, December 26, 1935, Ann Dvorak file, WB/USC.

5. Complaint for Declaration Relief, *Dvorak vs. Warner Bros.,* no. 396484, December 17, 1935, Los Angeles County Superior Court records, Los Angeles.

6. Paul A. Chase to Ann Dvorak, February 1, 1936, Ann Dvorak file, WB/USC.

7. Arthur Freston to Roy J. Obringer, February 4, 1936, Ann Dvorak file, WB/USC.

8. "Ann Dvorak Takes Stand in Fight over Contract," *Los Angeles Times,* February 15, 1936.

9. "Question Ann Dvorak on Film Roles in Suit," *Los Angeles Evening Herald and Express,* February 15, 1936.

10. "Is Ann Dvorak Able to Work?" *Los Angeles Examiner,* February 15, 1936.

11. "Question Ann Dvorak on Film Roles in Suit."

12. "Ann Dvorak Presses Studio Action," *Hollywood Citizen-News,* February 14, 1936.

13. "Film Star Denies Underweight at Suit Trial," *Independent Daily News,* February 15, 1936.

14. "Ann Dvorak Healthy Assert Doctors at Contract Suit Trial," *Los Angeles Independent Daily News,* February 19, 1936.

15. "Coffee, Ten Cups Daily, Made Ann Dvorak So Thin," *Modesto Bee,* February 19, 1936.

16. Memo of Decision, *Leslie C. Fenton and Ann D. Fenton vs. Warner Bros Pictures Inc.,* no. 396484, March 2, 1936, Los Angeles County Superior Court records, Los Angeles.

17. Ibid.

18. Ann Dvorak to Jack L. Warner, August 5, 1936, Ann Dvorak file, WB/USC.

19. Paul A. Chase to Ann Dvorak, March 8, 1936, Ann Dvorak file, WB/USC.

20. Ray Files to Roy J. Obringer, March 14, 1936, Ann Dvorak file, WB/USC.

21. Dvorak to Warner, August 5, 1936.

22. Louis B. Stanton to Freston & Files, March 12, 1936, Ann Dvorak file, WB/USC.

23. Roy J. Obringer to Ray Files, March 14, 1936, Ann Dvorak file, WB/USC.

24. "Court Hears Dvorak Plea," *Los Angeles Times,* April 5, 1936.

25. Arthur Freston to Roy J. Obringer, May 29, 1936, Ann Dvorak file, WB/USC.

26. Memo of Decision on Motion to Recall Minute Order, *Leslie C. Fenton and Ann D. Fenton vs. Warner Bros Pictures Inc.*, no. 396484, July 1, 1936, Los Angeles County Superior Court records, Los Angeles.

27. Warner Bros. Pictures to Ann Dvorak, July 22, 1936, Ann Dvorak file, WB/USC.

28. Paul A. Chase to Ann Dvorak, July 31, 1936, Ann Dvorak file, WB/USC.

29. Dvorak to Warner, August 5, 1936.

30. Roy Obringer to Ray Files, August 10, 1936, Ann Dvorak file, WB/USC.

31. Agreement between Warner Bros and RKO Pictures, July 31, 1936, Ann Dvorak file, WB/USC.

32. Read Kendall, "Ann Dvorak Insists on Right Roles."

33. Henry Sutherland, "Actors Do the Kissing, but Wally Does the Make Up," *San Francisco Chronicle*, September 22, 1936.

34. Katherine T. Von Blon, "Film Players Will Turn to Local Stage," *Los Angeles Times*, September 2, 1934.

35. Paul A. Chase to Ann Dvorak, September 22, 1936, Ann Dvorak file, WB/USC.

36. Roy Obringer to Abe Lastfogel, September 21, 1936, Ann Dvorak file, WB/USC.

37. "Smith Ballew Responsible for Funny Noise Epidemic," *Advance News*, February 11, 1937.

38. Read Kendall, "Around and about Hollywood," *Los Angeles Times*, October 17, 1936, 7.

39. "Domestic Pursuits of the Movie Stars," *Advance News*, February 9, 1937.

40. Louella O. Parsons, "Pete Smith and Robert Ripley to Collaborate on Film Shorts," *Los Angeles Examiner*, December 8, 1936.

41. "Princess Dress," *Spokane Daily Chronicle*, December 2, 1936.

42. "She Knows Her Vegetables."

43. Ibid.

44. Jimmy Starr, "Wally Smith Signed to Adapt Tunefilm *Convention in Cuba*," *Los Angeles Evening Herald and Express*, October 14, 1936.

45. "She Knows Her Vegetables."

46. Erskine Johnson, "Behind the Makeup," *Los Angeles Examiner*, May 23, 1937.

47. Ibid.

48. Louella O. Parsons, *Los Angeles Examiner*, December 23, 1936.

49. Warner, *My First Hundred Years in Hollywood*, 277.

15. Freelance Artist

1. Kendall, "Ann Dvorak Insists on Right Roles."

2. Complaint for Personal Injuries, *John J. Kelly vs. Ann Dvorak Fenton*, no. 410305, n.d., Los Angeles County Superior Court records, Los Angeles.

3. "Ann Dvorak Files Crash Suit Answer," *Los Angeles Evening Herald and Express*, March 23, 1937.

4. "Ann Dvorak Car Crash Suit Dropped by Court," *Los Angeles Examiner*, July 13, 1937.

5. Harrison Carroll, "Fenton under Knife; Mate Holds Hand," *Los Angeles Evening Herald and Express*, March 23, 1937.

6. Louella O. Parsons, "Syd Chaplin, Back in Hollywood, Amazed at Ten Years' Change," *Los Angeles Examiner*, May 8, 1937.

7. "She's No Lady," *Motion Picture Review Digest*, September 27, 1937, 85–86.

8. Frederic C. Otiman, "Hollywood Roundup," *Delta Star*, September 2, 1937.

9. Read Kendall, "Around and about in Hollywood," *Los Angeles Times*, May 19, 1937.

10. Alice Hughes, "A Woman's New York," *Washington Post*, January 14, 1938.

11. Agreement between Hal Roach Studios and Ann Dvorak, November 13, 1937, www.ebay.com (accessed March 19, 2011).

12. Server, *Sam Fuller*, 18.

13. Erskine Johnson, "Behind the Make Up," *Los Angeles Examiner*, April 8, 1938.

14. "Gangs of New York," *Motion Picture Review Digest*, June 27, 1938, 26.

15. Joseph Breen to Louis B. Mayer, October 17, 1935, Production Code Administration papers, MPAA Collection, Margaret Herrick Library, Center for Motion Picture Study, Academy of Motion Picture Arts and Sciences, Beverly Hills.

16. Selznick, *Memo from David O. Selznick*, 173.

17. "Ann Dvorak and Helen Mack Will Help Girl Hobos," *Los Angeles Examiner*, May 25, 1940.

18. Goldbeck, "The Mad but Happy Fentons," 77.

16. War

1. Jimmy Fidler, "Jimmy Fidler in Hollywood," *Los Angeles Times*, June 4, 1940.

2. "Sings on W-G-N," *Chicago Daily Tribune,* January 10, 1941.

3. "Ann Dvorak, 2 Other Brides Sail for Europe," unknown publication, December 15, 1940.

4. Woodbury, "A Glamour Girl Faces Real War," 32.

5. "Ann Dvorak, 2 Other Brides Sail for Europe."

6. "Variety Show Now on Boards at State," *Hartford Courant,* November 22, 1940.

7. Howard Fenton to "Pinky and Bettie," September 7, 1992, author's collection.

8. "Lord Barny and Bride Depart for England," *New York Times,* December 15, 1940.

9. Ann Dvorak Fenton, "War-time Crossing," *Hartford Courant,* January 19, 1941.

10. Ibid.

11. Ibid.

12. Woodbury, "A Glamour Girl Faces Real War," 54.

13. C. A. Lejeune, "Cocktail Time in London," *New York Times,* March 2, 1941.

14. Dvorak, "Invasion Village," 22.

15. Dvorak, "Gallant Troupers of King's Lynn," 10.

16. Foster, e-mail to Wagner.

17. Wadge, *Women in Uniform,* 377.

18. Dvorak, "I Lived in London," 66.

19. Woodbury, "A Glamour Girl Faces Real War," 54.

20. Dvorak, "I Lived in London," 66.

21. "Actress Writing Book for Women Mechanics," *Chicago Daily Tribune,* August 20, 1944.

22. Ann Dvorak Fenton, "Once Smart Piccadilly Grim in War Clothing," *Dallas Morning News,* July 7, 1941.

23. Dvorak, "I Lived in London," 66.

24. Canfield, "All through the Night," 50.

25. Hedda Hopper, "Looking at Hollywood," *Chicago Tribune,* October 26, 1945.

26. Louella O. Parsons, "Movie-go-Round," *Los Angeles Examiner,* April 13, 1941.

27. Fenton, "War-time Crossing."

28. Edwin Schallert, "Reel Notes Reeled Off Briefly," *Los Angeles Times,* July 12, 1941.

29. Warner, *My First Hundred Years in Hollywood,* 278.

30. Canfield, "All through the Night," 50.

17. Ann of All Trades

1. Scott, *The Battle of the Narrow Seas*, 56.
2. Canfield, "All through the Night," 50.
3. Woodbury, "A Glamour Girl Faces Real War," 54.
4. Ibid.
5. Ibid.
6. Lee Shippey, "Lee Side o' L.A.," *Los Angeles Times*, December 18, 1943.
7. Ibid.
8. Cecile Hallingby, "Acre in England Grows California Tomatoes," *Los Angeles Times*, October 24, 1943.
9. Woodbury, "A Glamour Girl Faces Real War," 54.
10. McFarlane, *Lance Comfort*, 42.
11. Foster, e-mail to Wagner.
12. Ibid.
13. Bates, *The World in Ripeness*, 125–26.
14. Underhill, "Reformed Vagabonds," 84.
15. "Bebe Daniels Heads Variety Troupe to Entertain Forces," *Stars and Stripes*, February 5, 1943; "Touring Stars Will Play at Red Cross in Belfast," *Stars and Stripes*, February 12, 1943.
16. Murray M. Moler, "Ann Dvorak Is Revising Camp Shows for U.S. Army," *Winnipeg Free Press*, February 2, 1945.
17. "'Man Bites Dog' at Troop Show," *Stars and Stripes*, February 15, 1943.
18. "USO to Bring American Stars to Forces Here," *Stars and Stripes*, February 19, 1943.
19. Dvorak, "I Lived in London," 67.
20. "Two New Shows Starting Today around GI Loop," *Stars and Stripes*, May 17, 1943.
21. Dvorak, "I Lived in London," 67.
22. "Backstage Story of a GI Drama," *Stars and Stripes—Features Special Supplement*, August 12, 1943.
23. "Actress 'Saves' Lane's Play in London," *Wisconsin State Journal*, August 6, 1943.
24. *Men and Women of Hawaii*, 594.

18. Shell Shocked

1. Dvorak, "I Lived in London," 67.
2. Hedda Hopper, "The Fentons Are Facing the Future," *Chicago Daily Tribune*, August 13, 1944.

3. Erskine Johnson, "In Hollywood," *Burlington (NC) Daily Times-News*, November 18, 1943.

4. Lee, "Lee Side o' L.A."

5. "Ann Dvorak Says Women Should Be Drafted," *Syracuse Herald-Journal*, October 14, 1943.

6. Erskine Johnson, "In Hollywood," *Helena Independent*, November 5, 1943.

7. Hopper, "The Fentons Are Facing the Future."

8. Ibid.

9. McKay, "Damsel in Success," 59.

10. Robbin Coons, "Ann Dvorak Is Back in the Movies After 4 Years in England," *Lubbock Avalanche-Journal*, July 30, 1944.

11. Rosalind Shaffer, "Ann Dvorak Back for Another Try at Movies," *Ogden Standard-Examiner*, October 22, 1944.

12. Ibid.

13. Moler, "Ann Dvorak Is Revising Camp Shows for U.S. Army," 6.

14. Edwin Schallert, "Ann Dvorak Considered for Lead with Powell," *Los Angeles Times*, April 25, 1944.

15. Lowell E. Redelings, "Acquanetta Set for New Film Thriller," *Hollywood Citizen-News*, March 9, 1944.

16. Edwin Schallert, "Hollywood Wins over Britain with Dvorak," *Los Angeles Times*, February 26, 1945.

17. Virginia MacPherson, "Ann Dvorak Finds Love Hinders a Screen Career," *Winnipeg Free Press*, March 23, 1945.

18. Sidney Skolsky, "The Gossipel Truth," *Hollywood Citizen-News*, July 3, 1944.

19. MacPherson, "Ann Dvorak Finds Love Hinders a Screen Career."

20. Hopper, "The Fentons Are Facing the Future."

21. Johnson, "In Hollywood," *Helena Independent*, November 5, 1943.

22. Hopper, "The Fentons Are Facing the Future."

23. Hedda Hopper, "Actress Ann Dvorak and Fenton Separate," *Los Angeles Times*, September 15, 1944.

24. "Ann Dvorak Marriage to Fenton a 'War Casualty,'" *Los Angeles Evening Herald and Express*, September 15, 1944.

25. Gene Handsaker, "Hollywood," *Plattsburg Press-Republican*, March 13, 1946.

26. Foster, e-mail to Wagner.

27. MacPherson, "Ann Dvorak Finds Love Hinders a Screen Career."

28. McKay, "Damsel in Success," 96.

29. Various real estate records, Los Angeles County Registrar Recorder/County Clerk records, Norwalk.

30. McKay, "Damsel in Success," 96.

31. Harry Corcker, "Behind the Makeup," *Los Angeles Examiner*, May 9, 1945.

32. Lowell E. Redelings, "The Hollywood Scene," *Hollywood Citizen-News*, March 30, 1945.

33. Harrison Carroll, "Dane Clark to Take State Bar Exam," *Los Angeles Evening Herald and Express*, October 8, 1945.

34. Louella O. Parsons, "Goldwyn Wants Joan Fontaine for *Bishop's Wife*," *Los Angeles Examiner*, May 12, 1945.

35. "Ann Dvorak Files Suit for Divorce against Fenton," *Hollywood Citizen-News*, October 25, 1945.

36. Louella O. Parsons, "Ronald Reagan Going Back to Work in *Stallion Road*," *Los Angeles Examiner*, December 3, 1945.

37. "Friends Report Ann Dvorak's Reconciliation," *Los Angeles Times*, January 15, 1946.

38. "Ann Dvorak Wins Divorce from Actor Leslie Fenton," *Los Angeles Herald-Express*, August 1, 1946.

19. Career Girl

1. MacPherson, "Ann Dvorak Finds Love Hinders a Screen Career."

2. Patricia Clary, "Ann Dvorak Upsets Theory of Only One Movie Chance," *Winnipeg Free Press*, October 30, 1945.

3. McKay, "Damsel in Success," 96.

4. Chierichetti, *Mitchell Leisen*, 212.

5. Lamour, *My Side of the Road*, 148.

6. *Masquerade in Mexico* file, Paramount Pictures production records, Margaret Herrick Library, Academy of Motion Picture Arts and Sciences, Beverly Hills.

7. Bob Thomas, "Hollywood," *Annapolis Evening Capitol*, October 20, 1945.

8. Lowell E. Redelings, "The Hollywood Scene," *Hollywood Citizen-News*, April 3, 1945.

9. Chierichetti, *Mitchell Leisen*, 215.

10. Jimmy Starr, "Film Chorine Gets an Acting Chance at TC-F," *Los Angeles Evening Herald and Express*, November 14, 1945.

11. McBride, *Frank Capra*, 525.

12. Louella O. Parsons, "Ann Dvorak Continues Amazing Return as 'Trail Town' Co-star," *Los Angeles Examiner*, June 25, 1945.

13. Clary, "Ann Dvorak Upsets Theory of Only One Movie Chance."

14. "Eisenhower's Home Town Cheers Movie 'Abilene Town,'" *Emporia Gazette*, January 15, 1946.

15. Harrison Carroll, "Behind the Scenes in Hollywood," *Bradford Era,* March 25, 1946.

16. Louella O. Parsons, "Lana Turner, Spencer Tracy Teamed in *Cass Timberlain,*" *Los Angeles Examiner*, March 22, 1946.

17. Felleman, *Botticelli in Hollywood*, 73.

18. McKay, "Damsel in Success," 59.

19. Felleman, *Botticelli in Hollywood*, 65.

20. Dick Peterson, e-mail to author, May 17, 2011.

21. "Reconciled in Los Angeles," *Lowell Sun*, May 20, 1950.

22. "Actress to Wed Dancer," *Stars and Stripes*, June 26, 1947.

23. Louella O. Parsons, "In Hollywood with Louella O. Parsons," *Los Angeles Examiner,* September 21, 1947.

24. "Ann Dvorak Debuts as Cafe Entertainer," *Port Arthur News*, December 15, 1946.

25. Louella O. Parsons, "Warners Take Option on Jackson's Fall of Valor," *Fresno Bee*, January 12, 1947.

26. Erskine Johnson, "In Hollywood," *Plattsburg Press-Republican*, February 20, 1947.

27. Virginia Mayo, in discussion with author, 2004.

28. John L. Scott, "Ann Dvorak Picks Up Her Career Where She Left Off," *Los Angeles Times*, November 2, 1947.

29. Parsons, "In Hollywood with Louella O. Parsons."

30. Ibid.

31. Louella O. Parsons, "Actor to Marry Ann Dvorak," *Los Angeles Times,* August 7, 1947.

32. Scott, "Ann Dvorak Picks Up Her Career Where She Left Off."

20. Broadway Bound

1. Agreement between Les Mitchell Productions, Inc., and Ann Dvorak, March 3, 1949, author's collection.

2. "Ann Dvorak Dotted for Telepix Series," *Daily Variety,* April 22, 1948.

3. "On the Air Waves," *Daily Variety*, November 9, 1949.

4. "Out of the Horn's Mouth," *Daily Variety*, November 2, 1949.

5. "On the Air Waves."

6. "My Secret Desire," admission ticket, author's collection.

7. Walter Ames, "Television, Radio, News, and Programs," *Los Angeles Times*, February 2, 1951.

8. Judaken, *Race After Sartre*, 55.

9. Lester Bernstein, "Meg Mundy Likes Role in Tighe Play," *New York Times,* July 29, 1948.

10. Lester Bernstein, "Contract Sent to Ann Dvorak," *New York Times,* August 12, 1948; Louis Calta, "Golden Considers Comedy by Actors," *New York Times,* August 19, 1948.

11. Janet Grayson, e-mail to author, June 30, 2009.

12. Sheilah Graham, "Linda Darnell to Play Negro Girl," *Hollywood Citizen-News,* June 27, 1949.

13. "Stage Pot Boiling on Rustic Circuit," *New York Times,* June 2, 1949.

14. "In Hollywood," *Plattsburg Press-Republican,* September 27, 1949.

15. Jane Wyatt, in discussion with author, 2003.

16. Edward Barry, "*Our Very Own* Called Best Film of Its Kind," *Chicago Daily Tribune,* September 15, 1950.

17. Annie Oakley, "The Theatre and Its People," *Windsor Daily Star,* October 8, 1949.

18. J. P. Shanley, "About Margaret Sullavan," *New York Times,* December 23, 1948.

19. Sam Zolotow, "Harmon Adds Two Prospects," *New York Times,* August 24, 1949.

20. "Chicago Visitors," *Chicago Daily Tribune,* September 7, 1949.

21. Ann Dvorak to Bill Brighton, October 5, 1949, author's collection.

22. Ann Dvorak to Bill Brighton, October 13, 1949, http://www.historyforsale.com/html/prodetails.asp?documentid=224424&start=1 (accessed July 30, 2012).

23. "25,000 Rooms 'with View' on Tap in Miami," *Chicago Daily Tribune,* November 27, 1949.

24. Ann Dvorak to Bill Brighton, n.d., http://www.historyforsale.com/html/prodetails.asp?documentid=224423&start=1 (accessed July 30, 2012).

25. Classified ads, *Los Angeles Times,* January 24, 1950.

26. "Ann Dvorak Asks Divorce from Dancer," *Los Angeles Times,* February 22, 1950.

21. Seasoned Professional

1. Wagner and Hagen, *Killer Tomatoes,* 62.

2. Hugh O'Brian, in discussion with author, 2007.

3. "Turner Classic Movies Announces the Network's Choices for 10 Great Overlooked Performances," December 2010, http://news.turner.com/article_print.cfm?article_id=5486 (accessed August 2, 2012).

4. Truffaut and Dixon, *The Early Film Criticism of François Truffaut,* 34.

5. Long, *George Cukor Interviews,* 46.

6. Agreement between Young & Rubicam, Inc., and Ann Dvorak, May 3, 1950, author's collection.

7. Edwin Schallert, "Heroic Actress-Spy of Philippines Helps Screen Her Own Torture Story," *Los Angeles Times*, January 14, 1951.

8. "Ann Dvorak Lists Current Picture as Her Favorite Role," *Evening Capitol*, May 25, 1951.

9. Schallert, "Heroic Actress-Spy of Philippines."

10. "Spy Story Opens at the Holiday," *New York Times*, July 4, 1951.

11. Richard L. Coe, "Mere Movie Based on Real Exploit," *Washington Post*, May 17, 1951.

12. "Ann Dvorak Lists Current Picture as Her Favorite Role."

13. William "Billy" Gordon papers, Margaret Herrick Library, Academy of Motion Picture Arts and Sciences, Beverly Hills.

14. Agreement between Twentieth Century-Fox Film Corporation and Ann Dvorak, January 27, 1951, author's collection.

15. Hedda Hopper, "Drama," *Los Angeles Times*, January 18, 1951.

16. Erskine Johnson, "New Elizabeth Taylor Romance Races Along," *Waterloo Daily Courier*, March 1, 1951.

17. Harrison Carroll, "Hollywood," *Farmington Daily Times*, March 9, 1951.

18. File 36734, p. 342, Los Angeles County Registrar Recorder/County Clerk records, Norwalk.

19. TWA Passenger Manifest, April 27, 1951, www.ancestry.com (accessed August 17, 2012).

20. Ann Dvorak to Bill Brighton, May 2, 1951, author's collection.

21. "Hollywood House Raided, 10 Seized," *Los Angeles Times*, April 7, 1951.

22. Dvorak to Brighton, May 2, 1951.

23. Leona Cary to Ann Dvorak, March 26, 1979.

24. "Highlights & Sidelights," *Long Beach Independent*, July 16, 1951.

25. "Ann Dvorak Wins Divorce Decree," *Ogden (UT) Standard-Examiner*, August 8, 1947.

26. "In Hollywood," *Plattsburg Press-Republican*, September 17, 1951.

22. Enter Nick Wade

1. Application for Social Security Account Number signed by Nicholas Wade, July 14, 1942, Social Security Administration, Baltimore.

2. 1930 Federal Census, https://familysearch.org/pal:/MM9.1.1/XHQN-64N (accessed August 24, 2012).

3. Ann Weiss (niece of Nicholas Wade), in discussion with author, March 2011.

4. Michael Theodore (nephew of Nicholas Wade), e-mail to author, December 30, 2003.

5. "Night Club Notes," *New York Times,* September 18, 1937.

6. "International Casino, New York City," *Architectural Forum,* November 1937, 385.

7. "New Apartments Being Provided in Various Parts of Metropolitan District," *New York Times,* July 11, 1937; "Entertainment in the Cafes," *New York Post,* May 29, 1937; "Entertainment in the Cafes," *New York Post,* November 13, 1937.

8. "Entertainment in the Cafes," *New York Post,* August 27, 1938.

9. "Woodside Cook Demands Wages," *Long Island Star-Journal,* March 10, 1939.

10. "Cook Not Paid, Boss Fined $1,000," *Long Island Star-Journal,* May 16, 1939.

11. Ramona Wade Guerra (granddaughter of Nicholas Wade), in discussion with author, July 2012.

12. Ann Weiss, e-mail to author, August 28, 2012.

13. Weiss, discussion.

14. Rudy Grau, in discussion with author, 2008; Weiss, discussion.

15. Marvin Kapelus, in discussion with author, June 2009.

16. Bob Francis, "'Street Scene' Emerges as Brilliant Job of Video Adaptation & Staging," *Billboard,* April 12, 1952.

17. "One-Week Stand," *Newsweek,* April 28, 1952.

18. Plummer, *In Spite of Myself,* 124.

19. Arthur Vergara, e-mail to author, August 30, 2012.

20. Jack Gould, "Radio and Television," *New York Times,* April 16, 1952.

21. Ann Dvorak to Manning O'Conner, December 4, 1951, author's collection.

22. Withdrawal request, signed by Ann Dvorak, May 5, 1955, Ann Dvorak file, Screen Actors Guild records, Los Angeles.

23. "Articles of Incorporation," file 309151, September 1955, California Secretary of State, Sacramento.

24. Louella O. Parsons, "Fred's Leaving June in July," *Washington Post and Times Herald,* June 4, 1954.

25. Ann and Nick Wade to Southwest Bank, June 5, 1956, document 51344, Los Angeles County Registrar Recorder/County Clerk records, Norwalk.

26. Document 51344, November 14, 1955, 244, Los Angeles County Registrar Recorder/County Clerk records, Norwalk.

27. *The Musician's Guide,* 78.

28. Library of Congress, Copyright Office, *Catalog of Copyright Entries,* 733.

29. Jordan, *Jim Reeves,* 144.

30. Anna Lehr to Arthur Vergara, July 4, 1967, author's collection.

31. Anna Lehr to Arthur Vergara, November 11, 1966, author's collection.

32. *Nicholas H. Wade vs. Southwest Bank,* civil case 26214, Court of Appeal of California, Second Appellate District, Division 2, December 27, 1962, 2.

33. Kapelus, discussion.

34. Weiss, discussion.

35. Guerra, discussion.

36. Kapelus, discussion.

37. Lisa Smith, in discussion with author, 2008.

38. Screen Actors Guild to Ann Dvorak, June 13, 1957, Ann Dvorak file, Screen Actors Guild records, Los Angeles.

39. Complaint for Divorce, *Ann Wade vs. Nicholas H. Wade,* file SM D-15862, June 3, 1957, Los Angeles County Superior Court records, Los Angeles.

40. Ibid.

41. *Nicholas H. Wade vs. Southwest Bank.*

42. Ibid.

23. Hawaiian Hopeful

1. Ligaya Fruto, "Whatever Happened to Ann Dvorak?" *Honolulu Star-Bulletin,* October 14, 1965.

2. *Men and Women of Hawaii,* 594.

3. Honolulu City Directory, 1962–63.

4. Chattel Mortgage, document 3394, book S860, p. 698, March 21, 1961, Los Angeles County Registrar Recorder/County Clerk records, Norwalk.

5. Fruto, "Whatever Happened to Ann Dvorak?"

6. Ann Dvorak to Arne and Mila Scheibel, July 19, 1969, author's collection.

7. Fruto, "Whatever Happened to Ann Dvorak?"

8. Ann Dvorak to Arne and Mila Scheibel, April 21, 1969, author's collection.

9. Dvorak to Scheibels, July 19, 1969.

10. Fruto, "Whatever Happened to Ann Dvorak?"

11. Dvorak to Scheibels, April 21, 1969.

12. Fruto, "Whatever Happened to Ann Dvorak?"

13. Dvorak to Scheibels, July 19, 1969.

14. Ann Dvorak to Arne and Mila Scheibel, September 3, 1969, author's collection.

15. Anna Lehr to Arthur Vergara, October 20, 1968, author's collection.

16. Ann Dvorak to Arne and Mila Scheibel, July 24, 1970, author's collection.

17. Weiss, discussion.

18. Rudy Grau, in discussion with author, 2007.

19. Anna Lehr to Arthur Vergara, January 11, 1967, author's collection.

20. Anna Lehr to Arthur Vergara, November 11, 1966, author's collection.

21. Anna Lehr to Arthur Vergara, January 14, 1967, and July 4, 1967, author's collection.

22. Anna Lehr to Arthur Vergara, December 20, 1968, author's collection.

23. Lehr to Vergara, July 4, 1967.

24. Anna Lehr to Arthur Vergara, September 21, 1968, author's collection.

25. Anna Lehr to Arthur Vergara, December 20, 1968, author's collection.

26. Ibid.

27. Dvorak to Scheibels, April 21, 1969.

28. Anna Lehr to Arthur Vergara, May 5, 1969, author's collection.

29. Anna Lehr to Arthur Vergara, July 29, 1969, author's collection.

30. Dr. Arnold Scheibel, in discussion with author, 2007.

31. Ibid.

32. Howard Fenton to "Pinky and Bettie," March 12, 1993, author's collection.

33. Ann Dvorak to Arne and Mila Scheibel, n.d., author's collection.

34. Ann Dvorak to Arne and Mila Scheibel, August 28, 1969, author's collection.

35. Ann Dvorak to Arne and Mila Scheibel, September 3, 1969, author's collection.

36. Ann Dvorak to Arne and Mila Scheibel, August 26, 1969, author's collection.

37. Dvorak to Scheibels, September 3, 1969.

38. Ibid.

39. Ann Dvorak to Mila Scheibel, August 25, 1969, author's collection.

40. Ibid.

41. Dvorak to Scheibels, September 3, 1969.

42. Anna Lehr to Arne and Mila Scheibel, August 31, 1969, author's collection.

43. Food Stamp Identification Card, November 1, 1974, Department of Social Services, author's collection.

44. Ann Dvorak, "The Rainbow Sunset," author's collection.

24. The End of Everything

1. Levy, "Top Hollywood Star Dies in Poverty and Squalor," 28.

2. Ann Dvorak to the Screen Actors Guild, March 20, 1975, and February 9, 1979, Ann Dvorak files, Screen Actors Guild records, Los Angeles.

3. Ann Dvorak, personal journal, October 21, 1977, author's collection.

4. Ibid.

5. Ann Dvorak to Joanie, August 31, 1979, author's collection.

6. William Wilde to Ann Dvorak, April 27, 1978, author's collection.

7. Dvorak, personal journal, October 21, 1977.

8. Leona Cary to Ann Dvorak, June 1, 1979, author's collection.

9. Levy, "Top Hollywood Star Dies in Poverty and Squalor," 28.

10. Polt, discussion.

11. Grau, discussion.

12. Levy, "Top Hollywood Star Dies in Poverty and Squalor," 28.

13. Leona Cary to Ann Dvorak, March 26, 1979, and May 28, 1979, author's collection.

14. Polt, discussion.

15. Levy, "Top Hollywood Star Dies in Poverty and Squalor," 28.

16. Small Estate no. 118163 PAU, file ISE00-0-11816, Circuit Court, First Circuit, State of Hawaii, Honolulu.

17. Levy, "Top Hollywood Star Dies in Poverty and Squalor," 28.

18. Certificate of Death 4966, State of Hawaii Department of Health, file ISE00-0-11816, Circuit Court, First Circuit, State of Hawaii, Honolulu.

19. Ann Dvorak files, Screen Actors Guild records, Los Angeles.

20. Small Estate no. 118163 PAU, file ISE00-0-11816 Circuit Court, First Circuit, State of Hawaii, Honolulu.

21. Paul Wroblewsk (owner of Only Show in Town), in discussion with author, December 2003.

22. Dvorak, personal journal, October 21, 1977.

Epilogue

1. Vidal, *Myra Breckinridge*, 211.

Bibliography

Albert, Katherine. "Why Leslie Fenton Came Back." *Photoplay*, February 1931.

Bates, H. E. *The World in Ripeness.* Columbia: University of Missouri Press, 1972.

Biery, Ruth. "Ann Dvorak." *Photoplay*, June 1932.

Bradley, Edwin M. *The First Hollywood Musicals: A Critical Filmography of 171 Features, 1927 through 1932.* Jefferson, NC: McFarland, 2004.

———. *The First Hollywood Sound Shorts, 1926–1931.* Jefferson, NC: McFarland, 2009.

Cagney, James. *Cagney by Cagney.* Garden City, NY: Doubleday, 1976.

Canfield, Alice. "All through the Night." *Screen Stars*, January 1945.

Chierichetti, David. *Mitchell Leisen, Hollywood Director.* Los Angeles: Photoventures, 1995.

Costello, Terrence. "The Newest Girl to Hit the Heights." *Movie Classic*, July 1932.

Davis, Bette. *The Lonely Life.* New York: G. P. Putnam's Son's, 1962.

de Kolty, Jeane. "Wide-awake Ann." *Street and Smith's Picture Play*, September 1932.

Dvorak, Ann. "Gallant Troupers of King's Lynn." *Illustrated*, March 8, 1941.

———. "I Lived in London." *Screen Guide*, December 1944.

———. "Invasion Village." *Illustrated*, February 22, 1941.

Ergenbright, Eric. "Hollywood's 'Love Runaways' Write Home." *Movie Classic*, March 1933.

Evans, Delight. "Watch Your Step, Ann Dvorak!" *Screenland*, October 1932.

Fairbanks, Douglas, Jr. *Salad Days.* New York: Doubleday, 1988.

Felleman, Susan. *Botticelli in Hollywood: The Films of Albert Lewin.* New York: Twayne, 1997.

Fenton, Howard. "Against All Odds." *Screenplay*, January 1934.

Finler, Joel W. *The Hollywood Story.* New York: Crown, 1988.

Goldbeck, Elisabeth. "The Mad but Happy Fentons." *Motion Picture*, August 1935.

Gussow, Mel. *Don't Say Yes until I Finish Talking: A Biography of Darryl F. Zanuck.* Garden City, NY: Doubleday, 1971.

Hall, Gladys. "The Public Never Forgets, Says Ann Dvorak." *Motion Picture*, February 1935.

Jamison, Jack. "Keep Your Eye on Ann Dvorak . . . !" *Modern Screen*, June 1932.

Jones, Carlisle. "Dreams Come Through." *Silver Screen*, June 1932.

Jordan, Larry. *Jim Reeves: His Untold Story; The Life and Times of Country Music's Greatest Singer.* N.p.: Page Turner Books International, 2011.

Judaken, Jonathan. *Race After Sartre: Antiracism, Africana Existentialism, Postcolonialism.* Albany: State University of New York Press, 2008.

Lamour, Dorothy. *My Side of the Road.* Englewood Cliffs, NJ: Prentice-Hall, 1980.

Lane, Jerry. "Danger Ahead for Ann Dvorak?" *Motion Picture*, September 1933.

Lee, Sonia. "Three Slants on the Ann Dvorak–Leslie Fenton Elopement." *Motion Picture*, June 1932.

Lehr, Ann, and Walter Ramsey. "What I Know about Ann Dvorak." Pts. 1 and 2. *Modern Screen*, October and November 1932.

Leibowitz, Ed. "The Idol Maker." *Los Angeles Magazine*, February 2009.

LeRoy, Mervyn. *Mervyn LeRoy: Take One.* New York: Hawthorn Books, 1974.

Levy, Paul F. "Top Hollywood Star Dies in Poverty and Squalor." *National Enquirer* [?], 1980.

Library of Congress, Copyright Office. *Catalog of Copyright Entries*, 3rd ser., part 5B, *Unpublished Music.* Washington, DC: Copyright Office, Library of Congress, 1955.

Lloyd, Ben. "An Extra Girl's Diary." *Photoplay*, July 1932.

Long, Robert Emmet. *George Cukor Interviews.* Jackson: University Press of Mississippi, 2001.

Loy, Myrna, and James Kotsilibas-Davis. *Myrna Loy: Being and Becoming.* New York: Knopf, 1987.

McBride, Joseph. *Frank Capra: The Catastrophe of Success.* Jackson: University Press of Mississippi, 2011.

———. *Hawks on Hawks.* Berkeley: University of California Press, 1982.

McCarthy, Todd. *Howard Hawks, the Gray Fox of Hollywood.* New York: Grove, 1997.

McClelland, Doug. "Ann Dvorak: Underground Goddess." *Film Fan Monthly*, May 1969.

McFarlane, Brian. *Lance Comfort.* New York: Manchester University Press, 1999.

McGilligan, Patrick. *Backstory: Interviews with Screenwriters of Hollywood's Golden Age.* Berkeley: University of California Press, 1986.

Bibliography

McKay, Margaret Morton. "Damsel in Success." *Motion Picture* [?], 1946.

Men and Women of Hawaii. Honolulu: Honolulu Business Consultants, 1972.

Mosley, Leonard. *Zanuck: The Rise and Fall of Hollywood's Last Tycoon*. Boston: Little, Brown, 1984.

The Musician's Guide: The Directory of the World of Music. New York: Music Information Service, 1957.

Newquist, Roy. *Conversations with Joan Crawford*. Secaucus, NJ: Citadel, 1980.

Olsen, Carolyn Roos, and Marylin Hudson. *Hollywood's Man Who Worried for the Stars: The Story of Bo Roos*. N.p.: AuthorHouse, 2008.

Parish, James Robert. *Hollywood Players: The Thirties*. New Rochelle, NY: Arlington House, 1976.

"Players' Personalities." *Photoplay*, September 1912.

Plummer, Christopher. *In Spite of Myself, a Memoir*. New York: Knopf, 2009.

Ramsey, Walter. "In Sickness and in Health." *Photoplay*, February 1936.

Ries, Frank W. D. "Sammy Lee: The Hollywood Career." *Dance Chronicle* 11, no. 2 (1988).

Scott, Peter. *The Battle of the Narrow Seas: A History of the Light Coastal Forces in the Channel and North Sea, 1939–1945*. New York: Scribner, 1946.

Selznick, David O. *Memo from David O. Selznick*. New York: Viking, 1972.

Server, Lee. *Sam Fuller: Film Is a Battleground*. Jefferson, NC: McFarland, 2003.

Smith, Jewel. "Chorus Cutie to Star." *Screenplay*, September 1932.

Sperling, Cass Warner. *Hollywood Be Thy Name: The Warner Brothers Story*. Rocklin, CA: Prima, 1994.

Stine, Whitey. *Mother Goddam*. New York: Hawthorne Books, 1984.

Strauss, Jerome. "They All Laughed at Her." *Screen Book*, January 1932.

Thomas, Bob. *Clown Prince of Hollywood: The Antic Life and Times of Jack L. Warner*. New York: McGraw-Hill, 1990.

Truffaut, François, and Wheeler Winston Dixon. *The Early Film Criticism of François Truffaut*. Bloomington: Indiana University Press, 1993.

Underhill, Duncan. "Reformed Vagabonds." *Motion Picture*, August 1944.

Vidal, Gore. *Myra Breckinridge*. Boston: Little, Brown, 1968.

Wadge, D. Collett. *Women in Uniform*. London: S. Low, Marston, 1946.

Wagner, Laura, and Ray Hagen. *Killer Tomatoes: Fifteen Tough Film Dames*. Jefferson, NC: McFarland, 2004.

Warner, Jack L. *My First Hundred Years in Hollywood*. New York: Random House, 1965.

Bibliography

Warwick, James. *Blind Alley: A Play in Three Acts.* New York: Samuel French, 1936.

Woodbury, Joan. "A Glamour Girl Faces Real War." *Stardom,* May 1943.

Yablonsky, Lewis. *George Raft.* Lincoln, NE: iUniverse, 2001.

Index

Index

Index

Index

Index

Index

Screen Classics

Screen Classics is a series of critical biographies, film histories, and analytical studies focusing on neglected filmmakers and important screen artists and subjects, from the era of silent cinema to the golden age of Hollywood to the international generation of today. Books in the Screen Classics series are intended for scholars and general readers alike. The contributing authors are established figures in their respective fields. This series also serves the purpose of advancing scholarship on film personalities and themes with ties to Kentucky.

Series Editor

Patrick McGilligan

Books in the Series

Mae Murray: The Girl with the Bee-Stung Lips
Michael G. Ankerich

Hedy Lamarr: The Most Beautiful Woman in Film
Ruth Barton

Von Sternberg
John Baxter

The Marxist and the Movies: A Biography of Paul Jarrico
Larry Ceplair

Warren Oates: A Wild Life
Susan Compo

Jack Nicholson: The Early Years
Robert Crane and Christopher Fryer

Being Hal Ashby: Life of a Hollywood Rebel
Nick Dawson

Intrepid Laughter: Preston Sturges and the Movies
Andrew Dickos

John Gilbert: The Last of the Silent Film Stars
Eve Golden

Mamoulian: Life on Stage and Screen
David Luhrssen

Maureen O'Hara: The Biography
Aubrey Malone

My Life as a Mankiewicz: An Insider's Journey through Hollywood
Tom Mankiewicz and Robert Crane

Hawks on Hawks
Joseph McBride

William Wyler: The Life and Films of Hollywood's Most Celebrated Director
Gabriel Miller

Raoul Walsh: The True Adventures of Hollywood's Legendary Director
Marilyn Ann Moss

Some Like It Wilder: The Life and Controversial Films of Billy Wilder
Gene D. Phillips

Ann Dvorak: Hollywood's Forgotten Rebel
Christina Rice

Arthur Penn: American Director
Nat Segaloff

Claude Rains: An Actor's Voice
David J. Skal with Jessica Rains

Buzz: The Life and Art of Busby Berkeley
Jeffrey Spivak

Victor Fleming: An American Movie Master
Michael Sragow

Thomas Ince: Hollywood's Independent Pioneer
Brian Taves

Carl Theodor Dreyer and Ordet: *My Summer with the Danish Filmmaker*
Jan Wahl